Contents

The Essential Guide to

Chartering and the Dry Freight Market

by

Nick Collins

Published by:
Clarkson Research Studies
12, Camomile Street,
London, EC3A 7BP,
England.
Telephone: 020 7334 3134
Facsimile: 020 7522 0330
E-mail: sales.crs@clarksons.co.uk
Web-site: http://www.clarksons.net

ISBN 0 900291 97 4

Cover design by Helix Design Partnership
Photograph courtesy of Bocimar N.V.

Printed by Halstan & Co. Ltd.,
Amersham, Bucks., England.

List of Figures

Acknowledgements

Some years ago Martin Stopford suggested that I should write a complimentary book on dry cargo chartering to the late Eddie Couslon's 'Guide for Tanker Brokers'. He identified that there was no book on dry cargo chartering written by someone at the cutting edge of the market. Most were written by shipping lawyers or arbitrators and did not cover the topics that Eddie did nor in the way he did. Having completed the book, I now realise why. The chartering market is a demanding place to earn one's living. Writing a book is, of course, also very demanding and time consuming. But they are very different disciplines and to do both simultaneously to an acceptable standard, which I trust I have done, was not at all an easy thing to accomplish. However, my thanks to him for the idea and invitation. I did enjoy the challenge.

I am also indebted to Eddie Coulson, of course, as I had in part an existing format to follow, especially in Chapters Three and Four where the mechanics of negotiating and the nature of ship broking are discussed. However, I found that discussing these issues and the meaning of charter party words and phrases without explaining the types of ships, what they do and why and without discussing the nature of the market itself, was like starting in the middle rather than the beginning of the story. Most commercial shipping people talk endlessly about ships, how they are employed and above all, the market. Yet I do not know of any book that addresses these issues from a commercial or chartering point of view. I therefore amended and expanded the topics covered to include an explanation of the types of ships, the supply and demand factors determining the freight market, freight derivatives and time charters which were not present in Eddie's book. There is much else including sections on the changing role of the Baltic Exchange and the future of chartering in the age of e-commerce. Much of the book's later chapters, however, are concerned with the legal interpretation of chartering phrases. I am not a lawyer and this is not a legal book but charter parties and shipping contracts are not normally negotiated by lawyers but by commercial shipping people and most of them know, or should know, what these phrases and concepts mean or imply. Nevertheless my sincere thanks to David Hughes of Jackson Parton, as I did need a good shipping lawyer to check what I had written in those chapters. He was able to give me many interesting pointers and insights and I am much indebted to him. I also owe thanks to Andrew Jamieson of ITIC who brought me up to date with the 1999 U.K. legislation, which has implications concerning brokerage. This book is primarily based, however, on my practical experience negotiating contracts over the past 25 years and it is not surprising perhaps, that over that time I have developed clear and strong ideas about some aspects of the profession. Some parts of the book are therefore deliberately opinionated. While not everyone will agree with each opinion, I hope they will find them well argued and above all, thought provoking.

Although the book is intended to be a snapshot of, and a guide to, the chartering market at the beginning of the twenty first century, I have been at pains to try to put it in a historical context. I have therefore tried to explain how we arrived at the present situation as well as today's developments and what that implies for the future. I have explained competing ideas and what charterers and owners argue about and why it is important. But however experienced anyone is, chartering is becoming increasingly specialised. I am therefore indebted to many of my colleagues who I tapped for information, many of them unknowingly. In particular, I owe thanks to Michael Grimwade, who reviewed early drafts of Chapters Five and Six and brought me up to date with developments in the grain chartering market. Thanks also are due to David Cherrett who read early drafts of Chapters One to Five and made many useful and constructive suggestions as to both styles and content. He is also responsible for Figures 2.14 to 2.17. Working with him for the past two years has helped crystallise many of my thoughts on freight, the nature of the market and the value a broker can deliver. My thanks also to Mike Rippingale who lent his many years of experience to give helpful comments on time charter practice in Chapter Seven. But despite all their assistance, the content and any mistakes therein are entirely my own responsibility.

Adrian Hughes of Clarkson Research spent a considerable amount of his private time and did a great job in cleaning up and re drawing most of the ship's plans in Chapter One. Cliff Tyler oversaw the production of the book. Michelle Crawley formatted it. Clarkson Research provided all the graphs. Associated Bulk Carriers allowed me to use their drawing in figure 1.32. BIMCO and the Association of Shipbrokers and Agents (USA) allowed me to reprint some of the key charter parties in Appendix 4. The Baltic Exchange allowed me to use their fixture list and reprint Baltic index material. Last, but certainly not least, Shipping Guides of Reigate allowed me to reprint their excellent load line map, which constitutes Appendix 3. My sincere thanks is due to all the above.

Most of all, since I spent many winter weekends writing the book, the biggest thanks to my family with whom I should have spent much more time and paid far more attention.

Introduction

Chartering is the process of negotiating and fixing a ship, usually for the carriage of a cargo at sea. It is an exciting profession and shipping is one of the most volatile, risky and exhilarating industries to be involved in, yet like many interesting professions, it only becomes so when the basics are mastered. The basics consist, among others, of some technical knowledge of ships, contract law, charter parties, the economics of supply and demand and a good degree of common sense. This book is designed as a guide on all the above.

When people involved in the shipping and chartering industry get together, they talk in technical and semi-technical terms, sometimes in abbreviated forms about the issues of their industry and in particular of the various sizes and types of ships and the parts of them. The charter parties, the contracts on which the ships are fixed themselves involve obligations concerning these ships, how they are constructed, managed and the dimensions and characteristics of certain parts of them. These various terms will initially be confusing to the layman. Thus, the first place to start in any explanation of chartering is with the ships themselves and this first chapter details the types and parts of ships and the trades in which they are involved.

The major topic that shipping people endlessly discuss is the freight market. The second chapter therefore, explores the freight market as a whole, its supply and demand constituents, how the market is measured and the advantages of controlling freight. The third chapter explains the mechanics of how the market works, the importance of the dissemination of information, risk management and the various roles of the broker. The fourth addresses guidelines for those working within, and especially negotiating in, the market. The fifth explores charter parties in general. The sixth and seventh are "what is at stake?" chapters which explore in detail the words concepts and phrases involved in voyage and time charter parties respectively; the crucial issues at stake in the negotiations and performance of a fixture, what is argued about and why. The last briefly examines protective clauses and the function and the importance of Bills of Lading. In total, this will provide the Essential Guide to Chartering and the Dry Freight Market that is promised in the title of this book.

What will constantly be apparent is that this industry is far from static. Indeed it is quite the contrary. Ships, the supply and demand determinants of the market, the market level itself, the different trades, charter parties and the issues that are negotiated are constantly changing. While this book is a snapshot of the chartering and freight market at the beginning of the twenty-first century it will attempt to explain, where necessary, how and why the present situation has arisen and where it might be likely to go.

1. The Ships

TYPES AND SIZES

The most numerous type of dry cargo ship to be chartered is undoubtedly the bulk carrier and it is this type of vessel, the cargoes it carries and the charter party terms involved in negotiating a fixture of a bulk carrier that this book will mainly be dealing. However, there is a significant, and in some sectors a growing chartering market for other types of vessels. Perhaps the easiest way to describe the types of ships is to classify them in groups. I have done so as the Bulk Carrier Group, the Container Ship Group, the Multipurpose Vessel Group, the Ro Ro Group and the Reefer Group. However, it is not quite as easy as it sounds as there is a great deal of overlapping. Some Ro Ro's have container capacity. Is it therefore a Ro Ro or a multipurpose vessel? Is the 'Conbulker' a multipurpose vessel? Into which group does a general tramp tweendeck belong? The answers to these questions are that they are artificial groups that assist in the explanation of the shipping and chartering market. Where I have chosen to put each type simply reflects where it is most appropriate to explain the purpose and origins of that type of ship. For instance, it is easier to explain the history and role of tweendeckers in the Multipurpose Group section, even though few in the industry would seriously refer to a general tramp tweendecker as a true multipurpose vessel.

The Bulk Carrier Group

This group's overriding character is that these are ships designed for and usually carry bulk cargo.

A bulk carrier is essentially a box into which bulk cargoes such as iron ore, coal, grain and sometimes break bulk cargoes such as steel, pipes, timber and other generals are loaded. Shipping people refer to the sizes of bulk dry cargo vessels as handy, handymax, panamax and capesizes.

Handy

This is an inexact term but most people involved in shipping would understand it to mean roughly any ship from 10,000 to about 35,000 dwt although some might bring the lower limit down and the higher figure up to 40,000 dwt. Below 10,000 dwt, however, bulk carriers might be known as **'mini bulkers'**. Whatever size limit is used, these ships carry a huge variety of cargoes. There are less handysize being built in recent years as economies of scale drive up parcel and ship sizes but they are still by far the most

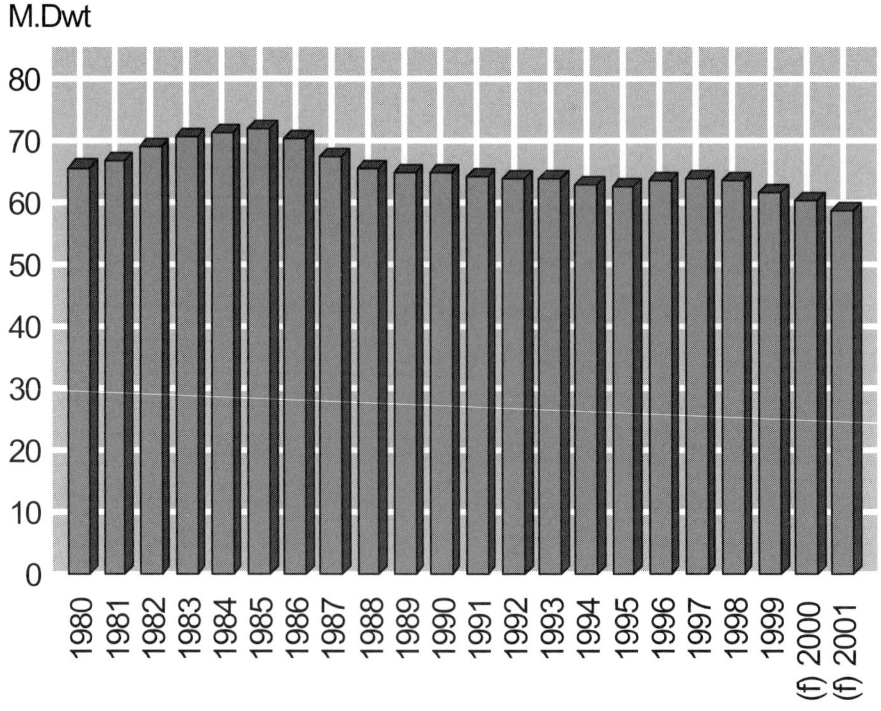

Figure 1.1

Handy size fleet development year by year in million dwt

numerous of the size groups and are therefore fixed more frequently than their larger and sometimes more headline hitting relatives.

At the beginning of the year 2000 there were 2457 ships (60.1 million tons deadweight) between 10,000 and 35000 dwt. This compares with 1327 handymax vessels, 1016 panamax and 524 capesizes. Therefore it is clear that despite the fact that both the handysize fleet as such and that its share of the shipping market as a whole is declining, it is still the most numerous of the size groupings by a long way. They are the workhorses of the market. Because less are being built the age profile is getting older. (See Figure 1.1 and 1.2).

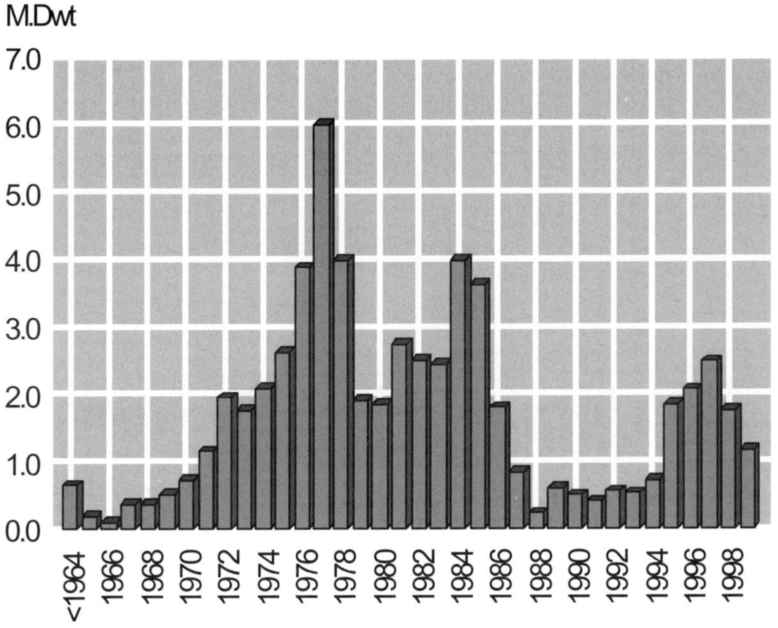

Figure 1.2

Age Profile Diagram of 10-35,000 dwt fleet at January 2000

Of the 2457 ships recorded, 46% were over 20 years of age and another 22%, between 15 and 19 years of age. This means that an incredible 68% of the fleet is over 15 years old and growing older. As one would expect with the trend towards economies of scale and the increasing volumes of trade, the trend within this size band is also towards larger ships. The highest percentage of old ships are therefore in the 10-20,000 deadweight group.

As noted above, the handysize fleet as a whole is shrinking and will almost certainly continue to do so. But its importance is reflected in that it accounts for about 23% by deadweight and 46% by number of the total bulk carrier fleet. Handysizes operate in an almost infinite number of trades. Most of them are geared, increasing the number of trades and ports they can use. Many of them work niche markets and are specialised. (See Figure 1.3 and the sections on the various specialist bulk carriers later in the Chapter).

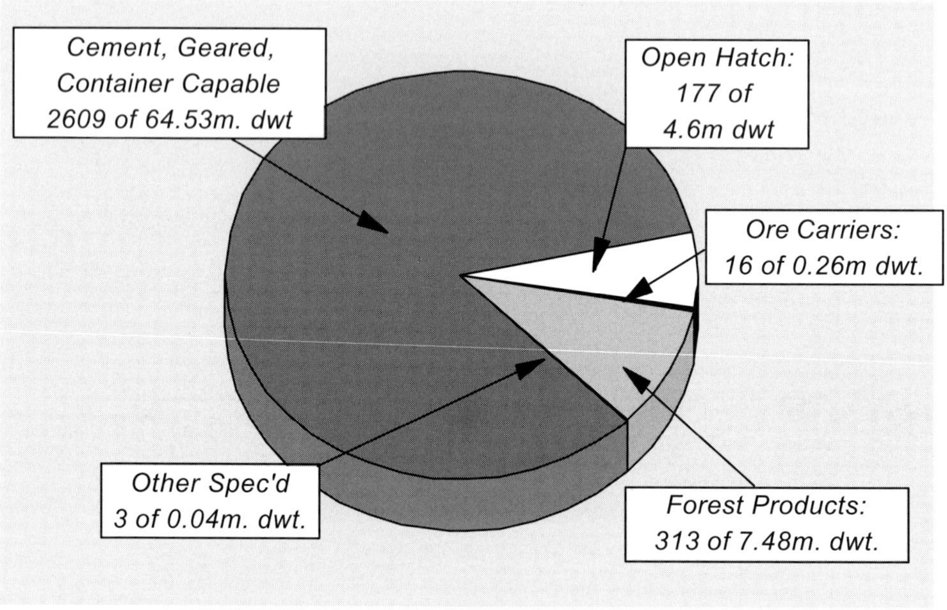

Figure 1.3
Specialised handy fleet

Because of the size of the fleet and the numerous general and specialist jobs they do, there is an infinite variety of deadweights, drafts, LOA's (length over all), beams and gear but a diagram of a typical 27000 dwt can be seen in Figure 1.4. The following are some typical handy size vessels with their dimensions and characteristics;

Age	Dwt	Draft	HH	Loa	Beam	Grain '000	Gear	Sp/cons
1979	19,610	9.52	4/4	158.5	22.4	857	4 x 25 t drks	12.5 on 21 +1.7
1982	23,194	9.95	4/4	160.4	24.6	1,103	4 x 25 t crns	14 on 21.8 +1.5
1982	27,652	9.60	5/5	165.5	27.0	1,229	4 x 25 t crns	13 on 22 + 0
1983	34,070	10.77	5/5	178.5	27	1,866	4 x 25 t crns	13.5 26/24+2
1997	27,288	9.82	5/5	175	26	1,322	5 x 30 t crns	14 on 24/24.5+0

A special category of handysize is the **'Laker'**, a ship that is able to transit the locks of the St. Lawrence Seaway and reach the Great Lakes of North

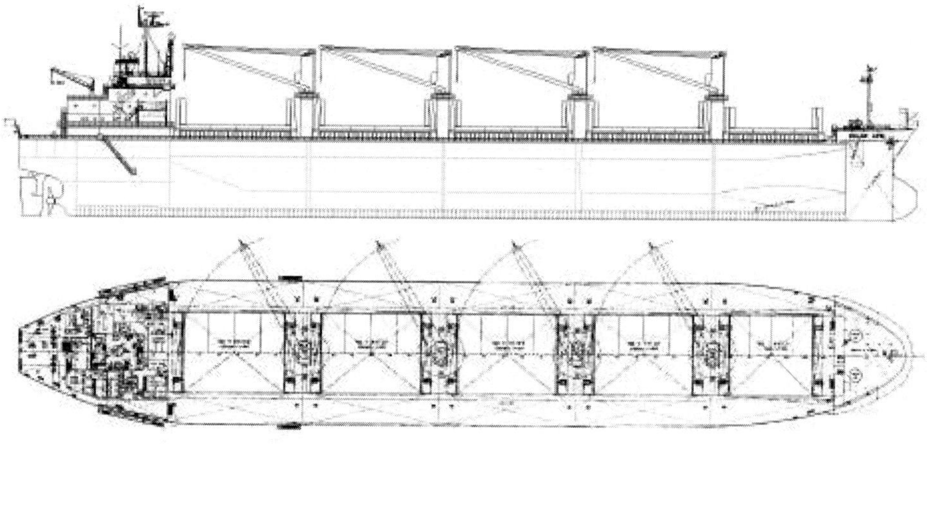

Figure 1.4

Plan of a typical handysize bulk carrier

America. The maximum dimensions are 23.77 meters beam and 222.5 meters LOA. If they are to enter they have to be fitted with equipment to go through the locks such as special ropes, fenders, fairleads, VHF radio and a stern anchor. The maximum deadweight is effectively about 28/32,000 dwt. The trade is restricted to the ice free season of April to December in the St. Lawrence. Ships that fail to sail out prior to the end of the season risk being frozen in.

These are not to be confused with ships designated for **Great Lakes trading only** which trade inside the Lakes as far as the St. Lawrence Seaway. With the beam limited to 75 feet and draft to 27 feet the only way to achieve satisfactory cargo capacity is to make the LOA much longer hence the curious very long narrow shape of these ships. There are other peculiar features to Great Lakes trading; the lack of severe waves and swell and hence stresses to the hull, the lack of corrosive salt water and the lack of grabbed handling appliances at load and discharge ports means the ships tend to last much longer than sea going vessels. The long narrow shape and the nature of the handling appliances determine the numerous hatch arrangements. Their efficiency added to the short distances involved led to the invention of the belt self unloader. (See later in the Chapter).

Handymax

This term denotes the maximum size of handy sizes before they reach panamaxes. It is another inexact term but handymaxes almost always have gear for loading and discharging whereas the panamaxes are usually gearless. Handymaxes can be roughly categorised as 35-50,000 dwt. This is a more modern fleet than the handysize fleet as this size has really replaced a great number of handy size trades as economies of scale have driven up parcel sizes. It is worth comparing Figures 1.1 and 1.5, the handy and handymax fleet development, which demonstrates this. At the beginning of 2000 there

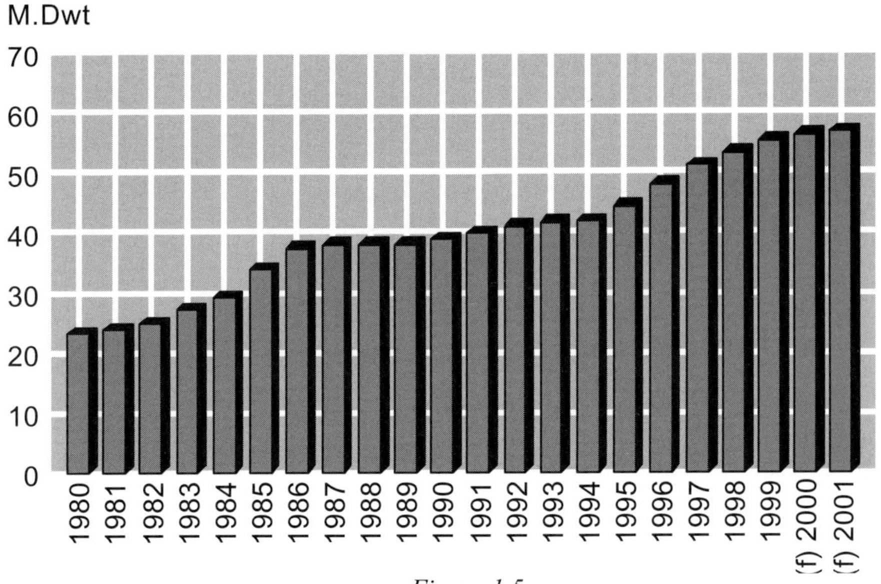

Figure 1.5

Handymax fleet development year by year in million dwt

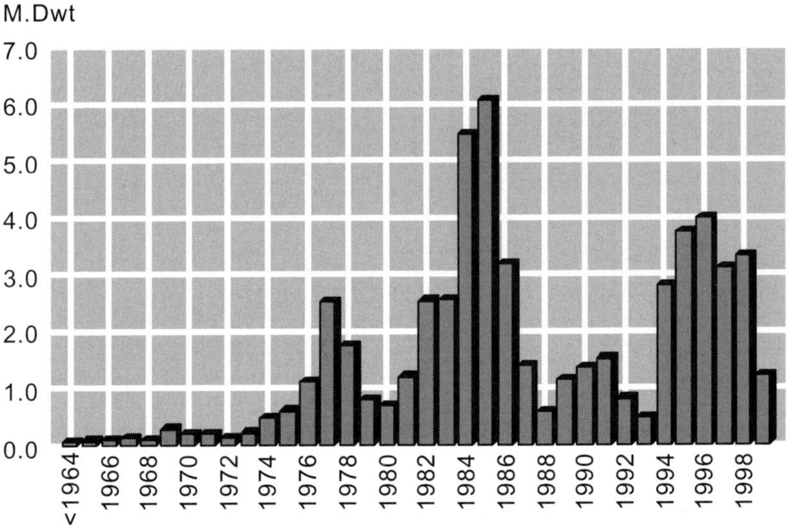

Figure 1.6

Age Profile of 35-50,000 deadweight fleet at January 2000

were 1327 ships of 56.1 million deadweight between 35,000 and 50,000 dwt and unlike the handy fleet's age profile, only 15% are over 20 years of age. (See Figures 1.5 and 1.6) and about 40% are younger than 10 years old.

Yet just as the handymaxes took over from the handysizes as parcel stems got bigger, the typical new handymax itself has got bigger throughout the 1990's as can be seen from the table on the opposite page. So much so that some of the modern ones are in excess of 50,000 dwt. The Tsuneishi 'TESS 52' (See Figure 1.7) has, according to its own publicity, the 'greatest deadweight at shallow draft of any handymax bulk carrier in the world' at 52,000 dwt on 12

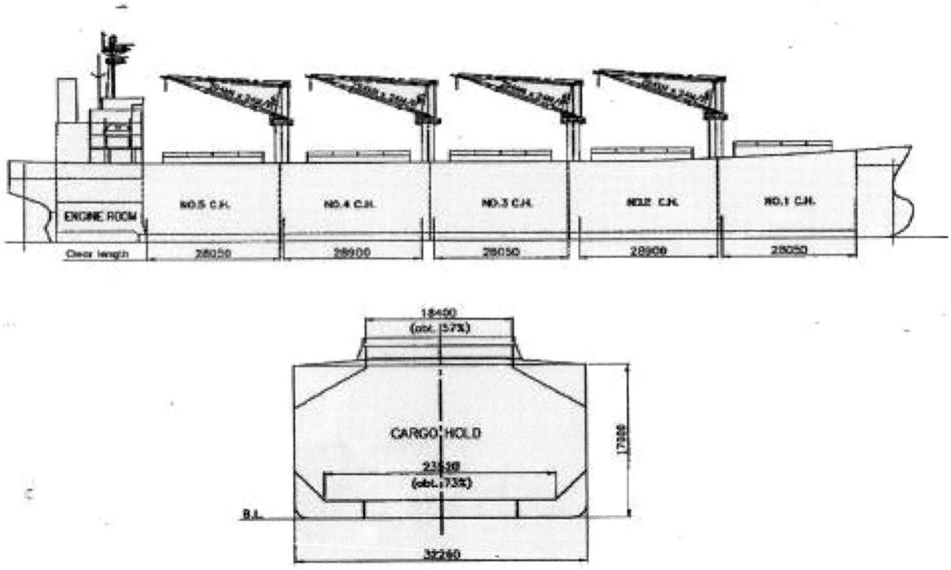

Figure 1.7
Plan of a TESS 52

metres scantling draft and can keep 41,300 mt on 10 meters. Its grain capacity is almost the same as the old late 1970's built 61,000 dwt Koyo panamax types and indeed it conforms to a panamax beam. Compare its characteristics in the handymax table with Koyo type in the Panamax table on page 11.

Between 35,000 and 50,000 dwt there are a whole range of bulk carrier types but in general the older handymaxes, often loggers, are in the lower end of this range and the modern ships, in general at the higher end. The following is a range of typical handymax bulk carriers showing the trend to increasing the deadweight, grain cubics, gear capacity but inevitably also the draft.

The development of the handymax bulk carrier

Year	Dwt	Draft	HH	Gr '000 cuft	Gear	Sp/cons	fittings
1983	36,850	11.02	5/5	1,686	4 x 25 t crns	14 on 28.6+2	logger
1991	42,035	11.2	5/5	1,859	4 x 25 t crns	13.5on24.5+0	
1985	45,202	12.3	6/6	1,920	4 x 25 t crns	13.3 on 27+2	
1994	48,131	11.71	5/5	2,060	4 x 30 t crns	14 on 32 +0	grabs
1999	52,000	12.00	5/5	2,422	4 x 30 t crns	14 on 28+0	

Panamax

This is an exact term. It is the maximum size of vessel able to transit the Panama Canal. The restriction is that the ship must have a beam not exceeding 32.2 meters. The usual draft restriction in the Panama Canal, except in cases of drought, is 39'6'' tropical fresh water. Panamaxes usually have deeper draft and thus do not load down to their marks or full draft when loading for a voyage via the Panama Canal. The standard stem size, for example, of grain from the United States Gulf to Japan via the Panama takes this into account and is 54,000 long tons 10 percent more or less in owner's option.

Designs have changed over the years. In the late 1970's the typical panamax, with a few exceptions, was 57/61,000 dwt. Throughout the 1980's the size of a typical new building gradually increased to 68/70,000 dwt and by the end of the 1990's it was 70/75,000 dwt. At the same time the draft and cubic capacity increased from around 12.5 to 14 meters and 2.5 million to 3 million cubic feet. The LOA, with a few exceptions, remained unchanged at between

225/230 metres. There is no physical reason for this but there are a few ports around the world with such restrictions, principally the main Japanese grain discharging ports. Most owners in general feel that this is such an important trade that they cannot exclude themselves from it. A few, however, have built 75,000 tonners and been able to have a shallower draft by increasing the LOA up to 250 metres. As long as they are not overbuilt there is definitely a niche in the market for this type. Most panamaxes are gearless but a few have been built with gear. Older vessels with 8 or 10 ton cranes had little opportunity to use them and some have subsequently had them removed. However, there is a profitably employed niche fleet of panamaxes with 25 ton gear with grabs which can trade to ports where there are no shore loading or discharging facilities.

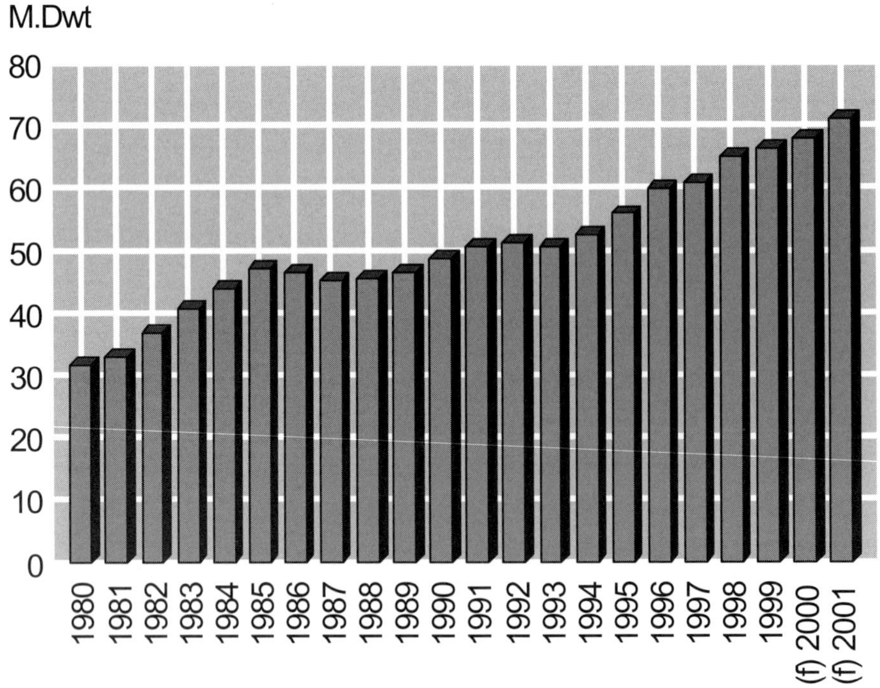

Figure 1.8
Panamax fleet development year by year in million dwt

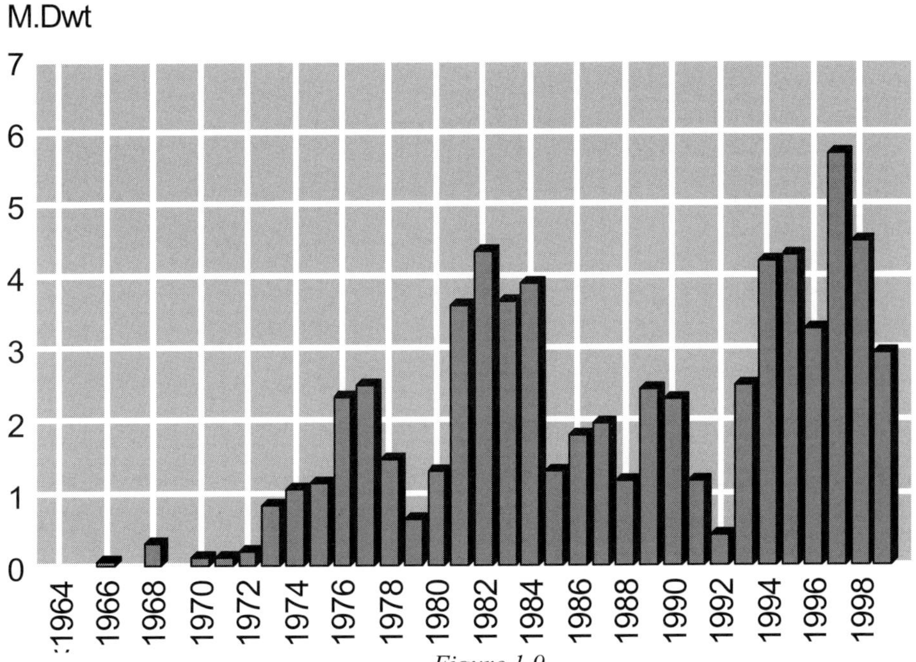

Figure 1.9

Age Profile of Panamax fleet at January 2000

Over the past 20 years the panamax trades have expanded both in number and volume, as indeed, has the fleet. At the beginning of 2000 there were 1016 vessels of 68.5 million deadweight of this type, 46% of them younger than 10 years old. (See Figures 1.8 and 1.9)

Typical panamaxes over the last 25 years indicating the development of size

Year	Yard	Dwt	Draft	LOA	Beam	HH	Grain	Sp/Cons
1975	Hitatchi	61,395	12.46	225	32.2	7/7	2,622,000	13-38/33
1976	Koyo	61498	13.04	222	32.2	7/7	2,429,000	13-32+2.5
1975	MHI	64,477	13.35	224	31.8	7/7	2,606,000	14/15-
1981	Hyundai	65,593	13.1	224.4	32.2	7/7	2,647,000	13/14-33+2
1985	CSBC	66,734	13.24	229.8	32.2	7/7	2,732,000	14-37/39+0
1985	Mitsui	69,621	13.258	222.7	32	7/7	2,829,000	13.5-32.5+0
1996	Namura	71,290	13.65	224.9	32.2	7/7	3,000,000	14-32/29+0
1996	Sanoyasu	70316	13.3	225	32.2	7/7	2,890,000	14- 28 +0
1996	B and W	75,265	14.3	225	32.2	7/7	3,007,330	14-36,5 +0
1998	NKK	74,761	13.79	225	32.2	7/7	3,095,930	14 35/29+0

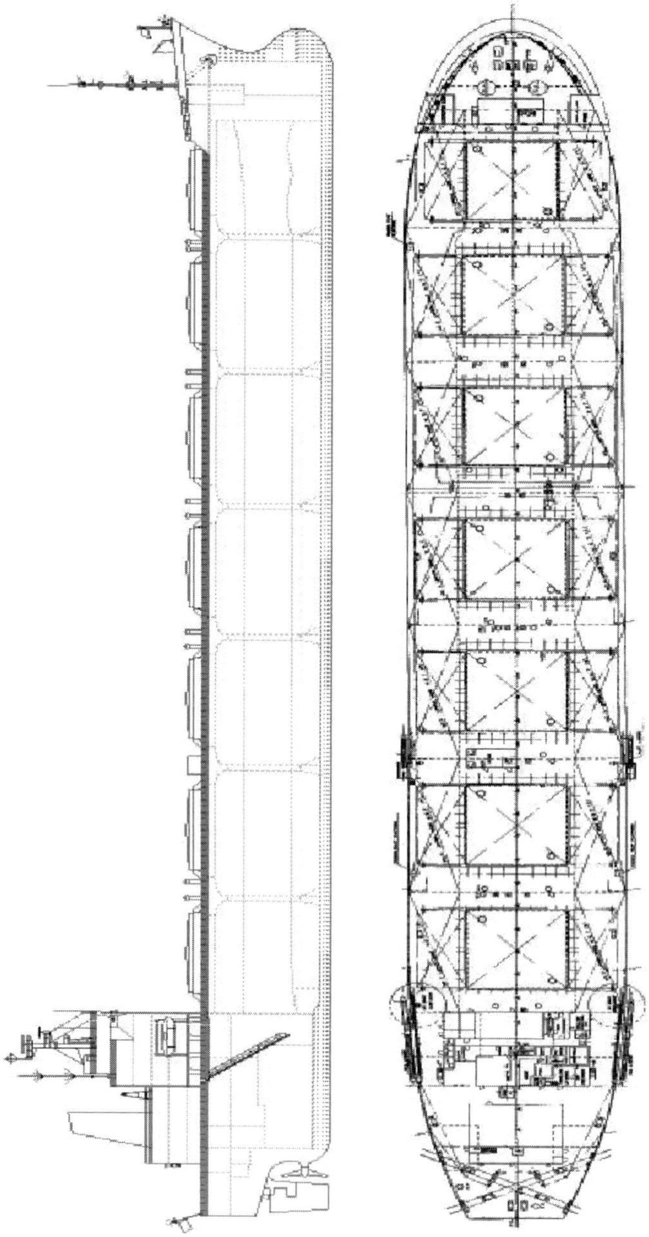

Figure 1.10
General Arrangement plan of a Panamax

It can be seen that the trend has been to increase the size and carrying capacity and a technical improvement in engine design as demonstrated by the speed and consumption.

The principal cargoes carried by panamaxes are grain, coal, iron ore, phosphates, bauxite, alumina, scrap and coke but occasionally steel products, and even the occasional cargo of sugar in the last two years. (See Figure 1.11).

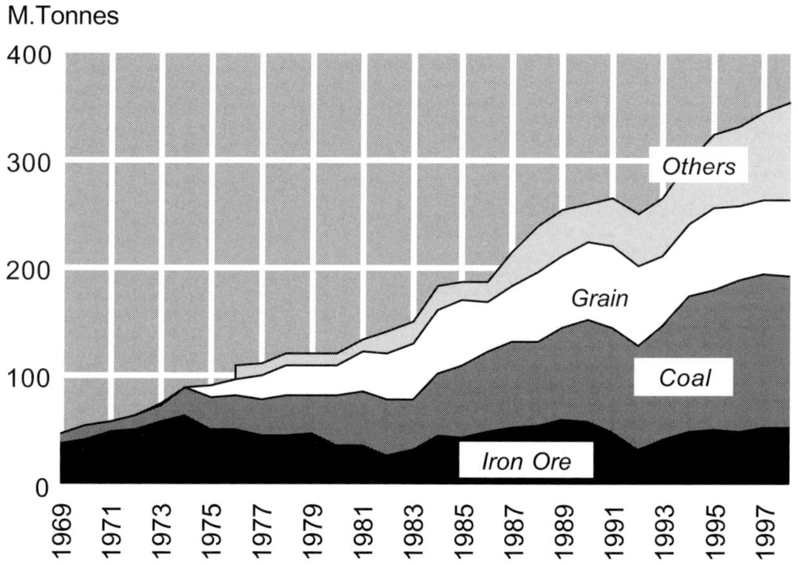

Figure 1.11
What does a panamax carry?

Capesize

These are vessels which being too large to transit the Panama Canal have to go from Atlantic to Pacific and vice versa via the Cape of Good Hope. But they need not trade in this pattern. There are plenty of inter Atlantic and inter Pacific trades which are designed to benefit from the economies of scale which the larger size brings. The cargoes they carry are mainly coal and iron ore. (See Figure 1.12). These trades have increased tremendously over the past 30 years, especially coal for use in power stations and the fleet has increased similarly. (See Figure 1.13). Technically defined as larger than 32.2 meters beam, they are, in most cases, commercially not worth building unless the beam is much wider.

The first capesizes were built in the late '60's and early '70's and some of these are still trading today. In many respects their designs and dimensions and the pattern of the mineral trades for which they were built have hardly changed. There were many 150/165,000 tonners built in the '70's, most of them ore/oil combination ships built for purpose built iron ore ports in Brazil, Australia, Japan and Europe and smaller bulk carriers of 100/130,000 dwt. In the early '80's the trend was to build bulkers rather than combination ships to cater for the growing steam coal trade and the popular size was 140/150,000 dwt. The trend increased so that by the late '90's the most popular size to build was 165/180,000 dwt.

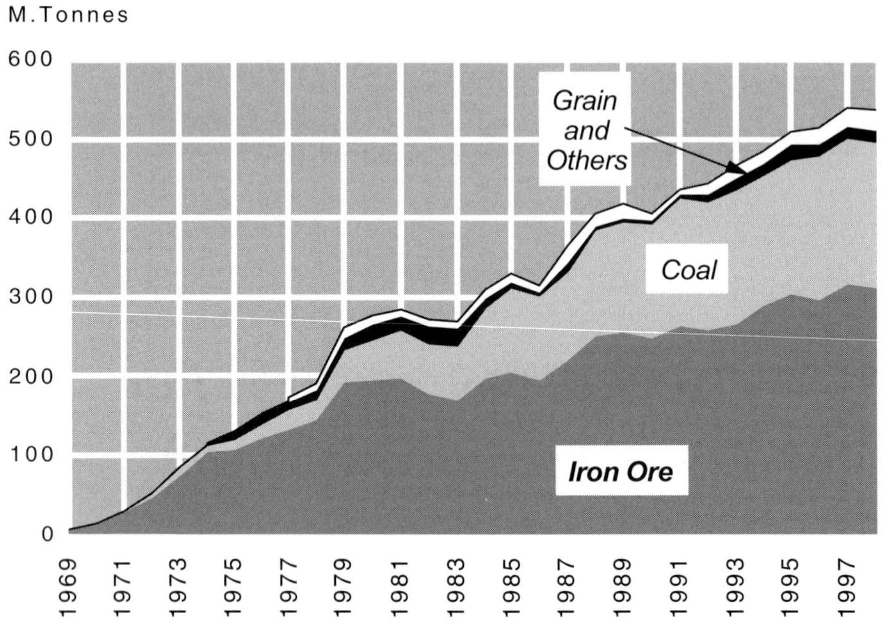

Figure 1.12
What does a capesize carry?

As with the panamax owners who bucked the trend with geared ships or with LOA's in excess of 230 metres, there were and are exceptions. For instance, there is a small fleet of modern 115/120,000 dwts which were built to cater for the West African ore trades on which only the oldest small capes were still trading. As it is, they have found their niche in other trades, especially shoehorning them into some ports where previously panamaxes were the largest size that could enter. At the other end of the scale, Koreans built a number of 211,000 dwts and even one 250,000 tonner to cater for the newly opened deep drafted port of Kwangyang and the considerable quantities of coal and iron ore being imported there.

At the beginning of 2000 there were 523 vessels of 82.1 million tons deadweight above 80,000 dwt with an age profile shown in Figure 1.14; It reflects the large number of capesizes built between 1995-1999. 32% are younger than 4 years old. However, a large number of the smaller capesizes are now quite old. In fact over 65% of those between 100-120,000 dwt are over 20 years old.

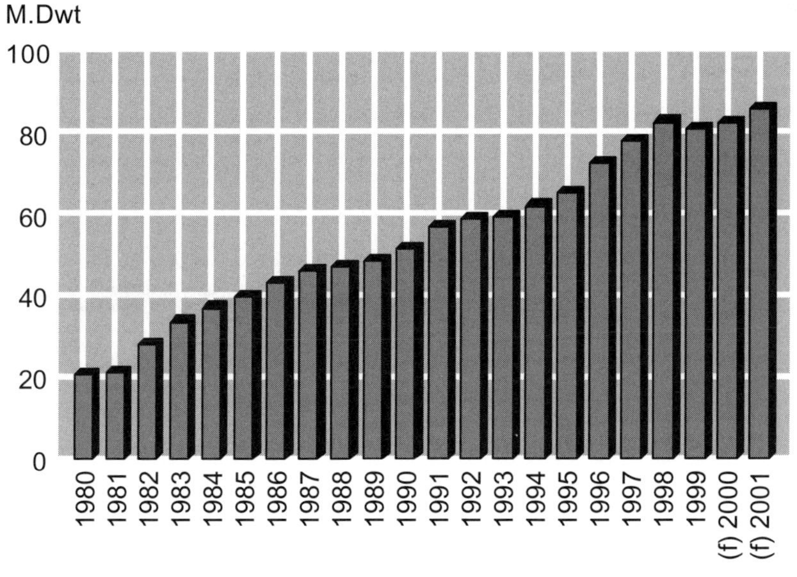

Figure 1.13

Capesize fleet development year by year in million dwt

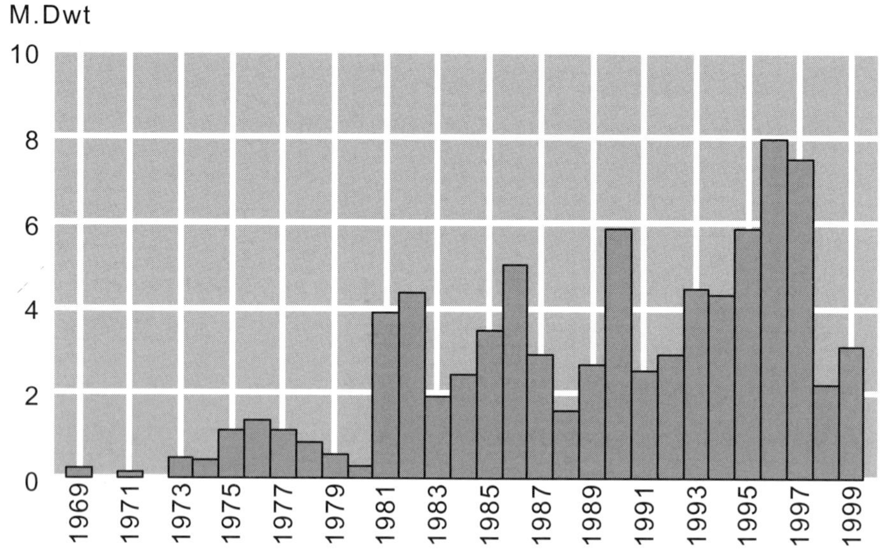

Figure 1.14

Age profile of the Capesize fleet at January 2000

Typical capesize bulk carriers demonstrating developments over the past 25 years

Year	Yard	Dwt	Draft	LOA	Beam	HH	Gr-'000cft	Sp/Cons
1973	MHI	129,542	17.6	261	40.7	9/9	5,562	11-37/46+2
1981	Hyundai	140,839	16.7	266.5	43	9/9	5,840	13-49/52+1.5
1986	CSBC	151,016	16.83	288.9	44.5	9/9	6,130	15/13.6-54+0
1993	Hyundai	160,849	17.5	280	45	9/9	6,215	14.5/14-50+0
1993	CSBC	150,000	17.3	270	43.4	9/9	5,906	14.5/13-45+0
1995	H and W	163,556	17.8	283.7	44.4	9/9	6,522	15.5/14.5-63+0
1997	Hyundai	185,800	18.0	291	48	9/9	7,045	14.5/15-58+0
1997	Daewoo	211,200	18.3	312	50	9/9	8,039	14.5/66L-57B
Modern 'baby cape'								
1993	Daewoo	123,737	14.5	266	40.5	9/9	4,800	15/14.25-47+0

The table demonstrates a general pattern of increasing size, improving dwt/draft ratio improving speed and consumption figures and a willingness to build up to a 45 meter beam for ships that can be generally traded on the open market up to about 175,000 dwt. A full discussion on the various merits of each design is not appropriate here but obviously if a ship is designed with a restricted LOA or beam then draft will suffer and vice versa. Notice the superior dimensions and speed and consumption of the modern 'baby cape', especially the draft compared with the similar deadweight 1973 built MHI type above.

Bulk carriers are the most widely chartered vessels. A full list can be found in the Bulk Carrier Register along with the main points that will need to be known regarding their employment. (See Figure 1.15).

Iran Azadi (Ex Oinoussian Friendship) 35,839 Dwt Log Carrier
Builder Nalkai S.B. Owner/Man. Iran Shipping Lines Flag Iran Callsign: EQPZ

Hull	M	Ft.	Tonnages		Hull & Class		Capacity		Holds/Hatches Dimensions		Cranes Derricks	Propulsion	
LOA	179.9	590	Dwt (m)	14,646	Built	197953	Ore cu.m		5 Holds	1@14.0% 10.5m	X 1 5 % 25t	B&W	28-A 6-cyl
Beam	28.4	93.3	Dwt		Class	LR	Grain cu.m	42,833		1@20.5% 13.4m	x 1 % t	HP	11,600B at 124
M. Depth	15.2	49.7	GT	10,774	S.Survey	01/02/891	W.Tank cu.m	3,000	5 Hatches	3@20.7% 13.4m	x 1 % t	Propeller	
Draught	10.3	36.9	NT	6,134	CRS No.	405675	Teu Total	572		@ % m	x 1 % t	Service Speed	15.0 Kt
Air Draft			SCNT		LR. No	76328387	Teu Hold	340		@ % m	S/Unloader 1/hrt	Consumption	37.0 1/day
TPC/I	43.6	109	PCNT		Ice Class		Teu Deck	232	Ballast	11,231t @ 636 1/hr	Conveyort 1/hrt	Bunkers	2,133 1
Safety & Other Details			LHP 1.70m. Log fined, Wbh in 3, 4 &5 holds only, Hvy. Cargo. Timber: dr. 10.87m. W. Tank Bleed. Cargo In 6.50m, Fr. Water General.										
Other Ex Names/Orig.			Oinoussian Friendship										

Figure 1.15

Part of a page of the Bulk Carrier Register

Within the Bulk Carrier group are catagorisations not only of size but of type. The 'Laker' and 'Great Lakes only' traders have been dealt with under 'Handy'. The following are some further examples.

Ore Carrier

Built for the carriage of ore only they have a very small cubic capacity reflecting the low stowage factor of iron ore. There are very few built these days except for dedicated trades with a bankable contract of affreightment as they are severely limited for trading on the spot market. Long contracts of affreightment enable ships to be tailored to the intended load and discharge ports and thus maximise economies of scale. Thus the largest dry cargo ship at 360,000 dwt is an ore carrier specially built for the carriage of ore from Brazil to the German steel mills under a very long term contract and the next largest is a 320,000 dwt ore carrier. She runs evergreen contracts to Japanese steel mill ports from Brazil one way and from Australia to European steel mills the other. It is very difficult indeed to trade anything larger than 200,000 dwt on the spot market at the present time as too many ports cannot handle either the LOA or Beam of the ship or indeed the delivered cargo quantity in one shipment.

Combination Carrier

They are able to load both dry and wet cargoes and became popular in the 1960's and '70's. The theory was that they could pay for the extra 15-20% building and running cost of a ship designed for dry cargo and oil by eliminating ballast legs in trading the ships. Thus a 160,000 ton combination ship, it was thought, could perform a Brazil/Japan iron ore voyage, then Arabian Gulf or Indonesia to Europe oil, then ore again minimising the ballast time. In practice this happened only with very few vessels in the '70's and '80's. The rest, however, improvised.

On good tanker markets they traded oil and on good dry cargo markets they traded dry cargo. Some did find combination trades. Brazilian iron ore into the Arabian Gulf then oil to Atlantic destinations including Brazil was one trade that lasted until recently but suffered as age and condition limitations imposed by the oil majors restricted the number of vessels that could perform. Another was iron ore from Chile to Japan and Europe, with oil from China or West Africa back to Chile until a pipeline from Argentina to Chile was built. One trade that has lasted until the present time with a large active combination fleet is in coal and grain in 50/100,000 tonners from the USA, Venezuala and Colombia to North Europe and the Mediterranean with North Sea and Mediterranean oil back. This trading pattern and the willingness of the combination carrier to carry coal to position itself back for the more lucrative oil cargo is actually the single most important factor setting freight rates on the vital North Atlantic dry cargo panamax and capesize markets.

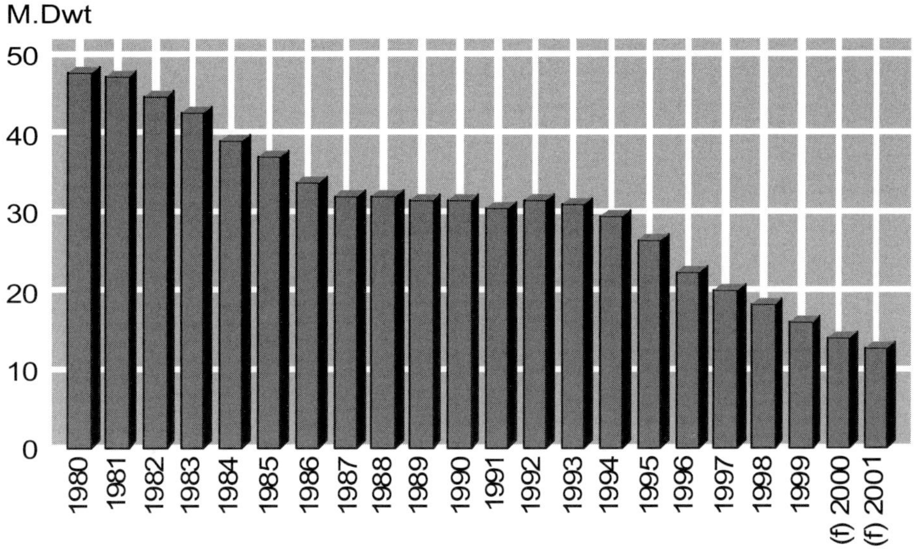

Figure 1.16

Combination Carrier Fleet Development year by year in million dwt

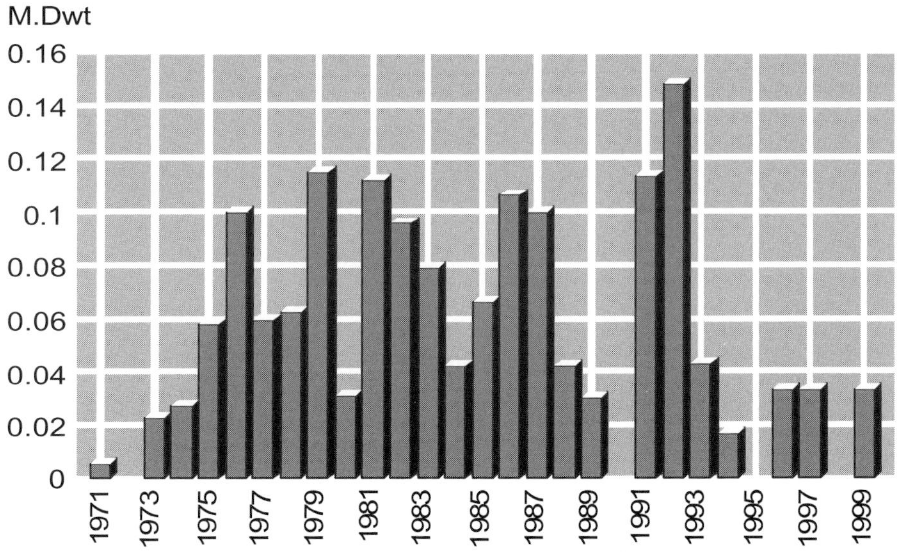

Figure 1.17

Age Profile of the Combination Carrier Fleet at January 2000

The various types of combination carrier (or **combo** for short) are:

Ore/Oiler

A combination ship allowing the carriage of ore and oil only having the small centre holds for carrying ore and the outer and centre holds for oil. The use of separate holds reduced the need for cleaning between oil and ore in the same cargo space but was wasteful and limited trading to ore and oil only. There are very few left trading.

OBO (Ore Bulk Oil)

A combination ship allowing oil and any bulk dry cargo in the same hold. More popular than ore oilers due to their versatility.

Probo

A concept which sought to eliminate ballast legs by combining the varied liquid products trades with dry cargo. Despite huge scepticism of the concept due to the stringent hold cleanliness demands for some types of oil products, the very few that were built are successfully trading as envisaged.

There obviously are niche's for some types of combination carrier and for a while some have traded very successfully indeed, but too many ore/oil carriers and OBO's were built in the '70's for the anticipated benefits. There has consequently been a reduction in numbers and they are not the influence on the market they were during the '80's and early '90's when the swing in and out of the tanker and bulk carrier trades affected the supply side of the market of both quite critically. At the beginning of 2000 there were 153 combination ships. Significantly, 83 of these were over 15 years of age. Indeed many of the older ones have been scrapped otherwise the imbalance of older ships would look even greater. The Cape sector of 81 ships represents 54% of the fleet by number and 71% by deadweight. There are also 56 Panamax Combo's (3.9 million dwt) and 15 handy combos. (See Figures 1.16 and 1.17).

At the peak of the dry cargo boom in 1995 there were only 7.3 million dwt of combined carriers engaged in the oil trades but over 17 million dwt in dry cargo. i.e. 70% of the fleet. But an improvement in tanker earnings and a decline in the dry cargo market accompanied by the scrapping of older vessels meant that less than 15% of the active combination fleet was operating in the dry cargo trades by the middle of 1999. With the increase in the market at the end of the summer of 1999 that went up to 18% but many of these older ships had become unsuitable for oil.

Belt Self Unloader

Some people, when talking of self unloaders are really thinking of ships with gear and grabs. In fact, geared and grabbed ships are commonly referred to as self-dischargers and although in the English language there is no difference in meaning between self discharger and self unloader, the shipping world tends to differentiate the two by this terminology. Of course, a geared and grabbed ship is able to self load as well but a self unloader cannot as it does not have cranes. It discharges by means of a conveyor belt on a boom which extends out from the side of the ship. The purpose built ships that do this employ the gravity feed system. (See Figure 1.18) This means that the sides of the holds are angled down to grates which, when open allow the cargo to slide down by gravity onto a conveyor belt. This carries the cargo along to another conveyor belt which lifts the cargo to the height of the deck where another belt on a boom will spew the cargo out at the place it is desired. The disadvantage is that much potential cargo carrying space is lost and the gear is expensive.

The advantage is that average cargo discharge speeds of 3000 tons per hour or even up to 6000 tons per hour can be achieved making the port stay very short and cheap. In fact they do not need to discharge at a port at all. They are

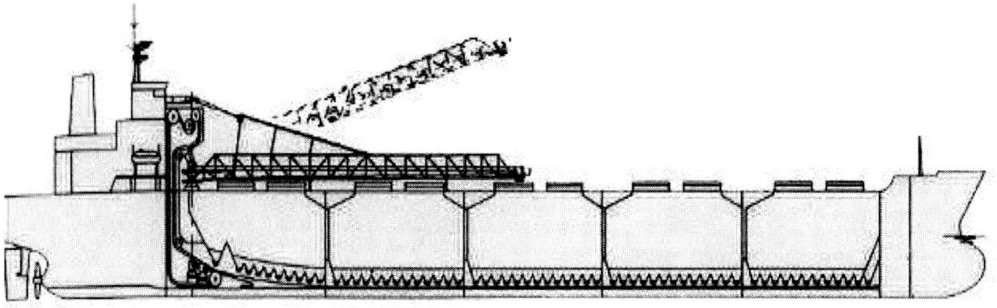

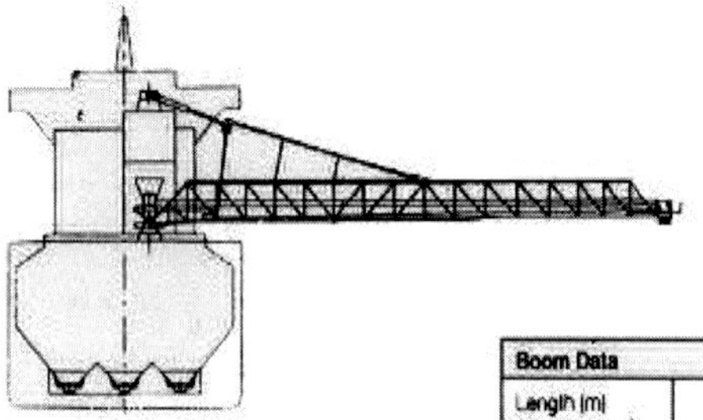

Boom Data	
Length (m)	82
Slewing (deg.)	± 90
Hoisting (deg.)	max. 18

Principal Dimensions of the Vessel	
Length between p.p. (m)	239
Width, moulded (m)	38
Depth, moulded (m)	21.5
Draught (m)	15.0
Deadweight (DWT)	96,000

Design Conditions		
Cargo	Coal, iron ore, grain, gravel, etc	
Unloading Capacity	Iron ore	6,000 t/h
	Coal	5,000 m^3/h
Power consumption at max. discharging capacity	about 2,200 kW	

Self-unloading gear of the M/V Western/Eastern Bridge

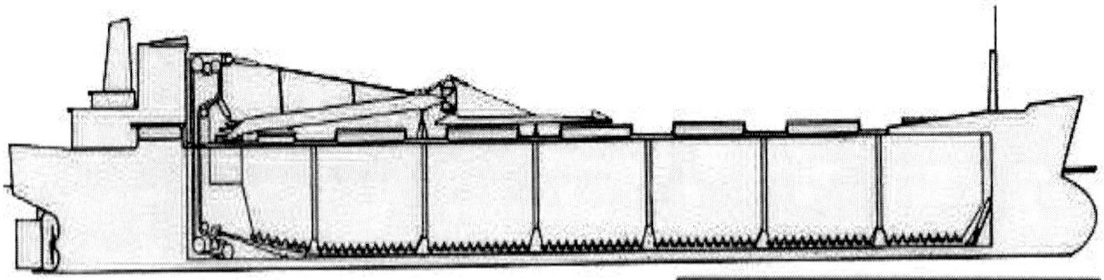

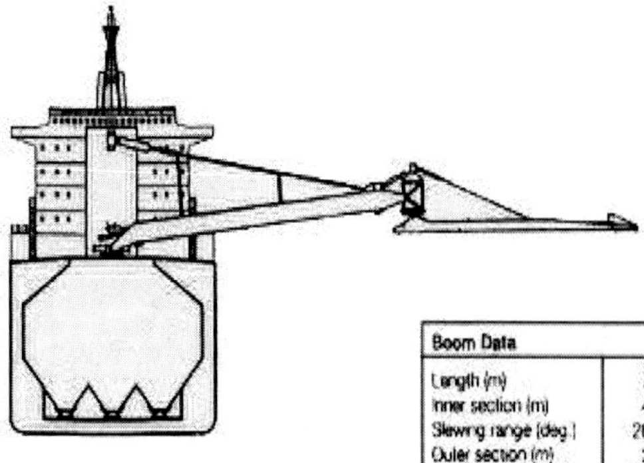

Principal Dimensions of the Vessel	*Innovator*	*Atlas*
Length overall (m)	227.7	227.4
Length between p.p. (m)	214.5	221.4
Width, moulded (m)	32.23	32.0
Depth, moulded (m)	14.2	19.2
Draught (m)	13.5	13.35
Deadweight (DWT)	62,500	67,800

Design Conditions			
Cargo	*Coal*	*Iron ore*	*Limestone*
Bulk density (t/m^3)	0.8	2.2	1.2
Max. lump size (mm)	50	50	400

Unloading Capacity	
Tunnel belt conveyors	1,500 m^3/h or 1,500 t/h
Cross conveyors	1,500 m^3/h or 1,500 t/h
Flexoift vertical conveyor (2x)	2,200 m^3/h or 2,250 t/h
Boom conveyor	4,400 m^3/h or 4,500 t/h

Boom Data	
Length (m)	76
Inner section (m)	46
Slewing range (deg.)	200
Outer section (m)	30
Slewing range (deg.)	300

Self-unloading gear of the CSL INNOVATOR

Figure 1.18

Two examples of Belt Self Unloader Designs

generally economic where the distance between load and discharge ports is very short and where the turn round for the ship is fast and reliable. They were first used in the Great Lakes where those conditions apply and they are now used increasingly in North America, north coast South America, Central America and in Europe in specialised trades with one in South East Asia. This is a classic niche market. Where the trade is longer than a very few days or there is a risk of other ships using the berth when the self unloader arrives causing delay, the economics of using this kind of a ship is destroyed.

There are other types of self unloaders which have been converted from standard bulk carriers. Having conventional holds, they take the cargo from the top of the hold by various means, sometimes a bucket system, occasionally a grab, which then deposits the cargo on the belt which then discharges in the same way. Being conversions these can be much cheaper but the discharge is much slower than the gravity feed system especially near the end of discharging each hold where the cargo at the sides and corners have to be collected. The average discharge rate of this kind of system is perhaps about 1000 tons per hour depending on the exact design.

Bulk Cement carrier

Cement clinker is an ordinary bulk cargo that needs no specialist ship and is discharged by grabs. Bagged cement is still carried in large quantities, usually in tweendeckers but occasionally in box hold bulk carriers in PVC coated jumbo bags lifted by plastic straps. More suppliers and receivers, however, now require the cement to be shipped in bulk. Some ordinary bulk carriers carry bulk cement. The provision of absolutely watertight hatch covers is obviously a priority. A hole is usually cut into the hatch cover and the cement blown in and sucked out by pneumatic pressure. These holes are made good to the owner's satisfaction at the end of the voyage. The holds must also be totally clean. However, there is a small fleet of specialised bulk cement carriers incorporating pneumatic cargo pumping and handling gear with

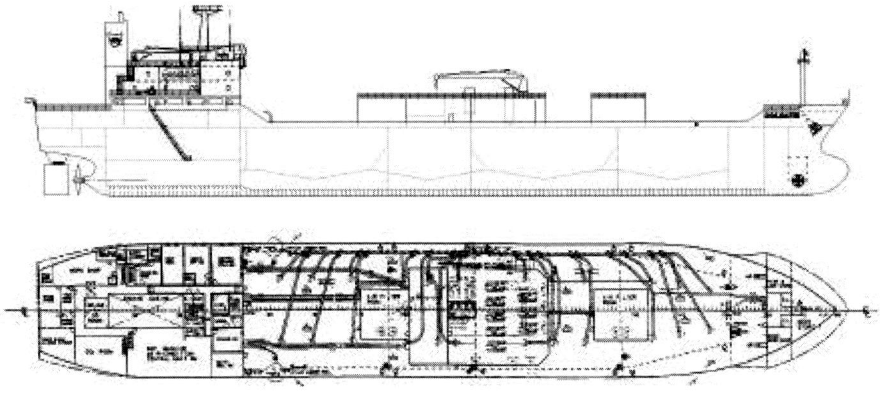

Figure 1.19
Example of a specialised Bulk Cement Carrier

totally enclosed holds and moisture control systems. These specialised ships are usually employed on long term contracts. (See Figure 1.19).

Chip carrier

Due to the high stowage factor of woodchips for the chipboard industry some ships were built with extremely high cubics especially for this trade. They were few in number and had to be fixed on dedicated long term contracts as they were very difficult to trade outside the cargo for which they were designed. They have a high freeboard, are fitted with gantry cranes, though shore based pneumatic equipment is often used.

Comparison of similar size and age bulk and chip carriers

Bulk Carrier built '90	**Chip Carrier built '90**
42,223 dwt on 11.2m	42,027 dwt on 10.3m
grain 1,870,300 cuft	grain 3,577,570 cuft
4 x 25 ton cranes	3 x 14 ton cranes self unloader
5 HoHa	6 HoHa
LOA 180 m	LOA 199 m
Beam 30.5 m	Beam 32.2 m
M depth 15.8 m	M depth 22.4 m

From the dimensions shown in the comparison of the bulk carrier and chip carrier above, it can be seen that the chip carrier has almost twice the cubic capacity as the similar sized bulk carrier and even more than the standard modern panamax. She manages this by being longer and wider but especially by having a much bigger moulded depth, despite having almost a meter less draft. This means that the **freeboard** (i.e. the distance from the water line to the deck) is far more. These characteristics make her difficult to trade outside the chip trade.

Open Hatch Bulk Carrier (Conbulker)

The open hatch bulk carrier offers a solution to the problem of access to the holds by having huge hatches which cover the width of the ship. This ship type can therefore load timber, pipes, steel coils, packaged cargoes and of course containers more efficiently than a standard bulk carrier with standard size hatches. This advantage is enhanced by having **box shaped holds**. This means that the holds are rectangular, the corners and sides not 'compromised' by the slopes of the wing tanks. The cranes are large enough to load the heaviest containers or other heavy cargo. This vessel type therefore

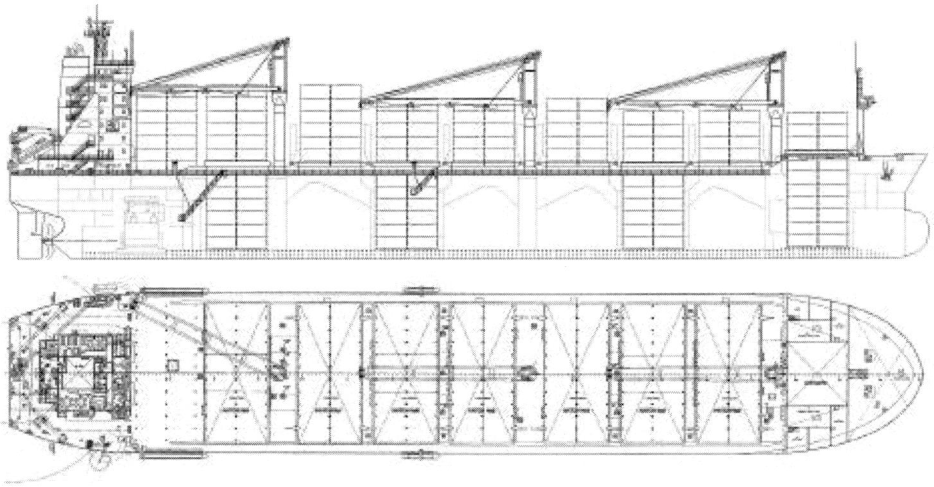

Figure 1.20
Example of Open Hatch type

sometimes has a role in the liner sector offering the option to carry containers on the outward leg and dry bulk on the return leg of a round voyage, especially useful in repositioning empty containers. Hence, they are often referred to as 'conbulkers'.

Two representative examples of conbulkers of different sizes.

1. 29,534 mt dwt on 10.02 m
   Box shaped, double skinned Open hatch Container Bulk
   Carrier built '98
   LOA 181/Beam 26
   36,311 cum grain/35,452 bale
   5 holds / 5 hatches
   5 x 30 ton cranes combinable
   Abt 14 on 23.5 MT IFO (180) no do at sea
   Port consumption idle 2.5 mt mdo. Gear working 4.5 mt mdo

2. 41,815 mt dwt on 12.2 m
   Box hold Open hatch type Container Bulk Carrier
   LOA /Beam 198.25 / 32.2
   52,783 cubic metres grain
   8 holds / 5 hatches
   5 x 41 ton cranes
   16 on 46 plus 4.5 blended

The concept of these multipurpose vessels, eliminating ballast legs, reminds one of the combination carrier and the problem with them is similar. When the more lucrative market, in this case the container ship market, is satiated with fast cellular container ships, there is no demand for conbulkers which are comparatively inadequate on both container capacity and speed. They therefore have to find a role with specialised 'breakbulk' and bulk cargo as best they can. When there is high containership demand which is unable to be satisfied by the cellular containership fleet alone, then these vessels will no doubt begin to command rates higher than they could achieve otherwise. It is the classic combination or multipurpose ship dilemma.

The Container Ship Group

Many ships can carry containers but when reference is made to 'container ships' what is meant is a dedicated, specialised fully **cellular** ship. All the major shipping lines use container ships and the chartering of them is mainly undertaken by liner companies. These are the same companies that used to use the liner type ships described under the "Multipurpose Group". They carry cargo in containers of two standard sizes laid down by the International Standards organisation (ISO), the 20 foot equivalent unit (TEU) and 40 foot equivalent unit (FEU). The structure of the ship is like an open box into which the containers are stacked. The holds are fitted with cell guides allowing the containers to be dropped into place and secured. The hatch covers are strengthened allowing the stacking of more containers above deck. In the most modern ones, the ships are hatchless which allows much faster loading and discharging.

This is a huge and very fast growing market. (See Figure 1.23). The first Container Register in 1995 listed 1800 vessels of 2.5 million TEU's. The 1999/2000 Liner Register which replaced it, however, details 2550 ships of 4.24 million TEU's. This is an incredible 40% increase in TEU capacity in only four years and the New Building order book will ensure a continuing strong growth.

As the market has evolved over the past 20 years it has polarised into several different size categories. There are now six identifiably different sectors. Like the bulk carrier group the newer ships are getting bigger overall and in each group.

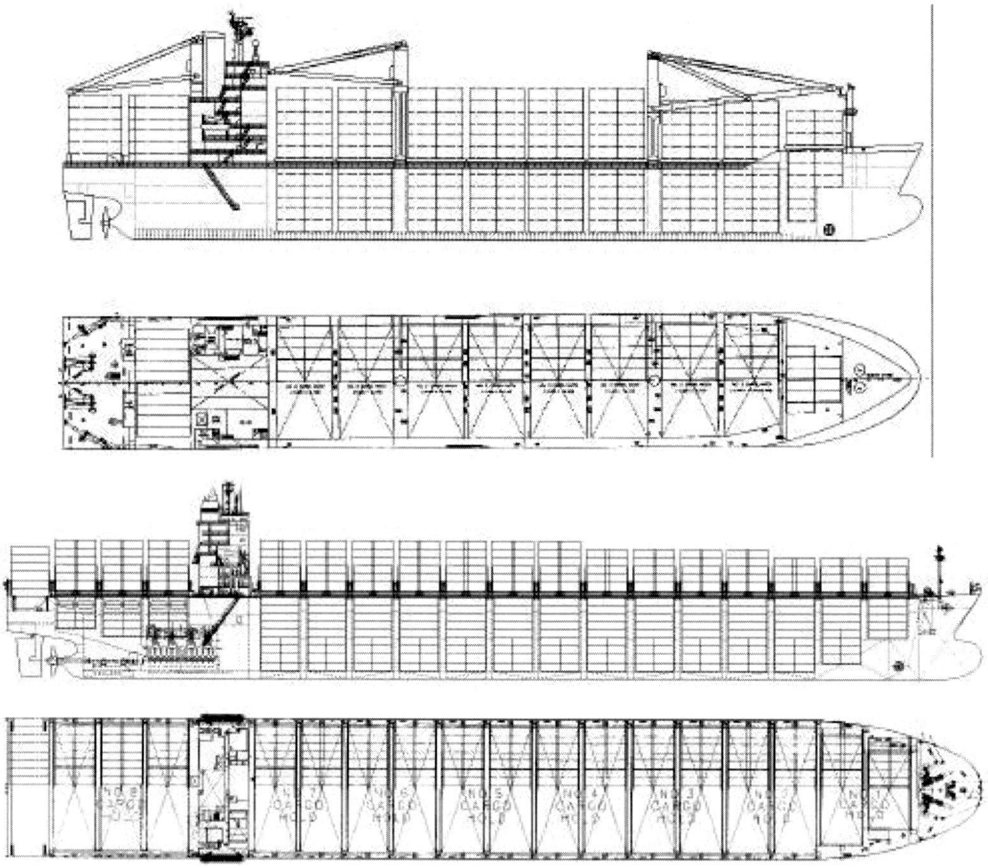

Figure 1.21

Examples of Feeder (top) and a post panamax Cellular container ship (below) - not to scale

Feeder

(100-500 TEU) The fleet grew rapidly in the 1980's but only about 3.5% per annum since 1985 and a spurt again since 1996. At 476 ships (18.7% of the whole fleet and only 3.4% of the TEU capacity), the proportion of this sector against the fleet as a whole is declining despite 22% having delivered 1995-1999. One third are fitted with gear and have an average speed of 14 knots, though the more recent vessels can achieve 15 knots. They are mainly employed on short haul operations feeding to main regional container ports from smaller ports and vice versa.

Feedermax

(500-1000 TEU) The very name suggests that like the bulk carrier size groups, the economies of scale are tending to increase the size of vessels on exactly the same trades as volumes expand. Half this fleet is geared with an average speed of 16.5 knots though modern vessels have an average speed of 17 knots. It also grew rapidly in the early '80's, then sustained steady growth followed by a spurt after 1994. Vessels built since 1995 amount to 43% of the fleet.

Handy

(1000-2000 TEU) The ships are small enough to be used intra regionally and large enough for the North – South trades where port restrictions or cargo volumes do not permit the use of larger vessels. 54% have cargo gear though the proportion is 65% for vessels built between 1991 and 1998. The average speed is 18.8 knots. This sector has grown by about 9% since 1990 and expansion continues.

Sub Panamax

(2000-3000 TEU) These are large versatile vessels used mainly in the deep sea trades. A growing proportion have cargo gear, now about 23%. They have an average speed of 20.6 knots. The growth rate follows a similar pattern to the feedermax with high growth in the early 80's then stable growth and large expansion from the mid '90's.

Panamax

(3000 TEU + maximum Panama Canal dimensions of LOA 294.07 and Beam 32.2) These are deep sea, long haul vessels. They have an average speed of 22.9 knots and none have cargo handling gear. It is a very rapidly growing fleet growing from only 8 vessels in 1980 to 321 in 1999 and with 41 on order it will continue to grow strongly.

Post Panamax

(4000 TEU exceeding Panamax dimensions) The most recent addition to the container fleet with the first appearing in 1988 and a classic response to volume increases and economies of scale. By the middle of 1999 the fleet had grown to 95 vessels with 50 more on order. The average speed is 24.5 knots. The definition of panamax and post panamax is becoming less appropriate as there are now 105 panamax containerships that have a nominal capacity greater than 4000TEU. The largest post panamaxes have a container capacity of over 7000 TEU's and further expansion at this end of the market can be expected.

* * * *

All these segments have different functions and thus different design characteristics. The larger the size the higher the speed. Although this is costly on fuel it allows less ships to be used on a service. The smaller ships used on regional short haul feeder trades call at many ports and therefore speed is less important but it can be seen that in all the size categories that the more modern ships are designed with higher speed capabilities. The smaller ships tend to call at less sophisticated ports so there is more likelihood that they will have cargo gear. They are known as **self sustaining** vessels. The larger ships which tend to call at sophisticated regional container ports with high volumes of container throughput are gearless relying on shore based container handling equipment.

During the period 1980-1999 the containership fleet grew at an average rate of 10.4% although in the period 1995-1999 it posted an average growth of 12.5%. The fastest growing sector in 1995/99 period was the post panamaxes with an incredible 57.5% followed by panamax at 15.2% and feedermax at 10.1%. The other categories managed between 5-18%.

Size Group	Age Range (Year of Build)																		Total		
Teu Range	25 Yrs & Over			20 to 24 Yrs			15 to 19 Yrs			10 to 14 Yrs			5 to 9 Yrs			0 to 4 Yrs			Average		
Average (m)	L	B	D	L	B	D	L	B	D	L	B	D	L	B	D	L	B	D	L	B	D
Feeder 100 - 499	102	16.2	5.9	107	17.0	6.2	113	18.7	6.7	116	18.3	6.5	105	17.1	6.2	102	16.9	5.8	106	17.2	6.1
Feedermax 500 - 999	167	23.3	9.3	157	23.4	8.9	141	21.7	8.1	147	22.5	8.2	129	20.8	7.5	127	20.5	7.4	139	21.6	8.0
Handy 1,000 - 1,999	211	28.1	10.3	199	28.1	10.4	183	27.9	10.5	175	26.9	10.0	169	26.0	9.6	170	25.8	9.4	179	26.8	9.9
Sub-Panamax 2,000 - 2,999	260	31.2	11.8	248	31.5	11.5	225	32.2	11.6	234	32.2	11.7	220	31.9	11.8	198	30.7	11.4	222	31.5	11.6
Panamax 3,000 & Over	290	32	13	259	32.3	13.0	274	32.3	12.5	270	32.3	12.3	271	32.2	12.4	272	32.2	12.5	271	32.2	12.4
Post-Panamax 4,000 & Over	-	-	-	-	-	-	-	-	-	275	39	13	283	38.0	13.5	293	40.8	13.5	289	39.9	13.5
Total Avg.	157	21.9	8.2	167	23.9	8.9	171	25.4	9.4	202	28.0	10.4	185	26.4	9.8	184	26.8	9.7	180	25.8	9.5

Note : Average dimensions are calculated on the basis of ships for which all three dimensions are known.

Figure 1.22

Container ship fleet by size and hull characteristics

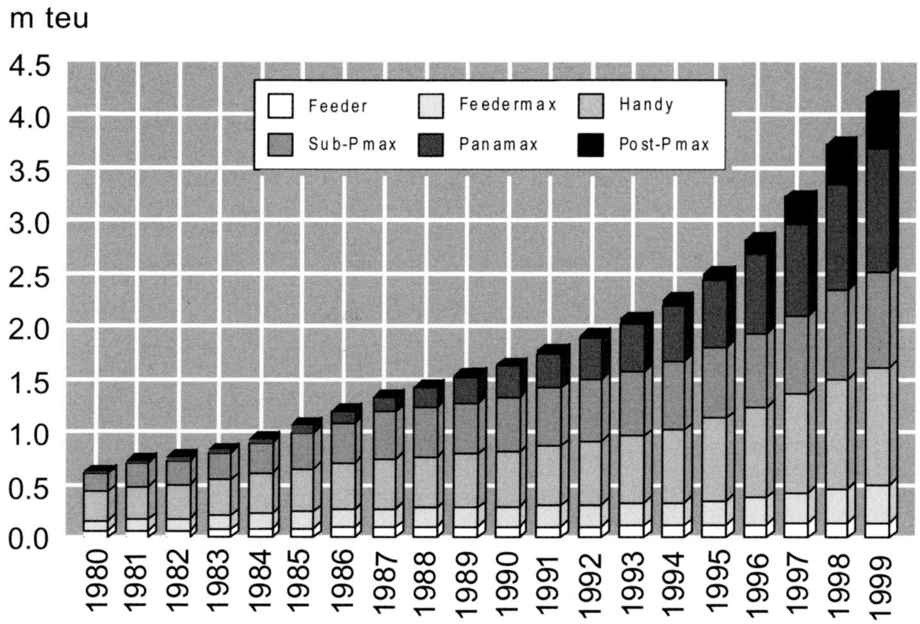

Figure 1.23

Historical development of Container Fleet

Some container ships can carry refrigerated containers that enable the large liner companies to compete with the traditional reefer. The containers are insulated and where a large volume of reefer cargo is carried the ship has a central refrigeration plant incorporated. For trades with small volumes containers incorporate their own refrigeration plant obtaining power from an electrical socket next to the container slot. These ships have replaced many traditional reefers on some routes and indeed containership reefer capacity now outstrip conventional reefer capacity. (See Figure 1.29).

A few entries from the Container Section of the Liner Register in Figure 1.24 demonstrates the details considered commercially important when chartering a container ship and in this example, both an older and new feedermaxes and a modern panamax with reefer TEU capacity are shown.

Polynesia — Owner/Manager: China Navigation Company — 701 TEU (100%)
Builder I.H.I — Operating Company: China Navigation Company — Flag Liberia — IRCS D5NZ

Hull	M	Ft.	Tonnages		Hull & Class		Capacity		Propulsion			
LOA	162.1	531.8	Dwt (m)	14,646	Built	1979/3	TEU (hmg)	673	Speed kts.	16.0	Sulzer	2 S.A. 7-cyl.
Beam	22.4	73.5	TPC		Class	LR	TEU Rfr.		Cons. T/day	28.0	HP	8,855B at 155
M. Depth	10.6	34.8	GT	10,774	CRS No.	90C751	Dwt/Teu	20.9	Bunkers t.	1,252	Propellor	1
Draught	7.7	25.2	NT	6,134	LR. Number	7805837	Hold/Hatch	5/8	Fuel Type	H	B. Thrust	1 x 600 kW

Other Details: LBP 155.01 m., Satcom, ID 1243224, Ballast 4054 t, Max Deck Tiers 3, Max Rows Across Deck 8, Adraft 41.76, S/Survey 2/98, SCNT 8958, PCNT 8464, Lwt 5606, Crew 26, Gear 5 x 25 C.

Portugal Bridge — Owner/Manager: Klaus Jurgens — 587 TEU (100%)
Builder Hugo Peters — Operating Company: Kawasaki Kisen — Flag Germany — IRCS DHMA

Hull	M	Ft.	Tonnages		Hull & Class		Capacity		Propulsion			
LOA	116.4	381.9	Dwt (m)	6,850	Built	1996/3	TEU (hmg)	335	Speed kts.	17.5	Wartsá	4 S.A. 9-cyl.
Beam	19.2	63.0	TPC		Class	GL	TEU Rfr.	104	Cons. T/day	20.0	HP	8,075B at...
M. Depth	9.2	30.2	GT	4,984	CRS No.	608340	Dwt/Teu	11.7	Bunkers t.	553	Propellor	1 Variable Pitch
Draught	7.1	23.2	NT	2,103	LR. Number	9123324	Hold/Hatch	2/2	Fuel Type	I	B. Thrust	1 x 410 kW

Other Details: LBP 107.80 m., Satnav/com, ID 21123670, Ice Class E, Ballast 2976 t, Holds 134 teu,Deck 453 teu, Bridge Aft, Shaft genekW, Adraft 36.00, S/Survey 4/96, Lwt 2925, CEx Antje Jurgens.

Portugal Senator — Owner/Manager: F. Laeisz — 4,545 TEU (100%)
Builder Hyundai H. I. — Operating Company: DSR Senator Lines — Flag Germany — IRCS DQVO

Hull	M	Ft.	Tonnages		Hull & Class		Capacity		Propulsion			
LOA	294.1	964.9	Dwt (m)	63,654	Built	1998/2	TEU (hmg)	3,355	Speed kts.	23.7	Wartsá	2 S.A. 9-cyl.
Beam	32.2	105.6	TPC	80.0	Class	GL	TEU Rfr.	350	Cons. T/day	151.0	HP	47,447B at...
M. Depth	18.4	60.4	GT	53,324	CRS No.	609028	Dwt/Teu	14.0	Bunkers t.	5,553	Propellor	1
Draught	13.3	43.5	NT	30,816	LR. Number	9147083	Hold/Hatch	6/17	Fuel Type	I	B. Thrust	1 x 1800 kW

Other Details: LBP 283.20 m., Holds 2307 teu,Deck 2238 teu, Max Rows Across Deck 13.

Figure 1.24

Typical Container page from the Liner Register

The Multipurpose Ship Group

There is a great deal of confusion about the meaning of this term. Multipurpose obviously implies a ship that can carry more than one type of cargo or do more than one job. Thus a combination carrier, strictly speaking, is multipurpose. What is normally meant by multipurpose, however, are those ships which are capable of carrying containers but are not fully cellular. The Liner Register 1999/2000 for example covers all non cellular ships which can carry in excess of 100 TEU's (excluding Ro Ro's and Conbulkers) and general cargo vessels over 5000 dwt including barge carriers and heavy lift ships. Some people include 'conbulkers' in their definition of multipurpose ship, as they can carry both containers and bulk cargo.

This is therefore potentially a very wide category and even on our restricted definition encompasses anything from traditional liner and tweendeck ships with container capacity to the modern multipurpose vessels. Figure 1.27 is part of a sample page of the Multipurpose section of the Liner Register and demonstrates this. It shows old general purpose tweendeckers, a Mark II Freedom, the plan of which is shown in Figure 1.25 and examples of modern multipurpose vessels including those with heavy lift and reefer TEU capability. There has been a need for a long while therefore for a clearer definition of this fleet. Some owners are too ready to label their ordinary tweendeck vessel as multipurpose for marketing purposes. I recently saw the following ship being marketed as follows;

MV........
Bahamas flag 1976
MPP Tween deck geared
15,051 mt on 9.061
4ho/6ha
g/b 711961/670577 cuft

14 derricks at 3.5 mt SWL
grain fitted, strengthened for heavy cargoes
Lakes fitted E/B aft
LOA/Beam 143.4/18.8

This is clearly an 'overaged' tweendeck ship with very limited gear and nothing much else, yet the owners market it as a Multipurpose **(MPP)** vessel. Many brokers also use the word too loosely. Even authors of books on shipping who are not in the forefront of the chartering industry have plainly been confused themselves and have limited their definition to fast tweendeckers or liner types. Thus, the following is an attempt to classify and clarify and it broadly follows the definition employed in the Liner Register.

Liner

The traditional general cargo ship used by the lines up until the late '60's and early '70's and now replaced by container ships would call at a considerable number of load and discharge ports on regular routes. They were usually a 15/16 knot tween or three decker which also had tanks for carrying liquid parcels of vegetable oil and a small refrigerated capacity. They could carry minor amounts of bulk parcels in the lower holds and mixed general cargo in the tween decks. They often had a great number of derricks including one heavy lift. They were designed to carry a mixture of cargoes but had a low container capacity due to narrow hatches, tweendecks, pillars, tunnels etc.. The advent of specialised bulk carriers, refrigerated ships and most of all, container ships with increased cargo volumes spelled the demise of these ships and they were obsolete by at least the mid '70's even though 39 vessels greater than 10,000 dwt were delivered in 1980 and a further 74 thereafter. Irregular shaped cargo compartments, small hatches, the difficulty of carrying containers and high consumption hastened their decline. Current ownership is dominated by Government controlled companies in China and Eastern Europe and the average age is about 23 years old. As a consequence of their obsolescence, there has been a steady stream of these ships to the scrap yard of late and the fleet is reducing rapidly. In 1980 there were 2570 vessels of this type (33.9 million tons). On the 1st July 1999, however, the fleet consisted of only 763 vessels (11.2 million tons).

The term "liner", while used to describe the type of ship, is obsolete regarding what they do and how they trade. The lines are now served by cellular container and non cellular multipurpose ships.

A typical liner type ship is described as follows;

M.V. ..
Flush tween/3 decker built '77
14,665 mt dwat on 9.49 m ssw
770,166 grain/706,897 bale
5ho/8ha (2/3/4 twin hatches)
3 decks in holds 1/2/3/4
tween deck in no 5 including classed reefer
4 x 22 ton Velle derricks serving holds 1/2/3/4
4x 5 ton cranes serving 2/3/4/5
1 x 8 ton derrick serving hold 1
Fitted for 288 TEU of which 80 on deck distribution / 36 fitted reefer plugs
15.5 on 37 (180) plus 2 mdo

These old liner types are now employed in the tramp trades and scrape a living carrying general cargoes such as bagged sugar and rice, for example, often in the third world.

Tramp Tweendecker

With a very few exceptions the last general tramp tweendeckers were built in the late '70's and early '80's. They were designed to do a multipurpose job of filling in gaps for the liner companies and trading break bulk and bulk cargo on the spot market and hence their inclusion into this rather broad, multipurpose category. With two decks, mixed general and especially bagged, cargo could be loaded securely. With large hatches bulk cargo was also loaded. Most of the older ones had their engine and bridge amidships but in the '60 and '70's the need for clear access to the cargo carrying spaces and reduced loading and discharging times meant that the newer ships of that time located the engine and bridge aft.

Many were less than 10,000 dwt but the most successful standard designs in the '70's were the I.H.I. Freedom and S.D. 14 of about 15,000 dwt with its competitor the GLR (German Liberty Replacement), but none were built after 1979. In an attempt to tackle the increasing economies of scale, a few 18/22,000 tonners were also built but they were not especially successful and

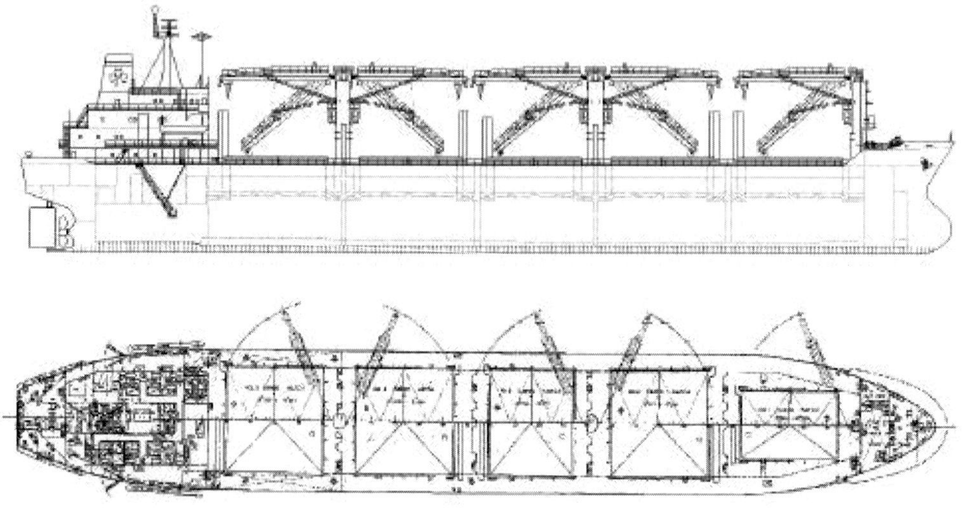

Figure 1.25
Example of a tweendecker(Freedom Mark II)

the tweendeck with container capacity was soon more popular, but again, soon eclipsed.

The specifications of these older types, which are still found trading are as follows;

SD14	14,800 dwt on 8.86	755,000 Gr/691,000 B	5hoha	12.5 on 20+2
Freedom	15,210 dwt on 9.05	711,000 Gr/671,000 B	5hoha	12 on 18.5+2

The SD 14 has the 5th hold as a single deck and the engine and bridge between hatch 4 and 5 and thus has the disadvantage of a shaft tunnel in number 5 hold, whereas the Freedom is tween throughout with engine and bridge aft. They both have various gear configurations with a minimum of 12 x 10 ton derricks but sometimes with one or two 20/30 ton and one 60 ton derrick. Figure 1.25 shows a plan of a Freedom Mark II of about 17,000 dwt.

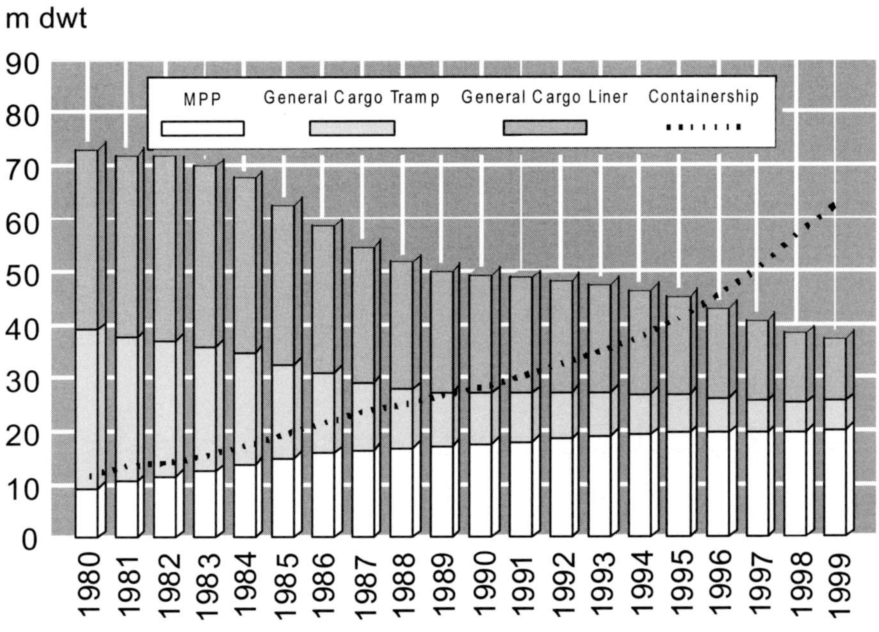

Figure 1.26 Changing fortunes !
The decline of the liner and tweendecker and the rise of the containership

Clearly tweendeck trampers quickly became inadequate for most regular lines, being too slow and not having purpose built container capacity. (Figure 1.26 tells the story).

But this sector of the market will be sustained for a few years, albeit at lower levels, by the continuing need for small general purpose vessels especially in areas of the world with low volumes of cargo and poor port facilities. The fleet has shrunk drastically, however, from 3,629 vessels of 30.1 million tons in 1980 to only 533 vessels of 5.4 million in mid 1999. These vessels find themselves squeezed between the logic of the economies of scale of using handy and handymax vessels and the drive to ship small parcels more efficiently in containers. Thus many of them are found, like the old liner types, trading in the third world with bagged general cargo such as rice, sugar, pulses and cement for example. Ownership is fragmented with only Chinese companies still operating a substantial number.

Multipurpose Vessel (MPP)

What is really meant by multipurpose today however is a vessel which can load both bulk, timber or general cargo including cars and containers. They have wide hatches and box holds with the dimensions designed for containers but are non cellular. They are generally fairly fast ships of 15-19 knots although the smaller ones tend to be in the 13-16 knot range. Most have gear in the 20-40 ton range in order to lift the heaviest containers. The handymax variety built from the '80's in general have a TEU capacity of about 1660 and have removable hydraulic container supports. The problem with these ships is that of their predecessors. Although they can handle a wide range of cargoes, they can not do it as efficiently as the specialised ships.

The following is an 'Astrakhan' type

17,850 dwt on 10.02 m
built 1986
MPP Tween with large hatches and quarterdeck in stern leading to tweendeck
4hoha
906,000 bale
553 TEU's fully fitted
4 x 12.5 ton cranes (combinable to 25 tons) serving all hatches
2 x25 ton derricks serving 2 and 3
1 x 125 ton derrick serving 3 and 4
15.5 on 32(180) plus 3 mdo

This ship has Ro Ro capability, reasonable heavy lift and TEU capacity. An ideal multipurpose vessel or a jack of all trades but master of none?

Heavy Lift Ships

These are sometimes classed in the multipurpose class as they are single or tween but usually tweendeckers and can carry bulk, break bulk or containers. In this respect they are the same as conventional ships except they have derricks or cranes capable of lifting cargo lifts of between 50 and 500 or more tons. They may also have container and / or Ro Ro capacity. Examples are the Astrakhan type mentioned above and the examples in Figure 1.27. Another slightly different one, but also marketed as a multipurpose vessel is as follows;

MV.......
Danish flag built 1991
MMPTween
4,110 dwt on 6 metres
SS 274 TEU's including 25 reefers
155 TEU's x 14 tons
131 TEU's x 20 tons

LOA 88.4/beam 15

186,030/173,207 cuft Grain

One box hold/hatch 50.11 x 11.79

2 cranes at 50 tons combinable to 100 tons

Gr/CO2/Elvent 30 a/c

13.5 on 8.5 gas oil

This ship can load almost any cargo and combination of cargoes including awkward shaped heavy pieces with the 50 metre hatch and 100 ton crane. With box holds she has good TEU capacity including reefer. The skill in chartering her will be to find charterers who can use her capabilities and thus be able to pay the best rate. If they cannot and the ship has to take bulk cargo,

Margaretha — 8,200 Dwt Multi-Purpose H/L
Builder J.J. Sietas — Owner/Manager Sal-Altes Land — Flag Antigua & B. — Call Sign V2L[illegible]

Hull	M	Ft.	Tonnages	Hull & Class	Holds & Hatches	Gear	Capacities	Propulsion
LOA	107.4	352.4	Lwt	Built 1992/12	Holds 1	2 x 200t C	Tot. Teu 461	M.A.N.; 4 S.A. 7-cyl.
Beam	19.9	65.3	GT 5,782	Class GL	Hatches 1		Homg Teu	HP 5,670B at 515
M. Depth	10.7	35.1	NT 3,152	CRS No. 607185	MaxH		Rfr Teu 30	Speed 16 kts
Draught	7.9	25.9	SCNT	LR. Number 9051739	Decks 2		Dwt/Teu 17.8	Bunkers

Other Details: LBP 98.60, Ice Str., 222 Teu Hld., 239 Teu Dk., Shaft General. 400 kW, 1 VPP, Bthrus 400 kW, Grain 9660 cu.m., Bale 9647 cu.m.

Maria Angelicoussi (Ex Sunmaria) — 16,934 Dwt Multi-Purpose "Freedom Mk II"
Builder I.H.I. — Owner/Manager Anangel Shpg. Ent. — Flag Greece — Call Sign J4[illegible]K

Hull	M	Ft.	Tonnages	Hull & Class	Holds & Hatches	Gear	Capacities	Propulsion
LOA	145.5	477.4	Lwt	Built 1978/1	Holds 5	4 x 25t C	Tot. Teu 558	Pielstick 4 S.A.107-cyl.
Beam	21.0	69.0	GT 10,274	Class AB	Hatches 5	1 x 10t C	Homg Teu	HP 6,000B at 480
M. Depth	13.1	43.0	NT 6,338	CRS No. 90D551	MaxH 18.8x15.6		Rfr Teu	Speed 14.3 at 17.7 t/d
Draught	9.5	31.1	SCNT	LR. Number 7718058	Decks 2		Dwt/Teu 30.4	Bunkers 780

Other Details: TPC 25.7, LBP 137.00, Satnav, 334 Teu Hld., 224 Teu Dk., Shaft General. 550 kW, 1 VPP, Bridge Aft, Ballast 6400 t, Grain 21240 cu.m., Bale 21070 cu.m. Ex.Sunmaria.

Maria Bonita — 21,610 Dwt Multi-Purpose H/L
Builder Mitsubishi H.I. — Owner/Manager Shinko Maritime — Flag Panama — Call Sign 3EHF5

Hull	M	Ft.	Tonnages	Hull & Class	Holds & Hatches	Gear	Capacities	Propulsion
LOA	155.5	510.2	Lwt	Built 1985/1	Holds 4	1 x 50t C	Tot. Teu 674	Sulzer; 2 S..A. 6-cyl.
Beam	25.0	82.2	GT 13,982	Class NK	Hatches 7	4 x 25t C	Homg Teu	HP 7920 B at ..
M. Depth	13.6	44.6	NT 8,462	CRS No. 90B895	MaxH		Rfr Teu	Speed 16 kts
Draught	9.8	32.0	SCNT	LR. Number 8315152	Decks 2		Dwt/Teu 32.1	Bunkers

Other Details: LBP 149.60, Crew 22, Grain 31000 cu.m., Bale 28979 cu.m., S/Surv. 6/95.

Maria G. (Ex Feleac) — 8,750 Dwt General Cargo Liner
Builder Galatz Shipyd. — Owner/Manager Navrom — Flag Romania — Call Sign [illegible]

Hull	M	Ft.	Tonnages	Hull & Class	Holds & Hatches	Gear	Capacities	Propulsion
LOA	130.8	429.1	Lwt	Built 1978	Holds 4	4 x 5t C	Tot. Teu	Sulzer; 2 S.A. 5-cyl.
Beam	17.7	58.1	GT 5,983	Class RR	Hatches 4		Homg Teu	HP 6,100B at..
M. Depth	10.2	33.5	NT 3,531	CRS No. 90A512	MaxH		Rfr Teu	Speed 16 kts
Draught	8.1	26.6	SCNT	LR. Number 7824508	Decks 2		Dwt/Teu	Bunkers

Other Details: LBP 121.20, Ice Str., Grain 11980 cu.m., Bale 11067 cu.m. Ex.Feleac.

Maria Green — 17,538 Dwt Multi-Purpose
Builder Scheldegroep — Owner/Manager HSS Holland Ship — Flag Netherlands — Call Sign PHAH

Hull	M	Ft.	Tonnages	Hull & Class	Holds & Hatches	Gear	Capacities	Propulsion
LOA	142.8	468.5	Lwt	Built 1998/9	Holds 2	3 x 60t C	Tot. Teu 962	Wartsila;
Beam	21.5	70.5	GT 11,894	Class LR	Hatches 2		Homg Teu 661	HP
M. Depth	13.3	43.6	NT 5,920	CRS No. 609869	MaxH 35.8 x 17.8		Rfr Teu 60	Speed 15.6 at 30t/d
Draught	9.7	31.8	SCNT	LR. Number 9164017	Decks		Dwt/Teu 18.2	Bunkers 1,386 t

Other Details: LBP 132.00, Ice 1A, 446 Teu Hld., 516 Teu Dk., 1 VPP, Bthrus, 750 kW, Bridge Aft, Ballast 5554t, Grain 710.71 cu.m., Bale 710.71 cu.m..

Figure 1.27

Sample page of Liner Register for Multipurpose Vessels

the extra cost of building such a sophisticated and expensive vessel are wasted and the advantages are lost.

There is a specialised heavy lift ship type which while having no cargo gear is **semi submersible.** Their design enables them to let in ballast water and submerge their decks beneath oddly shaped and heavy structures, such as work barges or oil rigs. They will then lift themselves up with the cargo on board in preparation for sailing. Strictly speaking this is not a multipurpose vessel but very specialised indeed. It is included here simply because it is in the Heavy Lift section.

The Ro Ro Group

Ro Ro is short for **'roll on roll off'** and means that cargo is loaded by ramps rather than through the hatches. There are many different types. Because of this, it deserves to be classified on its own and indeed it had its own Register before its amalgamation into the Liner Register. The Ro Ro market is enjoying a resurgence of interest and new building activity as new designs are conceived. There are four basic types, (i) the general purpose Ro Ro cargo ship, (ii) the Ro Ro/Lo Lo which is a Ro Ro cargo ship fitted with cargo handling gear which is not classified as a Ro Ro/Container ship, (iii) the Ro Ro Freight/Passenger ship or Ro-Pax for short and (iv) the pure car carrier (PCC) which is designed to be operated in the vehicle import/export trades.

Modern Ro Ro's are intended to maximise cargo handling productivity by optimising the internal arrangements of the ship such a dual level access, straight cargo lanes, square sided holds and automated lashing systems. Many of these features are being developed in short sea trades in northern Europe which incorporate passenger and Ro Ro ferry design. Demand and terminology for this trade can be demonstrated by a recent market order for small North Sea line quoting as follows;

ROPAX – 120 TRAILERS/ABT 1700 LM
60 DAYPAX- FREE HEIGHT MIN 4.5 M SPEED 18-19 KN
BOW DOOR PREFERRED
DELIVERY PPT ON NORTH CONT
3 OPT 3 MONTHS

It is interesting to note the characteristics important for the charterers; the length of the cargo lane (1700 metres), the capacity for trailers as well as cars, (4,5 m free height); day passenger capacity (60) and a specified speed which is obviously designed for maximising traffic and optimum times on the intended route. The Ro Ro market, however, is fragmented in design, ownership, use and geographical location. As we have seen, some double as heavy lift, passenger and container ships. Many are designed to load efficiently mixed cargoes that can be handled by forklift trucks such as bales, pallets, packaged timber and containers as well as wheeled vehicles.

They have hoistable car decks and often permanent cell guides on the weather deck. The Ro Ro decks are usually accessed by quarter stern ramps which are capable of carrying several hundred tons. There are much fewer Ro Ro's than container carriers and fill the role of lifting the cargoes that are not easily accommodated by container ships.

Pure Car Carrier (PCC)

The Pure Car Carrier fleet is the most specialised part of the Ro Ro fleet. These are specialised ships that can carry up to 6000 cars on hoistable decks which can be adjusted for the height of the vehicles and can therefore carry trucks and earth moving equipment as well as cars. The fleet comprises the more modern and larger Pure Car and Truck Carrier (PCTC) and the Pure Car Carrier (PCC). Their deck heights and internal arrangements are designed to maximise the carriage of these particular vehicles although modern designs incorporate adjustable decks and ramps, as many larger ships run as part of liner services. At the end of 1999 there were 427 vessels (5.4 million dwt or 1.63 million vehicles) with an average age of only 13.3 years. Many of the large (4000 vehicles plus) vessels are run on liner services on the East/West trades, mainly from Japan and Korea to Europe and America. The growth of Japanese and Korean car manufacturing in those areas meant that until the last few years that the fleet was not growing substantially but a resurgence in the last few years has led to a new building bubble as even old liner ships and reefers were being employed in car trades on a short term basis.

One variety of car carrier (but not PPC) that has disappeared, but that was important in the evolution of the car export trade from Japan was the car bulk carrier. These carried extra car decks that could be inserted in the holds after discharging bulk grain in Japan. The cars would then be loaded in Japan and discharged in the USA by a ramp. For a few years these ships competed well but Japanese shippers demanded tighter loading schedules than could be met by ships also involved in the bulk grain trade. In high car markets some bulk carriers were fitted with car decks but the ship did not have the ramp. They were called **lo-lo** or **'lift on lift off'** to differentiate them. They were obviously slower to load and discharge and worth less in the market.

These two types of ships used to dominate the Gulf/Japan grain market as it was the quickest cargo back to the load port area for cars back to the USA. They are mentioned because some grain charter parties still carry car deck clauses (See Chapter Six).

The Reefer Group

These are ships totally dedicated to the carriage of refrigerated cargo with insulated holds. Some cargoes like meat or fish need to be carried fully frozen at temperatures of up to minus 26 degrees Centigrade. Some like dairy products require just above freezing point and some like the important fruit trade require a controlled temperature allowing the fruit to ripen on passage. Modern vessels have their cargo spaces designed for palletised cargo and there may be reefer container capacity on deck on in the holds. They have competition from a substantial number of container ships which carry 'reefer slots' for refrigerated containers. At the beginning of 2000 the reefer fleet consisted of the 1350 vessels with 365 million cubic feet. This compares with 416 million cubic feet of reefer container capacity which overtook conventional reefer capacity in 1998. (See Figure 1.28). The reefer fleet now looks set for a long slow decline as there is little on order and 31% is over 20 years old and only 8% of the fleet is under 4 years old. Containership reefer capacity on the other hand looks set to maintain speedy growth. The 1000 TEU plus reefer capacity of the giant Post Panamax ships will in the future enable the lines to cater for even more peak crop movements, signalling a further decline for conventional reefer tonnage.

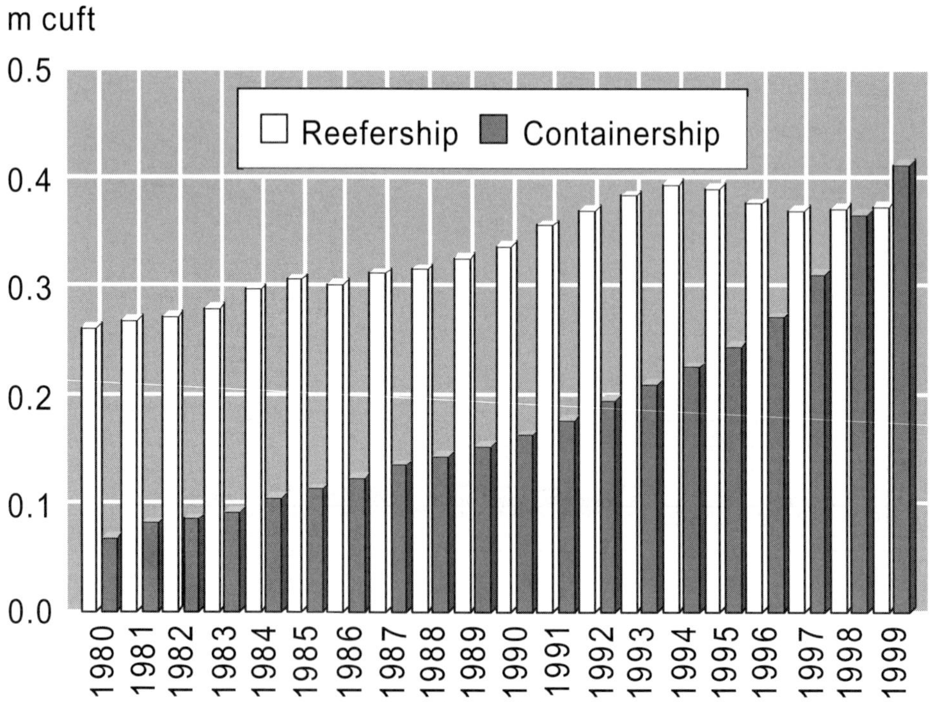

Figure 1.28

The growth of Reefer Container capacity

The fleet of small reefers under 100,000 cubic feet is a very old fleet with an average speed of 12.2 knots with no ships on order. The ships between 100/200,000 cubic feet have an average speed of 14.2 knots. Those of 200/300,000 cubic feet have an average speed of 16.4 knots with the age distribution evenly balanced but this sector of the fleet has been falling since 1993.

The 300/450,000 cubic feet ships have an average speed of 18.8 knots and is well balanced in age distribution. It is the 450/550,000 cubic feet sector which has been rapidly growing. In the years 1980 to 1999, the fleet increased by two and a half times but the order book in 1999 for this size was down to 7% of the existing fleet. They are mainly controlled by Europeans and have an average speed of 18.8 knots. The 550,000 plus cubic feet fleet also more than doubled during 1980 and 1999. They are very fast, averaging 20 knots with the most recent ships capable of in excess of 21.

Motovskij Zaliv — 13,1840 cu.m. Rfr Fish C.
Builder Mathias Thesen — Owner/Manager Mayfower Ship Mngt. — Flag Cyprus — Call Sign P3FZ4

Hull	M	Ft.	Tonnages	Hull & Class	Holds/Hatches/Refrig.	Capacities	Propulsion
LOA	152.9	501.8	Dwt 9,360	Built 1984	4 Holds 1 Decks	Pallets	M.A.N.; 2 S.A.5-cyl.
Beam	22.2	72.9	Lwt	Class NV	4 Hatches	TEU	HP 10,332
Draught	8.0	26.3	GT 12,383	CRS No. 90R818	Vent type Vert Circs/hr 90 Comp 12		Speed 18kts at 42t/d
M. Depth	13.6	44.7	NT 3,776	LR. Number 8421200	Min/Max C -30 -30 Diff Temps		Bunkers
Gear	2 x 10 D 7 x 5 D		Other Details	Cap. 465,589 cu.fr., LBP 142.02m., Ice Str., S/Equip.: Deck 2 & 3 in holds.			

Mulungisi (Ex Koala) — 12,443 cu.m. Reefer
Builder Uwajima Zosen — Owner/Manager S.A.M.A.M.A. — Flag Liberia — Call Sign ELKM5

Hull	M	Ft.	Tonnages	Hull & Class	Holds/Hatches/Refrig.	Capacities	Propulsion
LOA	149.0	488.9	Dwt 9.340	Built 1984/1	4 Holds 4 Decks	Pallets	Mitsub.; 2 S.A.7-cyl.
Beam	20.6	67.7	Lwt	Class NK	4 Hatches 8 S/Doors	TEU 40	HP 9,600
Draught	8.7	28.4	GT 9,057	CRS No. 90R693	Vent type Vert Circs/hr 90 Comp 15		Speed 18kts at 25 t/d
M. Depth	13.0	42.7	NT 4,268	LR. Number 8312643	Min/Max C -25 +15 Diff Temps 8		Bunkers
Gear	4 x 15 C		Other Details	Cap. 438,802 cu.ft., LBP 140.01 m., S/Survey 8/93, Deck Ht 1: 2.2m, Deck Area 4,9[illegible]			

Munsu (Ex Mun Su) — 1,207 cu.m. Rfr/Pallets
Builder Moen Slip — Owner/Manager Ergomax G.m.b.H.. — Flag Belize — Call Sign V3US2

Hull	M	Ft.	Tonnages	Hull & Class	Holds/Hatches/Refrig.	Capacities	Propulsion
LOA	51.6	169.3	Dwt 760	Built 1977	2 Holds 2 Decks	Pallets	Caterp. 4 S.A.8-cyl.
Beam	9.0	29.6	Lwt	Class BV	1 Hatches 1 S/Doors	TEU	HP 565
Draught	3.5	11.3	GT 398	CRS No. 90R819	Vent type Circs/hr Comp		Speed 10kts a4t/d
M. Depth	5.3	17.4	NT 121	LR. Number 7626126	Min/Max C -25 +25 Diff Temps		Bunkers
Gear	1 x 2 D		Other Details	Cap. 42,650 cu.ft., LBP 47.22 m., Ice Str., Norvest Reefer, Fjellhav, Tikal.			

Musashi — 5,738 cu.m. Reefer
Builder Kyokuyo S/yard — Owner/Manager Wako Kisen K.K.. — Flag Japan — Call Sign JIFN

Hull	M	Ft.	Tonnages	Hull & Class	Holds/Hatches/Refrig.	Capacities	Propulsion
LOA	120.8	396.2	Dwt 5,103	Built 1994	3 Holds 3 Decks	Pallets	B & W; 2 S.A.6-cyl.
Beam	16.6	54.5	Lwt	Class NK	3 Hatches	TEU	HP 4,070
Draught	6.9	22.7	GT 4,491	CRS No. 90S490	Vent type VertCircs/hr 90 Comp 9		Speed 16kts at 18t/d
M. Depth	10.0	32.8	NT 2,125	LR. Number 9087908	Min/Max C [illegible]		Bunkers
Gear			Other Details	Cap. 202,637 cu.ft., LBP 112.90 m., Deck Ht 1: 2.2 m, Ht 2: 2.2 m, Deck Area 2,320 sq. m.			

Figure 1.29

Part of a typical page from the Reefer Register

In short, while under threat from the Reefer Container, this fleet has shown a similar pattern of rapid development at the large size end of the market in response to volume, economies of scale and competition. The difference is that it looks as though it is coming to an end as the Reefer Containers take an ever increasing market share.

Figure 1.29 shows part of a typical page in the Reefer Register showing the important details for employment/chartering purposes but also the enormous diversity of designs especially in terms of numbers of decks and compartments. Figure 1.30 shows a small reefer with multiple decks.

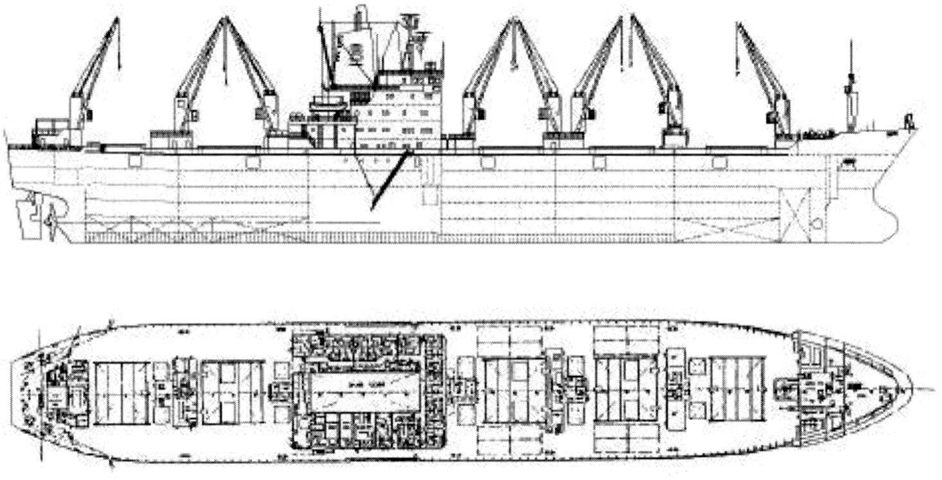

Figure 1.30
Diagram of a reefer vessel

Tugs and Barges

While not classified as ships, they can be and are chartered and in many instances are a vital part of the transport chain. Barges can be pulled by tugs or they can have notch in the stern into which the tug is secured rigidly and is pushed. The pulled barge is the usual cheap method and is satisfactory for most uses but the more rigid pusher does have advantages in manoeuvrability. As conditions require they can be open topped or have hatches. The latter obviously cost more but can transport perishable cargoes and can trade in far worse weather conditions. The flat top barges' main characteristic is that the cargo is always above the waterline. They are widespread in South East Asia. The Rhine and Mississippi barges are not flat top but have holds and thus the cargo is below the waterline.

Barges are mainly used for transportation on rivers where the drafts are shallow and there is need for small craft. In the Mississippi they are used for a variety of commodities especially grain. In Europe, the great river system of the Rhine distributes commodities in barges throughout Northern Europe and the Danube is beginning to achieve a similar role for Southern and Central Europe. In Indonesia open flat top barges carry coal down the Mahakam and Barito rivers to a transhipment anchorage or port. Usually the economies of scale mean that barges do not undertake deep sea voyages but where the conditions are favourable and the distances short there are examples. For instance coal from the Mahakam River is taken to the southern Philippines in barges and coal from the Barito river is barged straight over to northern Java. Some barges engage in coastal and short sea trades between northern European ports especially in the Baltic. Barges are also used to transport cargo to and from transhipment points where it is loaded and discharged by self loading and discharging vessels or off shore floating cranes.

Conclusion

For those engaged in chartering, it is unlikely that in the course of a career that they will be involved in all of these different types of craft. However, each of the ships and the trades on which they engage, impinge in some way on the others and it is likely that the Container fleet and trades will grow and therefore continue to affect all trades and ships to some extent. It is therefore important that everyone engaged in a sector of the chartering market at least be aware of the existence of the other sectors and the principles upon which they operate.

Much of the skill involved in chartering is in the thorough detailed and specialist knowledge of particular trades and types of ships. The principles and mechanics, on the other hand, of fixing an old tweendecker will be much the same as those when employing ships in an iron ore trade employing 150/200,000 tonners or a container ship for a period charter. These mechanics will be explored in later chapters.

This list of vessel types described above that can be chartered is not exhaustive. Specialised forest product carriers with extensive shipboard handling gear, offshore floating cranes, transhipment ships, cattle and sheep carriers, harbour tugs, platform supply vessels, drill ships, anchor handling tugs, salvage tugs, Lash Barges, oceanography, passenger and cruise vessels may also be chartered. However, this chapter is not meant to contain an exhaustive list. What it tries to do instead is give a flavour of the types of ships in the context of the trades for which they are designed and on which they are engaged. This should give an idea of the diversity, changing ideas, fashions and the issues that are involved.

The Future Development of These Fleets

As has become clear, shipping is an evolving industry. There have been many success stories as well as failures as a result of getting the evaluation of that evolution right or wrong. This is quite apart from the cyclical nature of the market (which will be discussed in Chapter Two) and the key question of getting the timing right. For example, combination ships bought as new buildings in the mid and late '70's and sold at the bottom of the market in the mid '80's never made a profit for their owners and never enjoyed combination trading as envisaged by their owners. But those who bought them near the bottom of the market in the mid '80's and traded them for the next ten years when new limited combination trades appeared and the market went up were able to trade profitably and sell well. One cannot help feeling that history may well repeat itself with multipurpose vessels and conbulkers. They are now virtually excluded from the container trades due to oversupply. Yet the container ship market will undoubtedly grow strongly in the long term. It is not inconceivable that while oversupply will depress prices further in the short to medium term, the long term growth of new container routes with limited volumes will open up new opportunities for these ships. But will they be able to hang on long enough under the present ownerships?

What are going to be the main trends over the next few years? Most have been identified but can briefly be summarised as follows;

1. Continuing strong growth of Container shipping. All bagged cargoes, bulk cargoes currently carried as part cargoes especially from draft limited ports and many of the minor bulk trades are all vulnerable to take over by container ships over the next few years.

2. Reefer trades will continue to be targeted by Reefer Container ships and in consequence, the pure reefers themselves are increasingly vulnerable as more reefer slots on container ships become available. The banana trade may be an exception.

3. The Handysize fleet of bulk carriers and tweendeckers will decline as they are squeezed by the economies of scale of large bulkers on the one hand and containerisation on the other.

4. The increasing effects of economies of scale in all fleets will be felt. Average sizes in all sectors will continue to increase.

5. In the container and reefer fleets, speed will be increasingly important especially in the large sizes.

SHIP TERMINOLOGY

The following will not be a comprehensive guide to every part of the ship or **vessel** but will cover those parts which are relevant for chartering purposes or that those involved in chartering will hear about. This may go beyond just the cargo carrying compartments or indeed what can be found in the relevant Register and will include what many charterers require owners to tell them about the ship or that is relevant to the voyage. This can be a huge amount of information especially for time charters. (See also Chapters Six and Seven – 'Ship's Description'). This section will not, however, attempt technical explanations better covered by books by Marine Architects.

The body of the ship is known as the **hull**, the front of which is the **bow** and the rear the **stern**. The frames of the vessel are covered by **shell plating**. The bow can be strengthened for trading in ice bound water and is then graded by the Classification Society as **Ice Class**. The **weather deck** is the top deck exposed to the weather into which the hatch openings are cut. The **superstructure** is the part above the weather deck, usually above the **engine room** which includes the **bridge** from where the ship is steered and commanded. Two plans of the ship are referred to in chartering. The **General Arrangement Plan (G.A. Plan)** shows the side elevation of the ship illustrating the cargo compartments, gear, engine room and superstructure and a cross section illustrating the shape of the holds and deck layout. The **Capacity Plan** including the deadweight scale shows the tonnages, cargo hold dimensions, bunker tank capacities and the principal dimensions of the vessel as well as where it was built and the hull number.

Tonnage

Ship's tonnage is measured by **Gross Registered Tonnage, Net Registered Tonnage (GRT/NRT) and Deadweight (DWT).** GRT and NRT are important for chartering only in so far as port charges and canal tolls are often measured by the GRT and NRT of the ship. They concern the internal volume of the ship and without describing the somewhat complex rules for measurement, roughly GRT means the volume of the vessel and the NRT the volume available for cargo. It is measured and assessed by the appropriate Classification Society. The Suez and Panama Canal Authorities have slightly different criteria for their measurements of NRT and GRT. These determine the charges payable for transiting these canals. Thus a ship will have a GRT/NRT, **a Suez GRT/NRT** and a **Panama GRT/NRT**. For chartering purposes, however, when we talk of a 70,000 tonner we mean a ship of 70,000 **deadweight** which denotes the weight of cargo she can carry.

The more exact term for deadweight (DWT) is **deadweight all told (DWAT)** which is distinct from **deadweight cargo capacity (DWCC).** DWAT is the total deadweight comprising everything on board including cargo, bunkers, fresh water, crew, stores, equipment and spare parts. What will interest a charterer most is the DWCC, the part available for the cargo. Thus a charterer interested in taking a ship on time charter will probably ask for the DWAT and the bunker capacity, fresh water capacity and 'constants' which are the stores, equipment and spare parts. They will therefore be able to calculate exactly the cargo carrying capacity which is the revenue earning capacity of the ship with any bunkering plan for a particular voyage.

The DWAT, and hence the DWCC, will be different depending on whether the ship is trading in 'Tropical fresh water', 'Tropical', 'Summer', 'Winter' or 'Winter North Atlantic' zones. It is normal to give the summer deadweight when describing deadweight but when calculating cargo intake it may be that a different one is applicable for a particular trade. The ship will be allowed to carry more cargo in summer and even more in tropical waters which are defined either according to the time of year or season or geographical location only as some are permanent. Thus a ship may carry more cargo on a route at one time of the year than another or if the ship is going from tropical through summer to winter marks the Master should have calculated his bunker burn so that the relevant marks are not under water because if this were the case, the ship would be illegally overloaded. It is measured by the **load line** or **Plimsoll mark** on the side of the ship (See Figure 1.31) and chartering staff for ship owners will have the deadweight scale tabulated for easy calculation of any potential cargo lift on a given draft. When the vessel has been loaded to her maximum permissible draft the vessel will be described as having loaded **'down to her marks'**.

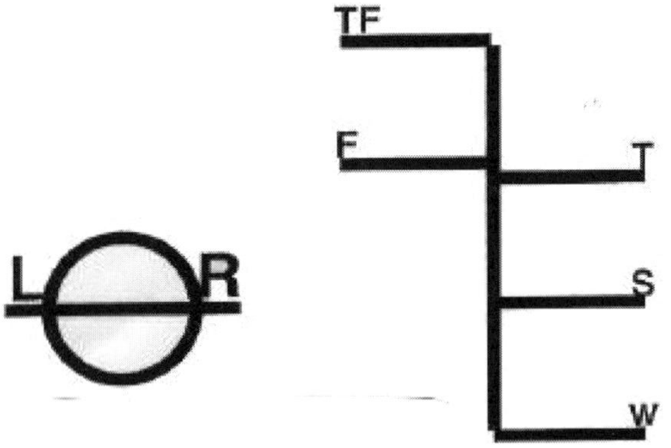

Figure 1.31
The load lines on the side of a ship

Occasionally **displacement** will be used as a means to measure ships at a berth or jetty. It means the amount of water displaced by the ship. This is calculated by adding the **lightweight** of the ship (the actual weight of the ship itself) to the amount of cargo, bunkers and constants she is carrying. A jetty, for example, may have a displacement restriction of 130,000 metric tons. Thus a ship of say 20,000 tons lightweight carrying 2500 tons of bunkers and constants may not carry more than 107,500 tons of cargo.

A further complication is that ship's tonnage is measured either in long tons or metric tons. Occasionally cargo tonnage from the United States is described in short or American tons. For clarity, the conversions are as follows;

Long Ton = 2240 llbs
= 1.12 short or American tons
= 1016.05 kilos or 1.01605 metric tons

Short Ton = 2000 llbs
= 0.892857 long tons
= 0.90718 metric tons

Metric Ton = 1000 kilos or 2204.621 llbs
= 0.98421 long tons
= 1.10231 short tons

The conversion factors;

	LT	ST	MT
LT	x 1	x 1.12	x 1.016
ST	x 0.893	x 1	x 0.907
MT	x 0.984	x 1.102	x 1

Other Ship Measurements Used For Chartering

Draft. This is the distance between the waterline and the keel and is important as many ports have draft restrictions.

Waterline to the top of the hatch coamings (WLTHC). It is this distance which is most important for chartering purposes as there are often restrictions at ports due to the position of the shore gear. If the ship is too high out of the water the shore gear is unable to swing round to load or discharge. At the loading port, for example, the ship will arrive empty and thus be higher out of the water. It is possible to minimise this by flooding the ballast tanks and a hold or holds to bring her down in the water. There are two types of **heavy ballast** where holds are flooded. **Seagoing heavy ballast condition** is when one hold is flooded. In a capesize this is usually No 6 hold which is strengthened accordingly. (See Figure 1.32).

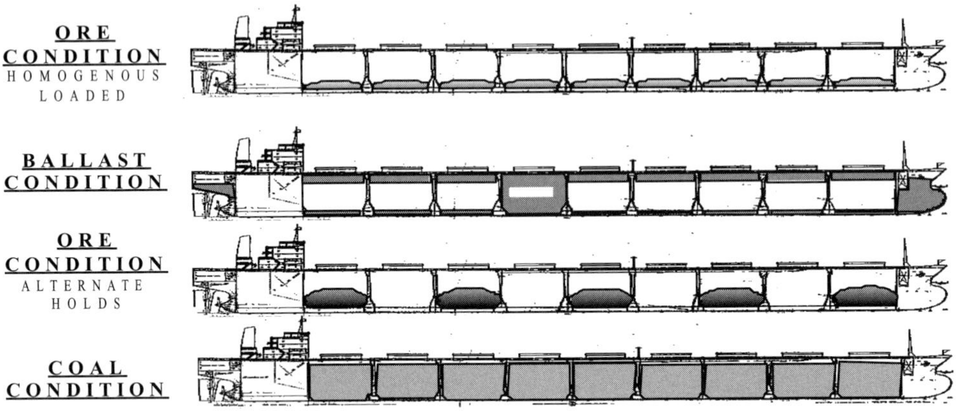

Figure 1.32
Capesize Bulk Carrier in various loaded/ballast conditions

In **harbour heavy ballast condition** an additional two holds of a capesize can be flooded to further reduce the WLTHC. Combination carriers which are designed to carry liquids as well as dry cargo are able to flood more holds. In a port such as San Nicholas, Peru, the loading arm height is such that only combination carrier capesize and specially designed 211,000 dwt bulk carriers can reach the WLTHC restriction.

Airdraft. This is the distance from the waterline to the top of the mast or whichever is the highest part of the ship. It is however, often wrongly used to mean WLTHC. Airdraft, properly described, is important in some ports. Genoa, for example, has an airdraft restriction due to the airport flight path. It is purely precautionary and artificial but if a vessel turns up exceeding it she will be refused entry. It is of great physical importance in river, canal or harbour navigation where clearances beneath bridges are important.

Freeboard. Connected to the above distances is freeboard, the distance from the weather deck to the waterline. Some vessels such as chip carriers and pure car carriers have higher freeboards than others. It makes the chip carriers for instance difficult to trade outside their dedicated trades. **Depth**, the distance from keel to deck, is also sometimes important in calculations about draft, freeboard and WLTHC.

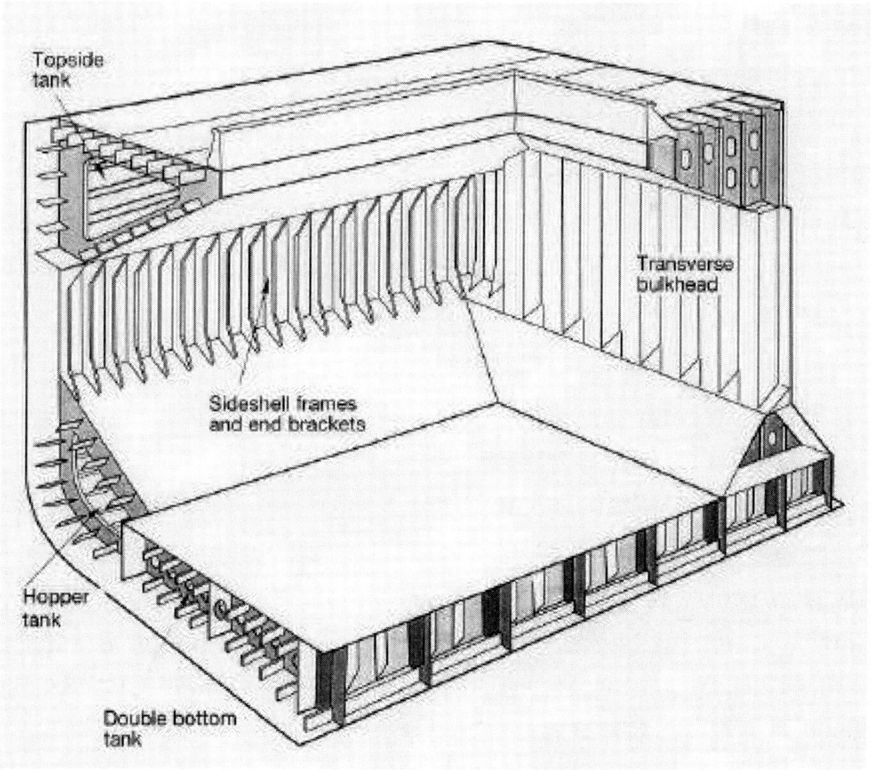

Figure 1.33

Typical Bulk Carrier Cross section

Deballasting rate/capacity. This is important in the management of freeboard or WLTHC during loading or discharging as the vessel has to de ballast simultaneously.

TPI/TPC (Tons per inch/centimeter). This figure assists in calculating the expected cargo intake where there are restricted drafts.

LOA – Length over all. The extreme length of the ship, important as many berths have restrictions either physical or imposed by the harbour master or port authorities.

Working area. The distance between the fore part of the first hatch to the aft part of the last. This distance is important if a berth is restricted in how far its shore gear will travel along the ship.

Beam. The external width of the ship, important for similar reasons especially the outreach of the shore loading or discharging gear. Also known as **extreme breadth** to differentiate if from **moulded breadth** which is the internal width.

Conversions to and from metric and imperial distance measurements are
1 meter = 3.28083 feet
1 meter = 39.3701 inches.

The Holds/Cargo Carrying Spaces

Grain capacity. The cubic capacity of the cargo space including hatchways measured in cubic feet or cubic meters. It is important when calculating the loadable quantity of any high stowing bulk cargo. For instance, iron ore as a very dense cargo stowing around 16 cubic feet per ton will not fill the cargo holds prior to her loading down to her marks. (See Figure 1.32) High stowing cargoes such as some grains, some coke, wood chips etc., however, will fill the holds without the ship being fully down on her marks. If a 61,000 tonner has a grain cubic capacity of 2,600,000 cuft., a full cargo of coke stowing about 65 cubic feet per ton would therefore only load about 40,000 tons. The **stowage factor** of a cargo is one of the key factors in assessing the workability of a cargo and calculating its worth in a voyage estimate.

Bale capacity. The same as above except that some older general cargo ships have **cargo battens** on the side of the holds. These perform the same function as the ceiling, or tank top (See below), that is, preventing bagged cargo coming into contact with the side of the ship which may form condensation and damage the cargo. The 'bale' is the capacity of the cargo space but measured from inside the cargo battens and thus it is the measurement used for calculating the intake of bagged and break bulk cargo.

Grain and bale cubic capacity is measured in cubic feet per ton or cubic metres per ton. The conversion is 1 cubic metres per metric ton = 35.8816 cubic feet per long ton. Despite international metrication, the stowage factor of bulk cargoes is still usually expressed in cubic feet per ton.

Bulkheads. The steel divisions across the vessel dividing the cargo compartments into separate holds and the holds from the engine room. They are usually corrugated to increase the strength and safety of a vessel.

Ballast tanks. Usually a typical bulk carrier has upper and lower **wing tanks** for ballast water. Ballast can also be carried in the fore peak tanks, in the double bottom and as was described in the "Airdraft" section, in a hold at sea in ballast or in port to reduce the WLTHC distance. (See Figure 1.32 and 1.33 "ballast condition"). Ballast tanks give a ship empty of cargo, immersion of the propeller and safe trim, improving steering. The lower wing tanks means that the holds have sloping upper faces which are described as **hoppered**

holds as opposed to **box holds** which have neither the upper or lower wing tanks hopper shaped. Box holds were created for the carriage of non bulk cargoes which obviously in hoppered holds leads to **broken stowage** or wasted space.

Self trimming. A sometimes contentious description of bulk carriers. Some owners will argue vigorously that no ship is self trimming. It has come to mean, however, that the ship can load bulk cargo without need for manual trimming of the cargo into the sides of the vessel underneath the deck to fill the air pockets that will develop. This is possible because the topside water ballast tank makes the shape of the top of the hold not box shaped but sloped, allowing free flowing bulk cargo to be stowed without the need to trim. These are the wing tanks or topside tanks which are also used for ballast and very occasionally loading of grain. (See Figures 1.32 and 1.33 and references in Chapter Seven in 'Ship's Description').

Box holds. Modern ship design allowing containers and timber to be loaded. (See Open Hatch, Conbulker section and Figure 1.20). Hold dimensions are important when pipes, containers, timber, etc. have to be loaded.

AHL-Australian Hold Ladders. In order to call at Australian ports, modifications to hold ladders demanded by the Australian stevedoring unions and the WWF are required for safety reasons.

Tweendecks. This is the intermediate deck between the weather deck and the tank top. (See Figure 1.26) 'Flush Tween' means that the tweendeck hatch cover fittings are flush with the deck and therefore there is no obstacle to the stowage of the cargo on the tweendecks.

Tank top. The bottom of the hold which is so called as it is also the top of the double bottom which is used for ballast water. (See Figure 1.33) In older general cargo ships there may be a ceiling consisting of wooden planks or **sheathing** sometimes laid on top to prevent cargo contact with the double bottom and to protect the tank tops against grab damage. This is done to prevent condensation damaging the cargo. Extra **dunnage** is necessary for bagged cargo and charter parties involving bagged cargo will normally allocate time and costs for this extra dunnage such as mats, boards, kraft paper etc..

Deeptanks. In older liner types, deeptanks running from the tank top to the lower or upper tweendeck were constructed which were suitable for the carriage of vegetable oil, palm oil etc on regular lines. They often had heating coils to enable discharge of the edible oil at the correct temperatures.

Hatches

Hatch covers. There are different designs reflecting different purposes. Loggers are likely to have pontoon hatch covers as they are strong and are able to have heavy logs loaded upon them. Other types are mechanical or hydraulic, some side folding, side pulling or fore and aft folding or sliding. They must be watertight. Some charter party clauses specify this explicitly rather than implying it in the phrase ‘seaworthy’.

Hatch coaming. The vertical plating around the hatch openings.

Gear

If a ship has gear it will have, unless it is a belt unloader, **cranes** or **derricks** or both. Derricks were used in older ships and still now for heavy lifts. They have to be rigged by means of ropes. Charter party references to parts of the derrick refer to winches, ropes, gins, slings and donkey boilers. Derricks are slower than cranes but can be rigged in **union purchase** which reduces the lifting capacity by half but increases the slewing speed. When fixing a ship with cranes or derricks on time charter, a charterer will, if unfamiliar with the type of gear or particular ship, want to know the slewing speeds, that is the cycle speeds from a jetty to the hold and back again.

Cranes are faster than derricks. There are two main types, **fixed** or **gantry cranes**. The fixed ones are usually centrally mounted on a pedestal although a few specialised ships have them mounted on the side. Gantry cranes run along the length of the ship on rails. Some cranes have **grabs** already fitted to make the ships self loading and self discharging. The grab size for normal bulk cargo will usually be between 8 and 15 cubic meters but scrap is discharged by orange peel grabs.

Fittings

Logs. Deck cargo of logs will need stanchions fitted to the side of the deck.

Container fittings. Cell guides are fitted in the holds and sometimes on deck so that containers do not need to be secured. This speeds up handling on fully **cellular** container ships.

Co2 fitted. A fire prevention mechanism.

Vent/Elvent. Ventilation of cargo is sometimes necessary. The commonest form of cargo damage is probably caused by condensation which is caused by the difference in temperature between the inside of the cargo hold and the outside temperature of the sea. This can be considerable and change a great deal with vessels in deep sea, long haul trades traversing various climatic zones. In tweendeckers and liner ships the sides of the holds are usually lined with cargo battens, strips of wood which serve the purpose of keeping break bulk cargo off the ship's sides and creating air flow channels round the edges of the cargo. Some bulk cargoes have a tendency to heat up and even self combust. If a build up of heat is detected, the main remedy is to shut down the ventilation. Most of the most recent tweendeckers will be equipped with **Electric ventilation** which is required for certain cargoes especially foodstuffs and the charterer will sometimes require a minimum number of air changes. Ships advertising themselves for such trades will state that they are electrically ventilated with say 25 or 30 air changes per hour depending on the capability of the equipment.

Dunnage. Temporary cargo separations, timber, plywood, kraft paper, etc to prevent contact with condensation on ship's frames and bulk heads and to properly stow and secure irregular shaped packages in the holds with each other. It all facilitates ventilation.

Butterworth Tank Cleaning system. on tankers and combination carriers, a method for cleaning and gas freeing tanks/holds after an oil cargo by means of rotating high pressure jets of water.

Coils. In a tanker or combination carrier or in older liner types in the deeptanks to heat the oil cargo when necessary.

IGS- Inert Gas system. For tankers and combination ships.

Materials and Management Issues

Ships built until the 1970's were constructed from mild steel. The rise in the cost of bunker fuel between 1973 and 1981, but in particular the second oil shock of the late 1970's, precipitated two major design changes. The most direct was the development of increasingly fuel efficient engines which have already been noted in the section on capesizes and panamaxes. (See the tables on the development of the handymax, panamax and capesize fleets, especially the improving speed and consumption). The second was the construction of ships in **high tensile steel**, which is much stronger than mild steel enabling the ship builders to build vessels with less steel. The yards could therefore build cheaper ships, more attractive in a depressed market. A typical 150,000 dwt capesize bulk carrier of the 1970's would have had about 24 mm thick plate and a lightweight of about 27/28,000 tons. A mid 1980s built ship, however, would have had these measurements reduced to 12/15 mm and about 18,000 tons respectively.

This affects the chartering market in two ways. More fuel efficient engines with better speeds and consumptions are more attractive to potential time charterers and will calculate a better daily return at a given freight rate. But because they have a smaller horse power they may be at a disadvantage in bad weather and lose time against the more powerful older engines. Secondly charterers taking high tensile built vessels for long period will take into account the record of the shipyard and the maintenance programme of the owners, as high tensile steel corrodes at the same rate as mild steel. It is fair to say that there is some concern in shipping circles about some of the early high tensile ships especially the cape sizes and especially following some losses of ships at sea where iron ore was carried after loading it at high speeds. The concern is that this high speed loading causes considerable stresses in the hull of the ship which is continually subject to **hogging** and **sagging** as each hold is loaded. This eventually weakens the whole structure leading in some cases to cracking in the hull and in extreme cases to the breaking of the ship's back. Sagging occurs when the centre of the ship sags under the weight of cargo. Hogging is the opposite where the weight of cargo at each end makes the end submerge deeper than amidships. Obviously, this also makes calculating the draft more difficult.

Navigational equipment. This includes direction finders, radar, gyro compasses and satellite assisted navigation. This increasing automation has led to another development over the past 20 years or so, that of significantly reduced manning levels on ships.

Flag. The flag indicates the nationality of the vessel, the country under who's laws the ownership is registered. This may be important for trading. Some flags are difficult or impossible to trade in certain areas such as **flags of convenience** in countries where the **ITWF** (International Transport Workers Federation) is strong. Why flags of convenience? There are two reasons. One is cost. Lenient taxation on income and capital gains, interpretation of tonnage measurements and crewing regulations has led to lower crewing costs. Many of these issues, however, have been addressed over the last few years by flag states. The real reason to register off shore, in a tax haven, in the name of a one ship company, is now to avoid corporate responsibility in the event of a disaster such as a spillage of bunkers in an environmental area for example. The anonymity of ownership in an off the shelf company, at a brass plate address in Monrovia or Panama leads to hire and freights being paid, through agents, elsewhere. However such cost and anonymity advantages can lead to questions and it can be an emotional issue in some shipping circles. Many ships found wanting by Port State Control Authorities are those flagged in third world countries with no maritime tradition but cheap costs, loose control and above all, a need for income (See "Conventions and Regulations" below).

Class. Classification Societies exist to ensure ships are properly constructed and maintained. To fulfil this role they make rules governing construction. They classify ships built according to its rules. The ones that are most respected are members of the **International Association of Classification Societies (IACS).** Some quality conscious charterers require in their charter parties that the vessel is classed only by a classification society that is a full member of the **IACS**. The Classification Society undertakes **surveys** throughout the life of the ship to make sure that they are kept in accordance with those rules. Every five years the vessel must undergo a **Special Survey** for hull and machinery. As ships get older the surveys become more onerous and expensive. In low markets, the anticipated cost of steel renewals required by special surveys may precipitate a decision to scrap the vessel. Some owners prefer that the ships are classified on a continual basis. The ships are required to keep the certificates of surveys undertaken by the classification surveyors on behalf of the flag states. These include the International Loadline Certificate, Safety Construction Certificate and Safety Equipment Certificate among others. Many charter parties require ships to be **'Lloyds +100 A1 or equivalent'**, which gives comfort to the charterer that the ship is kept to a minimum safe condition. The best known, apart from Lloyds Register (LR) are American Bureau of Shipping (ABS), Bureau Veritas (BV), Germanscher Lloyd (GL), Nippon Kaiji Kyokai (NK), Norske Veritas (NV) and Registro Italiano (RINA).

Arguments over the quality of the classification society or register has become as emotionally heated as that prevailing over the flag. Michael Grey, for example, writing in Lloyds List in May 1999 complained,

> 'There are some dreadful ship registers about, operated by truly awful people who are unashamedly on the make, faxing documents which legitimise rustbuckets and incompetent crew members around the world just as fast as they can get their hands on the money. Some of these are open registers and offer a refuge to the unprincipled, but others are bone fide national administrations that are either corrupt, incompetent, or seriously strapped for cash and are oblivious to the fact that their national flag fleet is not of an acceptable international standard. But there is, of course, no accounting for taste. It is a complete mystery to me why some of the world's most reputable shipping companies operate under quite

appallingly incompetent administrations. The truth is that they regard the flag as largely unimportant, and the register itself a legal document which facilitates a marine mortgage. Their ships could fly a tea towel from the ensign staff, but these dubious colours would not affect in the slightest their high standards and complete commitment to quality.'

It is true that while in general the general standard of quality has gone up, over the years, there still are some sub standard ships trading. Many charterers therefore do insist in their charter parties that among other things, that the ship should be classified only by those that are full members of the IACS.

P and I Club. This is a mutual association of ship owners to provide protection from large financial loss suffered by one member by contribution towards that loss by the member's funds. The P and I Clubs cover liability not insurable by the ship owner such as liability to cargo owners, collision liability not covered under hull insurance policy, damage to piers, removal of wrecks, personal injury, pollution liabilities, crew liabilities and defence costs. Their formation was spurred by the wide acceptance of the Hague Rules (See Chapter Eight) and the reluctance of marine underwriters to accept more than three quarters of the owner's liability for damage done to another ship in a collision. Charterers therefore have a great interest that the ship owner of the ship they are chartering is properly insured. Most charterers require that the vessel is covered by a P and I Club and some, that the P and I Club in question is and will remain a full member of the International Group of P and I Clubs.

Age. The age of the ship is important for the charterer as depending on the insurance policy conditions for the insurance of the cargo at sea, an **overage premium (AP)** is payable to the insurers of the cargo for ships over 15 or 20 years of age.

ITF or ITWF Approved/Blue Certificate. This certificate indicates that the owner has an agreement with the ITWF (International Transport Workers Federation) and the crew are being paid accordingly to ITWF specification. The description or separate rider clause of a charter party will often require the ship owner to guarantee that he has such an agreement and that in consequence no time will be lost through ITWF boycotts.

Ownership

Many ships are, as noted under 'Flag' above, owned by off shore, one ship companies. Others are owned by large corporations who are willing to put their corporate name in the charter party. Quite often when identifying parties to the agreement the word **disponent owner** or **timechartered owner** is used. In this case the ship is on time charter or bare boat charter. Thus, although the party controlling the ship is not the actual owner, for the purposes of employing the ship to a charterer this party assumes the responsibilities of ownership. He is called the disponent owner to distinguish him from the **beneficial owner**, which is the real owner who obtains the ultimate benefit of owning.

Conventions and Regulations

As a result of the tougher stance of governments about safety, spurred by series of accidents and losses over the last 15 years, resulting in reports such as 'Ships of Shame' in Australia, governments and government agencies have added to the regulations regarding safety. Among the current ones, old and new, are;

SOLAS - Safety of Life at Sea

IMO Code - Code of safe practice for Bulk Cargoes
(See Chapter Seven – 'Cargo')

ISM Code	- International Safety Management Code new charter party clauses are being added to cover this. (See Chapters Six and Seven)
Loadline	- Safety (from Plimsoll Line- Merchant Shipping Act 1876) (Load Line Certificate)
GMDSS	- Global Maritime Distress and Safety System
MARPOLL	- Maritime Pollution
OPA '90	- Oil Pollution Act 1990
Class Rules	- IACS –International Association of Classification Societies
STCW	- Standards of Training, Certification and Watchkeeping
USCG	- United States Coast Guard
AMSA	- Australian Maritime Safety Authority

Ballast Water Exchange- Environmental

Regional/Local Regulations - various

Most of these regulations are monitored closely. It was reported that during February 1999 for example, that the Australian Maritime Safety Authority (AMSA) held Port State Control inspections on 233 foreign flag and seven domestic vessels and as a result of which 12 were detained until their deficiencies were rectified. One panamax was detained for 48 hours while defects, among which were defective closing arrangements on the ballast tank air pipe, defective emergency batteries and corroded hatch inspection platforms, were rectified in the presence of a class surveyor. A capesize was detained almost as long due to non compliance of its 'Safety Manning Certificate'.

The Australian example above is not unusual. The shipping newspaper 'Tradewinds' reported in May 1999, 'Thirty two ships were held by the Japanese Maritime Technology and Safety Bureau's port state control inspectors during April. Similar to other areas in this part of the world many of the vessels detained were Chinese or Russian controlled ships flagged in Cambodia or Belize'.

Ships in the late 1990's have to carry numerous certificates with them to demonstrate that all safety regulations are being complied with so that they are able to produce them to the relevant authorities. Delays as described above can be costly to the ship owner and the economics of that particular ship. As regulations have become more stringent, charter parties have responded by adding clauses requiring not only compliance with the certificates but that the certificates should be carried by the ship as evidence of compliance. Delays due to failure to do so are usually stipulated to be for the owner's account. (See Chapter Six, 'The Ship's Description' and Chapter Seven, 'In every way fitted for the service').

Insurances For Ships/Cargoes

Cargo insurance
Hull and Machinery insurance (H and M)
Protection and Indemnity (P and I)
War Risk
Blocking and Trapping
Loss of earnings (LOE)
Defence
Charterers Liability Insurance
Mortgage Interest (for banks)

SHIP ECONOMICS

What is 'Breakeven'?

Some chartering will involve the chartering of the ship for a long period. The rate at which this is fixed will depend on the price of the ship, over how many years the vessel is to be **amortised** and the projected **running costs**. These are the variables that an owner must take into consideration. The calculation will vary depending on the assumptions in the calculation. Even if the ship is not chartered for a long period, the ship owner and his financiers will still have to make this calculation so as to have an idea of how healthy his business is. This subject is not central to chartering or the freight market but the ship does not arrive on a chartering manager's desk out of thin air. Some very basic understanding as a background is therefore necessary.

For example, if a new building capesize is priced at US$ 34 million, with pre delivery costs the total costs will add up to about US$ 35 million.

Amortisation, or the time that the ship is written down to scrap, would normally be calculated in the region of 12-15 years. But since the life of the ship will probably be over 20 years a bottom line of 20 years may also be calculated. Assuming a scrap price of US$ 150 per ton on a lightweight of 12000 tons, a nominal scrap value of 1.8 million dollars can be assumed. The calculation would therefore be $ 35 less $ 1.8 = $33.2 million. An annual depreciation of this over 20 years is $ 1,660,000 or a daily depreciation of $4,548. To this must be added the daily operating costs, that of crew, insurance, spares etc.. Depending on the type of crew, flag and management policy this may be as low as US$ 4,500 or as high as $ 5,500 daily. A dry dock provision of around $ 1000 per day should prudently be added even though the first three years of the vessel's life will be free of dry dock. Thus a provisional cost of between about $10,000 and $11,000 per day is calculated.

On top of this must be added the interest, the cost of borrowing the money, which will depend on the terms and interest rate that is able to be negotiated. It could vary from as low as $3,500 and as high as $5,000. This is a very rough calculation and because it is taken over 20 years would be considered very aggressive, although owners would calculate running costs in ways that reflected their own experiences. The results above might result in a cost of anywhere between a very aggressive $12,500 and perhaps, a more prudent $16,000 per day. Older ships' running costs are higher than modern ones as they invariably need more spares, more dry dock provision and increasingly expensive surveys.

Similar calculations could be made for second hand vessels with amortisation over fewer years. It has to be remembered, however, that prices fluctuate and that other newbuilding vessels in the market will have been bought at higher prices, which thus need a higher breakeven. They will also be competing with second hand ships bought at cheaper prices.

Voyage Estimating

The breakeven rate of the ship has absolutely nothing to do with what, at any time, is the market rate for that ship. To find the best paying market cargo it will be necessary to run a **voyage estimate.** No owner calculates the estimate in exactly the same way as another but the principals governing the estimate are the same.

The <u>income</u> is calculated by multiplying the estimated cargo intake by the freight rate. Cargo intake may be restricted by the deadweight of the ship, remembering that winter, summer or tropical marks may be applicable, the draft restriction at the load or discharge port or a canal and the cubic capacity of the cargo. There will be an overriding factor which will restrict cargo intake and therefore revenue. This must be identified before the calculation is made.

The expenses are the cost of bunker fuel, port charges, canal charges, commissions and freight tax if any. The reason why no owner's calculation is the same as another is because of the variables. These are:

1. Different distance tables will sometimes vary in what they quote as the distance between two ports. This is sometimes because of routing, for instance via the Indonesian and Philippine islands the route may be complicated by differing drafts which require differing levels of seamanship but most importantly are suitable for some ships but not others. For example, depending on the size and draft, a ship on a voyage from Newcastle, N.S.W. to East Coast India may go south bound or northbound through the draft restricted Torres Straight.

2. Some owners use a standard sea margin allowance for all calculations. Others use different sea margin allowance for different routes depending on their experience of currents and different weather patterns at certain times of the year. It should be appreciated that the real result, as opposed to the estimate, can be affected not only by weather (especially in winter) and currents but by tides, strikes and shore breakdowns. Owners will usually calculate a 5-10% margin for their sea margin allowance.

3. What is the optimum speed? This depends on the market level, the bunker price and where the vessel was last and should next be bunkered and at what price.

4. Cargo intake will also depend on the amount of bunkers on board and when, where and at what price the ship next bunkers.

5. Port charges will be calculated but different owners will allow slightly different amounts which depend on the exact method the port uses and what exchange rate is used to calculate from the local currency to the standard US$.

Once the income and expenses are calculated, the difference is divided by the number of days the voyage will take.

The first thing to write down at the top of every voyage estimate are the details of the voyage and the deadweight and speed and consumption of the vessel as follows;

MV LONDON

DEADWEIGHT 148,200

BALLAST 14.75 ON 43 PLUS 4 DO

LADEN 13.80 ON 46.5 PLUS 1DO

HAMPTON ROADS/ROTTERDAM COAL AT USD 4.50 PMT, JANUARY 10/20, 35000/25000 12 HOURS TT BENDS 3.75 PCT

Next, distances must be tabulated and days at sea and port calculated from them at the above laden and ballast speeds. This is important for the calculation of bunker costs.

ROTTERDAM		**SEA DAYS**	**PORT DAYS**
HAMPTON ROADS	3600	10.14	4.23
15PCT SEA MARGIN		1.52	
		11.66	
ROTTERDAM	3600	11.45	5.62
10PCT SEA MARGIN		1.15	
		12.60	
TOTAL		24.26	9.85
	GRAND TOTAL	34.11 DAYS	

The calculation of 3600 miles at 14.75 knots, the ballast speed, is straightforward, as is the same 3600 x 13.8 knots laden.

This calculation is based, as is customary in the capesize trades, on a ballast leg into the load port. All ships will be more economical in ballast than laden. The sea margin is a variable. Different owners will calculate differently. In this case the owner who obviously has experience of this particular ship at this particular time of the year on this route has decided to insert a 15 percent margin. In this case ballasting in winter in the North Atlantic against the current and prevailing winds is likely to be more difficult than in summer.

Different margins will be taken at different times of the year. It will also depend on the horsepower of the engine. A more powerful engine is likely to cut through heavy sea better than a lower powered engine but will be at a disadvantage in fuel consumption in calm seas. (See Materials and Management Issues above)

The port time is calculated on the loading and discharging terms. In this case it is easy because it is SHINC (Sundays and holidays included) terms. But if the terms were, for example, 10 days SHEX (Sundays and holidays excluded), an owner would almost certainly have to calculate 14 running days as he would have to take into account two possible weekends. The turn time is also added. (See Chapter Six - Laytime).

The result in this case shows that the voyage should take, for calculation purposes, 34.11 days. At the end of a voyage, prudent owners will compare the estimate with the actual performance.

The next part is the calculation of expenses and it is laid out as follows:

PORT CHARGES						
HAMPTON ROADS						USD 55,000
ROTTERDAM						USD 115,000
TOTAL PORT CHARGES						170,000
BUNKERS	DAYS		TONS		PRICE	
SEA	11.66	X	43	X	60=	USD 30,082.80
	12.6	X	46.5	X	60=	USD 35,154.00
PORT	9.85	X	4	X	100=	USD 3,940.00
	9.85	X	1	X	100=	USD 985.00
TOTAL BUNKER COSTS						70,161.80
TOTAL EXPENSES						USD 240,161.80

The port charges are available from agents at the ports. The bunker costs are calculated by the total days at sea multiplied by the sea consumption multiplied by the price of fuel and diesel oil where she will bunker. In this case is likely to be Rotterdam, which is a very large and competitive bunkering port. This is added to the diesel oil consumed while in port multiplied by 9.85 days by the price of diesel oil. Differences between owners' calculations will depend of where and at what price they last bunkered.

The revenue is a function of the cargo carrying capacity. This can be affected by the cubic capacity of the vessel and stowage factor of the cargo or by the draft, not forgetting to measure on the basis of whether this voyage is to be undertaken on winter or summer marks. In the case of Hampton Roads to Rotterdam, it is fairly simple as it will be governed by the 50 foot brackish water draft restriction at Hampton Roads, the vessel's constants and the bunkers on board.

DWT ON 50 FT	124,000 TONS
LESS BUNKERS AND CONSTANTS	1,800 TONS
CARGO INTAKE	122,200 TONS
RATE **USD 4.50** X 122,200 =	USD 549,900.00
LESS 3,75 PCT COMMISSION	20,621.25
TOTAL NET FREIGHT	529,278.75
FREIGHT	USD 529,278.75
EXPENSES	USD 240,161.80
SURPLUS	USD 289,116.95
OVER 34.11 DAYS	
NET TIME CHARTER RETURN PER DAY- =	**USD 8,476**

Now the owner knows what this ship earns for the business calculated so that he can compare it against other potential business. He can also compare it with his running costs or breakeven costs. However, he really has no option but to try to do the best on the market, whatever his theoretical breakeven costs are. Once he has fixed his ship he has helped create the market level for that kind of ship or that route. The following chapter will examine the nature of the market in more detail.

2. The Freight Market

MEASURING THE FREIGHT MARKET

The freight market is the market in which sea or ocean transport is bought and sold. The first thing any participant in the freight market will want to find out about is the latest fixtures on the routes on which he or she is specialising. A fixture is a completed agreement between a ship owner and a charterer for the hire of a ship or the carriage of the charterer's cargo. The most important guide to the market is the fixture 'rate'. This is the easiest and most common way that charterers and owners measure the market. For them it is a cost and income respectively. Bankers or analysts will look at the market a little differently and may want to measure it slightly differently. Market fixture lists are available from ship brokers, the Baltic Exchange, publications such as Lloyds List and groups such as Bridge News (who all obtain the details from brokers).

FREIGHT

As can be seen from Figure 2.1, the headline report of a **voyage** fixture will deal with main relevant terms which are; the name of the ship, the size of cargo, the loading dates, the freight rate usually expressed per ton of cargo loaded and the name of the charterer.

When participants in the market talk about the market rate on a particular route they are thinking in terms of the voyage freight rate in dollars per ton. For instance, if the market rate for a standard panamax shipment from the United States Gulf (USG) to Japan is U.S.$18, this voyage rate is readily understood to be the standard measurement of that route. The exact terms, the dates on which the shipment was contracted and any other relevant

The Baltic Exchange Daily Fixture List
18th August 2000

TIMECHARTER

"Obelix" 1982 194914 dwt 13.5 on 64 ndas dely Qingdao early Sept trip via W Australia redel China $22000 daily - Chinese

"Bunga Saga Dua" 1993 74696 dwt dely Portbury ed August/early Sept trip via US Gulf redel Far East $11500 daily - Shi Wei

"Militos" 1982 66919 dwt 14 on 35 + 1.8 dely US Gulf 25 Aug/5 Sept trip redel China $10200 daily + 225000 bb - Transfield

"Ocean" 1982 65650 dwt 13 on 37 + 2.5 dely China prompt trip via Australia redel dop Red SeaPG-Sri Lanka rge $8750 daily - Atlantic + Orient

"Alpha Gemini" 1985 65298 dwt 13.5 on 30 + 1.5 dely Vietnam 25/27 August 12 months trading redel w/wide approx $10400 daily - Chinese

"Eastern Venture" 1995 44500 dwt dely Progresso end Aug trip via NCSA redel UK/Continent $11250 daily - Navios

"Highland Trust" 1985 43000 dwt 13.5 on 25 + 2.0 dely Canakkale prompt trip via Black Sea redel US Gulf $8250 daily - WBC

"Santa Rita" 1996 41505 dwt dely Mississippi River prompt trip redel Far East $11500 daily - Changbai

"Silver Shing" 1996 40000 dwt dely mississippi River prompt trip redel W Mediterranean $10250 daily + 35000 bb - TGP

"Sea Rainbow" 1984 38000 dwt 13 on 23 + 2.0 dely S Brazil prompt trip via Plate redel US Gulf $9750 daily - Caytrans

GRAIN

"GIC TBN" 56/58000/5 hss US Gulf/Taiwan end Sept/10 Oct $22.85 fio 10000/4000 - MSK

"Spar 8" 30000 grains 55 Mississippi/UK prompt $17.25 fio 8 days - Cargill

"Wu Zhang Hai" 25000/5 grains 50' Rio Grande/Puerto Cabello 25 Aug/4 Sept $17.25 fio 4000/3500 - Alliance

COAL

"Marine Hunter" 160000/10 Bolivar/Hadera 6/15 Sept $8.70 fio 50000sc/30000sx - NCSC

"TBN" 70000/10 Gladstone/Ghent 30 Aug/13 Sept $15/15.25 fio 5 days sc - Sidmar

ORE

"Cape Lotus" 150000/10 Tubarao/Beilun + Baoshan 15/25 Sept $11.85 fio scale/30000sc - ERO

"Cape Equinox" 110000/10 narvik/Dunkirk E20 Aug/5 Sept $4.60 fio 6 days sc - Hanjin

"Pessada" 90000/10 Pointe Noire/Antwerp 25 Aug/5 Sept $5.75 fio 6 days sc - Cargill

Figure 2.1.
A typical Baltic Exchange daily fixture list

information may modify the market's view of that fixture, but that is the benchmark and the headline report.

HIRE

A **time charter** fixture report will detail the name of the ship, its description, the delivery date, the rate of hire and name of charterer.

As demonstrated in the previous chapter under 'Voyage Estimating', a ship owner, when fixing on voyage terms, will always equate the freight rate back to a time charter return and thus he will calculate how much the ship is anticipated to earn on a daily basis. In this way he can measure how he is performing against his running and amortisation costs. If one asks the question, 'what is the time charter rate for a trip from the Continent to Japan?', the answer is a rate in dollars per day but it is not so easy to measure in general terms as the voyage rate. For example, a 20 year old ship of around 61,000 dwt with 2,600,000 cubic feet and a speed and consumption of 13 knots on 32 tons of IFO plus 2 tons of diesel oil per day, will calculate one rate. A 1998 built ship, however, of 73,000 dwt with a cubic capacity of 3,000,000 and a more economical engine which may burn 13 on 28 IFO and no diesel oil will calculate differently. The latter ship will earn much more on a daily basis because the charterer can load more cargo and thus get more revenue and pay less in bunker costs.

The time charter market is thus less transparent for measuring the general market on a particular route. It is nevertheless, a very satisfactory measurement for owners, charterers and bankers on individual ships over a specified period as they will be able to assess the ship's income against their 'breakeven' cost.

TIME CHARTER INDEXES

The Clarkson indexes take the weekly market freight rate on a number of regularly traded capesize and panamax routes and converts them to a time charter equivalent on a standard ship. (See Figure 2.2). This is published in 'Shipping Intelligence Weekly'. For obvious reasons this is not perfect for every ship but given the inherent limitations it is as good a general measurement of earning capacity as any and it benchmarks how other ships

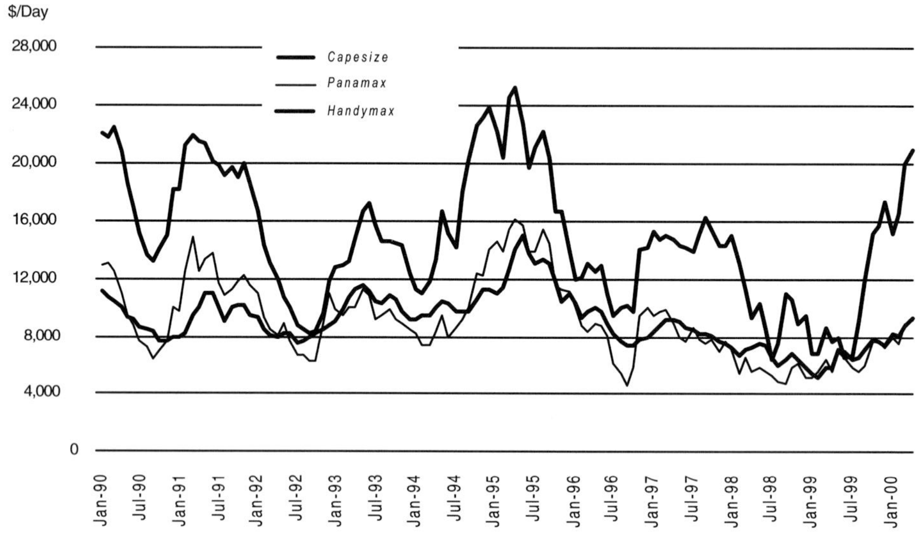

Figure 2.2
The Time Charter indexes for Capesize, Panamax and Handymax Bulk Carrier Spot Earnings

are performing. For the handymax routes which are more commonly fixed on time charter, the average inter Pacific, inter Atlantic, Atlantic to Pacific and Pacific to Atlantic rates for a standard 45,000 dwt vessel are averaged to produce the handymax index. This gives an accurate benchmarking mechanism. Figure 2.2 shows that the larger the ship, the more volatile are the swings in earning capacity when the market moves up and down. Other brokers also produce similar indexes. There is therefore a widespread, easily accessible fund of data. Since containerships are usually fixed on timecharter the same kind of indexes are also produced for the different sizes of these ships. (See Figure 2.3).

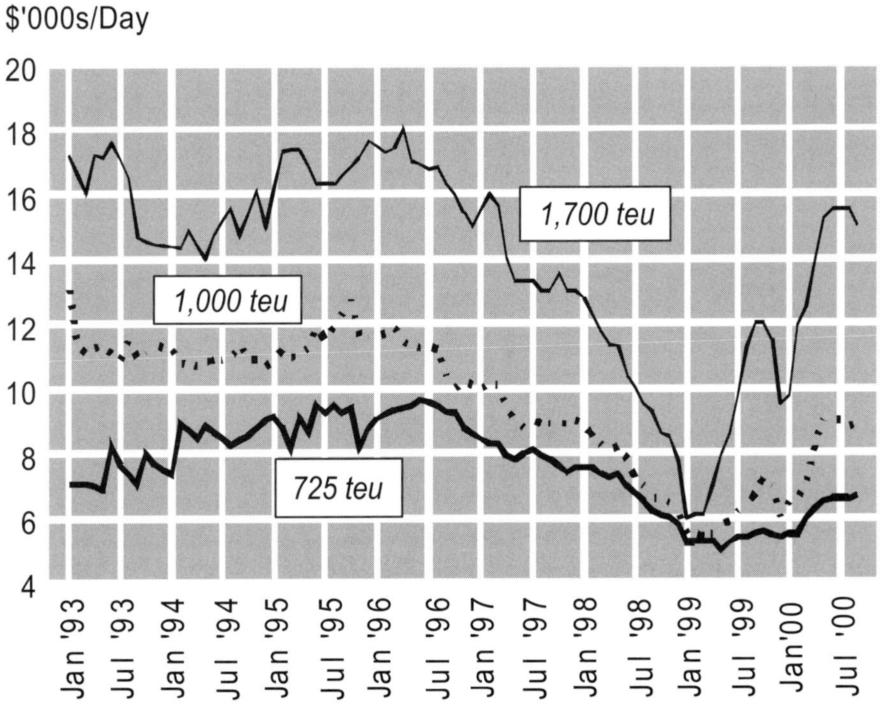

Figure 2.3
Clarkson's Container Ship Spot Earnings Indexes

VOYAGE INDEXES

A voyage index for the bulk markets can also easily be produced for the cape, panamax and handymax markets. Because it has been traded on the market known as BIFFEX (See Chapter Three - Freight Derivatives), the best known index has been the **BFI** or the **Baltic Freight Index**. (See Figure 2.4). This index evolved after it was introduced in 1985. For the first few years it included handy, panamax and cape voyage routes. The handy routes were taken out some years ago and a **Handymax index (BHI)** was created at the beginning of 1997. Three panamax time charter routes were inserted into the remaining cape/panamax index in the early '90's and in early 1999 separate panamax and capesize indexes, the **BPI** or **Baltic Panamax Index** and **BCI** or **Baltic Capesize Index** were created. The result is that there are now three separate indexes representing three of the bulk carrier markets by size. The tracking of the market can now be more size sector specific. The BFI disappeared in November 1999 to be replaced by the BPI as a traded index and by the **Baltic Dry Index** or **BDI** as a composite of the three size sector indexes to obtain a broad barometer of the dry cargo market. The constituent parts of the BCI, BPI and BHI are used as settlement mechanisms for **Forward Freight Agreements (FFA's)**. (See Chapter Three).

Freight indexes enable freight futures to be treated as a commodity. But freight itself is also a commodity.

FREIGHT AS A COMMODITY

Freight, as the most important measurement of the chartering market, is a commodity and like any other, it is subject to the laws of supply and demand of that commodity. The result is one of the most exciting and volatile markets in the world.

It will be noticed in Figures 2.5 and 2.6 how repeatedly freight rates or in 2.2, the market as measured by a timecharter index, has doubled and halved and more in the space of a very few months as they react to the supply and demand factors operating in this market.

What are these factors?

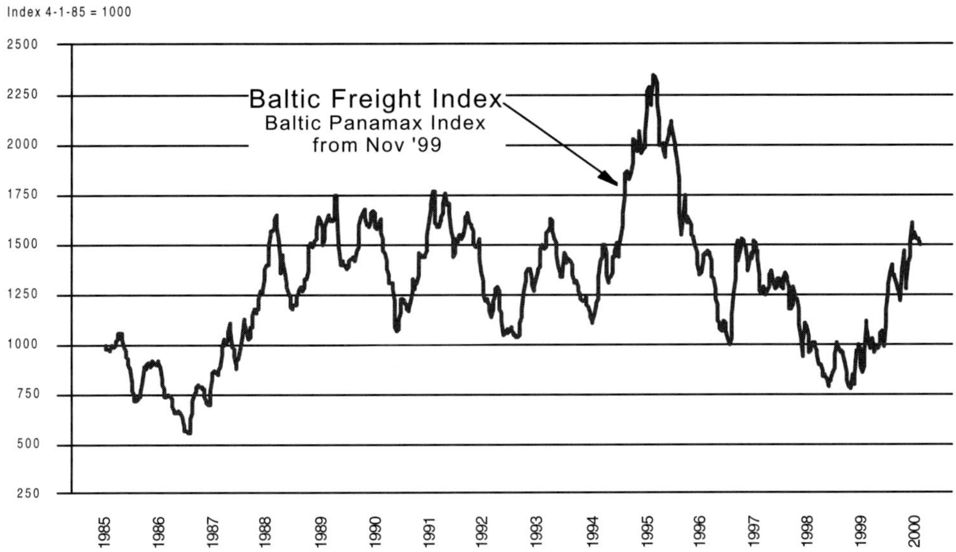

Figure 2.4.
The BFI since 1985

Supply

The supply factor in the shipping market is very simply the number, type and deadweight of ships in the market. This can be measured easily at any particular moment and the Shipping Intelligence Weekly and World Shipyard Monitor have the facts, figures and analyses.

The Autumn 1999 figures were as follows;

	Number of vessels	**millions of tons dwt**
10-35,000 dwt	2,467	60.3
35-50,000 dwt	1,318	55.7
50-80,000 dwt	999	66.9
80,000 and over	524	81.8

The supply side, or the availability of tonnage in the market, is a relatively straightforward calculation. Supply is calculated by taking the existing fleet and subtracting projected **scrapping**. Scrapping is modelled by analysts using three criteria. First the age of the fleet, determined by breaking the existing

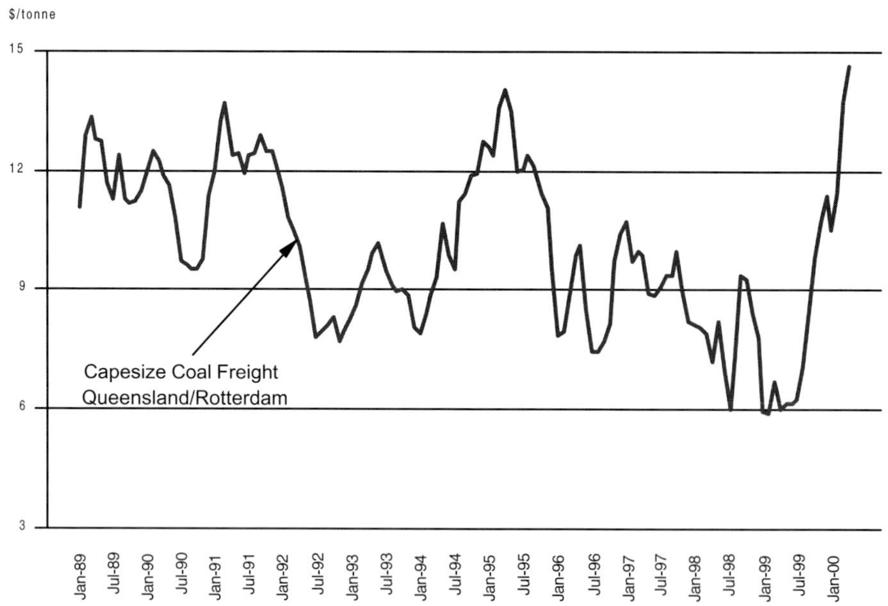

Figure 2.5

Queensland/Rotterdam voyage rates

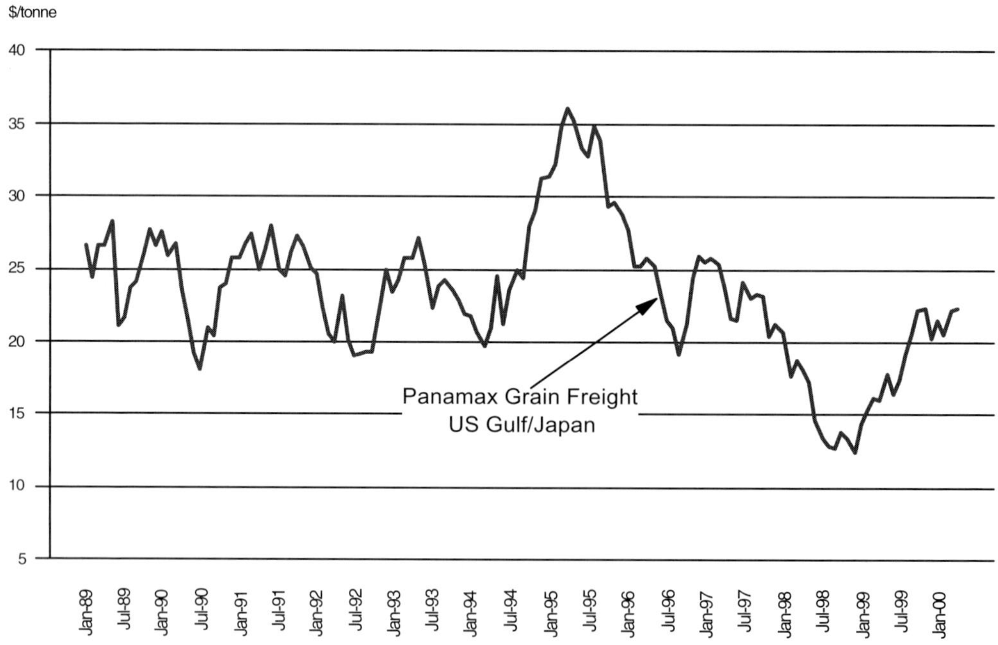

Figure 2.6

USG/Japan voyage rates

fleet down into **age profile**. (See Figures 1.2, 1.6, 1.9, 1.14 and 1.17). The greater the volume of old tonnage (traditionally vessels aged 20 years and over) the higher the likely volume of scrapping. The actual volume of tonnage scrapped will be determined by the level of the freight market. The final and least important variable is the scrap price, but this does not play a major role in calculations. Finally an allowance is made for additional removals, including conversions, lay ups and losses at sea. In recent years this figure has been statistically insignificant, but the industry correctly continues to be concerned at the level of bulk carrier casualties and the resultant loss of life.

Having calculated deletions from the supply side, the next stage is to calculate additions to the fleet. Forward **deliveries** are calculated by taking the **order book** (the volume of tonnage on order at ship yards around the world) and making a small allowance for slippage in the building schedule.

The balance of the fleet minus scrapping plus deliveries determines supply side growth, traditionally presented in percentage terms on an annual basis for a year or two ahead.

Figures 2.7 and 2.8 demonstrate the ingredients of the classic cycle. When the freight market and therefore ship owner's confidence is high, it fuels a rise in new building orders. When they are delivered some months or years later, often on a downturn in industrial production and thus demand, it precipitates a further sharp decline in the market as increased supply acts together with faltering or lower demand. This can be clearly seen in the 1994-99 period. However on a low market, confidence is also low and cash or credit tight. Orders and subsequent deliveries are therefore much fewer. When an increase in demand comes the market obviously responds by a sharp increase in rates and the value of ships. Notice the relatively low level of new building deliveries in the 1987-1993 period which obviously was a pre-requisite for the 1994-95 boom in the freight market.

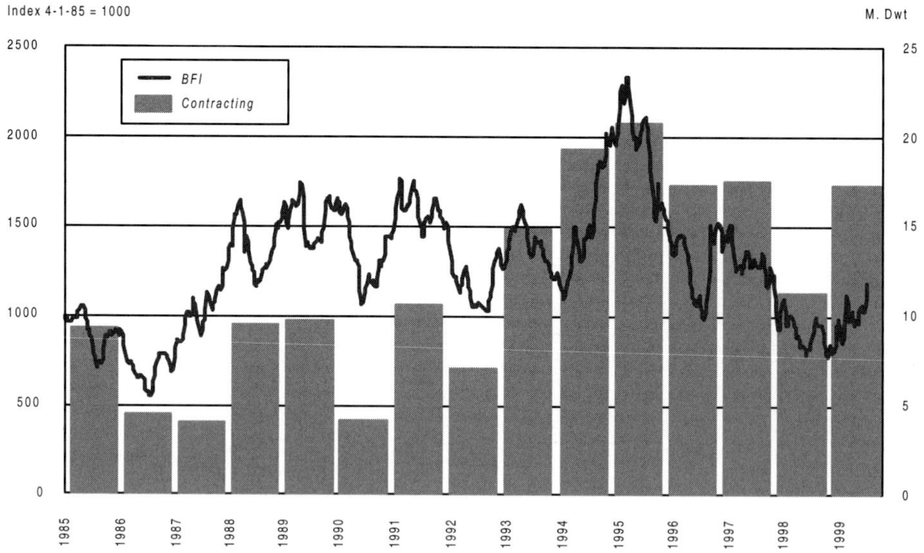

Figure 2.7

New building contracts and the market 1989-1999

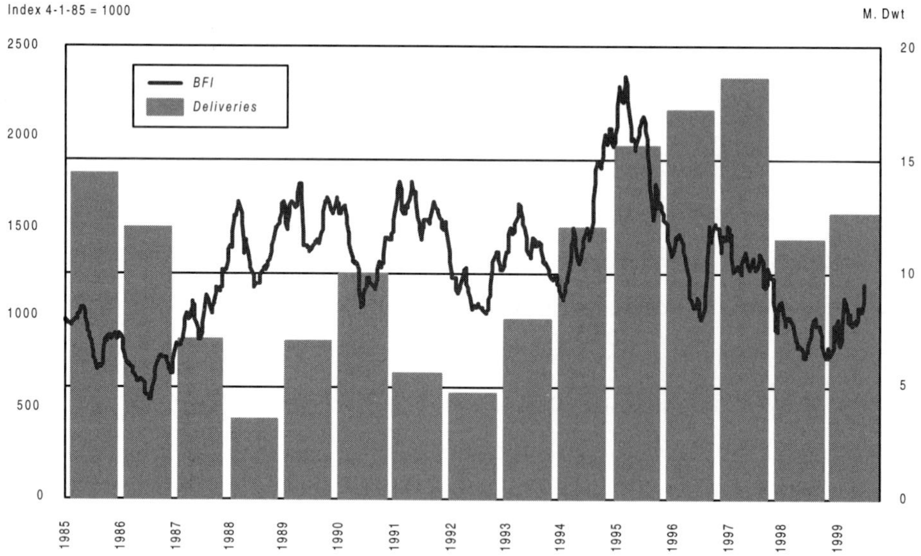

Figure 2.8

Market deliveries 1989-1999

Let us examine this demand side both in more general terms and concentrating on its specific components.

Demand

This is a much more complex subject than supply. It involves the health of the world's economy, especially of its basic industries, the steel industry being the most important for bulk shipping; the vigour of various commodity markets and the weather which has an effect both on the success or failure of harvests and also how much imported coal will be consumed in power stations in winter.

Demand is also affected by changes in the ton/mile ratio. For instance, if a European country switches its imports from the USA to Australia, the time taken for that voyage is increased significantly, thus effectively diminishing supply. In this way the price of commodities and in particular the movement of exchange rates which affect the delivered price in US$ is extremely important. Analysts will be monitoring large changes carefully. These factors do affect the way the markets move, especially in the short term.

However, basic demand is determined mainly by industrial demand and therefore there is a rough correlation between the freight and time charter market and industrial production. (See Figure 2.9). This is hardly surprising when it is considered that a large part of the overall bulk carrier use is for the carriage of bulk materials which are being transported for the steel and other heavy industries which constitute the demand side of the supply/demand equation.

A glance at the following table will demonstrate just how dependent on industrial production the demand side of the shipping market actually is.

Seaborne Trade	**1998**	**1999**
Iron Ore	**419** million tons	**418**
Steam coal	279	283
Coking coal	171	166
Total coal	**450**	**449**
Wheat/coarse grains	167	173
Soyabeans	41	39
Total grain	**207**	**212**
Bauxite/alumina	55	54
Phosphate rock	31	30
Sugar	37	37
Agribulks	93	93
Fertilizer	64	64
Scrap	46	45
Cement	45	45
Coke	11	12
Pig iron	13	12
Forest products	156	158
Steel products	189	174
Others	37	37
TOTAL	**1,851**	**1,839 MILLION TONS**

Bulk materials for the steel industry and steel itself (iron ore, coking coal, scrap, coke, pig iron and steel products) thus directly account for about 45 percent of the total bulk seaborne cargo carried. When added to the steam coal which is primarily for electricity production and to some extent cement production, to alumina and bauxite, the raw materials of aluminium production, the second most important metal in the industrial world and to cement, it can be seen that the seaborne transportation of these commodities, vital for the world's industrial production, comprise just over 65% of the total. The agricultural industry by comparison accounted in 1999 for a total of 438 million tons or about 22% comprising grain, agricultural products, sugar, phosphates, used for fertilisers and fertilisers themselves. However, the

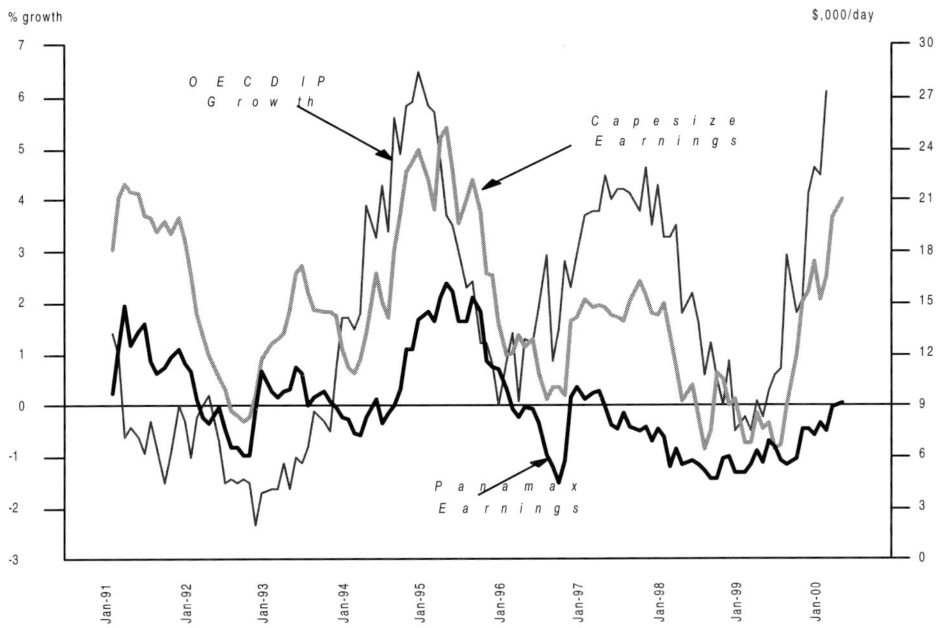

Figure 2.9
Industrial production and time charter returns

steadily upward trend in grain imports from about 100 million tons in the early '70's to the 213 million tons in 1999, as well as the rise in agricultural products, has been largely driven by the trend towards greater meat consumption in industrial and industrialising countries. The pre-requisite for this is the greater affluence which has accompanied industrial and industrialising societies.

Figure 2.9 demonstrates this close correlation over 10 years. Of course, there are discrepancies because this is only the demand side of the supply/demand equation but taken together with the supply side it can be seen that analysts will look at this very carefully. It is important to note that industrial production is not the same as GNP or GDP which includes, in the industrial economies, the increasingly important services sector.

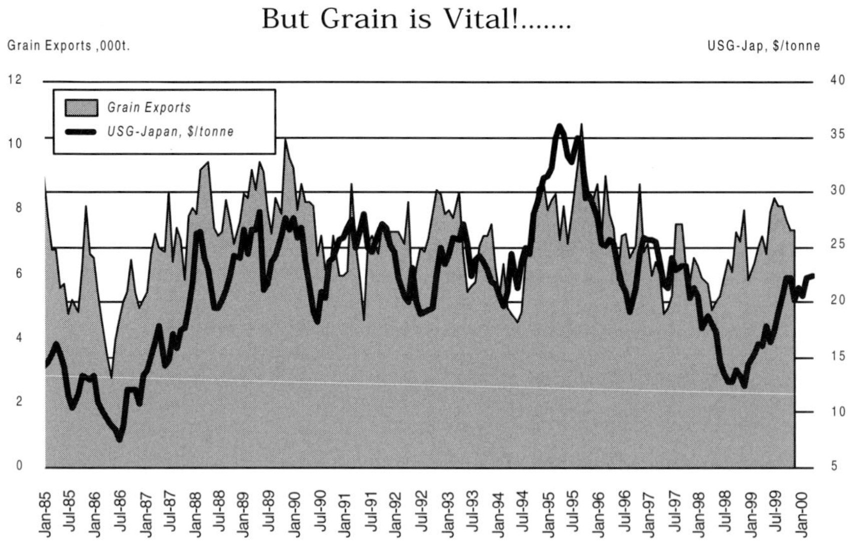

Figure 2.10

The correlation between US grain exports and U.S. Gulf to Japan panamx freight rates

There is a size sector factor to add to this simple model. While industrial production is the most important general factor for all types of ships, it is the steel industry in particular for capesizes, that is the most important demand factor. Figure 1.12 shows the predominence of iron ore and coal carried by

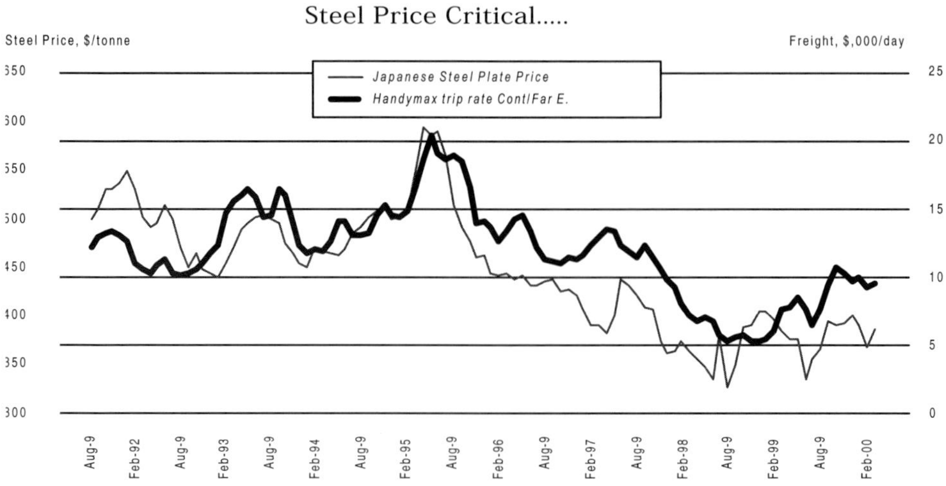

Figure 2.11

The correlation between the Japanese steel plate price and handymax trip rates

capesizes and the previous table shows around 580 million tons of seaborne iron ore and coking coal carried annually. Over 70% of capesize cargoes are destined for the steel industry. Its health is therefore a vital indicator for the capesize market.

However, in the panamax sector grain is a very important cargo (See Figure 1.11). The grain trade is, as a consequence, a major influence on the panamax market (See Figure 2.10).

Similarly when looking at the handy and handymax fleet it is the minor bulk trades that are the most important demand constituent and once again it is the steel industry that is by far the most important. Figure 2.11 demonstrates, for example, the close correlation between the price of steel and the time charter returns for handymaxes.

SUPPLY AND DEMAND

But what really drives the market? Supply or demand?

Of course it is the interplay of both factors which determines the level of the market, often with a dash of the 'x' factor, present in any market, sentiment. But for those at the cutting edge of the market it is plain that it is demand that drives the market up or down. This was true, for example, of the 1994/95 boom. It was no doubt aided by the restraint in ordering and deliveries of new buildings in the previous five years (See Figures 2.7 and 2.8) but it was demand driven. (See Figure 2.9). The acute fall in demand in 1995/96 and again in 1998, the latter as a result of the Asian crisis, led to a collapse of freight rates. Major bulk trades (iron ore, coal, grain, alumina/bauxite, phosphate rock) declined by 10 million tons (1 percent) while minor bulk trades decreased 40 million tons (3 percent). The freight market fall which resulted was no doubt accelerated by the over ordering and consequent high deliveries caused by the wave of optimism during the high market of 1994/95, (See Figures 2.7 and 2.8) which even survived the down turn in 1995/97 in some quarters. But the primary cause was the collapse in demand.

In short, over supply can cap a rise or accelerate a decline. Under supply can fuel a rise or cushion a fall. But demand is the driving force.

SHIPPING CYCLES

Figure 2.7 shows the correlation between supply of ships and freight and Figure 2.9 between industrial demand and freight. The classic shipping cycle thus occurs because as industrial production is high, freights are high. Optimism, apparently limitless opportunities and easy credit result in a glut of new buildings which are then delivered a year or so later just as industrial production has faltered, accelerating the fall in freight rates. On the other hand, ship owners on low markets have diminished earnings from their ships and are cautious or pessimistic and credit is tight. Few therefore have the confidence to order new buildings. Thus when demand picks up there is less supply to restrain a sharp market rise.

This is why the freight market is so volatile. The graphs of the freight market do not show gently undulating hills. They are positively alpine. When you add to the cycles where rates regularly double or halve, the fluctuations within the main cycles caused by droughts, seasonal grain demand and a whole host of temporary, isolated or micro factors, the result is extra volatility within the cycles.

The tendency is that between the cycles, the troughs are longer than the peaks. This was certainly true of the post war period until 1986/87 and interestingly, as far back as the 1850's which is as far back as have been recorded (See Figure 2.12). Since 1987 the cycles have become shorter (See

Figures 2.12 and 2.13) but even so, in general it is still true that there have been longer periods at the lower levels. This can be explained by the fact that owners and the banks who finance them are more optimistic as the market rises. A lot of money can be made when an owner buys at the bottom, enjoys a booming market and sells at the top. There are always optimists dreaming of being the next Onassis or Niarchos. But since they all act independently of each other, the large number of ships ordered generally far exceed the required demand making the troughs between the peaks that much longer. Because the world economy and in particular industrial production does not rise consistently and the new buildings are then delivered often in less promising economic times, this pattern will undoubtedly be repeated.

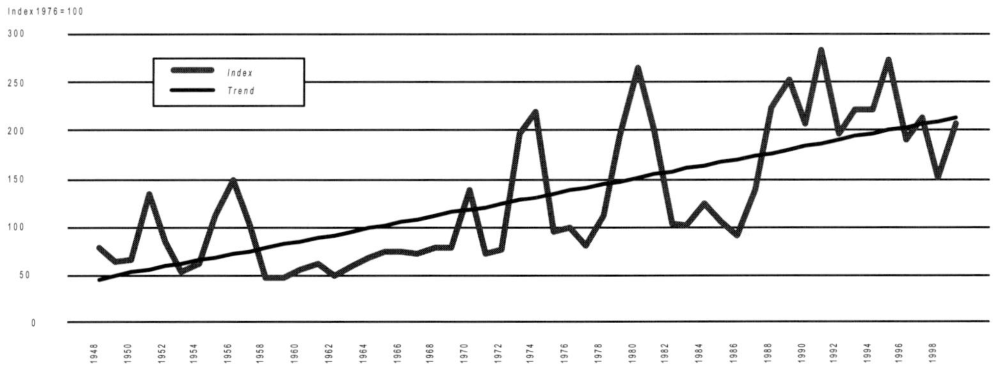

Figure 2.12

Dry Cargo cycles since 1948

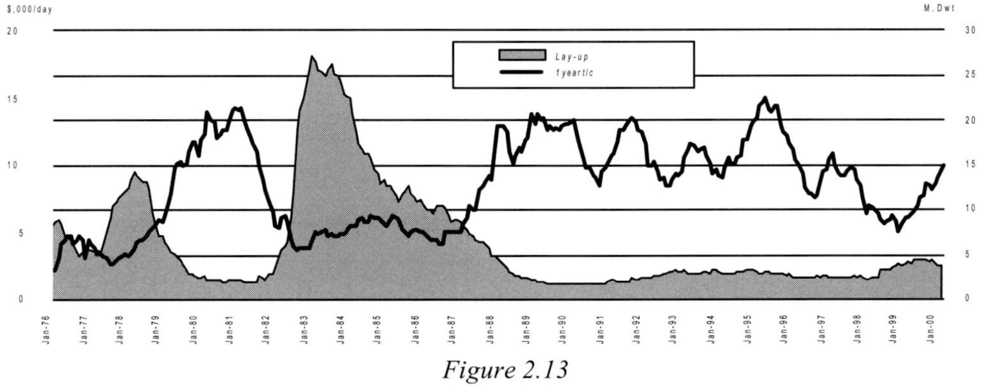

Figure 2.13

Greater volatility and shorter dry cargo cycles since late 1980's

As mentioned, these shipping cycles have been traced back to the 1850's*. Four cycles lasted 5 to 6 years, five 8 to 10 years, and three 11 to 12 years. But in the period 1987 to 2000, the cycles have become very short and essentially we have seen five distinct cycles in those 13 years. Each time the market declined, it bounced back almost immediately. This can probably be attributed to more sustained world growth, which has been more broadly based and the absence of the millstone of laid up tonnage. (See Figure 2.13). It also relates to the increasing integration of the global economy. It almost certainly has something to do with better information and analysis available, especially to shipowners and has probably been accentuated by receiver's greater reliance on the spot market than was previously the case. But one result has been greater volatility within the cycle.

But why does it react so violently? The graphs of historical freight or hire rarely show gentle rises or falls. The capesize market between the two months mid August and end October 1999, for example, doubled in freight rates and tripled in time charter rates. Why such a violent swing? A good analogy is to think of a set of scales. Pile a heap of small coins on one side of the scales. Let them represent the supply of ships. The market is over tonnaged. Ships are scrapped. Coins are therefore taken away. Supposing industrial production is increasing, the coins are put on the opposite side of the balance. Nothing happens at all to the supply/demand balance until the coins are more or less equal. The scales quiver. Only one more coin, just that little extra demand, makes the balance crash to the opposite side. And so it is with freight market. Of course, even in the freight market there are tempering factors. These can be for example, the ability to delay cargoes, to parcel up to larger sizes, to switch loading areas to one closer to the destination lowering the ton/mile ratio or even to buy from an inland origin. Nevertheless volatility is the name of the game. This has led to the need to hedge the freight risk. The various ways this can be done will be dealt with in Chapter Three.

** See "Maritime Economics" by Martin Stopford*

FREIGHT AND OTHER COMMODITIES

As freight is an independent commodity with its own unique set of supply and demand criteria, it deserves to be looked at separately. Yet it is often treated by those who buy and sell cargoes as something that is barely understood, rather tiresome, but that has to be added to and therefore part of the price of the commodity they are trading. Whether cargoes are bought CIF or FOB it is a grave mistake to view freight in this way. The markets for coal, grain and alumina, for instance, react quite differently than the market for freight.

It can be seen in graphs 2.14, 2.15, 2.16 and 2.17 that although there is some small degree of statistical correlation between the FOB price of coal, grain, and steel plate and freight rates appliciable to routes on which these commodities move in significant volumes, this should hardly come as a surprise. After all, these are bulk commodities involved in industrial production or at least the industrial world and thus a key element in the demand side of the supply/demand equation. It is interesting to note that the price of steel plate and the iron ore Brazil to Japan capesize route shows the closest correlation. This, once again, highlights the importance of the steel industry on the demand side of the equation. But it is equally interesting to note that alumina and steam coal pricing has hardly any correlation at all. There is, in fact, no more correlation between freight and most industrial or food commodity prices than there is between those commodities themselves.

When there is trouble in the world's economy, for instance, it usually has a bearish effect on demand across the spectrum of commodities, each one differently, however, due to the different nature of those commodities. Thus we can see that if there is a common pattern to all these commodity/freight graphs, it is simply that during this period they tend to start high and finish lower. What happens in the middle has more to do with their own individual supply/demand criteria.

CONTROL OF FREIGHT

If freight, as an independent commodity, reacts differently from other commodities, then those who understand it will want to control it. The principles of buying and selling cargoes are quite straightforward. The buyer and seller can effect the sale **CIF** or **FOB**. CIF or **C&F** means **'Cost, insurance and freight'** or **'cost and freight'** respectively, which is the delivered price at the port of discharge including the freight. This means the supplier, seller or an intermediate trader is responsible for the freight. FOB means **'free on board'** which means that the cargo is delivered to the buyer at the port of origin or supply. This means therefore that the receiver, buyer or an intermediate trader is responsible for the freight. Careful attention to the freight markets can present buyers, traders and sellers with opportunities to make money, sell cargoes they would otherwise not have sold, or buy cargoes cheaply they would not otherwise have been able to buy.

What are the advantages and disadvantages of controlling the freight element in a sale involving seaborne transportation?

One advantage is that not all suppliers or receivers want to control the freight. They are often untutored or uncomfortable with the freight market or they may simply wish someone else to take the responsibility. If this is the case, an old, disparaging joke is that for suppliers who like to sell FOB, it actually means 'free of bother'. But not controlling freight also means that control over one of the price elements in the delivered cost is lost. The party controlling freight has a commercial advantage. Assuming both parties have the capability to do the freight, what are the issues?

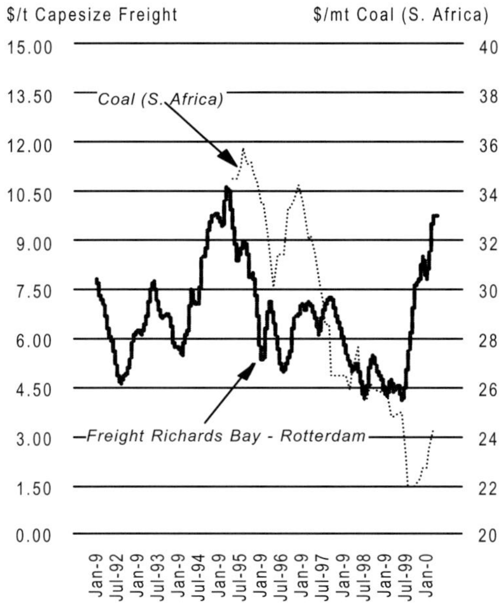

Figure 2.14

Coal/Freight Correlation

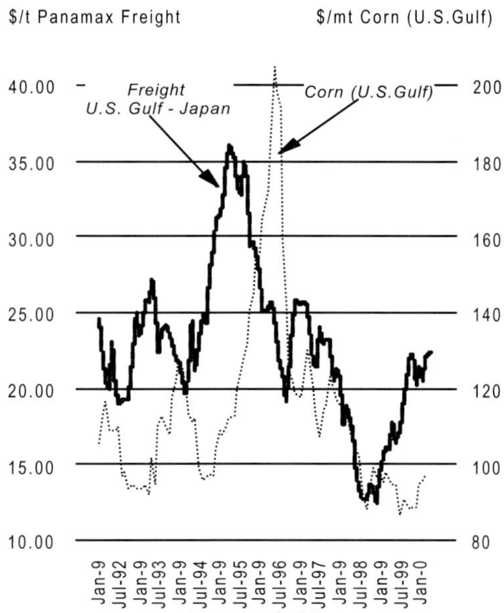

Figure 2.15

Grain/Freight Correlation

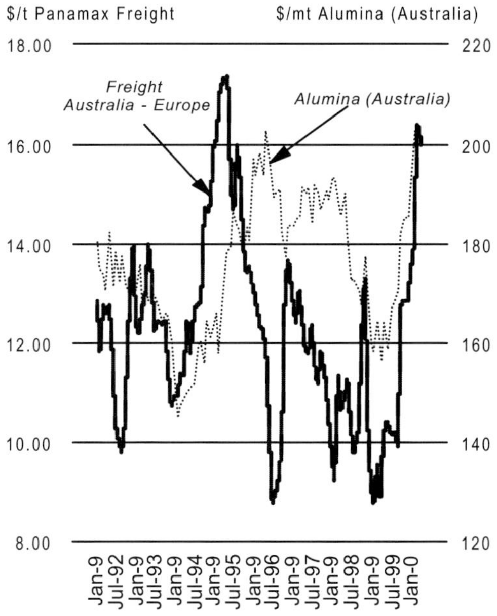

Figure 2.16

Alumina/Freight Correlation

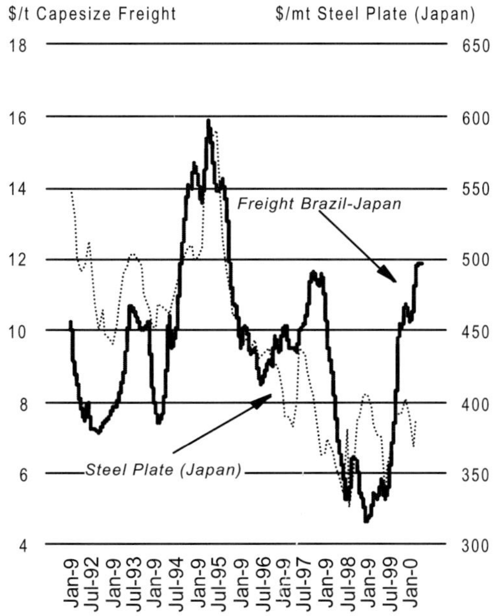

Figure 2.17

Steel/Freight Correlation

COST

Theoretically, a FOB price plus freight should add up to the quoted CIF price. If that is the case the decision as to who controls the freight will either be mutually agreed, be a test of wills, or one party will feel that there is a greater operational value in the control of freight than the other. However, it is more often the case that the freights given or assumed by the shippers (sellers) on the one hand and the receivers (buyers) on the other are not consistent with one another. One reason is that some ship owners will have special relationships, perhaps based on previous or on-going business, with one but not the other. If they have the most aggressive freight in the market then the party they support will have the best delivered cost, assuming that the seller is not manipulating the FOB price. Another reason is that one party may take a view on the market without attempting to cover freight and the other will try to get the best available market freight.

Where does the advantage lie in this relationship?

This varies considerably owing to the circumstances surrounding each participant in the prospective deal and this simple model ignores the important role of the trader. However, in general terms, given a level playing field, since the buyer has the last word to accept or not, the advantage will lie with him. His options are; (1) he can accept a CIF offer if the delivered price is more competitive than the FOB plus the freight he has negotiated himself; (2) he can try to beat the freight element that has been offered in the CIF price; (3) if there are a number of competing sellers he can use more leverage on each one of them. If this is the case, ship owners are more likely to give a competitive rate to the receiver rather than a competing supplier whose offer may fail for reasons quite other than the freight. The receiver will have the last word. But it is not only a question of delivered cost.

CONTROL OF THE SHIPPING OPERATION

Whoever controls the freight and shipping controls the practical aspects of the shipment such as the quantity shipped, the exact dates of shipment and the probable dates of delivery at the discharge port. Benefits can arise in a number of ways. Quantities can be aligned with stem, market or stockpile considerations. The exact time of loading can be aligned with stem, stockpile or expected berth occupancy considerations. This latter advantage is considerable in busy ports or berths where the elimination or reduction of demurrage is of paramount consideration. Missing an available berth by a small margin only to see one or more ships arrive ahead in the queue can not only put the expected arrival of the cargo badly out of schedule but the resulting demurrage can be hugely expensive.

Furthermore, some contracts of affreightment (COA) can incorporate different sizes, different load ports, a minimum and maximum number of cargoes to be loaded and even options to extend the period of the contract. **Flexibility and options are the keys to a successful freight policy. While these options are secondary to the base requirement, they can quite often be manipulated to considerable financial and logistical advantage. For instance if the market rate goes above the contract rate, optional cargoes can be declared. If not, they need not be and spot cargoes can be fixed at the lower market rate. The contract has thus not only hedged the sale of the cargo and capped the price but given opportunities to improve that price by managing the contract by means of monitoring the freight market and locking in lower freights if they become available. If the market rates increase for instance from the Pacific and decrease in the Atlantic, the buyer who controls freight may be able to trigger cheaper delivered costs with spot cargoes purchased from Atlantic origins rather than Pacific.**

Are there extra responsibilities when controlling freight?

The only extra responsibilities will be the need to insure the cargo, which is easily and relatively cheaply done and to employ the people to fix the contracts and manage the contract. This means watching and understanding the freight market. The cost of employing a competent person to do this is often a worthwhile investment depending on the company's business, structure and volumes of cargo. Competent brokers can also be employed to look after the Principal's interest for no fee since their remuneration comes from brokerage anyway. The best ones may, for the right company, be willing to give a value added service which would include strategic and tactical advice, statistical analysis and post fixture and operational services. The laytime statements will also have to be looked at by the party controlling the freight. But so they will also if that party does not control the freight at one or other of the ports. At least, if the party knows about freight and laytime statements, the other party is unlikely to take undue advantage. One of the broker's jobs is to assist in finalisation of laytime statements and accounts.

CONCLUSION

Whoever controls the freight becomes a participant in the chartering market along with the ship owners and operators. It is a market which as can be seen from Figures 2.2, 2.5, 2.6, 2.9 and Figures 2.12 to 2.17 is outrageously volatile. Yet these risks can not only be minimised, they can be made to work for the participant. In deciding how the participant should position himself in the market, the most important commodity is information. But the way this information is analysed is crucial. How that information is obtained, how to get the best analysis of that information and how to hedge the freight risk is the subject of the next chapter.

3. The Broker

THE SHIPBROKER – WHAT'S IN A NAME?

The profession of 'shipbroker' means different things to different people. In Japan and Korea, for example, the term 'shipbroker', is only used for the intermediary broker. But in Europe the word 'shipbroker' is used to identify a variety of chartering functions. Professional chartering staff employed by ship owners or their exclusive agents or representatives or by charterers are referred to and refer to themselves as 'shipbrokers'. This is why a leading British shipping company's chartering staff have the designation 'Broker' on their name card, yet when they travel to Japan they have new ones made which read 'Chartering Department' so that their hosts do not misunderstand their role.

There are scores of companies which, especially in London, represent a charterer or an owner. They typically represent no other client. They call themselves brokers but they are not independent. Yet many brokers working for independent companies are used, usually by charterers but also by owners, on an exclusive basis to represent their interests. Other brokers in the same company could represent another company who may be a competitor. It is a complex world of interdependent interests.

The word 'Broker', however, does imply the independent intermediary between the ship owner (or his representative or broker) and the charterer (or his broker or representative). Indeed, most people would probably initially think in these terms. The word 'Broker' in this book is, unless qualified, used to denote the independent intermediary. But those involved in chartering do it from quite different points of view. Owner's brokers and charterer's brokers obviously look at the market from different perspectives. Independent shipbrokers are, in the main, the competitive element whose job it is to act as intermediaries and while having allegiances and relationships, their job is to put the business together as they are paid solely by commission and not by the clients. They are therefore, an entrepreneurial lot. A ‘Lloyds List’ article of March 1993 reporting about the ship broking industry bouncing back after a depressed market and the Baltic Exchange bomb wrote, ‘A broker is a rare breed needing to be a salesman, legal expert, financial wizard, geographical genius, cool headed in a crisis and able to react rationally in a split second to any opportunity that presents itself.’

This sounds impressive but how do they deploy these skills and what is their role?

THE ROLE OF THE INDEPENDENT SHIPBROKER

Information

The oxygen of any market is information. Information is what makes a market work. Gathering that information requires time, effort, people, equipment and a network of contacts. It therefore needs a specialist at gathering and interpreting that information. It is no longer possible to be a general shipbroker and know almost everything about every market. Detailed specialist knowledge on certain areas, trades, sizes, commodities or charterers is always in demand as the ship owner, charterer, or his representative will often need to learn about a different market depending on where his ship is or what he has to fix. Furthermore, ‘there is need for a conduit through which information can flow from various sources, some of whom may not be seeking to attain objectives from the same point of view’ as Eddie Coulson wrote in his excellent ‘Guide for Tanker Brokers’. It is a fast moving market. Many ships and charterers are negotiating constantly. Traders need to know freight rates in order to sell cargoes. All Principals need up to date information on which ships are interested in what cargoes, why and at what rates, what cargoes need to be lifted in certain areas at certain times. There is an enormous diversity of interest, volatility and variety in the market place. While Principals demand the information there is a need for someone to gather it and make sense of it.

At its very basic level this will entail background and reference information. The Lloyds Register is a well known comprehensive Register of all vessels. The Clarkson Registers, obtainable in book or disk form, are also standard reference works. Examples are seen in Figures 1.15, 1.24, 1.28 and 1.30. There are also research publications available covering all areas of every shipping market. The 'Shipping Intelligence Weekly' gives the most comprehensive weekly analysis of every shipping market including freight rates, prices, volumes and sales. Monthly publications give an over view of the supply ('World Shipbuilding Monitor') and demand ('Dry Bulk Trade Outlook') situations. The 'Clarkson Shipping Review and Outlook', a six monthly publication, does just what it says. It gives a detailed review of the markets over the previous six months and attempts some tentative predictions. Investment decisions will be of a higher quality when this kind of background information is taken into account. These successful publications are designed especially for the shipping markets and one of the most important is the chartering market. The reason for their success is mainly because the industry is both hungry for the oxygen of up to date and comprehensive market information which is collected from brokers and for an analysis of aspects of the market which is done by shipping analysts working with brokers.

Furthermore, newspapers and magazines report shipping and chartering matters. 'Lloyds List', for example has a daily section on the dry cargo chartering market. (See Figure 3.1) The source for this information is brokers.

Summer predictions less than sunny for carrier

THE anticipation of summer appears to have placed the majority of the dry bulk carri er sectors in the doldrums. While modern panamaxes put on a positive front in the Atlantic and Pacific, the ca-pesize market seems reluc tant to proceed with any new gains, and the handysizes remain mixed in outlook.

Movement in freight rates has been slight and range bound in either direction over the past week, and the majority of trading has been at best flat. Flashes of inspiration have been lacking and the market seems content to trade near unchanged levels.

With June just around the corner one might be forgiven for adopting a summer lack lustre attitude but while some aspects of the dry bulk carrier sector remain buoyant, the potential for in-

GRAIN

US Gulf to Egypt-Vessel to be nominated, 55,000t ± 5% heavy grains, $15.50, fio, 10,000t/ 6,000t, mid June. (Charterer not reported)*

US Gulf to Trinidad - *Nassau Paradise*, about 27,000t grains, $12.00, fio, 7,000t/6,000t, end May. (Skaarup)*

COAL

Richards Bay to Hadera

- *Cape Kestrel*, 140,000t ± 10%, $10.25, scale load/20,000t SHex, June 20-30. (NCSC)*

Hampton Roads to Taranto — SCF vessel to be nominated, 90,000t ± 10%, $7.80, fio, 30,000t SHinc/30,000t SHinc, May 30-June 8. (Ilva)*

Richards Bay to Koper Vessel to be nominated, 60,000t ± 10%, $11.50, fio, scale load/ 20,000t SHinc, end May-early June. (Enel)*

ORE

Tubarao to Beilun and Baoshan — *Treasure*, creased demand and activity remains a possibility.

Most shipbrokers believe that this summer will bring a traditional lull to the market, and the effect of this opinion will no doubt bring a 'slow down' element into trading. The advent of Posidonia in the coming weeks will also compound an early summer tone. However, there are two months until the traditional August holiday and therefore plenty of time for the unex pected to play a part in freight rate trends.

Freight rates across the board are healthier this year than they have

140,000t ± 10%, $10.75, fio, scale load/30,000t SHinc, June 5-17. (Safore)*

MISCELLANEOUS

Constantza to Bandar Khomeini— Vessel to be nominated, 20,000t alumina, $29.00, fio, 2,500t/3,000t, prompt. (Irisl)*

DryBulk

Jennie Harris

Damietta to South Korea — Vessel to be nominated, about 14,000t sugarbeet pulp pellets, about $40.00, prompt. (ACT)*

TIMECHARTER

Pacific Vitality (165,794 dwt, Hong Kong, built 1996) delivery Baoshan June 25-30, about 2 years, low $18,OOOs. (Cobelfret)*

Polycarp (152,065 dwt, Norwegian International Register, 13.8k on 43t + 2.5t, built 1990) delivery west coast India prompt, trip via Richards Bay, redelivery Spain, $19000s daily. (Cargill)*

Filippo Lembo (74,500 dwt, Italian, 14k on 34t, built 1997) delivery Praia Mole early June, trip via river

been for some time. In addition, the indus try also has the autumn to look forward to, with many predicting that seasonal de-mand will boost the market further. However, there are concerns, especially in the panamax sector, that the final quarter may cause prob lems for freight rates, as many newbuildings are expected to come on line. Until then, owners and charterers are determined to enjoy the best the market can offer. The remaining spring activity should provide sup port in the week ahead.

• Japan's Food Agency has bought 149,950 tonnes of feed barley and 14,010 tonnes of feed wheat at tender. Ship ment of the barley must be made by September 30, and the wheat by November 30. The agency previously pur-chased 14,060 tonnes of feed wheat and 150,000 tonnes

Plate, redelivery China, $11,800 daily plus $280,000 ballast bonus. (Cosco-amended)*

Caya (73,867 dwt, Panamanian, 14k on 32t, built 1997) delivery dropping outward pilot Portbury May 23-24, trip via east coast South America, redelivery China, $12,350 daily. (Dreyfus)*

Ruby Crest (73,330 dwt, Panamanian, 13.5k on 32t,

Figure 3.1

Lloyds List daily market report

H. CLARKSON HANDY SIZE MARKET REPORT – WEEK ENDED 8TH JAN 1999
==

BATLIC-CONT-MED-BL SEA/FAR EAST

SINCE OUR LAST REPORT RATES WOULD SEEM TO HAVE JUMPED FROM BOTH AREAS. THE MAIN INTEREST IS FOR THE LARGER GOOD GEARD HANDYMAX TYPES AND IN PARTICULAR FOR THE BLACK SEA WHERE THERE IS A DEFINATE SHORTAGE FOR PROMPT/EARLY FEB DATES. RATES THERE ARE EXPECTED TO RISE SLIGHTLY MORE BEFORE LEVELLING OFF.

THE STEELS FROM THE BALTIC ARE ALSO BEING SOURCED MORE THROUGH ST. PETERSBURG IN RUSSIA WHICH HAS AN ICE PROBLEM AND IS ALSO OUTSIDE IWL. LIMITED TONNAGE IS ABLE OR WILLING TO TRADE THERE SO RATES WOULD HAVE APPEARED TO HAVE INCREASED SIGNIFICANTLY. IN REALITY THOUGH THERE IS A GOOD VOLUME OF JANUARY TONNAGE SO A TWO TIER MARKET FROM THE BALTIC/CONT IS EXPECTED TO EMERGE WITH TONNAGE NOT WILLING ST. PETERSBURG ACHIEVING LEVELS WHICH ARE NOT FAR FROM THE PRE-CHRISTMAS RATES OF LOW 5'S FOR HANDYMAX TYPES.

FIXTURES WHICH HAVE EMERGED ARE AS FOLLOWS:-

A/C COPENSHIP FIXED THE CHETTINAD TRADITION BSS DEL LOWER BALTIC FOR A TRIP TO BANGLADESH AT USD6400 SHE IS 85 BUILT LI FLAG – 43,589 ON 11.319 CRS 4X25 5 HO 5 HA ABT 13.5 K ON 24 MT IFO 380 PL US 1.5 MT MDO

A/C MARTRADE TOOK AND IRANIAN 34,000 TONNER FOR BL SEA/PMO AT USD5300 BSS DEL CANAKKALE

THE 49,000 DWT 83 BUILT VESSEL HIDIR SELEK WAS FIXED FRO BL SEA/FAR EAST AT USD6100 BSS DEL CANAKKALE TO METALINVESK.

A/C PANOCEAN TOOK THE 94 BUILT 27,000 DWT 'WAVELET'FOR A TRIP VIA MOROCCO TO THE FAR EAST WITH FERTS AT USD4000 BSS DOP CASA DELIVERY. OWISE VARIOUS OTHERS WHERE RUMOURED BUT DETAILS HAVE NOT YET SURFACED.

US GULF

WITH A LACK OF EARLY TONNAGE IN THIS AREA WE HAVE SEEN AN IMPROVEMENT IN THIS MARKET SINCE THE BEGINNING OF THE YEAR. AT THE EARLY PART OF THE WEEK IT WAS REPORTED THE ÇAPRICORN'82 BLT 37000 DWT GEARLESS FIXED TO MAN SHIPPING DEL NCSA TCT CONT AT USD 5250 DLY FOR A TRIP TO EUROPE WHILST A 41000 DWT BY THE END OF THE WEEK THE SERAFIN TOPIC 82 BLT 37000 DWT 4/25 CR HAD FIXED TO ELKEM FOR A TRIP TO NORWAY AT USD 6750 DLY.

ON THE GRAIN FRONT TRADIGRAIN COVERED US GULF/ALGERIA 25000/5 PCT THE RATE LEVEL WAS SAID TO BE AROUND USD 15.60.

DREYFUS WERE RUMOURED TO HAVE COVERED GULF/IRELAND 1/1.2 MILL ON TC BASIS – LEVELS WERE NOT REPORTED.

WE HAVE SEEN AN INCREASE IN THE BALTIC HANDY ROUTE USG/CONT FOR 1.4/1.6M GR 55' OF 27 CENTS SINCE 31 DEC TO USD 11.10

SOUTH AFRICA
=============

THE SOUTH AFRICAN OPERATORS HAVE RETURNED FORM THEIR CHRISTMAS HOLIDAYS KEEN TO COVER THEIR REQUIREMENTS RESULTING IN A BUSY START TO THE NEW YEAR. IT HAS BEEN AN ENCOURAGING START TO JANUARY WITH A GOOD NUMBER OF FIXTURES CONCLUDED.

RATES FROM SAF TO ATLANTIC DESTINATIONS ARE HOLDING UP WELL AND IN A FEW CASES RISING AS MODERN HANDYSIZE TONNAGE IS IN SHORT SUPPLY AND ENQUIRY PLENTIFUL. RATE LEVELS FROM SAF TO SINGAPORE/JAPAN RANGE ARE STEADY WITH LESS ENQUIRY AVAILABLE BUT WITH THE FAR EASTERN MARKET FALLING AWAY, THERE WILL BE LESS INCENTIVE FOR OWNERS TO FIX THEIR VESSELS EASTWARDS UNLESS THERE IS A PARTICULAR REASON TO DO SO. INDEED, TONNAGE OPEN IN S/E ASIA – FOR THE FIRST TIME IN MANY MONTHS – IS CONSIDERING BALLASTING TO SOUTH AFRICA FOR EMPLOYMENT AND IF RATES CONTINUE TO TUMBLE, IT WONT BE LONG BEFORE CHARTERERS WILL ONCE AGAIN LOOK FOR TONNAGE OPEN IN MALAYSIA/INDONESIA/SINGAPORE AREA TO COVER THEIR ORDERS FORM SOUTH AFRICA. AFTER A BRIEF FLURRY OF ACTIVITY FROM PLATE/BRAZIL FOR END DEC/ELY JAN POSITIONS, ENQUIRY FROM ECSA SEEMS TO HAVE DRIED UP WITH LITTLE ENCOURAGEMENT FOR OWNERS IN THE NEAR FUTURE.

Figure 3.2

Example of broker's report

FIXTURES
=========

WESTMAN CY 1979 TWEEN 18,500 MT DWT ON 9.95 M 949,398 GR 5 HO 7 HA DKS 1X60 DKS 1X35 DKS 5X22 DKS 1X 10 13 ON 18 (1500) + 2.3 MDO A/C MUR DELY DURBAN TCT REDELY FULL MED USD 4200 DLY 20/25 JAN

SEA PHOENIX LI 1985 BC 40,473 MT DWT ON 11.02 M SSW 1,792,151 GR 5 HO 5 HA CRS 4X25 13 ON 25 MT (180) + 1MT MDO

A/C MUR DELY SAF TRIP US GULF OPTION FEAST USD 6500 DLY 17/25 JAN

SEA MERIT CH 1985 BC 37,451 MT DWT ON 11.22 M SSW 1,807,209 GR 5 HO 5 HA CRS 4X25 GRABS 13.25 ON 26 180 + 0.1 DO

A/C SOUTHERN CHARTERING DELY SAF TCT REDELY SPORE/JAPAN 19/23 JAN REGION USD 6500 DLY

NEPTUNE JACINTH SG 1985 BC 21,644 MT DWT ON 9.688 M 946,523 GR 4 HO 4 HA CRS 3X30 DKS 1X25 LOA 151.9 4 BM 24 15 ON 18 MT (2500) + 1 MT MDO A/C IVS DELY R.BAY 6/9 JAN TCT REDELY UK/CONT USD 5500 DLY

GREAT LAKER MY 1987 BC 28,358 MT DWT ON 10.57 M SSW 35,284 GR 5 HO 5 HA CRS 4X25 13 ON ABT 17 MT (18 0) + 1.8 MT DO

A/C MCL DELY APS R.BAY TCT REDELY US GULF 8/15 JAN USD 6100 DLY

ANDREAS A MA 1978 BC 27,868 MT DWT ON 10 M 1,240,394 GR 5 HO 5 HA CRS 4X22 GRABS 12 ON 21 IFO (180 C ST) + 2.5 MT MDO

A/C ANKER KOLEN 25,000 10 PCT COAL DURBAN/GEBZE 5/15 JAN 6000 SHEX/5000 SHINC REGION USD 13.50

FAR EAST

THE NEW YEAR HAS BROUGHT WITH IT VERY LITTLE CHEER FOR OWNRS. THE MODERATE AMOUNT OF ENQUIRY SEEN HAS BEEN OUTWEIGHED BYTHE AMOUNT OF SURPLUS TONNAGE, A SITUATION WE SEE REMAINING UNTIL AT LEAST THE END OF JANUARY. THE PREMIUM THAT HAS BEEN PAYED FOR TONNAGE IN THE PACIFIC OVER THE ATLANTIC HAS COMPLETELY VAPOURISED. SIGNIFICANT FIXTURES OF LAST WEEK SAW A SPOT HANDYMAX IN SINGAPORE BALLAST TO SOUTH AFRICA TO GET FIXED AND A HANDYMAX NB DEL EX YARD TCT VIA AUSSIE REDEL USWC AT USD 5500.

FIXTURES
=========

"American Trader" 1994 45262 dwt dly Nopac Jan trip Singapore-Japan range $6600 daily + $70000 bb

"New Ample '' 1989 42248 dwt 14 on 22 dly Vancouver mid Jan trip Singapore-Japan range $5900 daily + $ 40000 bb – Hanjin

"Pacific Splendor " 1984 41373 dwt dly nantong prompt trip Taiwan $7000 daily – Sinochart

"Handy Silver'' 1983 24404 dwt dly W Australia Jan trop S E Asia $5000 daily + $30000 bb – Pacific Carriers

BALTIC HANDY INDEX 5 JAN 99

INDEX 703 (DOWN 31 FROM OUR LAST REPORT DTD 21 DEC)

ROUTE 1-43,000 DWT CONT/FAR EAST-USD 5036(5001)

ROUTE 2-43,000 DWT TP R/V-USD 6050(6417)

ROUTE 3-43,000 DWT FAR EAST/CONT-USD 6493(6930)

ROUTE 4-43,000 DWT T/A R/V-USD 5092(5220)

ROUTE 5-USG/CONT 1.4/1.6.M 55'-USD 11.00(10.83)

ROUTE 6-BRAZIL/CONT 28/32000 53'-USD 12.00(12.67)

Figure 3.2 (continued)
Example of broker's report

'Tradewinds' has a more informal approach but a cursory glance through any copy will reveal that it too is constantly in contact with brokers and indeed, dependent on them, for the latest market information and gossip. The Baltic Exchange publishes a daily list of fixtures. The source of this list is information from shipbrokers. (See Figure 2.1).

Any publication will to some extent be historical. Even a broker's market report (See Figure 3.2) will reflect what has been done in terms of fixtures. But it should be more than that, going into greater detail about particular markets, trends and give a feel to the pace of the market. Yet all this gives the impression that the broker spends his life writing reports. On the contrary. He spends most of the time on the phone picking up the latest information of who is trading at what levels for what dates and disseminating this to his clients with his conclusions about the direction of the market and his recommendations.

In a competitive situation owners will support the broker who is able, with the best information, to put the owner in a position to fix the cargo if he wants it. The owner always has the option not to fix the cargo but if he wants it, he will need to know what he has to do to fix it. In the same way a charterer needs to know what he has to do, at any particular time, to fix the most suitable or cheapest ship. He will not be able to do so without this up to date market information.

Options

A thorough base of information will lead to an appreciation of the available trading options. For a shipping company these may be which cargoes are paying what rates, which charterers are reliable, which pay and perform professionally, which ones can take the ship for a long period or contract, etc.. For a charterer this may mean what rates can be obtained with which ships on what dates, whether it may be better on time charter or voyage, whether to cover the cargoes on the spot market or on a contract etc. etc.. With all the options explained, the well informed Principal will be in a position to make the best decisions.

Market advice

Having looked at the variety of options, which one should the owner or charterer take? Should the charterer fix, for example, one ship or another at similar rates but different demurrage rates, ETA's and cargo lifts? This will depend on the risk of congestion, the realism of the load and discharge rate, whether there is risk in the given ETA, whether the charterer wants a large or small cargo within the charter party limits and a number of other concerns. What will be the impact on demand of a forthcoming harvest, a crop failure, a drought or other natural disaster? Some of these criteria will be known only to the charterer but some will better be known by the broker who is at the sharp end of the market and whose job it is to constantly talk to many owners and charterers about their business. In this way they build up experience which can be lent as market advice. In my experience, the best results in the chartering market have been obtained with the broker and Principal working together closely, trusting each other's expertise. In other words, if the broker is good, he will assess the market accurately and the Principal's position in it and advise him how he should act and position himself without fear of losing business. Good brokers are worth their weight in gold. But to get the optimum results the Principal also needs to be professional. Getting the best out of the brokers depend very heavily on how the Principal acts. I have known ones who work brilliantly with brokers using each other to effect the best result and others who through ignorance or arrogance or both contrive to get it wrong most of the time, despite having all the necessary information and advice.

There are a very few charterers who try to avoid using brokers. They are mainly from newly developing countries who do not fully understand how the market works and fail to understand the value of information and advice a good broker, properly and professionally used, can give. They erroneously believe that they will save 1.25 percent if they contact a handful of owners directly, believing that all owners give roughly the same market rate as if there was a liner conference rate. This is because they fail to realise the diversity of interests in the market and how creative a good broker can be, when taken into confidence, in finding alternative ways of achieving what the charterer wants or needs. They also fail to realise that an owner loves to talk to a new charterer directly without the protection of his broker. They may also have been exposed to local 'brokers' who have not got the professionalism nor the information and resources that brokers in more established centres are privileged to have around them and thus do not appreciate the added value to be gained by using a good broker sensibly.

Strategic Advice

Broking should not simply be, however, the mechanical execution of a fixture. Principals usually require to know if the market is likely to rise or fall and thus how to position themselves. As was demonstrated in Chapter Two the freight market is a cyclical market and within those cycles there are factors which make for volatility within broad trends.

The greater volatility especially of the period 1987-2000 described in Chapter Two (See Figures 2.5, 2.6 and 2.13 to 2.17 for example) has meant that professional advice on the ingredients of the freight market is needed more than ever before. To position oneself wrongly in the cycle can not only lose a great deal of money. It can literally risk bankruptcy.

Just as large stockbrokers have research teams and analysts, the largest shipbrokers have research departments whose insights and analysis are available to close clients. A front line broker who has not got the benefit of this research and analytical capability is at a grave disadvantage as against those brokers that have such additional support. A Principal investing large sums of money or taking positions without using such independent advice and analysis is making the investment a great deal riskier than if he did. His own in house analysis will not be independent and it will necessarily be taken from a narrow standpoint. Broking companies with the capability of delivering high quality independent shipping analysis as part and parcel of their ship broking activities are therefore likely to be in greater demand as their usefulness becomes appreciated. Furthermore the broker's knowledge of what others are doing in the market will also help clarify what course the Principal should follow. This kind of advice is liable to help save them or make them, especially in fast moving markets, millions of dollars.

This has, and is, changing the role of the broker. As mentioned in Chapter Two, the volume of information available compared with 10 years ago is huge. Shipyards, governments and economic bodies are much more willing to release data. The rapid development of computer technology has enabled that data to be processed and presented faster and easier. Not only can lists of particular vessel types in particular locations be produced at the touch of a couple of buttons but answers be given to more difficult questions. If a Principal involved in the steel trade wants to know, for example, the effect of currency movements on the steel trade to decide whether to take a vessel for cargo on voyage charter or for a short time charter period, today's spreadsheet programmes can plot the correlation between weaker Asian currencies, for example, and the effect on steel exports. In other words the analysts can produce increasingly sophisticated results. Broking companies with such capabilities can put such analyses on the desks of clients who reward the broker through brokerage or fee income.

Ship broking services from the larger companies have therefore caught up with the standard practice of stock broking companies for those clients willing to use brokers not just for the execution of a fixture but as strategic shipping advisor.

Negotiating Buffer

When two parties wish to conclude a contract it is often useful to have a third party between them who can negotiate, advise on market conditions and suggest compromises or solutions where the Principals are in opposition. This is even true and sometimes especially true when the Principals know each other well and often they insist on it. The negotiating function of the broker is of course the most well known. The proper execution of a fixture is of paramount importance and will be examined in detail in Chapter Four.

Administration of the Charter Party or COA

This includes drawing up the charter party in accordance with the negotiations making sure the vessels are nominated when they are supposed to be, that the ETA's are given to everyone's satisfaction, that freight is paid on time, that laytime statements are agreed and that any disputes are solved in, as far as possible, a practical, commercial and amicable manner. Efficient performance in this area is just as important and essential as the fixing of vessels and the providing of accurate information and good advice. Renumeration in the form of commission is linked to the performance in properly recording and efficiently monitoring the charter party terms and conditions. A good professional service should also ensure the client's goodwill.

Assistance in resolution of disputes

A broker should be able by a professional approach to a negotiation or shipping problem be able to avoid many disputes. But if there is a dispute, the fact that he is a professional, independent intermediary means that he may well be able to suggest creative compromises or point out at an early stage what can be done of a practical nature to get the voyage or period completed in a mutually satisfactory way before the problem gets out of hand or into the hands of lawyers or arbitrators.

BROKER OR CONSULTANT?

The broker requires a thorough and expert shipping knowledge which leads to the ability to engineer solutions as much as up to date market knowledge in order to bring business opportunities to the Principals. This multi-functional role, especially the advisory role of a shipbroker brings into question whether it is increasingly one, at least in part, of a consultant.

It is useful to contrast the role of a consultant who will recommend and advise but never has to pick up the pieces if there is a problem thereafter with the broker who, by contrast, has a vested interest in making sure the contracts work in a practical way. On the other hand the advice and information functions of a broker are very similar to that of a consultant. As we have seen the broking company's role is multi-functional; that of a collector of information and conduit for that information, negotiator, executor of the deal, administrator of the physical workings of the contract, and strategic advisor or consultant.

The broker traditionally is remunerated on a 'no cure, no pay' basis. In other words he takes the risk that his investment in time, effort and money, not to mention free information, will result in a fixture or not. If it does, he is paid a commission from the freight or hire. A consultant or legal advisor is paid an hourly or daily fee plus expenses whether or not the deal is finalised or not. His income is regular and paid as earned, but a brokerage in bigger deals could amount to more but spread over the length of the contract or time charter. The broker's costs will also continue through the administration of the contract.

While the disciplines involved in broking and consultancy are to some extent different, it is likely that the broker's role in future will more and more encompass the provision of quality information, statistics and analysis of trade and shipping data, as well as a thorough knowledge and appraisal of the spot market. A military General directing the strategy of battle cannot judge the whole battle while permanently in the front line in one particular place, nor can he properly judge as a 'Chateau General' 50 miles behind the lines. Similarly, advice which is the product of statistical analysis as well as front line spot market experiences, is likely to be a superior product than one based on only one of these ingredients.

I recently met a charterer who had taken the advice of a consultant on his shipping strategy. This advice was now treated as sacrosanct and written in stone as company policy. Without knowing who the consultant was, it was obvious from that policy that he was not someone who was 'on the market' or in the front line on behalf of industrial companies. If he had been he would have known what was available and would never have recommended such a costly and rigid strategy wrapped up in the guise of 'risk management', when other methods and strategies would have given him the same degree of cover without the rigidity.

Because of their expertise, brokers are now being brought into complex projects as advisors or consultants at a very early stage. Where someone is proposing to open a mine or build a power station or alumina plant on a greenfield site, for instance, logistical questions need answers at a very early stage. These questions might be: If I build a jetty what is the relationship between the cost of extending it into deep water and the freight benefits that come with deeper draft? I can buy discharging equipment that will discharge at 25,000 per day or 40,000 per day. What would the freight differential be between these two alternatives from a number of selected ports? Will the cost of building a terminal outweigh the costs of using geared and grabbed ships or floating discharging solution? In short, what is the most reliable and cost effective solution? Project shipbrokers working with port engineers or port consultants will have a far better chance at arriving at the optimum logistical solution than only one of these. It is interesting to see examples of ports who have rejected brokers input and those that have worked with them. In Indonesia in the early '90's there were coal mines which gave one example of each. Despite broker advice that in Tanah Merah they were building too expensive a port in the wrong place they went ahead and ended up with what in effect is a hugely expensive barge loader. Another mine that was working with broker's ideas and recommendations at the same time was constructing flexible reliable and cheap loading solutions.

In conclusion, the broker is needed to gather and make sense of market information, and being on the market, knows what is and what is not possible because he knows what other charterers and owners are doing, proposing and thinking. The broker is, of course, necessary as the intermediary executing the fixture. However, in some cases he has taken the role of strategic advisor and project broker. The twin computer and information revolutions has meant that those broking companies with the resources, can provide better quality information, up to date market appraisal and sophisticated analysis and make sense of it. While improved means of communications threaten the role of the intermediary who cannot add any value to the fixing of a ship, the same revolution offers the broking industry an opportunity to not only survive but to thrive and prosper.

How many brokers?

The number of brokers a Principal should use varies with the exact circumstances and the nature of the business. It is also very subjective. Some conclusions can, however, be drawn from the differing way owners and charterers look at the market.

A ship owner's business is, by its very definition, shipping and the employment of ships. He must therefore have access to all the employment opportunities that exist. Since many charterers use just one broker he will have to talk to them anyway. In short, it will be sensible for the owners to talk to a number of brokers, as many of them may have something to offer and as mentioned at the beginning of the chapter, he will use that broker who puts him in a position to fix the cargo that he wants at that time. In practice he will find that he is drawn to the same limited pool of brokers almost every time depending on the sector of the market. Some owners employ chartering staff to fulfil this function of covering the market while others, such as many of the London Greeks' have an agency agreement with a company that employs a broker to do nothing else but represent the owner and fix his ships.

A Charterer's business, at least the cargo interest, on the other hand, is only partly about shipping. The cargo interest which charters ships may be a coal mine, a grain importer, a steel mill, an electricity company or sugar refiner. That is their business. They will want to use the shipping industry only in a service capacity. But it is unlikely that they will want to get involved in it any more than that. Nevertheless, if there are substantial volumes of cargo they will need to fix them competitively and professionally and they must have some kind of freight strategy. Because their main business is not shipping they need independent advice. They should, therefore, unlike the ship owner, restrict the number of brokers they use to a very few. The exact number depends of the nature of the business but in general my recommendation would be no more than three and in many cases just one.

The advantages of having one broker is that he should act as part of the charterer's company. He should have access to the charterer's confidential information and with his knowledge of the shipping markets be able to think how to position the charterer in the market and develop a freight strategy. The position can be likened to that of the company's legal advisor. Just as a company would not appoint two or three or more competing lawyers and expect to get the best independent advice as if they were working solely in that company's interests, why talk to a number of brokers and expect the same? One reason might be that the charterer thinks he can distinguish good and bad advice. But this is only likely to apply to someone totally immersed in shipping as a profession. It cannot apply to someone who does it only part time. Moreover, an exclusive broker can approach the market with a degree of stealth when confidentiality is desirable. This is increasingly required by charterers who do not want their competitors to access their buying, selling and trading activities via the shipping market.

Thus, just like legal advice, shipping advice has to be 'out-sourced'. In either case, the obvious policy is to appoint the legal advisor that has the expertise on that particular legal issue or the broker/advisor that has the expertise in the particular markets that the charterer is interested in and who, moreover, has strength in depth, research or analysis capabilities and a knowledge of the freight derivatives market (See below). This is the kind of company that can act as a kind of strategic advisor as well as an executor of chartering fixtures.

Yet there are very few companies that can do this. The freight market is, as we have seen, a cyclical market and inevitably, from time to time hits low periods. Low markets mean low commissions and low income. Since they are invariably paid in US$, the strength of the broking company's home base currency is also a factor and if it is strong against the dollar at a time of a low freight market, brokers can go bankrupt. The early and mid 1980's saw, not only the demise of a few ship owners but of a whole raft of shipbrokers. The depression of 1996/99 witnessed the end of a few more. The tendency has been therefore, for there to be fewer broking companies in the main centres as many of them disappear or consolidate into larger units. This tendency accelerates in times of low markets. It is, of course, mirrored among ship owners. In the late 1990's we witnessed for example, the merging of NYK and Showa, Mitsui and Navix (Navix itself was a merger of Japan Line and Yamashita Shinahon), P and O Bulk Carriers with Shougang, P and O Containers with Nedlloyd, P and O Ferries with Stenna Line and A.P. Moller with Safmarine (Containers).

Large ship broking companies with research departments, freight future capabilities and strength in depth are therefore in a potentially advantageous position as they possess the most valuable commodity in the market; information. Most sensible players in the market try to gain access to that information. There may be various ways but the most obvious is to become a valued client who does business through that company.

FREIGHT DERIVATIVES

The Futures Market (BIFFEX)

In recent years a new area of risk management in the shipping market has evolved. Traditionally, a contract of affreightment or a period time charter was the only way a charterer hedged against a future rise in freight rates or owners guarded against a fall in their earnings. Both involved the physical delivery of a vessel or physical delivery of a cargo. As we have seen, brokers advise on the merits and details of these various freight strategies.

In 1985, however, the industry developed the Baltic Freight Index (BFI), a basket of freight rates for various routes, indexed on the basis of 1000 points on the 1st January of that year. A panel of international ship brokers assessed the rates of the constituent parts of the index daily. These were audited by the Baltic International Freight Futures Exchange. In November 1999 the BFI was replaced as a traded index by the Baltic Panamax Index (BFI) but it is assessed and audited in the same way.

Future prices of this index known as BIFFEX can be traded on the LIFFE (London International Financial Futures Exchange) in order and hedge physical freight positions. The daily index is announced by the Baltic Exchange at 13.30 hours London time. Traders 'buy' or 'sell' their estimates in ten dollar units, for future months. Like other futures markets, the price is determined by market expectations of the future. For example, if in May the BPI is 1100 and the price for October is 1165, it means that October is expected to be higher than May. At the end of October, the actual price for October is settled. Let us assume the actual end October price is 1200. The trader who bought an October unit back in May at 1165 in anticipation of the market rising was right. He is paid the difference (1200 minus 1165 = 35 x USD 10 = USD 350) by the trader who sold October in the hope of a fall. The financial performance of the contract is guaranteed by the London Clearing House. The Baltic Exchange now publishes Capesize, Panamax and Handy, size specific indexes. Its constituent parts are still a basket of routes.

As already mentioned from November 1999, the BFI ceased to be the traded index, being replaced by the BPI (Baltic Panamax Index). The BCI (Baltic Capesize Index) and BHI (Baltic Handy Index) are not traded as indexes but individual component routes of those indexes, and of the BPI, are traded as Forward Freight Agreements (FFA's).

BIFFEX FREIGHT
FUTURES REPORT 14 August 2000
PLEASE CONTACT: IAN BLAND
ROBIN KING/ANDREW JAMES/ANDREW LUNT/
TEL: 44 (0) 20 7334 3151 FAX: 44 (0) 20 7283 9412 TELEX: 887811 CLDRY G

CLARKSON
SECURITIES LIMITED

BPI	USD/DM	USD/Yen	UK/USD	IFO (Rot)	HSFO
1568 (-4)	2.1635	109.38	1.5058	132	126

Biffex Futures

	Close	Previous	+/-	High	Low	Vol.	O.I	Previous	+/-
Aug	1600	1595	5	1600	1600	5	20	20	0
Sep	1610	1620	-10	1605	1605	2	4	4	0
Oct	1625	1620	5	1625	1625	2	74	76	-2
Jan	1625	1620	5				5	5	0
Apr	1635	1630	5				5	5	0
Jul	1365	1360	5				0	0	0
Oct			0				0	0	0
Jan			0				0	0	0
Total						9	108	110	-2

Futures Comment

BIFFEX showed marginal improvement today, registering 5 points up across the board with the exceptio n of the September position which lost 10 points. The BPI lost 4 points (1568).
BDI 1637 (-3)
BHI 1107 (u/c)
BCI 2246 (-4)

FFA values:- August 23, 40, September 23, 95, October 24, 25.

BPI Routes and Implied Rates

	Rates	Previous	+/-	Implied Aug	Implied Oct	Implied Jan
1.USGulf/NCont	15.421	15.443	-0.022	15.736	15.982	15.982
1a.TransAtlantic	11400	11411	-11	11633	11814	11814
2.USGulf/Japan nc	23.471	23.471	0	23.95	24.324	24.324
2a.Skaw-Pass/Twn-J	11388	11413	-25	11620	11802	11802
3. NoPac/Japan	15.843	15.871	-0.028	16166	16.419	16.419
3a.TransPacific Round	11369	11431	-62	11601	11782	11782
4. F.East/Europe	10994	11033	-39	11218	11394	11394
Average of 4 BPI TCs	11287.75	11322	-34.25	11518	11698	11698
Index	1568	1572	-4	1600	1625	1625

Any research and/or analysis contained in this report has been produced by us and may have been acte d upon by us for our own purposes and has not been procured for the exclusive benefit of clients. This report is directed onl y at non private customers and must not be passed on to anyone who is not such a person. Nothing contained in this report shall construe d as or constitute an offer on our part to buy sell any commodity or future referred herein. We are regulated by the Securities and Fut ures Authority (SFA).

Figure 3.3
Example of Biffex Trading Report

DATE		01/11/99	
BALTIC HANDY INDEX		**961 (SAME)**	
Index Routes	Description	Weighting	Average USD/Day
H1	43,000 DWT CONTINENT/FAR EAST	25%	11,000
H2	43,000 DWT JAPAN-SK/NOPAC or AUSTRALIA RV	30%	6,699
H3	43,000 DWT SINGAPORE/AUSTRALIA/CONTINENT	15%	5,963
H4	43,000 DWT CONTINENT/N or S ATLANTIC RV	30%	8,500
	AVERAGE OF THE 4 T/C ROUTES		8,040
Ongoing Trial Routes			USD/MT
T1	1.4-1.6M 55' US GULF/CONTINENT - GRAINS	-	14.76
T2	28/32,000 53' BRAZIL/CONTINENT - GRAINS	-	16.34

Figure 3.4

An example of the Baltic Exchange's daily BHI report

The point of trading an index is that on a basket of routes broadly covering the bulk carrier market or the Panamax sector of the market for example, ship owners, charterers or traders can speculate or hedge against future freight rate volatility without ever taking delivery of a ship or cargo. Why would they do that? Firstly, it is much simpler and quicker to trade futures contracts than physical contracts. It takes seconds only as only one number on a set contract is being fixed, while a physical contract may take hours, days or even weeks depending on its complexity. Secondly, they may be aware of a general need to hedge freight risk forward but without actually having physical business to fix at that time.

The individual component routes of the BPI and BCI are shown below and of the BHI in Figure 3.4. These are the brief descriptions. They are actually very specific in detail which need not concern us in this overview.

Baltic Panamax Index (BPI)

1. 55,000 10% light grain (55) US Gulf/Cont 10 SHEX

1a. TA Round Voyage for 70,000 dwt, max 15 yrs, 3 million cuft grain 14 on 30

2. 54,000 5% HSS US Gulf/Japan 11 SHEX

2a. T/C trip del. Skaw-Gibraltar redel. Taiwan-Japan for same vessel as in 1a

3. 54,000 5% HSS NoPac/Japan 11 SHEX

3a. TP Round Voyage for same vessel as in 1a

9. T/C trip del Japan-S Korea redel. Skaw-Gibraltar for same vessel as in 1a

Baltic Capesize Index (BCI)

1.	120,000 10% coal Hampton Roads/Rotterdam 6 SHINC	
2.	160,000 10% iron ore Tubarao/Rotterdam 6 SHINC	
3.	150,000 10% iron ore Tubarao/Beilun + Baoshan Scale/30,000 SHINC	
4.	150,000 10% coal Richards Bay/Rotterdam Scale/25,000 SHINC	
5.	150,000 10% iron ore W. Australia/Beilun + Baoshan 18m SWAD Scale/30,000 SHINC	
6.	120,000 10% coal Newcastle/Rotterdam 35,000/25,000 SHINC	
7.	150,000 10% coal Bolivar/Rotterdam 50,000/25,000 SHINC	
8.	Trans-Atlantic Round Voyage	*basis 161,000 dwt, max*
9.	Del. ARA-Passero redel. China-Japan	*10 years, 176,000 cum 280*
10.	Trans-Pacific Round Voyage	*LOA/45m beam 14/14.5 K on*
11.	Del. China-Japan redel. ARA-Passero	*52 FO/NO DO*

The Over The Counter (OTC) or Forward Freight Agreement (FFA)

The problem with the BFI as a risk management tool for the shipping industry, however, was its imprecision. The BFI was a basket of freight routes and ship sizes as well. This was adequate for getting the general direction of the bulk carrier market, but unsatisfactory for an accurate hedge on a particular size sector or a particular route. If a grain trader is buying and selling grain for the Japanese market, for example, he will want to hedge the USG/Japan HSS grain future freight rate. He will not care about Hampton Roads to Rotterdam in capesizes or any other route which constituted the parts of the Baltic Freight Index or even the size specific Baltic Panamax Index.

As a result of this industry pressure, a new and more precise derivative instrument was developed by brokers in the early 1990's, the Forward Freight

CLARKSON
SECURITIES LIMITED

PANAMAX AND CAPESIZE
FFA REPORT 14TH AUG 2000

PLEASE CONTACT: ROBIN KING/IAN BLAND/ANDY JAMES/ MARK RICHARDSON
TEL:44 (0) 20 7334 3151, FAX:44 (0) 20 7283 9412
TELEX:887811CLDRY G

BPI	BDI	BCI	USD/Dm	USD/Yen	UK/USD	180cst Rdm	380cst Rdm
1568(-4)	1637(-3)	2246(-4)	2.1635	109.38	1.5058	132	126

PANAMAX FORWARD FREIGHT AGREEMENT INDICATIONS:

	1. US Gulf/Cont		2. US Gulf/Japan		3. NoPac/Japan	
	Bid	Offer	Bid	Offer	Bid	Offer
Aug	15.25	16.50	23.40	23.65	15.50	16.50
Sep	14.50	16.50	23.85	24.05	15.25	16.50
Oct	14.50	16.25	24.20	24.50	15.00	17.00
Nov	14.50	16.50	24.10	24.50	15.00	17.00
Dec			23.50	24.50		
Jan			23.50	24.20		
Quarts			23.25	23.60		
BPI	**15.421**		**23.471**		**15.843**	

	1a. TA Round		2a. TCT East		3a. TP Round		4. Feast / Cont	
	Bid	Offer	Bid	Offer	Bid	Offer	Bid	Offer
Aug	11000	12250	11200	11650	11250	11500	10650	11000
Sep	10800	12600	11500	12000	11350	11750	10750	11250
Oct	10800	12600	11850	12750	10800	11750	10750	11250
Nov			11600	12750	10800	11750	10500	11500
Dec					10500	11750		
BPI	**11,400**		**11,388**		**11,369**		**10,994**	

Average of the 4 BPI TC Routes:

	Bid	Offer
Q4 00	11500	11700
Aug-Dec '00 (5 Mth)	11400	11600
Q1 + Q2	11000	11300
Oct 00 – Jun 01 (9 Mth)	11200	11550
Aug 00 – Jul 01 (12 Mth)	11000	11450
Oct 00 – Sep 01 (12 Mth)	10900	11250
Jan 01 – Dec 01 (12 Mth)	10600	11000
BPI 4 T/c Av	**11,288**	

Comments:
Panamax G/Jpn Oct continued its recent push up with buyers noting and feeling comforted by today's arrest in the Rt2 index's fall. Physic- ally however the bears are still pointing to the ppt and ballasting tonnage in both atl and pacific oceans. Capes suffered from Euro hols with a lack of input. Short-term tone as per the end of last week; easier with excess prompt tonnage.

Figure 3.5

BCI & BPI Freight Futures broker's report

Agreement or FFA. In essence the FFA is akin to financial market swaps. It is an over the counter (OTC) instrument. In other words, it is a contract solely between two counter parties who agree to buy and sell respectively the future freight rate on a particular route and is not traded through an exchange. It is a simple $/mt price agreed for that route and settled at the end of the given period between the two counter parties in accordance with the price quoted on the BPI, BCI or BHI for that route and that route only. But critically, like an exchange traded future, it is a cash settlement. There is no physical delivery.

Being a cash instrument, it can be settled much quicker than a physical contract. It also allows a buyer (or seller) to secure a freight price he or she will pay without actually limiting the trader to a particular carrier. The beauty of this is apparent, for example, where a trader likes one particular owner to perform his contract (because through experience the owner understands his business) but the price the owner quotes forward is too high at that particular time. The trader can then buy an FFA at the forward price and settle the physical lifting with his chosen owners at a later date safe in the knowledge that he has already locked in the price he is paying for the freight. The one potential danger is that being an OTC, it is dependent on the financial strength of the counter party for payment. Unlike BIFFEX, the London Clearing House does not guarantee payment as it is not traded on the Exchange and there are no deposits or margin calls. In a futures trade, the price is guaranteed by the Exchange, so payment is always forthcoming. Nevertheless, when confident of the performance of the counter party, the FFA offers a flexible and specific method of hedging and it has become hugely successful with growing volumes traded while BIFFEX volumes have declined. The spreads for FFA's are obtained from freight futures brokers and these themselves are an indication of the market. (See Figure 3.5) Over time, they have become increasingly sophisticated and can be not only for 'spot' fixtures on that route, that is within a month, but even contracts such as quarterly voyages over one year. They have become an increasingly important instrument to the broker's risk management tool kit that he can offer to his clients.

The Changing Role of the Baltic Exchange

Following a brief explanation of the Baltic indexes, it is now relevant to consider the changing role of London's Baltic Exchange. The Baltic, as it is referred to for short, is still a significant factor in the chartering industry, but not all in the way it was. If this book had been written 20 years ago or so, there would have probably been a more extensive and self congratulatory section on the Baltic. It would have given a brief history of its coffee house origins starting in 1744 to become the world's premier and oldest international shipping Exchange. It would have detailed how brokers met and exchanged information and offers on the floor of the Baltic and the importance of face to face contact.

But between the mid 1970's and the mid 1990's the Baltic faced not only a membership crisis but one which went to the heart of its very function and identity. Its problem in the 1970's was its complacency in rapidly changing times. Patterns of trade had changed and were continuing to change, other chartering centres were growing in importance and the twentieth century communications revolution was just about to go into its final critical phase which would accelerate and universalise global contact even further.

By the 1970's phone and telex made verbal and written communications to most parts of the world quick and in many cases instantaneous. The fax was in its infancy and the mobile phone and e-mail as yet unheard of. Many members and the institution of the Baltic itself had a belief, however, that nothing in ship broking would change substantially, that London was and always would be the world's pre-eminent shipping exchange and that this was because of the institution of the Baltic Exchange itself. This belief could thrive because apart from the increased speed of communications, little had changed since the mid nineteenth century when the laying of submarine caldes had revolutionized communications and shipping became truly international with the Baltic as the international market place. Then, brokers would visit the Baltic several times a day making notes and rush back to the office to send telegrams containing new cargoes, positions and offers. A century later brokers visited less often but there was more that was the same than was different.

The inability to admit to the possibility of change was demonstrated in part in its excluding females to membership in 1966 (previously not a factor) at a time of liberalising social and work place attitudes and also in an unhealthy amount of time discussing dress codes on the trading floor. The bar on women was rescinded against much opposition in 1974 and about the same time members were permitted on the floor of the Exchange in pastel coloured shirts rather than white which had been the rule hitherto.

This particular blend of conservatism and complacency was reflected in the journal of the 'American Bureau of Shipping Surveyor', May 1976 edition* which recorded, 'more information is available and more face to face contact takes place than anywhere in the world.... its members are confident that the Baltic Exchange will remain a key factor in shaping international commerce and agree.... that there is no substitute for its services'.

However, Baltic membership which peaked at 2834 one year later in 1977, was down to 1749 by 1992 having registered a steady decline year on year*. The floor of the Baltic which had been full for much of the day in the 1950's and '60's and was full from midday to 2pm each day in the 1970's, began to lose its attraction. Brokers stopped attending to concentrate on trading in their offices where they were accessible, especially those working the Far East markets and on the cape size and panamax markets. They were not accessible

* *Quoted in "The Baltic Exchange" by Hugh Barty King*

on the Baltic whose communication system was not keeping up with the latest technological developments nor with the changing attitudes of members. It had ceased to be useful to them. Business was being conducted by phone and fax and by the mid '90's by e-mail.

Personal relationships were still important but they were certainly not a commodity of which a Baltic had a monopoly and they were not in themselves enough in a competitive trading environment. However, it should be noted that to put the problem in context, other exchanges such as the London Stock Exchange faced similar problems and challenges.

The Baltic knew that something had to be done. But what? Change was always going to be difficult with a structure in which the Chairman was appointed for one year only, the year before he retired as chairman of a member company and therefore only as a part time job and was part of the reason for the delay in responding to these new challenges in the 1970's and 1980's. The strategic business review which was called for and submitted in 1992, reported that the Baltic needed to reconsider its whole purpose and function! It was no longer needed primarily as a trading exchange. Its future 'lay in building on its reputation for high ethical standards and as an international shipping and commercial club'.

It is necessary here to make the distinction between the Baltic Exchange and the London market. They are often, mistakenly, talked and written about as though they were the same thing. During this period of loss of direction of the Baltic, some of its member companies on the other hand adapted well to the rapidly changing conditions. While some did perish, especially in the period of the unprecedented freight rate depression of 1982-87, a number of others built up and dramatically expanded their business in the rapidly expanding global market place. Arguably, London brokers increased their importance as a centre of dry cargo chartering. London brokers had been working international third party business since the nineteenth century. Unlike the British shipbuilding industry which relied on the declining domestic shipping companies and eschewed competing internationally until well past the point at which it was too late*, broking companies went far afield for business. They built up valuable new business in the developing shipping areas of the world such as the Far East and South America, in new commodities of growing importance such as steam coal or in certain key sizes or types of ships such as container ships.

By the late 1990's, however, primarily as a result of the direction given by the strategic business review and in the last few years of the twentieth century in particular by vigorous leadership, the Baltic Exchange itself can be said once again to be of growing importance.

Where does that importance now lie?

First and foremost, the Baltic motto, 'Our word our bond' is of continued vital importance in a commercial atmosphere where negotiations are quicker than ever before. This principle of holding a broker's word as binding has recently been upheld in the United States after a dispute involving twelve years of litigation and is the benchmark of honesty expected by Principals dealing with each other and through brokers world wide, whether they are members or not.

But one of the most important bases upon which the Baltic and the London market in general has been built over the last fifty years has been the large number of foreign owners who chose to make London their business base and in particular the 'London Greeks'. Their demand for high quality and up to date trading information has made London the centre for chartering information, much of which can be used for other clients, if necessary. It also

* *"The Development and Decline of British Shipbuilding" by Sir Robert Atkinson*

should not be forgotten that London is a major centre for the trading of commodities such as grain, sugar, metals and of late, coal. It is of great advantage when trading those commodities to be able to give delivered prices, which of course include freight.

But recently it is not only the owners, charterers, traders or shipbrokers that are joining (or rejoining) the re-focused Baltic but maritime lawyers, arbitrators, P and I Clubs and bankers involved in shipping. In 1999, thirty major maritime law firms were registered as members. The 40 members of the London Maritime Arbitrators Association (LMMA) are also members. Nor is it only London based companies but shipping and trading companies world wide. The Baltic also now operates a successful dispute resolution service, which it boasts, recovered around two million dollars for members in 1998. It alerts members via its web site and monthly bulletins of charterers and owners who are in default and keeps an archive of defaulters that can be consulted at any time.

The Baltic Exchange's daily fixture list (See Figure 2.1) is probably the first place to start any broker's dry cargo market report. It has its own e-mail facility for members. It insists that members hold P and I cover for at least 100,000 pounds sterling, a potentially valuable insurance for clients.

The Baltic Freight indexes are, as has been demonstrated, the ones that are consulted and traded on a daily basis by the industry world wide. Because the input comes from the world's pre eminent brokers in their specific trades and administered by the Baltic, it is regarded as the only independently audited range of indexes. If members have a problem with one of the rates which make up the traded index they have the right to query and an immediate audit and enquiry will take place.

Finally, at long last it seems to have a restaurant of quality, which adds to the more open and friendly atmosphere. Although it still has some way to go, it has overcome the fatal attitude that it is important simply because it is there. It now sees itself instead as providing a service to its members, one which by the nature of the world today and the shipping market itself, will continually change. It has and is re-inventing itself along the lines laid down by the strategic review and is "building on its reputation for high ethical standards and as an international shipping and commercial club".

Maritime London

As part of this, it also sees and presents itself as one part of all the maritime services sector of London. They call it ‘Maritime London’ as a convenient shorthand. This is part of the re-defining and re-focusing process and is very sensible. London is, after all, also the largest insurance, financial and legal centre in the shipping world and contains the largest ship’s register.

A Baltic submission to the Transport Sub Committee at the House of Commons in January 1999 listed the ingredients of ‘Maritime London’. First, under the Baltic umbrella, London has the largest community of international shipbrokers. It estimated that London’s share of the market is between 30 and 50 percent. It also has a substantial and probably higher percentage of tanker chartering and sale and purchase negotiations. London also operates the only freight futures market in the world for which the Baltic provides a range of settlement indices, the importance of which has already been examined.

Outside the Baltic, the investment banking community in London is large and active. In 1996 it was estimated that London’s loan book amounted to some 6 billion pounds sterling with the annual transaction volume in the range of 1.5 to 3 billion. About 30 percent of marine risk (both hull and machinery and cargo) is placed in the London market. Third party liability arranged by the

Protection and Indemnity Associations account for almost 80 percent of the total world cover. English law is applied to shipping disputes more widely than the law of any other country. London is therefore the principle centre for maritime law and the world's leading centre for maritime related arbitration. The largest classification society is Lloyds Register accounting for 21% of the total world fleet but London also has large branch offices of the other major societies. There are many other maritime related services; publishing, consultancy, engineering and accounting. The United Nations Maritime Organisation is also based in London. It is difficult for any other chartering centre to compete when London contains so much inter-related shipping services as well as the extensive trading activities. Indeed, most other chartering centres while important, are local or regional in the sense that they service local or regional needs and do not attempt to fix foreign ships to foreign charterers in the way that London does.

There are exceptions and the above is not to demean other chartering centres. Many of them also have important related maritime industries. The world's largest and most significant ship building industries as well as large domestic shipping and chartering companies support the broking community in Japan, Korea and China in a way inconceivable elsewhere. Japanese steel production which varies between 90 and 100 million tons annually is totally dependent on imported raw materials in bulk carriers, most of which are provided by domestic owners, including the largest owner of bulk carriers in the world. Korea and Taiwan are similarly significant industrialised countries with large steel industries dependent on imports and also heavily dependent on imported steam coal for the production of electricity. Their chartering supports a large domestic fleet and a significant number of local brokers. The Piraeus and Oslo markets are underpinned by important local independent ship owners. Hamburg is the centre for a number of important container ship owners. Melbourne and Sydney as the chartering centres for the huge mineral, grain and sugar exports of Australia are also important. These are only examples and many more can be cited all over the world. Nevertheless, when I have worked in foreign centres, the daily dialogue with London brokers was by far the most important to gather the information quickly and efficiently. London still is the most important centre for market information. This is true irrespective of the decline of the Baltic Exchange between the 1970's and 1990's.

However, the revival of the Baltic in the 1990's reinforces London's importance as a chartering and commercial maritime centre by acting as a marketing tool for all the maritime services, increasing the services of the Baltic for members in the way of information via web sites and at the same time being a benchmark of high quality for the industry as a whole.

One welcome change in the Baltic from the 1970's is in its attitude. Contrast the attitude of complacency described by the commentator in the American Bureau of Shipping Surveyor in 1976 quoted previously with the words of the chairman of the Baltic to the Transport Sub Committee in January 1999. 'Although Maritime London was built on the back of Empire trade routes and the coaling stations, with the central core of a strong domestic fleet, it has nevertheless thrived now that the British fleet has dwindled. Nevertheless it would be foolishly complacent to imagine that the mutally inter-dependent services are not fragile'.

Quite so. The communications revolution means that chartering can now be conducted anywhere as long as the parties have a phone. London as a chartering centre is always vulnerable to rising costs of doing business, possible changes in the tax regime, the continuing communications revolution and competition from other maritime centres. It thrives currently because of its continuing concentration of expertise, its concentration of ships, it size, its inter dependent and in some cases dominant maritime industries and its time zone between the Far East and the Americas. The Baltic Exchange has recognised that it represents and must nurture the London market's chartering expertise. It owes its existence to its members, not the other way around. No longer does it delude itself that it is more important than its constituent parts. If this continues it can do the London market and the shipping industry in general a great deal of good in the future by providing expert leadership where there had previously been none.

A Lloyds List editorial of October 1999 praising the Baltic's initiatives in the 'important matter of determining a twenty first century role for the exchange', went on to look to that future.

'The vision proposed by the directors, in which the exchange would broaden its terms of reference to become an electronic platform, market information source and data base, a more international forum, yet remain an integral part of Maritime London offering a wider range of relevant services and available skills is an excellent starting point.

London remains the principal maritime centre and needs a physical manifestation of this, where the various elements of this huge global presence can meet.

Facilities for meetings, entertainment, arbitrations and inquiries, research and expertise, along with a friendly ambience attractive to 'out of town' and associate members would seem to be imperatives.

An available and comprehensive voice for the industry would be useful. In short, the world's best international shipping centre and club, where every element of this disparate industry can find a welcome'.

Information Technology, e-Business and the Future of Chartering

Just as the Baltic Exchange has had to adapt in the face of faster communications it is now the assumed wisdom that chartering in general will have to change to meet the demands of new technology. At the beginning of the twenty first century this is all very much in its infancy and no one knows for sure how this will affect chartering and the role of the broker but there has been a lot of ill informed comment on the subject. The following is therefore designed as a rough guideline to what is a very fast changing scene.

First, we must differentiate between the provision of information on line from interactive trading on line.

As has been demonstrated, shipping and the freight market is all about information. It always has been. We have seen the forms in which this information is accessible. The broker has always had a central role in the collection and dissemination of information but a vital role is also played by specialist magazines, registers, newspapers, the Baltic fixture list etc.. Technology has enabled the Baltic fixture list to be available on the Baltic's web site and Registers in CD form. However a large leap forward in the availability of shipping information occurred in early March 2000 when Clarksons launched 'SIN' or 'Shipping Intelligence Network'. This web site contains, among other things, daily news and gossip, full fleet profiles, the Shipping Intelligence Weekly, thousands of graphs from time series detailing all sectors of the shipping market, dry, wet, sale and purchase and much reference material. It is even possible to arrange for specified research data to be relayed daily to a web page specially designed to the customer's requirements. It is too early to assess the impact of this system but I suspect that this is the kind of on line information system that will be the essential tool of the shipping industry in the next few years. This is because it can be accessed by anyone with a computer anywhere in the world, from the office, the home, the airport or on holiday with the information being updated daily from a commercial shipping data base. In short, information is getting more plentiful and easier to obtain. The leading information providers will always be not only those with the best information but those who can most effectively present that information.

What, however, about on line trading? In the 1999/2000 technology frenzy, a number of e-commerce companies were started with a view to trading cargoes and fixing ships on line. What is their future? Is chartering to be conducted in the future on the internet, on auction or bid sites? I think that some charterers will try this but I also suspect that the majority of chartering will continue to be conducted with the intermediary broker.

Some markets are just numbers. Freight futures, for example, have a pre-arranged contract so that the only thing negotiated is the headline number. Just like stocks and shares, this is therefore a natural candidate for on line trading and fixing. Chartering vessels is, however, much more complex. As the remainder of this book will demonstrate the freight market is only partly about the headline rate. Fixtures are often made in only a few days, hours and sometime minutes but it is not simply a numbers game. Charterers, especially receivers, may well see some merit in an on line auction based on their own charter party which has to be agreed without alteration. For them it is cheap, quick and easy. But in the immediate shipping market, any e-market place will have to be organised by some one who knows where the ships are and who has the capability to alert players to this market. The broker is therefore simply changing the tools of his trade.

There are, of course, already a number of shipping web sites but so far they have tended to attract only the cargoes that cannot be easily fixed by the traditional methods. This is usually because the business can only be done at rates well below the market level. These sites are not interactive and owners rarely use them as they get no story or feel for the cargo. The effect is similar to a broker just sending a message quoting a cargo. Busy owners often ignore such messages unless they are followed up with a phone call. What an owner needs is information. Is this cargo firm or is just a rate check? What is the charterer's rate idea? What is the competition? When are the charterers in a position to work? Can the charterer manage to load the ship two days earlier than they have quoted? Does the charterer mind if the ship loads 150,000 if what is quoted is 135,000 10%? Can you really discuss stowage plans, complex terms or the merits of this or that clause, on line? What about the key issue of timing? Only a conversation can convey these and many other issues that usually need to be addressed.

It seems therefore that while there will be some deals done for some charterers on line, that we are some way from eliminating the role of the market expert broker especially in his advisory role.

CONCLUSION

This Chapter has explored a number of important issues under the heading of "The Broker". It has emphasised the central and crucial role of risk management the modern broker has in the freight market. The issues and questions discussed were, what is a broker? What are and will be his functions in the future, his crucial advisory and analytical role, how a Principal should use a broker, freight derivatives, risk management and the changing role of the Baltic Exchange. Yet if cargo is to be moved and ships are to be employed, brokers, owners and charterers have to negotiate and fix. How this is done while avoiding the many dangers is the subject of the next chapter.

4. Chartering and Negotiating Guidelines

CHARTERING PRACTICE

The modern chartering industry and the job of the modern shipbroker is demanding. There are more cargoes, ships, trades, nationalities, charterers, and owners than ever before. Moreover, there is a faster pace of change in politics and economics and a greater degree of volatility in the shipping market itself. Currencies fluctuate, sometimes wildly. Freight futures have to be watched as well as the physical market. Communications are, in the main instantaneous, even to and from the remotest and poorest parts of the world. The broker today must be more competitive in maintaining, seeking and developing business. It is difficult to think of any other industry in which contracts are negotiated within a few days, if not hours.

Under the pressure of difficult negotiations conducted at speed, often by telephone, mistakes and errors of judgement can have disastrous consequences. In this demanding environment, care must be taken to give the most professional advice, conduct negotiations in a serious and business like way and make sure all clauses in the charter party complement each other. When these guidelines are ignored the broker may well become liable for substantial claims. Huge Principal companies with large chartering portfolios have switched broker allegiances due to the most experienced of brokers making an error by ignoring the basic principles. All this must be done without jeopardising the essential creativity of the role.

INVESTIGATING THE PRINCIPAL

If a new and previously unknown Principal approaches a broker it is wise not to take him at face value. A diplomatic request for information as to his financial standing and previous experience in chartering, for instance, should produce information. If genuine, the new client should be only too willing to provide evidence of his credentials. It is difficult for the broker who has been brought up in an environment of trust which is vital when negotiating and enshrined in the Baltic Exchange motto, 'My word, my bond', not to take what he hears at face value. But it must be investigated to the best of the broker's ability. Hard though it may seem, it is better to lose a piece of business than to be drawn in to one which goes badly wrong. If it does not sound or feel right, it probably isn't. Many years ago a broker approached me with what appeared to be a very convincing story of what cargoes his Principal wanted and why. However, I was uncomfortable with both the explanation and the source and therefore ignored it. He continued to hawk the business round to others and eventually fixed some cargoes. It was, in fact, an elaborate and clever lie and it resulted in one of the biggest shipping frauds in recent history. For those brokers that were taken in, it was time consuming, expensive and a career damaging event. The lesson is clear. Know exactly with whom you are dealing!

RECOMMENDING A CLIENT

It is very common for a broker to be asked to comment on the financial standing or reputation of a Principal. Great care must be taken with the answer. If the Principal is recommended, the broker may well be called to account should it transpire that the recommendation is not supported by the behaviour of the Principal either during negotiations or in the fulfilment of the contract. On the other hand, the broker is equally at risk if the broker were to denigrate the Principal, by passing on disparaging or inaccurate rumours.

A charterer may be well known but he may try to charter in the name of a similarly named off shore subsidiary with no assets which only comes to light after the fixture is complete. Who can know the financial status and behaviour of every company? The only way to deal with this is to be extremely cautious. When conducting negotiations always make sure the charterer's full style and domicile is correct.

The phrase, 'First Class Charterer' or 'Owner' is sometimes seen. The party using this term is either seeking to protect the identity of their Principals who either do not wish their presence to be known in the market or their broker does not wish their identity known. It is, however, a totally unprofessional approach to the market. First, it is not likely to flush out the best rates as busy ship owners will be unlikely to take time to calculate a business when they do not even know the name of the charterer or if it is serious or not. In case the business is so confidential, it is better to ask a friendly and discreet broker who is familiar with that sector of the market and who therefore will be able to find the best rate without circulating the enquiry to the market. But secondly and more importantly for the security of the broker, it is impossible to define 'First Class'. A broker who receives an enquiry so marked should on no occasion pass this on without comment. Even when the broker knows the company is a well known, 'blue chip' company who wishes their identity to remain confidential, it is still best to avoid the phrase altogether. Even charter parties involving these companies can involve disputes and the opposing party is likely to be upset if he thinks he was led into the fixture by the broker's representation and that this party is now behaving badly, however financially sound it may be.

The broker should confine information to that which he knows to be correct*. This would usually be what business the company is involved in, what ships they have fixed or what charterers the owner or operator has fixed and how

** For a more detailed examination from a strictly legal point of view of many of the issues discussed in this chapter see "Shipbrokers and the Law" by Andrew Jamieson*

they performed especially with regard payments of freight and demurrage/despatch settlement.

If information is received about a company it is best to pass it on advising the source of the information. If the charterer is unknown it would be prudent to add, 'We pass on the above information which we have received from........as brokers only and without guarantee and would suggest owners/charterers make their own investigations'. If the broker inadvertently and innocently passes on inaccurate information without such comments he may be liable for substantial claims for negligence and misrepresentation when charterers fail to pay freight or some other misdemeanour.

CONFIDENTIALITY

The broker owes a duty of care to the Principal. One way it can be demonstrated is by following the Principal's wishes regarding confidentially. If is often necessary to keep business confidential because clients demand it. Very often the reason is because it is possible to find out what competitors are doing through the chartering market. If an Electricity company, for example, hears of a competitor on the market with a cargo of coal, he will almost certainly know from which coal mining company it is buying, what loading and discharging rates are, the freight rate and through a series of other calls will build up a picture of his competitor's business. If the company requires confidentiality therefore, how should the broker approach the market? He will have to bear in mind that the market will be very interested in a cargo and will want to find out which ship has fixed it at what rate. Even if you try to hide it, one of the broker's jobs is to track down this kind of information by seeing which requirements get covered, which ships get fixed and even if no one will divulge the details, make educated guesses about what has been done. To execute a fixture privately it must be in the hands of one broker only. He must approach very few owners and only on a direct basis, emphasising to those owners the confidentiality of the requirement. How does the charterer know that the market has been covered properly? This comes down to the skill of the broker. He should know where the ships are, which owners can keep information confidential and which ones have a tendency to leak information. He should know what the market rate should be and be able to get it for his charterers.

DERIVATIVE INVESTMENT ADVICE

In order to give investment advice and place derivatives business (FFA's and BIFFEX) a broker has to be accredited by the SFA, the Securities and Futures Authority, the financial police of the City of London. A shipbroker who has not got an SFA accreditation is not allowed to give investment advice but he can, of course, give a market opinion on quoted prices.

MISREPRESENTATION

A broker should never misrepresent facts or information to anyone. If a broker is representing a Principal and acting on his behalf, he can be expected to protect the Principal's interests in the sense that he only puts one side of the argument and does not disclose his own client's weakness to the counter party's broker or representative. What he must not do is misrepresent facts. For example, if the client has to nominate a ship the same day and therefore has to fix quickly it would not be acting in the client's interests to admit that. It is perfectly reasonable to say or imply to a possible counter party that the charterer may have some flexibility on dates, is considering using larger or smaller vessels or that if the rate asked by the owners was too high that the charterer would seek to defer the shipment. If the charterer is faced by what by market standards is an expensive charter then the charterer would and should be exploring such alternatives anyway. But deliberate misrepresentation may not only have legal consequences but make the broker's career very short lived. It is perfectly possible to get the reputation as a good, professional broker and 'straight shooter' while protecting your Principal from the market or his own misjudgements.

VALUATIONS

Brokers are sometimes asked by owners or banks to value their ships on the basis of a specific period time charter. It is more common for sale and purchase ship brokers to be asked to value the market price of the vessel but it is also relatively frequent in the chartering market. Brokers have got to be accurate in this to the best of their professional ability. Pressure may be applied by an owner to a broker to give a valuation that suits the owner's purposes with the banks. Yet the object of asking the broker is for an independent and professional judgement from an expert. If they succumb to pressure, the consequences can be devastating. The headline in the 'Independent' newspaper of April 1998 in the Business section entitled 'U.K. Shipbrokers incompetent' is something that no shipbroker likes to see, least of all the company that is alleged to be incompetent. The story was of a group of U.S. insurance companies who were considering suing two U.K. shipbrokers who were alleged to have got the sale valuation of a fleet of ships wrong by a factor of 100 percent. While this was never actually pursued in court, the adverse publicity was obviously unwelcome. The message is clear. Valuations must be honest, independent and professional. Brokers must also give these valuations with the appropriate disclaimers and on the basis of the ship being in good condition or in the case of voyage contract rate valuations, the exact terms, drafts or any other considerations must be included.

THE LEGAL POSITION OF THE INTERMEDIARY SHIPBROKER

The Baltic Exchange handbook states, 'A broker negotiating as an intermediate between ship owner and charterer is deemed to warrant that he has the full authority of a Principal to contract on the terms of an offer which he transmits. If for some reason it transpires that he did not have the necessary authority he may be liable in an action brought by the person who receives the offer and accepts it'. In the case of two Principals negotiating through two brokers for example, if the second broker makes a mistake and he passes on an offer which is accepted, he could be liable for an action from his Principal if the mistake is to his detriment, for breach of warranty of authority with negligence. If the first broker makes the mistake and the second broker innocently passes on that inaccurate offer and it is accepted, then the second broker could still be liable for an action for breach of warranty of authority without negligence. He may have recourse action to the first broker who made the mistake. It is therefore important to make sure that the companies with whom the broker is dealing are financially sound and of good reputation.

AVOIDANCE OF ERRORS

Description of Vessel

An offer will usually commence with a description of the vessel and possible details of the vessel's previous cargoes and her itinerary. This is part of the charter party. It is therefore advisable to get this description from the owner and not rely on descriptions from computers or registers. The flag may have been changed or there maybe a typographical error in one of the figures. It is for similar reasons that assumptions should not be made about estimated times of arrival (ETA's) of ships. This can be crucial for a charterer and when given by the broker it is a warranty. The ship owner may have a different ETA than that assumed by the broker's estimate based on distance for any number of reasons; knowledge of an engine problem giving a deficiency of speed, bunkering en route, knowledge of bad weather lying ahead, the need to call into a port for spares etc.

Negotiating

If possible, confirm all offers given by telephone as soon as possible in writing by fax, e-mail or telex. This is good practice and frequently saves arguments later on. In the same way, confirm all approvals given. It is especially important where the counter party's English is poor or the telephone connection is bad.

Negotiating papers

Once concluded the broker should send a recap of the fixture with the full details to both owner and charterer. Indeed, if fixed on subjects the broker should send a recap of main terms agreed and subsequently of all terms agreed. The fixture is clean at the point at which both parties have fully agreed. There is no actual need to have a charter party or to sign it. This does not make the contract. The contract is made when the parties have agreed. However, the parties will be able to prosecute the fixture professionally if they are provided with a record of the terms agreed in the form of a charter party as soon as possible. That is the broker's job.

If there is a dispute as to the wording of the recap this will either be because there has been a misunderstanding or each party has a different interpretation of a loosely worded phrase or that the broker has misled one or both parties. The broker must seek to avoid these situations by being careful and precise. There is no need to be pedantic but it is important to be professional. If there is a dispute, the arbitrator or lawyer will seek to discover the intention of the parties. It is therefore very important to have all the notes and papers relating to the negotiations. These must be placed in the fixture file. This will help resolution of a dispute, will shed good light on the broker as careful, prudent and business like and add support to those occasions when his word is disputed by one of the parties.

NEGOTIATING TERMINOLOGY

Indication

This is what it says. It is an indication of what one party is likely to be able to agree. It is given in good faith and if attractive to the recipient he often asks for it to be converted into a firm offer. But it is not an offer. It can be a prelude to a negotiation but is not part of a formal negotiation.

Offer and Counter Offer

Just as the broker must be careful in what he says and how he says it as described above, care must also be taken in the techniques of negotiations. One cannot offer for two or more businesses or ships at the same time. Quite apart from the practical difficulties of negotiation if both were accepted at the same time it would present severe difficulties. An offer should, as a matter of good practice, expire before another is made. This is perfectly acceptable, ethical, fair, businesslike and moreover, effective. It is possible to offer 'subject unfixed' or 'subject open'. Indian government cargoes are worked in this way. But it is not done widely. The reason is very simple. It is not effective. It does not engender trust, feel or goodwill, which are essential elements to any successful business venture. Neither does it necessarily get the best rates. Most owners will not be bothered to play the game. If someone is caught trying to do it, word will get around the market very quickly and will look upon him with suspicion in future. When a new party enters the market they will be given all the benefits of any doubt and all will make the presumption that the player will play by the unwritten market rules to make the market work effectively. It is very difficult and time consuming to recoup trust once it has been damaged.

If an offer is 'clean', that is without subjects, and it is accepted, then the fixture has been concluded. If, however, the recipient replies that he rejects the offer entirely but makes an alternative proposal that is also an offer. If the recipient accepts some parts of the proposal but rejects or amends other parts then this is a counter offer. The distinction is important. We often see replies to offers made with a preamble along the lines of; 'Herewith charterer's counter offer'. There then follows a detailed proposal. It implies that the charterer has accepted the terms of the owner's offer on which the charterer has not commented. It implies that this is an 'accept/except' offer. However, it could easily be that the charterer wanted to reject the owner's proposal entirely and the fact he missed out certain terms means that he wanted to discuss them later. It is such lack of clarity that are the seed beds of unnecessary disputes. It is therefore advisable to use the following terminology:

Accept/Except

This counter offer accepts some parts of the last offer but not others. It is the easiest to follow in a long negotiation as the parts which are in dispute are highlighted with every counter offer and are, in a successful negotiation, whittled down until there are none.

Repeat last offer, except

This is an offer. It rejects the last offer from the other party and maintains the last offer in the format last given but only changing it in some aspects so stated. These changes will either be concessions to the other party or some new needs.

Decline your offer and offer

This is a complete rejection of the offer received, possibly because despite the fact that the rate looks promising, it is in the wrong format and on the wrong terms. Nevertheless, it is worthy of a detailed new offer in reply on the terms that this party will accept.

At the beginning of the negotiations it is usually, but not always, the owner who makes the offer. This will probably be brief and contain the details of the vessel offered, the trading limits of the voyage, the position of the ship and the remuneration required. The charterer will then usually respond with a detailed reply incorporating some of the information given by the owner but incorporating the terms which the charterer requires. In this case it is likely to be in a, 'decline your offer and offer as follows' format. If the owner knows the charterer's business well he may well offer on the terms required immediately. If there have been previous fixtures between the owner and the charterer on the same or similar route he may well say, 'As per last fixture except'. The changes may well be the name and description of the ship, the dates and the freight rate only.

Each party is at liberty to change its mind or introduce new items into the negotiations at any time until the contract is agreed in its final form. However, the brokers and chartering staff should try to avoid doing this as it does not give an impression of trust, competence and professionalism on the part of the party changing the terms.

Reply Times

Offers, counter offers and subjects will often have time limits on them beyond which they are not valid or binding. This time limit must be clear and unambiguous. It is the communication to the Principal, not the broker, that is the vital time in determining when an offer has been accepted or a time limit has expired. Thus the words, 'reply 1400 hours' begs the question which day or date, and where. It should read, 'reply to owner's office by 1400 hours London time today the 25th October 1999'. There is no room for misunderstanding in this. The reply has got to be received in the owner's office, not to the broker who may not be able to get through to the owners. The time and date is specified. Some years ago a London owner gave an offer for reply 0900 hours London the next day. The broker sent the offer out verbatim. The charterers confirmed the offer clean the next day at 0845 but the broker could not contact the owner till 0915. The owner insisted the offer was out of time and he was free. The charterers insisted that they had confirmed within time. If the broker had made it clear that the offer was for reply to the owner and not by implication himself, he would have been covered.

Although they are in common usage, the words, 'immediate reply' or 'prompt reply' are inexact and it is advisable not to use them if at all possible. It is safer to use a time even if it is only two or three minutes away.

Subjects

An offer, counter offer or fixture will frequently have a subject which must be cleared before the contract is binding. They are used when the charterer has to check that the cargo is still available on the dates provisionally booked or that the cargo has been sold;

The most common subjects are;

1. **Subject stem.** The charterer requires to verify that the cargo will still be available at the load port.

2. **Subject shipper's approval.** The charterer requires to verify that the cargo suppliers will accept the fixed ship at the load berth and that the cargo is going to be available on the agreed dates.

3. **Subject receiver's approval**. The charterer must check with the receiver or cargo buyer that the vessel, its expected arrival date and cargo size are acceptable before confirming the ship is fully fixed.

4. **Subject head charterer's approval.** An owner or operator may have taken a cargo on a 'TBN' or 'to be nominated' basis and finds that when the charterer nominates the dates, he does not have a vessel on position. He therefore has to fix in a vessel to cover it or to **'sublet'** or **'relet'** the cargo as he is permitted to do. When fixed 'on subjects', one of those subjects has to be head charterer's approval as they have not been a party to fixing the vessel. They may or may not also be the receivers or the shippers but there may be a chain of sublets/sub charterers.

5. **Subject management approval or Subject Board of Directors (BOD) Approval.** This is a subject that should be used with care. In most spot single fixtures the person negotiating on behalf of the ship or cargo should have full authority to fix. Those that try to use this subject tend to give the impression that they are unsure of themselves and that negotiations are likely to be slow. It will therefore tend to work against getting the best rate. However, in long term contracts or time charterers or fixtures which are of a complex nature, if the commitment is clearly of a long term strategic nature, it is usually understood by both sides that it will need the sanction of management or the board of directors. In such cases, it may be better to spell this out in the negotiations.

6. **Sub Sale.** The sale of a cargo is either being negotiated or subject to a tender in which case a number of charterers may be trying to fix freight.

7. **Subject owner's approval of charterers.** If the charterer is unknown to the owner, he will need to check on the company's background and

performance which will necessitate talking to other owners, BIMCO and perhaps the charterer's bank.

8. **Subject details**. When a fixture is done on main terms it is usual to specify 'subject details'. The main terms will comprise the name and description of the ship, the load and discharge ports, the cargo quantity, the rate, demurrage, the laytime for loading and discharging, any other monetary term, the commission and the charter party form. The details will tend to comprise terms which are not contentious. It is possible to fall down on 'details' but it is not usual.

   However, there is always the doubt about what are 'details' and what are 'main terms' especially given some apparently inconsistent decisions in American courts. Any term which could involve a monetary gain or loss should be mentioned in the main term negotiations. Thus issues such as overage insurance, crew war bonuses and turn time, for example should be in the main terms. But for the avoidance of doubt, instead of 'sub details', the words **'subject mutual agreement of all outstanding charter party terms'** will be clearer. This will also make any potential problem due to differencies in interpretation of English and American law on what is a 'detail' superfluous, as the parties have clearly agreed that all outstanding terms have to be agreed before there is a fixture. These outstanding terms or details should then be cleared as quickly as possible in a businesslike manner.

   It is sometimes a source of contention in international business if one side delays looking at these terms. For instance, Japanese who are used to fixing with other Japanese find it inconceivable that a fixture concluded subject details would fall down. They therefore often tend to regard these details as something that can be left to a later time. Europeans, on the other hand, will want the fixture wrapped up quickly so they know that they are

'clean fixed'. When these business cultures clash it is wise to err on the side of caution and get the outstanding terms agreed promptly.

9. **Others.** In a negotiation either side may put any subject they wish to on the negotiations. 'Subject survey' or 'Subject satisfactory survey' may be a condition in case of a long term time charter where the charterer wishes to check the physical condition of the ship rather than simply rely on the written description. 'Subject financial closure' may be the subject on a contract of affreightment which depends on banks' financing the whole venture of which the shipping is just a part.

When a vessel is fixed 'on subjects' it means that the owner is bound to the contract until the time for the subjects to be removed or not has passed. Until that time the owner cannot negotiate the vessel at least on a firm basis for any other business. The owner will therefore usually try to restrict the declaration time to the shortest possible period.

It is advisable for a broker when notifying a party that all subjects are cleared that a record is made of the time and date and from whom and to whom the information was conveyed. If there is no one at the recipient's office, it is advisable to send a telex or fax confirming the deal, recording the time. The counter party should then be advised that it has not been possible to locate the Principal but has confirmed it in writing to the office and that a reconfirmation may be necessary. The date of the charter party will be the date on which the subjects are lifted.

ANATOMY OF A NEGOTIATION

The basic elements of a negotiation leading to a main terms recap are the name of the Charterer, the name of the ship and its description and depending whether it is time charter or voyage charter the following points.

<u>For Time Charter</u>

Delivery
Redelivery
Period or nature of the trip
Trading area and exclusions
Dates (Laycan)
Permitted cargo/exclusions
Hire/ballast bonus
Bunkers on delivery/redelivery
Commission structure
Charter party form
Subjects

<u>For Voyage Charter</u>

Loadport
Discharging port
Cargo description and quantity
Loading terms
Discharging terms
Dates (Laycan)
Freight
Freight payment
Demurrage/despatch
Commission
Charter party form
Subjects

There may well be other things of importance that are included. In a voyage charter for example, main terms may well include turn time, optional ports, whose agents, freight payment details, who pays for which dues and taxes and notice of readiness terms. For a time charter it may well include a bunker quality provision and trading and cargo exclusions. This will depend on the trade, but the above elements must be present. They are the barest of bones of a recap of a fixture.

How does it work in a negotiation?

Let us take a charterer's requirement and see how it might be marketed and negotiated. This may be read in conjunction with Chapter Six and Appendix One. The following fictitious order might have been circulated as follows;

ACCOUNT COLLINS
130,000 MT 10 PERCENT COAL IN BULK
1SB NEWCASTLE/1SB ROTTERDAM
15/30 DECEMBER
35000 SHINC BENDS
12 HRS TTBE
2.5 ADDCOMM
BEST OFFERS

This covers the bare essentials of the order giving size, load and discharge ports and terms, dates and commission. Brokers will be able to locate the main candidates from these initial facts.

One owner might have offered as follows

FIRM REPLY TO OWNER'S OFFICE BY 1000 HOURS GENOA TIME TOMORROW 30 OCT 1999
ACCT COLLINS MINING OF SYDNEY, AUSTRALIA
MV LUCIANO PAVAROTTI
ITALIAN FLAG 1989 BULK CARRIER
165,213 METRIC TONS DWT ON 17.61 M SSW
6,214,913 CUFT GRAIN
9 HOHA
LOA 279.9 / BEAM 45
OPEN TOKYO BAY 1ST DEC
130,000 MT 10 PERCENT COAL MOLOO IN BULK
EXPLOAD ABT 130,000 MT
1SB NEWC/1SB ROTT
15/30 DEC ETA 15 DEC
35,000 MT SHINC BE
12 HRS TT BE USC

FREIGHT USD 11.00 PMT FIOST
DEM USD 14,000 DHDLTSBE
SUB DETS 2.5 PERCENT ADDCOMM PLUS 1.25 BROKERAGE

This gives the charterer the details of the ship so that they can immediately see if she is suitable. It specifies the domicile of the charterer so that the owner knows he is fixing to a substantial company and not an offshore subsidiary. The owner gives his freight and demurrage rate and repeats the terms given except he qualifies the 12 hours turn time with USC (unless sooner commenced). (See Chapter Six). The freight is based on **'free in and out trimmed'** to protect the owner from any possible extra costs. It means 'free' to the owner and differentiates it from **'gross load'** where the owner pays for the cost of loading. The broker would have passed this on making sure that the reply was specified to owner's office. It is fair to say that depending on the circumstances the broker should also give some background as to the market situation, competing ships and owner's attitude to this and other possible cargoes.

Assuming that the charterer feels that this is an offer he wishes to pursue he will counter to it. He may take into account that the ship is relatively modern, that she is currently giving an ETA at the beginning of the laydays so that in case of delay there are 15 days in which she can still reach the port and perform the cargo lifting. Last, but certainly not least, he may think that the initial offer of freight is a reasonable one compared with 'last done' and the other offers he has received. He will then make a full firm counter with all the relevant main terms. It would look like the following:

CHTS DECLINE YOUR OFFER AND OFFER FIRM REPLY TO CHTS BY NOON LONDON TODAY AS FOLLOWS
ACCT COLLINS MINING OF SYDNEY
ALL NEGOS AND/OR EVENTUAL FIXTURE TO BE KEPT STRICTLY

P AND C
MV LUCIANO PAVAROTTI
DESCRIPTION AS PER OWNER'S OFFER
PLSE ADVISE VESSEL'S FULL ITINERARY
ETA NEWCASTLE 15 TH DECEMBER
EXPECTED INTAKE 130,000 MT

130,000 MT 10PCT MOLOO COAL IN BULK
LOAD - 1SB NEWCASTLE CHOPT 1SB PORT KEMBLA
DISCH- 1SB ROTTERDAM CHOPT ZEEBRUGGE CHOPT 1SB ANTWERP
LAYCAN DECEMBER 10/30 1999 (TBN TO A 15 DAY SPREAD UPON FIXING)
LOAD - 35,000 MT SHINC (LOCAL HOLIDAYS EXCL)
DISCH- 35,000 MT SHINC (LOCAL HOLIDAYS EXCL) CHOPT 25,000 MT SHINC (LOCAL HOLIDAYS EXCL)
12 HRS TT BENDS
NOR ATDNSHINC WIPON, WIBON, WIFPON, WECCON. IF THE VESSEL FAILS CUSTOMS CLEARANCE OR FREE PRATIQUE THEN TIME FROM FAILING UNTIL PASSING NOT TO COUNT.
FREIGHT(S)
BASIS 35,000 MT SHINC DISCHARGE
USD 10.00 PMT FIOT BASIS ROTTERDAM DISCHARGE
USD 10.00 PMT FIOT BASIS ANTWERP DISCHARGE
USD 9.85 PMT FIOT BASIS ZEEBRUGGE DISCHARGE
FOR 25,000 MT SHINC DISCHARGE
USD 10.20 PMT FIOT BASIS ROTTERDAM DISCHARGE
USD 10.20 PMT FIOT BASIS ANTWERP DISCHARGE
USD 10.05 PMT FIOT BASIS ZEEBRUGGE DISCHARGE
DHD USD 11,000 LAYTIME NON REV BENDS
FREIGHT PAYABLE 90 PERCENT WITHIN 10 BANKING DAYS

AFTER S/R B/L BALANCE UPON SETTLEMENT OF ACCNTS.
CHABE
DRAFT RESTRICTIONS AT BOTH LOAD AND DISCH PORTS TO BE OWNER'S RISK AND RESPONSIBILITY
SHIFTING BETWEEN ANCHORAGE AND/OR WAITING BERTH TO LOAD/DISCHARGE BERTHS NOT TO COUNT AS LAYTIME EVEN IF THE VESSEL IS ON DEMURRAGE
EXTRA INS IF ANY DUE TO VSLS AGE/FLAG/CLASSIFICATION OR OWNERSHIP TO BE FOR OWNER'S ACCT
SUB OWNER'S ACCEPTANCE OF CHT'S AMWELSH C/P
SUB STEM AND RECEIVER'S APPROVAL LATEST 2 WORKING DAYS AFMT
2.5 PERCENT ADDCOMM

For the meanings of the above abreviations and terms and what is at stake in each of them see Appendix One and Chapter Six. However, it will be noticed that the charterer is careful to get the itinerary of the vessel so as to double check the ETA especially since the laydays cancelling has to be narrowed. The charterer needs the option of 2 load and 3 discharge ports. He did not circulate the order like this because any ship agreeing to perform Newcastle/Rotterdam could and would do the alternatives but he initially wanted to attract offers by keeping it simple. Notice the exclusion of local holidays. This is not always usual although more charterers are attempting to make it standard that local or 'Super holidays' (i.e. Christmas, New Year, Easter etc. where applicable) do not count especially if the port in question is not working on those days. In this case, as the laydays/cancelling cover the Christmas period, it could be important. Notice the 12 hours turn time without the USC (unless sooner commenced) that the owners offered. Notice the exclusion of time counting if vessel fails to clear customs or free pratique. Notice there is no time stated when the charterer has to declare which load and discharge port is applicable (which is important for the quantity loaded) and when the declaration of which discharge rate is applicable. Notice also that for avoidance of all doubt, the charterer has specified that the draft restrictions are owner's risk and responsibility. Notice that the owner is being asked to accept the charterer's pro forma unseen.

Since this is a very comprehensive offer the owner decides to counter on an accept/except basis. He goes back as follows:

A/E REPLY TO OWNERS BY 14.30 LONDON TIME TODAY
ITINERARY- ETA TOKYO BAY TO DISCHARGE COAL 24 NOV 1998
ETS 1ST DECEMBER THEN BALLAST TO LOADPORT
ESTIMATED INTAKE 130,000 BASIS ROTTERDAM
120,000 BASIS ZEEBRUGGE
12 HOURS TT USC
BASIS 35000 DISCHARGE RATE
FREIGHT USD 10.50 ROTT
USD 10.50 ANT
USD 10.35 ZEEB
BASIS 25000
USD 10.70
USD 10.70
USD 10.55
CHTS TO DECLARE LOADPORT ON FIXING AND DISCHARGE PORT AND DISCHARGE SPEED ONE DAY PRIOR ETA LOADPORT
DEM USD 12000
FREIGHT WITHIN 7 RUNNING DAYS
BALANCE WITHIN 20 DAYS OF COMPLETION DISCHARGE
SUB MUTUAL AGREEMENT OF AMWELSH P/F – PLSE SEND FOR OWNERS TO STUDY
END

However the fixture is eventually concluded after this, the main points of contention will have been isolated and now can be argued about and negotiated. The broker will be able to take the charterer's first offer and make the full and comprehensive recap from that and the amendments agreed thereafter. From this he will be able to draw up the charter party.

This is an example of a simple voyage negotiation of a bulk cargo with well known ports and standard terms.

Let us examine the recap of something a little different. This again is fictitious but based on similar trades that do exist. We will assume that the negotiation has proceeded along sensible lines outlined above and produced the following main terms recap.

ACCT STEEL-CO OF BEIJING
RISING STAR TBN MAX 25 YEARS MIN 15 TON CRANES
FREE EXTRA INS UP TO 20 YEARS - EXTRA INS DUE TO VSLS CLASS, AGE (OVER 20 YRS) FLAG, OWNERSHIP, REGISTRY TO BE FOR OWNS ACCT AGAINST ACTUAL VOUCHERS
PERFORMING VESSEL TBN LATEST 7 DAYS PRIOR ETA LOADPORT
CHTS APP OF SAME TO BE LIFTED WITHIN 24 WORKING HOURS OF NOM.
FULL OR P/C IN OO OF 35,000 MT PIG IRON –ONE GRADE
1SB KLAIPEDA CHTS GTEE 10.6 M/ 1SB AA SHANGHAI AND BEILUN ROUGHLY 50 /50 EACH DISPORT QUANTITIES DISCH AT EACH DISPORT ASCERTAINED BY INDEPENDENT DRAFT SURVEY– ROUTING VIA SUEZ
IF P/C THIS CARGO IS BASE CARGO- OWNERS INT TO COMPLETE WITH OTHER CARGOES IN GEOG ROT- BUT HAVE THE RIGHT IN/OUT GEOG ROT.

CARGO TO BE LOADED IN SEPARATE HOLDS FROM OTHER CARGOES
NO OTHER PIG IRON ALLOWED FOR CHINA DISCH
4000 MT SHINC LOAD –NOR CAN BE TENDERED FRM 0800-1800 HOURS SHINC - USD 7000 DEM HDLTS/ CQD DISCH (EXCEPT IF CARGO CANNOT BE DISCH DUE TO LACK OF DOCUMENTATION CHTS TO PAY DETENTION CHARGES AT USD 7000/DAY PR
20/27 NOV 1998 TBN TO 7 DAY SPREAD WHEN NOM PRFRMNG VSL
FREIGHT USD 20.50 PER MT FIOST
90 PCT WITHIN 7 BANKING DAYS AFTER COMPL LOADING
B/L TO BE MARKED 'FRT PAYABLE AS PER C/P' BALANCE FRT WITH DEM/DES LATEST 30 DAYS AFTER COMP DISCH
IF CHTS REQUIRE 'FRT PREPAID' B/L THEN SAME TO BE RELEASED ON RECEIPT OF TLX FROM CHTS BANK TO OWNS CONFIRMING THAT THEY HAVE IRREVOCABLY REMITTED FREIGHT AS PER C/P –INCLUDING REMITTANCE DETAILS, VALUE AND DATE.
CONGEN B/L TO BE ISSUED
CHABE
AGENTS AT DISPORT-PENEVICO
1.5ADD AND 1.25 BROKERAGE
O/WISE SUB MUTUAL AGREEMENT OF CHTS EXECUTED P/F

All the main points of this rather more complex fixture are set down. Due to the draft limitation which the charterer has been good enough to guarantee in this case, the owner has taken the opportunity to ask for part cargo option and clearly has the intention of booking other cargo for Far East destinations. However it must be loaded in different holds. **CQD (or customary quick despatch)** discharge has been agreed. This is usually a dangerous thing for an owner to do as it is fairly meaningless in terms of guaranteeing a discharge rate. But there are areas of the world where if an arrangement can be made with influential people within the port or at the receiving end, for quick berthing and discharging the freight premium for agreeing such a risky term can be more than off set. The official port load and discharge rates in China are much slower than what can really be achieved especially with local influence. This is why all owners that are well connected there are happy with CQD. Notice, however, that if the delay is on the charterer's side because of documentation then a detention charge is payable. This is prudent from the owner's point of view. Notice the freight payment terms and the stipulation from the owner that freight has to be paid prior to 'pre paid' Bills of Lading being released. If not, the owner is in fact, saying that he has received the freight when he has not!

A simple time charter negotiation can be seen below on an entirely different trade. This is for a short period for a 'Laker' for the duration of the Lakes season. The owner knows what is involved in Lakes trading so he makes a fairly comprehensive offer from the outset. This pattern is usual for time a charter and unlike voyage charter. In the latter case the charterer needs to explain to the owner all the terms on which he has to calculate. In time charter the owner has to explain the details of the ship and the terms on which he is prepared to let out the ship to the charterer. This may be read in conjunction with Chapter Seven and Appendix One.

OFFER YOU FIRM REPLY TO OWNER'S OFFICE BY 10 AM LONDON TOMORROW
M.V. LAKES TRADER
PAN/82
29,611 MT DWAT ON 10.5 M
19,200 MT DWAT ON 26 FT FRESH WATER
182.2/23.1 LOA/BEAM
34,618 CUM GRAIN IN 5HOHA

4 x 16 TON CRANES
13 ON 22 (180) PLUS 2 MDO

ACCT CANADIAN LAKES SHIPPING CO.
DEL DLOSP ANTWERP
LAYCAN 16/25 MARCH 1998
WW TRADING INC GT LAKES IN SEASON
TRADING ALWAYS WITHIN IWL EXCEPT GT LAKES/ST LAWRENCE TRADING ONLY, AA EXCEPT FOR RIVER PLATE ALWAYS VIA SB(S) SP(S).
CHTS LIBERTY TO BREAK IWL ONLY FOR GREAT LAKES/ST LAWRENCE TRADING
REDEL DLOSP/PASSING BOSTON/BAHIA BLANCA RANGE, CHOPT SKAW/PASSERO RANGE
NO GREAT LAKES/ST LAWRENCE TRADING UNTIL 10 DAYS AFTER OFFCIAL OPENING
PERIOD TO REDEL BETWEEN 1st NOVEMBER/20 DECEMBER 1998
HIRE USD 7700 DAILY INC O/T
BOD 450/500 MT IFO AND 45/55 MT DO
BOR SAME QTY AS ON DEL
PRICES OWNS REVERTING
SUB MUTUAL REVIEW OF PREVIOUS C/P DATED 17 APRIL 1985
5 % TTL COMM HERE
SUB CHTS MNGMNT APP DECL BY COB LONDON MONDAY 25 FEB 1998

Charterers counter as follows and the negotiation quickly becomes a trade on the essentials only.

CHTS A/E REPLY TO CHTS BY 12OO HOURS LONDON TODAY
NO LAKES ENTRY PRIOR 0001 HOURS 4TH APRIL

US 7000 DAILY
BUNKER PRICE BENDS 65/110
OWNERS A/E REPLY 2 PM LONDON TODAY
NO LAKES TRADING PRIOR 0001 HOURS 5TH APRIL
HIRE USD 7250

The simplicty of this negotiation is helped by the fact that the parties have fixed before as evidenced by their use of a previous charter party on which to base the fixture. The charterer therefore does not need to ask a lot of questions about the ship. He has it all on record anyway. The issues here are really just the rate and the dates when she can safely enter the St. Lawrence/Great Lakes, the so called First Open Water (FOW) and safety margin. This is a safety issue as it will still be icy. There is a large redelivery range. The owner allows the charterer to trade in the River Plate and go safely aground which is necessary there. One would have to assume that there is a good chance of a negotiation at this stage leading to a fixture.

5. Charter Parties

DEFINITION

A Charter Party is a contract under which two parties have agreed to effect a transportation by sea. This will necessarily involve the use or hire of a vessel. The origin of the term is from medieval Latin, "charta partia" or in French, "charte partie", a divided charter or contract. This is a reference to the fact that two copies were prepared, one for the charterer and one for the owner. The English version of the word is a corruption of the French. The first pre-printed example still surviving is from 1813. There is no need for a special pre-printed form but it is usual to fix on one of a number of standard forms of charter party. Each will usually have a number of printed clauses which will cover established and common requirements. These will frequently be common to various forms of charter party. There is no rule that states these printed clauses must be used. The parties are free to use whatever format and wording they desire and to omit, amend or add to such clauses. However, the wording of many usual clauses has been established for a long time and in most cases has been considered in court cases and legal interpretations given to their meaning.

Whether or not a charter has been made depends on the ordinary rules of contract law. That means it does not need to be signed to be valid. Indeed, a written agreement need not exist at all. If owners and charterers have agreed all essential terms in correspondence by telephone, fax, telex etc. contract law determines that a binding contract exists whether a charter party has been drawn up or not. However, it is very inadvisable to fix on this basis. For this reason, most fixtures are concluded on charter parties. Due to the complexity of most agreements, at the very least, the charter party should act as an 'aide memoire' and record of what has been agreed and what should happen in certain circumstances.

CHARTER PARTY FORMS - THE HISTORICAL CONTEXT

Many charter party forms have their origin in the late nineteenth and early twentieth centuries. All of these have been amended from time to time in an attempt to bring them up to date. However, they usually continue to carry outdated wording concerning machinery and equipment that no longer is used.

When I started working in the chartering industry in the mid 1970's I was struck how 'old fashioned' it was. There were even a few brokers around who had fixed sailing ships! Aspiring brokers were taught at courses preparing themselves for the I.C.S. exams about Liberty ships, the famous war time convoy vessels bought and traded after the war by entrepreneurs, and liner vessels with engine and bridge amidships which were rapidly becoming redundant rather than modern bulk carriers. Fleet analysis was done by 'T2' equivalents. T2's were the wartime convoy oil tanker! The Baltic Exchange had only just admitted women as members and relaxed the dress rules so that it was now possible to wear a pastel coloured shirt rather than the obligatory white one hitherto. Charter party forms usually designated by their year of revision, their headings or introductory words often in copperplate writing, looking as though they were imitations of 'Magna Carta' and about to be unfurled by a medieval Town Crier, still contained wording applicable to a much earlier age. General wordings like 'tight, staunch and strong', (most charter parties); 'the reach and burthen of the ship' (Baltime) instead of the carrying capacity; and the 'tackle, apparel, provisions and furniture', instead of the gear and equipment of the ship were used. Ships were referred to as 'steamers'. The detailed contractual terms talked about giving notice by telegraph. Others referred to 'pitmen and trimmers', 'stokeholds', that the 'bunker coals to be kept properly separated from cargo', (Amwelsh '53), 'donkey boilers', 'steam winches', 'gins slings and falls' and 'grates and stoves' (NYPE '46).

The Amwelsh '53 did not really look much different from the old Welsh Coal Charter Party. Even the '79 adaptation kept the same format and changed very little. In other words, the format and phraseology in a document made in 1979 were taken from one originating in 1896!

All this could partly be explained (but perhaps not wholly excused) because in the previous 20 or 30 years the shipping industry had undergone a technical change so vast the word 'revolution' is perhaps not far short of the truth. In 1945 the world's merchant fleet consisted of liners and tramps, few of which were larger than 20,000 dwt. Most had derricks and were turbine powered. But thirty years later, by 1975, specialised bulk carriers of 55-75,000 dwt and 100-165,000 dwt were common, trading into specially built ports, terminals and wharfs in Australia, Brazil, the USA, Europe and Japan. Container ships had appeared and were expanding their operations fast. Car carriers were trading cars and grain in specialist trades. Virtually all ships were being built with engine and bridge aft to increase the loading and discharging efficiency. In short, specialist ships had taken the place of the older general cargo ships. That was the revolution. The changes that have happened since then, while profound for those involved, have followed the trends set earlier. Many of these '70's built ships are still trading and apart from being less fuel efficient are not out of place in today's market. For instance, the largest container ships increased in size from 2000 TEU's in the early '70's to over 7000 TEU's by the end of the 1990's, but along the same lines. Ship design technology has certainly improved with more efficient engines, better hatch covers, INMARSAT and anti-fouling paints, for example. Improved technology has meant that ships carry a smaller crew. Yet they are recognisably the same types of ship as were trading in the '70's and in many cases on the same trades (See Chapter One).

The chartering industry has, however, changed rather drastically since the 1970's. This modernisation has been described in detail in Chapters Two and Three. Furthermore, most negotiations are now usually conducted almost entirely in metric measurements (deadweight, cargo quantity, bunker quantity, length, breadth, draft and cubic capacity) rather than in imperial measurements or a combination of both, although cubics and stowage factors are probably better understood and usually expressed in cubic feet. The ICS exams now admirably reflect a more modern industry. Charter party forms have been amended, in some cases many times. The Gencon and Orevoy even use a user friendly box format. We have seen that there is an now an active derivatives market in OTC (over the counter) products (FFA's) as well as Exchange traded futures (Biffex). And yet the industry still uses old charter party forms as a base for seaborne contracts, sometimes when modern ones are available. Why?

It is because the shipping industry is unique in that contracts are negotiated within a few days or even hours that printed forms have been established. For understandable reasons all parties involved in a negotiation concentrate initially on the most commercially important elements which are called **'main terms'**. These main term agreements are then grafted onto a charterer's pro forma which are based on established forms.

Most large charterers have charter party pro formas, many of them based on old and outdated forms onto which a series of more modern and relevant additions, deletions and rider clauses are added. When these charter parties were first introduced they were intended to be comprehensive with no need for extra clauses. The gaps for load and discharge ports, dates and freight and demurrage were simply filled in and the document signed. Today, almost all of these older forms have a style of wording that needs clarification in the form of inserts in the main body of the charter party and by rider clauses which typically number around fifty but sometimes many more. The result can often be a messy and difficult to read main body. Some charterers have, partly for this reason and partly for reasons of corporate identity, in recent years, written their own tailor made charter parties which have tried to define the obligations of each side more precisely and arrange them in a more logical order. The BHPVOY (BHP), 'Envirocoal' (Adaro), 'Damsalt' (Dampier Salt), GKE, KPC (Kaltim Prima Coal), CSR, ESB (Irish Electricity Board), and Posco (Pohang Steel) charter parties are good examples. This follows the trend in the tanker industry where many oil companies have their own tanker forms. Other charterers have adopted 'new' independent charter parties. Perhaps the 'Norgrain' and 'Orevoy' are the most successful.

So why aren't the modern, updated, independent forms more frequently used?

Many charterers prefer to use their pro-formas, based on the older forms, because they are simply more familiar and comfortable with their terms set out in rider clauses which have been imposed onto older charter party forms. If this is a 50 year old form, it will not matter to them since they have amended it continuously, adapting it over the years to incorporate modern ship's equipment, usage and phraseology reflecting decisions of the latest court cases or their own experiences. When a charterer fixes 'main terms' with an owner he has never fixed with before, he will not give them a blank pro forma which is obviously outdated and have to spend days or weeks negotiating replacement clauses. He will give them an executed copy of a charter party which incorporates all additions, deletions and amendments agreed by other owners in the recent past. This will form a very good basis for negotiation and in some cases will be accepted in full, sometimes with the qualification, 'with logical amendments'. This practicality as well as familiarity with old wording which may have been subject to legal interpretation are some reasons why the latest Gencon '94, Amwelsh '93 and NYPE '93, which have at long last organised the charter in a more logical and modern way, are still not used as much as the older varieties with grafted on clauses.

But the reason that these modern forms are unpopular in the market is not only charterer's inertia or familiarity and comfort with what they know. Partly, it is because the appearance of these forms is lamentably late. They incorporate wording in common use in rider clauses for the past 15 or 20 years anyway. These new forms, in this respect, are only playing 'catch up'. If the required clauses are in the rider clauses in older charter parties, why change? Furthermore the reason some charterers went to the trouble of writing their own form was partly due to the fact that their needs were not being catered for already in independent charter party forms. Lastly it is because many charterers feel that some of them are seriously flawed and that a great opportunity has been missed.

Criticism of these forms, however, is easy but attempting to produce a new or updated independent form that is both relevant and that would be widely accepted is far from a simple business. Just because there are old fashioned words and phrases, it does not mean to say that if you were to simply delete them, the result would be immediately hailed as the greatest breakthrough in shipping since the invention of the 'iron clad'. New charter parties, to be successful, have to fulfil a need. If they do not, however well written, they will not be adopted by charterers who will feel no necessity of using them. That, to a very large extent is regrettably the case in the 1990's with the Amwelsh '93, Gencon '94 and NYPE '93. The jury is still out on the Sugar '99 but BIMCO have attacked the form and many of its clauses are being resisted by owners. It is too early to tell in the case of the Gentime, only having been introduced in September 1999, but there has been no immediate take-up. Thus with the exception of the special case of the Polcoalvoy '97 which despite its complexities, because of the way Polish coal is sold is necessary, and the Synacomex '90, all the independent charter parties issued in the 1990's do not seem to have been widely accepted by the market.

Old forms have, for the most part, been adapted very adequately by charterers and owners in the market. Disturbingly for charterers, delicate and traditional balances have been changed in some of the new forms. The new Amwelsh 1993 for example is, on the face of it, a splendidly logical and comprehensive document. Yet, no doubt subject to pressure from owners, the authors of the form have altered the balance between the charterer and the owner that prevailed in previous Amwelsh forms and in some cases to the detriment of good chartering practice in general (See specific examples in Chapter Six). It is true that these can be altered back by negotiated amendments but why should a charterer tempt fate like that? It must be remembered that it is the charterers who declare what charter party form they use. The NYPE 1993 is more modern and logical in that it incorporates clauses that are not found in the older version's printed clauses but these clauses are standard rider clauses in the older forms that have evolved in the market anyway.

Having negotiated main terms, the owner will want to see the charterer's pro forma. Whether it is a private form, or a charter party based on a new or old standard form, they will assess it on its merits, on the state of the market, their perceived bargaining power and on the basis of whether other owners have accepted it previously.

Nevertheless the continued use by some charterers of older traditional forms which have outdated, imprecise or insufficiently comprehensive clauses for modern usage can be a potential problem. The structure of these charter parties has been necessarily messy. Outdated and useless clauses are deleted. Others are added in boxes at the side or in rider clauses. The computer has partly come to the rescue by being able to have the charter party forms on the word processor so that inserts can be made in the text without the need for box inserts at the side. But even so there is often no logical order. Clauses concerning laytime, for example, are found all over the document. Additional rider clauses have to be added. There is therefore a danger that an old form with a series of standard additional clauses, which have amendments and new clauses grafted on, then becomes itself amended in subsequent charter parties giving rise to contradictions between printed and additional clauses and between additional clauses themselves. This can lead to costly and time consuming disputes.

This is one reason why new charterers often decided to start from scratch and in the absence, until the '90's, of the possibility of more relevant forms issue their own private form incorporating fully worded and precise clauses in logical order. That there is so much case law concerning inadequately phrased or contradictory clauses should be a case of concern and vigilance for those involved. Even so, the evolution of charter parties is a continuous process. New interpretations and conditions will arise. New clauses are therefore needed before long, even on a comprehensive modern form. However, these documents are negotiated and often produced under time pressure and too little attention is sometimes paid to the wording of those contracts and clauses within them and how applicable they are to the contract negotiated. Yet huge sums of money are at stake. This is one reason for a clear understanding of the issues at stake, which will be discussed in Chapters Six, Seven and Eight and the care that must be taken which has been discussed in Chapter Four.

TYPES OF CHARTERS

Bareboat (or Demise)

The charterer leases the vessel from the owner and takes full control and management of the vessel, appointing the Master and crew. The charterers provide stores, bunkers and undertake repairs, insurance and dry docking. There are three 'Barecon' charter party forms to chose from.

Timecharter

The charterer hires the vessel for a specified period of time within certain pre arranged geographical limits. The commercial control of the vessel lies with the charterer who directs the Master and crew but the management and maintenance of the vessel and the appointment of Master, officers and crew remain with the owners. The charterer is responsible for arranging and paying for bunkers and all port charges. The remuneration, payable by the charterer, is called 'hire' and is usually paid every 15 days, 30 days, semi-monthly or monthly. If the vessel is unable to trade for a period of time through some fault of the ship and/or owners or through an accident, the charterer does not pay for such 'off hire' periods.

The main type in constant use is the 'New York Produce Exchange 1946' (NYPE) issued by the Association of Shipbrokers and Agents (USA) Inc.. This charter party originates from 1913 and although many times amended, still has to have many standard deletions, additions and rider clauses to bring it up to modern usage. References in the preamble to steam winches and donkey boilers for instance are always deleted. Clause 20 which addresses miscellaneous fuel use refers to 'grates and stoves'. This goes back to the days of coal fired ships when the crew's quarters were equipped with grates and stoves for burning coal. An updated version, called the ASBATIME was introduced in 1981 and recommended by FONASBA. A 1993 version of the NYPE was recommended by BIMCO but neither of them are as popular with charterers as the old '46 version. Nor is the loose and owner friendly wording of the 'Baltime' the choice of many charterers these days. The NYPE '46, albeit heavily amended, is still the most popular basis of most time charter agreements. In September 1999 a new charter party, the 'Gentime' was introduced by BIMCO but it is too early to tell if it will be successful.

Voyage charters

The charterer will charter part or the whole of the carrying capacity of the ship to carry a cargo loading at a named port or ports or at an agreed number of specified ports and discharge the cargo at a named port or ports or an agreed number of specified ports or a range of ports. The responsibilities of management, maintenance, crewing, provisions, payment of bunker fuel, port charges, appointment of agents, remain with the owner. The charterer is obliged to provide the agreed cargo and pay the freight usually on a per ton, per cubic metre or on a lump sum basis. Unlike the time charter, payment is based on the actual cargo carried and thus the owner's risk is the duration being extended by weather or port delay and in some cases, increases in bunker costs.

Unlike tanker chartering there are many different types of voyage charter parties dependent on area of origin and cargo type. More than 50 charter party forms have been approved, at one time or another, by the Baltic and International Maritime Council (BIMCO), which is an organisation designed to protect shipowners. Among other activities, they issue or approve a number of well known and widely used charter party forms. Some of the standard charter party forms have been in existence since the late nineteenth or early twentieth century. This is why, even on recently amended forms there are often many deletions, additions and rider clauses incorporating accumulated wisdom, experience and legal decisions which help to clarify the intentions and define the obligations of the parties. Over the last few years, the general trend has been for charterers to use fewer standard forms and more private tailor made forms.

For instance in the coal trade, the 'Amwelsh' is now dominant, even in Australia, having more or less supplanted the 'Auscoal'. Among the Amwelshes, it is still the Amwelsh '79 that is being used the most, with the '53 version coming a distant second. Having been successfully adapted over many years, the 1993 version has totally re-written the form. The amended layout with each clause having headings is easier to read and make the order of the clauses more logical. But few charterers have yet gone to the trouble of changing their pro forma to this updated version. Under time pressure in negotiations it is often easier to take the 'last done' charter party as a base rather than have an owner go through a completely new, virgin form. As briefly mentioned earlier, a further reason can be found in the break with tradition with earlier 'Amwelsh' terms, making them more owner favourable. These will be discussed in detail in Chapter Six. The South Africans tend to use the specially designed 'Richards Bay Charter Party'. This was written for the coal producers over 25 years ago by the best coal freight broker in South Africa at that time when the South Africans first started exporting coal in large size vessels and has survived the test of time well. It rarely has to have more than four or five rider clauses. Polish exports are dominated by the evolving 'Polcoalvoy' charter parties.

Two of the main Indonesian suppliers have had their own private forms from when they first started exporting in the late 1980's and early 1990's. They were also written and designed by brokers, the KPC charter party by the same broker who wrote the Richards Bay Coal charter party and the 'Envirocoal' charter party by this author.

In the grain trade, the 'Baltimore Form C' (BFC), Synacomex and 'Norgrain' tend to be predominant, even being used by some River Plate charterers where the 'Centrocon' used to dominate. Each grain house has adapted the BFC to incorporate its own 'standard' terms except in the case of Cargill who have adapted a 'Euromed' charter party which is now used as a multi origin and multi destination form.

The 'Norgrain' (North American Grain Charter Party 1973) was an attempt to write a new up to date form, rather than further attempt to adapt very old forms. The evolving nature of shipping however was proved yet again, however, when it was itself amended in 1989. It may well be that in the next few years charter parties for individual routes become standardised. However, the nature of the grain business is such that it has until now proven difficult to persuade the major grain houses to cooperate on standardising an industry wide, route specific form. The industry is extremely competitive, secretive and propriatorial. The margins on the trades are so small that freight is a very important part of the bottom line on their trade.

Iron ore charterers tend to use the 'Riodoceore', 'CORE7' and 'Orevoy' while the Japanese charterers still favour the 'Nipponore'. Sugar charterers have tended to use the Sugar '77, although the recently introduced Sugar '99 may replace it in the market. Unlike the new BIMCO inspired Amwelsh and Gencons, the Sugar '99 was written by members of the sugar industry and has tightened up some clauses and tipped the balance more in favour of the charterers. Fertiliser charterers often use the 'CORE7' but there are many others in use such as the 'Africanphos' and 'Ferticon', for example.

General cargoes, most coastal cargoes and any of the above can be and are, fixed on the 'Gencon', the most widely used general charter. The major criticism of this charter party is that it requires the addition of an undue number of additional clauses to cover issues normally covered by the standard clauses. In one sense this may be the reason for its continuing use. It is adaptable and flexible. Most charterers want or need to add their own clauses on to a base charter. If the base charter is long, irrelevant and potentially harmful to them, they will simply not use it. A short and simple document that is well known, even if it is known as inadequate and outdated, may be preferred as a base for the charterer's terms. Some charterers, however, as mentioned, construct their own private forms, tailor made for their trade and requirements. They will almost certainly incorporate some similar wordings in many of the clauses.

Consecutive Voyage Charters and Contracts of Affreightment (COA's)

These are multiple voyage charters either with the same ship in the case of consecutive voyage or with a variety of ships at the owner's option in the case of COA's. They may well incorporate more options in terms of loading and/or discharging ports, quantities and term but are based on the same voyage forms as single voyage charter parties.

EXAMPLES OF SOME CHARTER PARTY FORMS

General

GENCON 1922 (74/76/94)	- Issued by BIMCO- General - From '74 box type. The charter party most widely used for all commodities, especially small ships
MUTIFORM 82	- a charter party issued by FONASBA – widely praised - little used
NUVOY 1984	- Polish general form
WORLDFOOD 1986	– Private form for Worldfood
VOLCOA 1982	- Issued by BIMCO for COA's but almost never used

POSCO C/P (amended 1997)	- issued by Pohang Iron and Steel for coal/ore imports
BHPVOY	– private form issued by BHP for their own cargoes

Grain

BALTIMORE FORM C 1913 (1963/74/75/76/82)	- general purpose grain
NORGRAIN- 1973 (1989)	- general purpose grain
CENTROCON- 1934 (1937/50/74)	- River Plate grain - issued by UK Chamber of Shipping - little used now
SYNACOMEX 1974 (1990)	- general purpose grain - European origin grain
EUROMED 1983	- Cargill developed form from Synacomex
GRAINVOY 1966 (1974)	- box form similar to Gencon but little used
AUSTWHEAT 1989 (1990/91)	- issued by Australian Wheat Board - wheat
AUSBAR 1975 (1980)	- issued by Australian Barley Board - barley
COSCO GRAIN 1990	- issued by COSCO especially for Chinese shipments

Coal

AMWELSH 1953 (1979/93)	- has become the most widely used
RICHARDS BAY COAL C/P	- specially designed form for Richards Bay exports
POLCOALVOY 1971(76/95/97)	- Used extensively for coal from Poland - box form
SOVCOAL 1962 (1971)	- Previousy used for Soviet coal exports
AUSCOAL	- Box type for Australian coal but has lost ground to the Amwelsh and now rarely used
ENVIROCOAL C/P 1991	- Private form for P.T. Adaro
SAFANCHART NO 2 '74	- Mainly handies from Durban, Maputo and Richards Bay

N.B. – there are a number of other redundant charter parties for trades which now hardly exist

Ore

CORE7	- A standard ore form in wide use
NIPPONORE	- Favoured by Japanese charterers for Japanese imports
OREVOY 1980	- Tended to be adopted by the newer small steel mills
RIODOCEORE	- For Docenave's Brazilian exports but now has wider use

STEMMOR '76 (1983)	- For Phibro, adapted from CORE7 now used by others
GENORECON 1962	- Issued by BIMCO but now superseded by other charter parties
LABRADORE ORE	- Seven Islands/Baltimore, Philadelphia or Newport News
SAN JUAN BAY ORE (1959 /1961)	- little used, if at all, these days
SCANOREOCON 1962- (1966)	- For Narvik, Lulea, Oxelusund cargoes
LAMCON	- Lower Buchanan ore – no longer in use
MAURITANORE 1988	- Shipments from Mauritanea only
SOVORECON	- Soviet charter party

Fertilisers

CORE7	- Designed for ore but also used for fertilisers
AFRICANPHOS '50 (1987)	- Box layout from Morocco only
KEMIFERT	- Kemira's private form
FERTICON 1942 (1950/1974)	- General use- issued by UK Chamber of Shipping
FERTIVOY 1978 (1988)	- Private form used by Canpotex
FERTIDUTCH (1950/73)	- Dutch exports
GENFERT	- General fertiliser form
FERTISOY 1991	- Issued by Russian authorities

FOSFO PHOPHATE C/P	- Old American form for Tampa cargoes
RED SEA PHOSPHATE	- Old form for Red Sea origin

Salt

DAMSALT	- Dampier Salt private form
CORE7	- Occasionally used for salt

Sugar

SUGAR '77	- The most widely used charter for sugar by a long way
SUGAR '99	- Update of the Sugar '77 attacked by BIMCO
CUBASUGAR	- Cuba origins only- very old form
FIJI SUGAR 1977	- Specific trade and charterer
MAURITIUS BULK SUGAR (MSS)	- Specific trade
AUSTRALIA/JAPAN BULK RAW SUGAR 1998	- CSR own form for Japan destinations. They have separate own forms for each destination.

Cement

CEMENCO (1922/74)	
CEMENTVOY 1990	- For bulk cement and clinker

Timber

SOVCONROUND 1969	- Soviet charter party
BLACKSEAWOOD	- Ditto
SOVIETWOOD 1961	- Ditto
NUBALTWOOD 1964	- Ditto
NANYOZAI 1967	- For the log trade from South East Asia to Japan
BEIZAI 1964	- American logs and lumber to Japan

Timecharter

NEW YORK PRODUCE (NYPE 1913 adapted 21/31/46)
- The market standard

ASBATIME (1981) an adapation by the Association of Shipbrokers and Agents (USA)Inc (ASBA)- not as popular but some charterers have adapted it as their own private form.

NYPE '93- another revision in conjunction with BIMCO and the General Council of British Shipping- as yet little used except for long period time charters.

FONASBATIME	- Issued by FONASBA but little used
BALTIME 1909	- Amended 1920/39/50 - Has lost ground to NYPE
SINOTIME	- Especially made for Chinese
LINERTIME 68	- Revised in box form in 1974- little used

BHPTIME	- Private form for BHP
KLAVTIME	- Private form for Klaveness - Based on Asbatime
BOXTIME	- BIMCO form for the container trade
GENTIME	- Issued by BIMCO in September 1999. So far untested by the market, box format
BARECON 'A'	- Standard bareboat charter party
BARECON 'B'	- Bareboat charter party especially used for new buildings
BARECON '89	- Amalgamation of A and B- box type

In assessing the relative commercial use of these charter parties it is worth putting them in the context of the amount of bulk coal, ore, grain, phosphates etc. actually moved by sea and therefore under charter parties of one type or another. The following are the 1998 figures.

Iron Ore	**419** million tons
Steam coal	279
Coking coal	171
Total coal	**450**
Wheat/coarse grains	167
Soya beans	41
Total grain	**207**
Bauxite/alumina	55
Phosphate rock	31
Sugar	37
Agribulks	93
Fertiliser	64
Scrap	46
Cement	45

Coke	11
Pig iron	13
Forest products	156
Steel products	189
Others	37
TOTAL	**1,851 MILLION TONS**

Although it cannot be measured in any meaningful way, in view of the Amwelsh's predominance in coal chartering and the volumes of coal moved by sea, it is likely that it is the voyage charter party form on which most tonnage is contracted The Gencon is probably the most used voyage charter party in terms of numbers of shipments.

THE LAWS GOVERNING CHARTER PARTIES

Statute laws- Passed by Act of Parliament, for example the Merchant Shipping Acts. In certain circumstances recourse to the courts may be made to clarify the meaning of an Act of Parliament but the courts must seek to carry out the wishes of Parliament.

Common law- Decisions by Judges on some matter set a precedent for similar matters brought before the Court. It is therefore continually evolving. It is not unusual for precedents to be changed but they provide guidance for future decisions.

Customary law- It is not necessarily codified but commonly accepted by all as they are the practices that have been in existence for a substantial period of time.

International law- Conventions passed internationally at International Conferences, the United Nations, etc. are ratified by the UK and then incorporated into English Law by Parliament passing a Statute. They have therefore become Statute Law but originate outside England. A good example is the Carriage of Goods by Sea Act 1972 which is an Act of Parliament giving effect to an International Convention.

Custom of the trade- This may be taken into account in an arbitration but is not in itself a law.

CONDITIONS AND WARRANTIES

Charter party terms can normally be divided into two main categories, **Conditions** and **Warranties.** The breach of a Condition goes to the heart of the contract or shows an intention by the defaulting party not to be bound by the terms of the contract. It therefore entitles the aggrieved party to be relieved from further performance of the contract and recover damages; or the contract may be maintained and damages recovered in the option of the injured party. An example would be the payment of freight. A breach of a Warranty would not, on the other hand, destroy the basis of the contract but the aggrieved party could be entitled to receive damages. Legal rulings over the years have tended to blur these distinctions and there is sometimes a third catagory called "innominate obligations" which span both the others where the innocent party may have the right to treat the contract as terminated, depending on the severity of the breach. An example might be speed and consumption in a time charter. A failure to reach the speed by one knot would be a breach of warranty. A ten knot deficiency may well be regarded as a breach of such severity to be regarded as fundamental and therefore allow the charterer to terminate the contract. The breach of any term could result in damages depending on the gravity of the breach.

DRAWING UP CHARTER PARTIES

Charter parties and addenda are documents reflecting an agreement on a transaction to be carried out and thus are always written in the future tense.

As will be demonstrated in forthcoming chapters, although charter party wordings have developed legal meanings, because many are still drawn up or based on very old forms, it is essential that the rider clauses and amendments to the main body are as clear and precise as possible. Many a judge on deciding the interpretation of charter party clauses has criticised the drafting of both established and rider clauses.

The aim of drafting a contract should be clearly to express the rights, obligations, penalties and intentions of the parties concerned. Inconsistency between clauses should be avoided. One of the broker's duties is to assist in the construction of clearly worded clauses and try to advise the Principals to avoid loosely worded clauses.

Where a typed or rider clause is in conflict with a printed clause on the standard Charter Party, the Arbitrator or Courts will often take the view that as the parties went to the trouble of constructing a special clause and attaching it to the standard clauses, that the intent of the parties was to override or modify the standard clause. However, great care should be taken in drafting clauses so that they clearly express the intent of the parties and that the various clauses work with each other rather than against each other.

For instance, one judge remarked in a case where a Centrocon arbitration clause was illogically grafted onto another charter party fixed for consecutive voyages, 'The wholesale lifting of common form clauses, without adaptation, from contracts for which they were designed, into other contracts to which they can only be made to apply with difficulty, is constantly occurring in the field of charters and Bills of Lading and does no credit to the art of the chartering broker'.

Some charterers require a 'Duplicate Original Charter Party'. In this case the original should be headed up, 'Original' and the duplicate headed up 'Duplicate Original'. Both should be signed.

Any changes mutually agreed should be expressed in a second document known as an Addendum. It should refer to the original charter party, the date on which the changes were agreed and then clearly set out the changes. This should be signed by both parties in the same way as a Charter Party.

Charter parties should be drawn up by the broker promptly. While one party signs the document, the other should be sent a working copy as soon as possible. The original charter party is usually, though not necessarily, retained by the owner.

SIGNING CHARTER PARTIES AND ADDENDA AS AGENTS

If a Principal authorises the broker to sign the charter party he must sign it in such a way as to show that he is acting as an agent for the Principal and not as a party to the contract. He should also show in detail the source of his authority. For example,

'For Owners/Charterers

By telex/fax authority timed.........dated.......... received from.........

For and on behalf of (Broking Company name)

Signed by Director

As Agents only.'

It is now time to examine in detail the two main types of charter party forms.

6. The Voyage Charter Party; Words, Phrases and Concepts. What is at Stake?

THE VOYAGE CHARTER BASIC CONCEPT

The basic obligations under a voyage charter party are that the charterer provides and loads the cargo. The owner, in turn, carries and delivers the cargo to the discharge port. It involves the utilisation of the vessel's cargo carrying space on a per ton, per cubic metre or lumpsum basis. The terms of the charter party therefore, deal with the efficient carriage of the cargo from load to discharge port, the ship's compliance with all regulations, the time that charterers allow for loading and discharging, the payment of freight etc.. The charter party attempts to define responsibilities, allocate costs and provide mechanisms to solve problems in the event of the unexpected.

Although the issues that are negotiated and described below, can get detailed and complex, it is worth stepping back and reminding oneself of what a voyage charter is all about. The charterer is obliged to provide the agreed cargo, pay the freight and also the demurrage if the agreed laytime is exceeded. The management of the ship, crewing, arranging and payment of bunkers, port charges and appointment of agents are the owner's responsibilities. The safety of the ship and safe navigation is always (and this is true in time charters as well), the responsibility of the Master. It follows that the risk of delay because of weather is also the owner's.

This chapter will address the issues at stake both legally and commercially for owners and charterers regarding the various clauses, words, phrases and concepts and the differences between some of the main charter party types in how they address these issues.

THE SHIP'S DESCRIPTION

In older charter parties, it was common to give the bare essentials of the vessel only; the deadweight, draft, cubic capacity, gear and number of holds and hatches, and maybe not even that. This is no longer the case. As a reflection of this change it is worth comparing the Sugar '77 and Sugar '99 charter parties, clauses 1 and 2. In the twenty two years that separates them, the description, which took up eight lines in 1977, now comprises thirty one. The difference includes the inclusion of a few extra details such as the union purchase capacity of the gear, the last few cargoes and the requirement that the tunnel shaft, if any, has to be floored over. But more importantly, there are four sub clauses whereby the owner has to *'(a) guarantee that the vessel is fully insured for Hull and Machinery risks..... for the duration of the voyage';* who with and how much, *'(b) guarantee that the vessel is fully P and I covered..'* and with whom; *'(c) guarantee that the vessel will not change flag, class, ownership, managers, P and I Club coverage of this charter party without charterers prior consent (d) guarantee that the vessel carries and will do so for the duration of the voyage all certificates and other documentation whatsoever required by her flag, state authorities and/or the authorities at any place of call under this charter party'* and that vessel complies with the ISM Code. The Sugar '99 is the only voyage charter party issued since the ISM's introduction and thus the only one to have it as a printed term. Indeed, it reinforces this new look by a **'Certificates clause'** (Clause 35) which says, *'If required by Charterers, Owners undertake to issue or otherwise supply, any letters or certificates in connection with vessel's classification, registration, age, flag, gear, details of vessel's entry* *into P and I Club or any other certificates required by Charterers'*. In other charter parties it is usually the subject of a rider clause, sometimes very extensive.

It is normal for a port or jetty which is solely used for one bulk commodity to have its own rules and regulations, for example, the Richards Bay Coal Terminal Regulations. It is usual therefore for the charterer to add a rider clause which requires the vessel to comply with the **regulations of the port**. Some charterers require that a copy of them is attached to the charter party. This is unnecessary. A simple clause could, and sometimes does say, 'The vessel shall comply with the Port Regulations and any amendments will automatically apply and form part of this contract'.

Many grain charter party rider clauses now reserve the right to physically inspect the vessel at any time before loading (where convenient). On grain COA's charterers also reserve the right to refuse the nomination of a vessel by reason of head ownership and trading history, for example, recent arrests, failure to pay creditors etc. in order to avoid potential problems. Many rider clauses in these charter parties, are prefaced with the words, 'Owners warrant that.....'. Failure to comply with any of the warranties gives the charterer the right to deduct from the freight the charterer's estimated and actual losses (including threat to commodity sale).

Some charterers also go into great detail about the **suitablity** of the ship for the voyage or trade including **Oil Pollution responsibility** and **P and I coverage.** The following is a particularly stringent example.

> 'Vessel shall be in every way suitable for the transport of the cargo with hull, machinery and equipment in a thoroughly efficient state with all necessary certificates, records and documents and permissions for such

transport. The vessel shall comply with all governmental regulations applicable to vessels engaged in such transport including, but not limited to, regulations concerning the environment including certificate of financial responsibility relating to oil pollution, longshoring, cargo gear and equipment on board. If any work is not permitted due to failure of the vessel to comply with such regulations, or its country of registry or nationality of crew, any delays and or expenses to charterers resulting therefrom shall be for owner's account.

The vessel shall be classed and maintained in class 100A1 with Lloyds Register of Shipping or equivalent class by an IACS member classification Society and not scheduled for break up after completion of the voyage. Vessel to be insured for not less than its full commercial value with Lloyd's underwriters or other first class underwriters or insurance companies of at least similar reputation and standing. In addition, performing vessel to maintain Protection and Indemnity (P and I) cover save in the highest amount generally obtained by first class prudent owners of fleets of vessels of similar type, size, age, trade, purpose and flag as performing vessel with a Protection and Indemnity Club which is a member of the International Group of Protection and Indemnity Clubs. Any expenses to charterers resulting from vessel not maintaining class or insurance shall be for owner's account. The vessel is suitable for grab discharge. The vessel is a gearless single deck self trimming bulk carrier with bridge and machinery aft. Owners warrant vessel has not called Cuba or North Vietnam. Vessel may be rejected for loading if the vertical distance from the waterline to the top of the highest hatch coaming exceeds..... at any time while alongside the loading berth. Any extra insurance due to vessel's class, ownership, age shall be for owner's account. Owners acknowledge and warrant that the vessel shall comply with all port regulations at the ports covered in this charter party. Vessels shall be fully suitable in characteristics and dimensions for all ports covered by this charter party'. (Compare 'Description' in Chapter Seven).

An **ISM Clause** is now fairly standard in both voyage and time charter parties after the ISM Code came into operation on the 1st July 1998. The **"International Code for Safety Management and Pollution" (ISM Code)** not only requires good management in matters of safety and seaworthiness. It requires the owner to prove he has undertaken a series of detailed safety related measures. The clause often states something like;

"The requirements of the International Safety Management (ISM) Code are hereby incorporated into the terms of the charter party. Owners warrant that a safety management system in accordance with the ISM Code is in operation both on shore and on board the vessel and that they possess a valid Safety Management Certificate (SMC). Owners shall supply charterers with a copy of the SMC and when required by charterers, owners shall provide a report of safety audits carried out internally or by the vessel's flag administration. Non compliance with the requirements of the ISM Code shall be deemed a breach of the charter party."

The BIMCO ISM Clause is;

"From the date of coming into force of the International Safety Management (ISM) Code in relation to the Vessel and thereafter during the currency of this charter party, the owners shall procure that both the Vessel and 'the Company' (as defined by the ISM Code) shall comply with the requirements of the ISM Code. Upon request the Owners shall provide a copy of the relevant Document of Compliance (DOC) and Safety Management Certificate (SMC) to the Charterers. Except otherwise as provided in this charter party, loss, damage, expense or delay caused by

> failure on the part of the owners or 'the Company' to comply with the ISM Code shall be for the Owner's account."

In general, time charter parties have far more extensive description clauses as the charterer is taking on the responsibility for running and paying for the whole ship, not just renting the carrying capacity. However, it is perfectly legitimate to have rider clauses covering the description of the ship referring to its ability to safely carry the cargo as agreed. A grab discharge clause is perhaps the most common. On bulk carriers it may be no more than a single sentence guaranteeing that the ship is suitable for grab discharge. The Amwelsh '79 (clause 19) instead simply says, 'No cargo is to be loaded in deeptanks or similar places in accessible by reach by grabs' and the '93 version (clause 23) updates it to, 'No cargo shall be loaded in any cargo compartment inaccessible to reach by grabs'.

For a tweendeck vessel it may well be much more extensive. A typical example would be as follows;

> "Owners guarantee that the vessel is suitable for grab discharge. No cargo is to be loaded in tweendecks, deeptanks, ballast tanks or other places inaccessible to grabs. Any extra expenses incurred for discharging from places not accessible to grabs for owner's account and time not to count. Any deeptanks, shaft tunnels or other projections to be adequately protected against grab damage. Wooden ceilings to be in adequate condition for grab discharge. Any cargo battens, tweendeck hatch covers and hatch beams to be removed from holds and stowed away from loading and discharging gear".

Occasionally, a clause will require the ship to have at all times a safe, secure and accessible gangway from the jetty to the ship. In default of this, loading and discharging operations may be stopped and time not to count.

A questionnaire is sometimes attatched to the charter party which includes all relevant tonnages, distances, and measurements, the P and I Club and insurance details etc. It may also specify that the Master and key officers speak English.

For certain trades, an **ITF or ITWF** clause may also be necessary, obligating the owner to provide a ship, manned with a crew complying with the requirements of the **International Transport Workers Federation.** It will provide that should it be delayed due to non compliance or lack of the certificate to prove compliance, the owner is to be responsible for the consequences. A comprehensive example is, "Owner confirms that all officers and crew are employed under an agreement recognised by the ITWF. The vessel has a valid ITWF (Blue Card) on board (No -------). Owners are responsible for any time lost and damages resulting from work stoppage due to the interference of labour organisation, whether directly or indirectly incurred, due to the vessel's flag or her country of registration and/or the terms and conditions under which the crew of the vessel is employed or for claims resulting from the vessel's previous employment or another vessel managed by the owners".

SEAWORTHINESS

The words, *'tight staunch and strong and in every way fit for the voyage'*, (Clause 1 of the Amwelsh, Norgrain and Synacomex), and *'in every respect fitted for the voyage'* (Riodoceore), imply and warrant seaworthiness. These phrases not only mean that the ship is safe to put out to sea but that all its machinery and equipment work efficiently, that bulkheads are not cracked, that all weather deck and hull openings such as hatches, doors and ramps have been tightly secured with seals etc. and are maintained in good order and that no faults on the ship will interfere with its efficient prosecution of the voyage or trip. These are standard wordings and are never changed. In any event, the ship owner has common law and statutory duty regarding seaworthiness. There are also obligations in the 'Carriage of Goods by Sea Act' which are usually incorporated into the charter party by means of a Clause Paramount. (For a full discussion on the issues see Chapter Eight).

The Act does not, however, give a guarantee or warranty of seaworthiness. Under the Act the owner only undertakes to '*exercise due diligence*'. It is expressed in the Ferticon '74 and at length in the Norgrain '89 (Clause 36) which states that the owner should '*exercise due diligence to make the ship seaworthy and to have her properly manned, equipped and supplied and neither the vessel nor the master shall be held liable for any loss or damage or delay to the cargo for causes excepted by US Carriage of Goods by Sea Act 1936 or the Canadian Carriage of Goods by Water Act 1970, or any statutory re-enactment thereof*'.

The importance of seaworthiness is fundamental as the most important obligation of a carrier is to deliver the cargo in the same condition as it was received.

Full consideration must also therefore be given to the stowage of the cargo, load distribution, separations and securing, that might effect seaworthiness just as much as the hull, machinery and equipment. The Gencon '76 (Clause 2) states, *'Owners are to be responsible for loss of or damage to the goods or for delay in delivery of the goods only in case the loss, damage or delay has been caused by the improper or negligent stowage of the goods....... or by personal want of due diligence on the part of the owners or their managers to make the vessel in all respects seaworthy and to secure that she is properly manned, equipped and supplied, or by the personal act or default of the owners or their manager'*. Often an insertion is made here to make the responsibility crystal clear. 'Owners and Master to be responsible for proper stowage'. This then would over ride the continuation of clause 2 which says that the owners are not responsible for loss or damage from other causes that would come under the term 'seaworthiness'. It continues, *'Damage caused by contact with or leakage, smell or evaporation from other goods or by the inflammable or explosive nature or insufficient package of other goods not to be considered as caused by improper or negligent stowage even if in fact so caused.'* This is sometimes deleted and when the implications for the charterers are considered it is hardly surprising. Other charter parties dealing with bulk cargoes do not usually have such clauses dealing with break bulk cargo. Further comments on the extent of the Master's and the charterer's responsibility will be found in this Chapter under 'Stevedores and the Loading/Discharging Clause' and in Chapter Seven under 'Loading, stowing, dunnaging'. It is one of the most contentious and debated points in chartering.

THE SHIP'S POSITION

A lazy, but unfortunately common way of describing this in the preamble of the Amwelsh, where after the word '*now*', the blank space which should be for the position of the ship, is often left blank or filled in with the words, 'now trading' or 'now trading', ETA 20th November'. This should be avoided. If the vessel is not trading but in dry dock or repairing, it is not accurate. Under certain circumstances it could be construed as a breach of charter party. A claim for damages could result if the vessel is delayed and proven damages sustained because of an unrealistic ETA based on a false declaration of '*trading*' rather than 'repairing' for example. It is better to specify the full itinerary, for instance, 'now discharging Tokyo Bay with current ETS 15th November with ETA load port 22nd November, all going well', or 'now drydocking in Singapore with ETS 19th September and ETA loadport 20th September', as the case may be. The charterer will be informed as to the exact position while not harming the owner who gives the position as advice and a warranty. The only reason the owner may not want to be precise on the position is if he wants to misrepresent it but it is much more likely that the charter party is drawn up in a sloppy fashion by the broker. The same principal goes for the Gencon, (Boxes 8 and 9) and any rider clauses giving the itinerary. In case of contracts of affreightment this space can be left blank, as positions will be covered in a nomination clause incorporated in the rider clauses.

SAFE BERTH/PORT

The charter party will often provide that the charterer may load or discharge the vessel at a named port or sometimes an unnamed port within a geographical range. As a result the owner must seek protection against the charterer nominating a port or berth which the vessel cannot physically enter or where for some reason, the vessel might be prevented from loading or discharging. (See also Lightening/Lighterage). General criterion of 'safe' port or berth is that the vessel can enter, use it and leave it safely and is free from any danger which could be avoided by good navigation and seamanship. The port should have general aids, tugs and pilots where the port warrants such assistance. The port, however, would not be unsafe because of some temporary danger or difficulty such as a period of low tides. The port may be 'safe' for some ships but not others. For instance, a larger ship than is usual at a port may need additional tugs which the port does not have. This may make it unsafe for her but not for other smaller vessels.

The fact that the charterer must nominate a safe berth and port does not relieve the owner and Master from their responsibility to ascertain the safety of a port for their vessel and to take proper action to avoid endangering the vessel. If the charter party names a port or berth without the words 'safe', this places upon the owners the burden of ensuring that the vessel can load and discharge at that named port/berth. It is not unusual for the owner to agree this if he is familiar with the berth or port. The charter party form will not always provide the word 'safe' and leave the space blank for whatever the parties mutually agree.

ALWAYS AFLOAT

Owners will often ask or even insist that at the load/discharge port, that the vessel lies 'always afloat'. This means that no part of the hull or keel touches the bottom while at the berth or in the port. However, some ports need the owner to agree **'safe aground'**. The Synacomex '90 has the option, one of which has to be deleted. This means that at low tide the vessel will sit on flat mud. An example are the up river ports in the River Plate. It is not deemed 'safe' if the ground is rocky and is liable to damage the hull of the ship. **NAABSA (not always afloat but safe aground)** is the main term abbreviation which covers this provision.

'WITH ALL POSSIBLE DISPATCH'

This wording from the Amwelsh '79 which describes how the ship will sail to the load and discharge port is slightly different from the Norgrain, Synacomex, Riodoceore and Amwelsh '93 which states that she must proceed, **'with all convenient speed'.** Variations in other charter party forms include **'all possible speed'** or **'all reasonable speed'.** The use of the words, 'all possible' has implications, especially in low markets, to the saving of fuel costs by operating at reduced speeds. In high markets the owners will probably want to perform the voyage as quickly as possible as fuel costs will be a minor concern in relation to the revenue from freight rates. In low markets fuel costs tend to become increasingly important. The exact relationships will depend on the price of fuel. If the charter party wording does say 'all possible', owners should either seek to negotiate 'all convenient' or obtain the charterer's permission before instructing the vessel to proceed at less than 'all possible' speed. Otherwise this could lead to disputes. If the speed of the voyage is important it is recommended that charterers deal with this issue specifically. Otherwise the use of 'all convenient speed' is fair to both parties.

NOTICES AND LOADING/DISCHARGING PORT ORDERS

Older charter parties will refer to the **sailing telegram** but this clause in whatever form, will cover the notices the Master must give to the load and discharge port, the charterer and possibly other parties. The point is that the charterer and relevant authorities must be aware of the position of the ship in order to get the cargo ready, to prepare for discharge, to plan berth schedules in busy ports etc.. Owners usually agree to what charterers reasonably require to efficiently effect their business.

The authors of the new Sugar '99, however, seem to have got rather carried away in clauses 12 and 20. For instance, the words, *'owners to be responsible for all consequences and damages of whatsoever nature and howsoever arising in the event of owner's or master's failure to keep charterers fully informed of any change in the ship's position prior to loading,'* is a wording which gives a licence to the charterer to make claims for changes of only a few hours. This kind of delay can easily occur in bad weather or adverse currents. It seems unnecessarily onerous when the owner has the obligation of keeping the charterer constantly informed and specifically if the ship is delayed for more than 24 hours. Furthermore, the charterer has the option, unique in a voyage charter party, in clause 24, of placing a tracking device on the ship. There is more than a whiff of overkill in this clause, bearing in mind what the charterer reasonably needs.

'OR SO NEAR THERETO AS SHE CAN SAFELY GET'

This is often added to the standard wording, which says that the vessel has to proceed to a named port. It applies if access to the port is initially prevented but within a reasonable period of time access will be permitted. This will apply for instance if there is congestion or a low tide and the ship has to wait outside the port. What is reasonable must be decided by commercial considerations, the nature of the voyage the ship is to perform and the interests of both the parties. Whether the place is sufficiently 'near thereto' is decided by whether both parties would consider, as reasonable persons, to be in a proximity of the place she is required to proceed.

Owners will often ask for the words **'always accessible'** after the named port. This is partly an alternative but is more comprehensive in terms of access.

'ARRIVED SHIP'

The issues involved in 'or so near to as she can safely get' described above, also can relate to the legal question of what is an 'arrived ship'. In the case of a **berth charter party** (that is one which specifies the destination as a specific berth rather than and unnamed berth in a specified port) it does not become arrived until she is at the berth. Laytime therefore begins to run once she is ready to load and a valid **Notice of Readiness** is given to the charterer according to the provisions of the charter party. Therefore, any time lost before the vessel can get to the berth is borne by the owner unless there is provision to the contrary.

Under a **port charter party,** (one which specifies the destination as a port or range of ports) delay in berthing would normally be for the account of the charterer. Additional phrases are often requested by owners to clarify that time counts when the ship is ready to load or discharge rather than when the port is ready to load or discharge the ship. A series of contradictory legal cases in the USA and UK as to when a vessel is an 'arrived ship' is the cause. The issues that have been debated in the courts are; whether the ship is within the 'commercial area of the port'; what is the definition of 'commercial area of the port', whether an anchorage outside the port counts if it is regularly used or is in a queue for a berth and therefore subject to port authority control etc..

A modern rider clause to an old charter party will therefore set out in great detail the circumstances under which a Notice of Readiness (See below) may be given. More modern charter parties such as the Norgrain '73 (Clause 17b), the Norgrain '89 (Clause 18b), the Synacomex '90, the Sugar '99 (Clause 19) and the Amwelsh '93 (Clause 6b) provide detailed wording. There is no provision in the printed form of older charter parties, which is why it is normally addressed in detail in the rider clauses. In tailor made, modern, private forms it is usually dealt with in detail. It is often agreed that time counts 'on arrival at or off the port'.

NOTICE OF READINESS (NOR)

The purpose of a Notice of Readiness from a ship is to inform the shippers or receivers that the vessel is ready to load or discharge. The laytime for loading (or discharging) will not start to run until the owner has given notice as required by the charter party. It does not need to be accepted to be valid, unless it is specifically stipulated. It is usually an uncontentious issue and NOR's can usually be given in writing by telex or cable. The charter party should stipulate whether the NOR should be tendered in office hours, on weekdays only, or can be tendered at any time. The shorthand chartering term for this is **Shex Notices** and **Shinc Notices.** It is perfectly possible to have Shinc laytime but Shex notices.

A clarification often asked for by the owner in giving the NOR is the addition, **'whether in port or not, whether in berth or not, whether in free pratique or not, whether customs cleared or not'**. This is usually referred to in the main terms as **WIPON / WIBON/ WIFPON/ WCCON**. It refers either to how notices are given or when laytime starts. It means that if the ship is waiting for a berth and is in every respect ready to load or discharge, but is prevented from doing so or even entering the port, laytime will still commence as per the above stipulations, even if she has not cleared customs or got free pratique.

Pratique is the permission from the port's health authorities for a ship to use the port. The officers and crew must be free from symptoms of infectious disease. Before the ship arrives the agent will report to the port's health officer on the Master's behalf that the ship is healthy. He will then permit the agents to transmit **'free pratique'** by radio to the ship. When the ship arrives at the port the Master will confirm the agent's declaration. However, if the vessel is not found to be in free pratique, an appropriately worded charter party may well stipulate that time does not count.

Very often a charterer will stipulate that if a vessel fails to clear customs or pratique, which is therefore a fault of the ship, then time will not count from time of failing to the time she passes. This is likely to be a contentious issue if this does arise, as when she does finally pass, another vessel may well have berthed preventing her from loading/discharging. Charterers obviously then may find it unfair that they have to pay for waiting time that was the fault of the ship. In order to obviate this, the charterer may therefore require that time will not count from time of failing until she is actually at the berth to commence loading/discharging. The stipulation that time will not count until she is '*in all respects ready to load*' is not the same thing if she cannot berth due to another ship occupying the berth.

TIME COMMENCING AFTER NOR AND TURN TIME

If a vessel is fixed for laydays of, for example, the 20th but arrives on the 18th, she can tender NOR on the 18th but laytime would not start until 0001 hours on the 20th unless the charterer wished to commence loading earlier and by mutual agreement they agreed on an earlier commencement. If the charterer wants specific protection there may be a stipulation in the charter party that NOR could not be tendered until 0001 hours on the first day of the laydays.

When time starts after NOR, however, often differs. The Gencon provides that laytime commences *'at 1 p.m. if notice of readiness is given before noon and at 6 am next working day if given during office hours.'* The Amwelsh provides for **'Turn Time'**. Although it is not called that in the main body of the charter party, it is referred to as such in the main terms negotiations. It is the number of hours after which laytime starts. It can be anything from 6 to 24 hours and is referred to in lines 28 of the Amwelsh '53, line 27 of the '79 version and lines 62/63 of the Amwelsh '93. Its origin is in the time permitted for the charterer to make the necessary arrangements to prepare the ship for loading/discharging. If the charterer was able to make those arrangements faster then laytime would start earlier. It was therefore usually accompanied by the phrase, **'unless sooner commenced'** or **'unless used'.** If sooner commenced, a further addition is that 'actual time used to count' or 'half time used to count'. Some charterers, however, ask for turn time whether sooner commenced or not or **'even if used'**. Owners will probably calculate the extra time into their calculation whatever the terms and if 'unless sooner commenced', will deem it a bonus if time commences earlier. Charterers should therefore think carefully about the need and financial wisdom of this particular clause and its variations.

LAYTIME

Laytime is an agreed period of time, expressed in hours or days, in which the charterer undertakes to load and discharge the vessel. It is triggered by the Notice of Readiness.

Recent promotional material, advertising computer laytime calculation software proclaimed, 'Laytime calculations are one of the most laborious, objectionable and time consuming tasks people in the shipping world have to cope with. But on the other hand, accurate laytime calculation can save a lot of money'. This is a pretty good way to grab the reader's attention as a prelude to promoting their software. But there is also a great deal of truth in it if the laytime excludes various periods in varying circumstances. Most of the time, however, it is fairly straightforward.

Laytime may be **reversible**, which means that time not used at the loading port can be used at the discharging port or **non reversible** which means that it cannot be and must be calculated separately. If reversible is required it should be stated as the standard clauses of charter parties treat them as separate or non reversible.

The laytime will typically be either **Shex** or **Shinc** or **Fhex** or **Fhinc.** That is shorthand for **'Sundays and Holidays excluded'**, **'Sundays and holidays included'** and for predominantly Muslim countries, **'Fridays and holidays excluded'** and **'Fridays and holidays included'**. Occasionally Saturdays will also be excluded **(SSHEX** or **SATSHEX** or **Saturday afternoon (SATPMSHEX))** or from Friday evening to Monday morning such as '1700 Friday preceding a holiday to 0800 Monday or the day following a holiday excluded'. The exact times will vary according to the custom of the port. Thursday afternoon in Muslim countries may similarly be excluded. (**TAFHEX or TPMFHEX**) This is self explanatory but the Shex or Fhex will often be qualified by **'Even if used'** or **'Unless used'** or **'unless sooner commenced'**. This obviously refers to how the laytime is calculated and if the ship is worked even in an excluded period. A further qualification that is often used is to add **'unless used when only half time actually used to count'**.

Laytime is usually fixed by reference to certain days, **running days, working days**, **weather working days, 'days of 24 hours', or '24 consecutive hours'.** Often, however, laytime is fixed by reference to a quantity of cargo per day or weather working day etc.. Sometimes further qualifications are used such as 'at the average rate of' or **'tons per hatch day'** or **'per workable hatch'**.

In the case of self dischargers or belt self unloaders it may be termed **'as fast as can deliver'**, or **'as fast as can'.** In this case it is usually necessary for the charterer to guarantee a minimum **take-away** speed. If a self discharging panamax, for instance, can discharge at her maximum speed at an average of 20,000 SHINC per day but the on-shore conveyors can only take the cargo away at an average of 10,000 per day, it is obviously the latter figure that governs the maximum discharge speed.

'Working day of 24 hours' or 'working day of 24 consecutive hours' are important distinctions as 'consecutive hours' works in favour of the owners when the port does not work consecutive hours and normally has break times. This is increasingly rare, especially for modern ports handling large volumes of bulk commodities.

It is advisable when describing loading or discharging rates, to use the phrase, the **'average rate of',** as ships will be loaded and discharged at different daily rates during the course of a loading or discharging operation lasting several days. It is particularly true of discharging bulk cargo where an unloader is able to achieve very high discharging rates, 'creaming' cargo from the top, but slowing down appreciably when remaining cargo is lying at the bottom and sides of the holds. Thus a cargo which may have achieved a discharging rate of 40,000 tons in the first day may well slow down to less than 5,000 in the last day as bulldozers collect the cargo from the furthest reaches of the holds and bulldoze it to the centre for the unloader to discharge it. It would be fairly typical to have a charter party speed specifying an 'average' discharging rate on which laytime is calculated. All this may appear to be obvious and unnecessary but arbitrations have been held on the lack of such a simple and obvious word. Perhaps the most comprehensive and satisfactory wording is, 'For the purpose of calculating laytime, the cargo as described in the Bills of Lading shall be deemed to be loaded/discharged at the average rate of.........'. This defines the purpose of describing the rate of cargo loaded in one day (i.e. for calculating laytime) and obviates any pedantic owner's claim if, in fact, the cargo is discharged slower on some of the days.

Clause 6 of the Gencon '76 and '94 provides for the cargo to be loaded and or discharged, *'within the number of running hours as indicated in..... weather permitting, Sundays and holidays excepted, unless used in which event time actually used shall count'*. Normally the charterer will determine the terms based on his experience with the cargo, port, stevedores and equipment. The owners may seek to clarify them if they find them imprecise. The terms agreed will be inserted into the charter party's main body.

Terms and phrases used in these clauses have been subject to varying interpretations. In many legal systems **'weather permitting'** and **'weather working day'** have been given the same meaning but English law has always made a distinction. 'Weather permitting' means interrupting laytime if weather actually prevents work while 'weather working day' qualifies the length of laytime and prevents laytime from running if the weather would not have permitted work even if no work was intended, planned or possible. This is both clearer and also more favourable to the charterers. If, for instance, a vessel is waiting at an anchorage due to congestion and laytime has commenced, it can be stopped if there is rain that would have stopped the loading or discharging of the vessel, even though no loading or discharging could take place. If the vessel is already on demurrage, however time continues. See 'Demurrage' below.

In a 1983 case, a judge's summing up appeared to give 'weather permitting' the same meaning as the traditional meaning of 'weather working day'. However, although commented upon at the time, it seems to have had no affect, since in practical terms, owners and charterers are still agreeing laytime statements on the basis of the traditional interpretation and chartering is conducted on the traditional assumptions. It is therefore advisable for a charterer to continue to use 'weather working day' and the owner to try and get 'weather permitting' if there is a risk of congestion at a rainy time of the year. The Amwelsh '93 has broken with Amwelsh tradition in using 'weather permitting' instead of 'weather working day'. The Gencon '76, Synacomex '90 and Norgrain '89 use 'weather permitting' and the Sugar '77 and '99 'weather working day'.

Complications in laytime calculation can arise when the laytime period is fixed by reference to the number of working or **workable hatches**. English courts have construed that a hatch ceases to be workable once it becomes full on loading or empty on discharge thus differentiating **'per workable hatch day'** from **'per hatch day'**. Thus under 'per workable hatch day', the rate of loading or discharge reduces as loading/discharging continues. However, this type of wording is a rich source of disputes.

Imagine holds of different sizes with different loading or discharging rates at each hatch due to one gang at one hatch and two at another, for example.

Some holds will therefore be completed a long time before others. It will therefore be appreciated that 'per hatch day' is more advantageous for owners than 'per workable hatch day'.

'Workable hatch', as has been explained above, means that there must be cargo in the hold below. It does not refer to the crane or derrick above it. This means that in the case of a vessel with 4 cranes and 5 hatches which self loads or discharges, laytime is calculated on the 5 hatches that have cargo in the holds below, not 4 hatches that are being worked by the 4 cranes. '**Available**' can also be defined as 'workable'. These phrases can be summarised as follows;

Per hatch day laytime = $\frac{\text{Quantity of cargo}}{\text{Daily rate x number of hatches}}$

Per workable hatch day laytime = $\frac{\text{Largest quantity in one hold}}{\text{Daily rate per hatch x number of hatches serving that hold}}$

Some charter parties contain provisions requiring waiting time to be counted as laytime even though the ship is not at the berth. Clause 6©of the Gencon provides that, *'time lost in waiting for berth to count as loading or discharging time, as the case may be'*. Laytime provisions apply to waiting time. In other words, 'Sundays and holidays' in a Shex charter party or bad weather in 'weather working days' qualify waiting time. Owners will usually ask for the **WIBON, WIPON, WIFPON, WCCON** provisions discussed in 'Notice of Readiness' above to cover themselves. Some charter parties will specify that time used in shifting from anchorage to berth or between berths is not to count as laytime, and whose expense it should be.

Some ports have their own Scale load rate which applies in all cases. Richards Bay, for example, has a scale applicable for minimum 25,000 to over 140,000 cargo in thirteen stages. The Polcoalvoy charter party also has set loading scales from alternative Polish coal ports.

As can be appreciated, owners and charterers will attempt to calculate laytime most advantageously to themselves. Thus the wording of laytime clauses must be as clear as possible.

Some rider clauses will specify time limits for when laytime statements and demurrage and despatch statements shall be submitted, agreed and paid. Usually supporting documentation is requested to verify the laytime statements.

FREIGHT

Freight is the consideration paid by a charterer to the owner for the carriage of a cargo by an owner's ship. How freight is to be paid, when and by whom will be specified in the charter party. Usual terms would typically be, for instance:

1. Payable on signing and releasing Bills of Lading.

2. 90 percent payable 5 days after signing and releasing Bills of Lading. Balance within 30 days after discharge with demurrage/despatch calculation/settlement.

3. Payable before breaking bulk, (B.B.B.) i.e. before commencement of discharging.

It should be noted that the number of days after which freight will be paid may be qualified. The words **'banking days'**, **'working days'** or **'running days'** may be used. They refer to the type of days in the country from which the freight is being paid and will exclude holidays and weekends if 'working' or 'banking' is used, but not if 'running', which means continuous, is used. It is an important distinction for the owner's cash flow. 10 banking days could really mean 14 running days, or even more in case of holiday periods. It may mean, in extreme cases, that the vessel will arrive at the discharge port before the freight is due. If this is a danger, owners should try to include the words, **'but in any case, before breaking bulk'.** Another slight variation is, **'upon right and true delivery'**. This is ambiguous but implies at the time of discharge. In this case, the right of **lien** is a great deal harder to exercise in practice. (See Cesser Clause, below).

On the day freight is **'payable'** it should have been received in the owner's bank. In other words, the charterer should have instructed his bank to remit the freight well before the due date. Understandably, owners tend to get very upset if there are delays. If a charterer gets a reputation for delaying freight it tends to mean that when an owner is faced with a choice between a charterer with a good reputation and one with a bad reputation regarding freight payment, that they will choose the charterer who pays on time. In other words, the charterer who performs badly ends up paying for it in the end in some intangible way.

The charterer cannot, unless there is a specific agreement otherwise, withhold all or part of the freight because the quantity delivered is less than what is stated on the Bill of Lading or because the cargo is damaged or contaminated. If there is a loss of cargo, the aggrieved party must claim damages, not withold freight.

The method of freight payment is usually specified **'free in and out trimmed'** or **FIOT.** Alternatives are **FIOSpT** or **'free in and out spout trimmed'** and **FIOST** or **'free in and out stowed and trimmed'.** This means that the cost of loading and discharging is free to the owner who pays the port charges only. This is to differentiate if from liner or gross terms where they pay both. Sometimes it is expressed as, 'Freight in full of all port charges, pilotages, consular fees, light duties, trimming, lighterage at loading/discharging ports', which means that the owner pays the port charges and other expenses specified.

Freight is usually calculated and **'paid on the Bill of Lading weight'**. Occasionally there maybe variations on this. The Riodoceore charter party for example stipulates that the freight is paid on *'out turn weight or in case of non weighing at port of discharge, Bill of Lading weight less....... percent.'* Main term negotiations for iron ore that retain this term usually state, '.......percent **ILOW'**, meaning **'in lieu of weighing'**. Typically it may be anything from 0.5 percent to 1 percent. The owner will invariably factor this into his calculation of freight. Thus, charterers must weigh carefully the arguments for and against the practice. On the one hand it is likely that if the cargo is loaded wet that during the voyage she will lose some moisture and therefore weight. On the other hand they will probably have to pay for more onerous terms in a slightly higher freight rate. This is yet another charter party clause which is often changed these days to reflect payment on the Bill of Lading weight. The Symacomex '90 stipulates payment *'on nett Bill of Lading weight less 0.50 percent.'* The Amwelsh charter parties, even the '93, still has the freight being paid, *'in accordance with the dock or railway weight'*, which is hardly ever the case in practice and is almost always changed to reflect payment on the Bill of Lading weight. It is curious that the Amwelsh '93 which has changed so much else, has failed to change this outdated term.

In some cases the freight may be paid on a **lumpsum** basis. In this case it is up to the charterer to utilise the deadweight and cubic capacity of the ship and load as much cargo as possible. In effect, it shifts responsibility of maximising the cargo from the owners to the charterers. This method is often employed when a mixture of cargoes is to be loaded. The charterer will have to be given individual hold cubics and even the dimensions of the holds depending on the nature of the cargo.

Usually there is a clause which states that freight is **'deemed earned on shipment, ship and or cargo lost or not lost',** even though it is actually paid somewhat later. A variation of this wording is, **'the freight shall be deemed earned as cargo is loaded on board and shall be discountless and non returnable vessel and or cargo lost or not lost'.** This clause places the freight risk upon the charterer by making the freight earned and payable irrespective of carriage and delivery of the cargo. It is therefore wise for the charterer to take out insurance on both the cargo and freight. The new Sugar '99, however, states that estimated freight (less commission, estimated loading despatch and extra insurance) is paid within 7 days of sailing from loadport but that freight is deemed earned, on *'safe arrival of the vessel and right and true delivery of the cargo at destination'*. The implication is that if anything happens to ship and cargo between payment and delivery, the owner must pay it back. The owner will therefore have to insure against this eventuality instead of the charterer. In the grain trades, Andre have also required *'freight deemed earned on safe delivery of cargo'*. In a low market charterers have such leverage over owners. In a fast and upward moving market it would seem that while arguing about this small matter, the more important matter of fixing the freight is delayed, usually a bad thing for charterers in a bull market. Charterers will no doubt decide whether it is worth insisting on this.

This Sugar '99 clause also departs from the norm by stating, *'owners to advise their New York corresponding bank, otherwise charterers not to be responsible for late receipt of freight by owners'*. This is to protect charterers from delays of receipt of freight by owners when paid on time due to the well known delays that can occur in the transfer of U.S. Dollars via New York banks. It is a novel, but perhaps not totally illogical or onerous term and indeed may have some merit if it helps prevent the inconvenience of late payments due solely to banking delays.

Some countries impose **taxes on freight**. This is usually the subject of a rider clause allocating which party has the responsibility to pay it. It will usually say 'Freight and cargo taxes to be for charterer's account'. This is because it is the receiver, or importer, who is ultimately liable to pay the tax. The Synacomex '90 says, in the main body *'All charges and dues levied on the cargo shall be for charterer's account and those levid on the vessel for owner's account'*. However, if this is not the subject of a specific clause, the implication is that the owner will have to pay as it is a tax on the remuneration that he has received. It is therefore advisable for owners to cover this point specifically if the vessel is liable to call at a port in a country where it is applicable. BIMCO publishes a handbook on freight taxes to advise the latest situation country by country so owners can be better informed when calculating and negotiating their vessels's employment. Some nations have bi-lateral agreements exempting ships owned or managed in their countries. The Sugar '99 has a new extensive clause (Clause 8) allocating specific taxes in nine countries. For instance, for Brazil it reads; *'Brazilian Merchant Marine Renewal Tax, Quota da Provedencia, Contribuicao da Uniao and Port Utilisation tax to be for shipper's account. All other customary taxes and/or dues on the vessel to be for owner's account'*.

Deadfreight is the freight on cargo agreed by charterers to be loaded but not actually loaded. If the charterer fails to load what he has agreed to load despite the ship having the space and deadweight to load it, he must pay freight as if he had loaded it.

REGULAR TURN

That the vessel shall be loaded in regular turn, is specified in the Riodoceore but not in general in other charter parties and not in this charter party for the discharge port. It can be an important point at some steel mills which may need a particular product when ordering on a 'just in time' basis. It can happen that a ship arriving first has to wait for a later ship which berths first for this reason. It might also happen that on a high market a vessel nominated under a contract of affreightment has a much lower demurrage rate and the charterers keep it waiting rather than incur the higher demurrage penalty. If this happens an owner may lose the next business. For most industries it is not an issue, as unless there are special circumstances it is in the charterer's interest to load and discharge the ships as they arrive.

LAYDAYS/CANCELLING (LAYCAN)

This is the stipulated span of days, the first day of which the charterer is obliged to accept the ship if presented for loading and the earliest day the owner can demand loading to be commenced. The time on the first day is sometimes specified. In the Norgrains for example '0800' is stated. The Amwelshes have said '9 am' until the Amwelsh '93 changed it to '0800' hours.

The last day of the laydays is the cancelling date. If the vessel has not arrived at the place required by the charterer within that date, the charterer has the right to cancel the charter party. The Norgrains specify a time of '1200 hours' on the cancelling date as the last time the vessel can be delivered and the Amwelshes, '9 am' except the Amwelsh '93 which states '1700 hours'. These times are often amended during negotiations. Rather perversely, the Riodoceore mentions the cancelling date prior to the laydays. The Norgrain and Amwelshes more logically put the same issue in the same clause (Clause 4 in the Norgrain, Clause 15 in the Amwelsh '79 and Clause 5 in the

Amwelsh '93). The box layout of the Gencon should make this easy. But even the Gencon '94 has a box (21) for cancelling, ETA (9) and present position (8) but not for commencement of the laydays. Nor is this mentioned in the printed form, necessitating a rider clause on an essential point.

If the vessel is ready earlier than the laydays, the charterer is not bound to use the ship before the commencement date and time. If he wishes to do so, however, he may by mutual agreement at the time. Occasionally, a clause stating that 'time actually used before commencement of laytime shall count' is used, or better still, 'Provided charterers consent to loading before laydays commence, any such time actually used shall count against laytime'.

The charterer, under most charter parties, is under no obligation prior to the time when the option to cancel arises, to declare to the owners whether or not the charterer will cancel the vessel. The vessel must therefore proceed to the loading place whether or not she is badly delayed or not until the charterers declare one way or the other whether she is cancelled or continued. An extension to the cancelling date may be negotiated and if agreed will be covered by an Addendum to the charter party.

However, the Gencon '76 gives the owner the right, in case the vessel is not *'ready to load on or before the date,'* to demand whether or not charterers cancel '*at least 48 hours before the vessel's expected arrival at the port of loading'*. The Gencon '94 goes a stage further. Clause 9(b) says, 'S*hould the owners anticipate that the vessel will not be ready to load by the cancelling date, they should notify the charterers thereof without delay stating the expected date of the vessel's readiness to load and asking whether the charterers will exercise their option of cancelling the charter party or agree to a new cancelling date. Such option must be declared by the charterers within 48 running hours after the receipt of owner's notice. If the charterers do not exercise their option of cancelling then this charter party shall be* *deemed amended such that the seventh day after the new readiness date stated in the owner's notification to the charterers shall be the new cancelling date'.*

This is obviously a very favourable clause for the owners and where delivery dates are crucial may not be accepted by charterers. The Amwelsh '93 has departed from Amwelsh tradition and for the first time inserted a similar clause (lines 50/58 in clause 5) but goes even further still. Whereas the Gencon clause specifically states that this may only happen once, the Amwelsh '93 states, *'Should the vessel be further delayed, the owners shall be entitled to require further declarations of the charterers in accordance with this clause'*. It hardly encourages charterers to go to the trouble of changing their pro formas to this otherwise admirably simplified and comprehensive form if it contains such potential complications for them.

Promoters of this type of clause would say, however, that forcing the owner to actually tender notice before knowing from the charterer whether he is cancelled or not is crude and unfair. But in practice if a ship does look as though it is going to miss its cancelling, the charterer will deal with the consequences and make a decision when he can on a case by case basis. The real problem is that it has the potential to encourage some owners in pressing circumstances to agree a laycan they have little hope of meeting in the secure knowledge that they can invoke this clause later when charterers have little chance of securing an earlier vessel. Furthermore, the Richards Bay Coal Terminal Regulations for example, which are usually, and should be incorporated in charter parties when fixing from Richards Bay, specify that if the vessel arrives after the cancelling date and the charterers accept the ship, that she will join the queue of vessels and time will not count. Such a penalty encourages owners to be circumspect, cautious, prudent and properly professional when they agree to the laydays. But clauses that run counter to port regulations, as will happen if fixing on an unamended Amwelsh '93 for Richards Bay loading, are bound to lead to problems and disputes.

DEMURRAGE

If the ship is detained for longer than the allowed laytime, the charterer must pay the owners a fixed sum for exceeding the time allowed and this is known as "demurrage". It is usually expressed as '.......dollars per day or pro rata'. The rate of demurrage is a matter of negotiation but should have some relationship to the vessel's current market time charter value. Demurrage arises for a breach of the laytime provisions of a charter for which there are liquidated (that means pre-determined) damages which is its legal definition. Unless there is an express agreement, it is payable for the whole period between the expiry of time allowed and the completion of loading or discharging. This is often expressed by the maxim, 'Once on demurrage, always on demurrage'. This is the basic premise but may be broken by specific mutual agreement. Such an example would be, 'time taken shifting from anchorage to the discharge berth is not to count, even if on demurrage'. If the words, 'even if on demurrage' were not specifically written in, the maxim would apply. The Sugar '99 tries a new departure in the strikes and force majeure clause (28) by attempting to break the 'once on demurrage rule' in case of strikes or force majeure. It is a point of dispute with many owners.

Most charter parties do not limit the demurrage period and it is difficult to see the benefit of doing so. The Gencon '76, however, provides that 'ten running days on demurrage at the rate stated per day or pro rata '. If the charter party does not contain demurrage provisions or if the fixed demurrage penalty period has expired before loading or discharge has been completed the owner will be entitled to claim **damages for detention**. These are unliquidated (that is, not a pre-determined sum) and therefore determined under national laws which adopt different approaches. It is therefore highly advisable to have a demurrage clause for an unlimited time in the charter party. It is good to see the Gencon '94 has eliminated this rather bizarre limitation.

The Gencon '76 states that demurrage is *'payable day by day'*. The Gencon '94 says that it is, *'payable upon receipt of owner's invoice. In the event that demurrage is not paid in accordance with the above, the owners shall give the charterers 96 running hours written notice to rectify the failure. If the demurrage is not paid at the expiration of this time limit and if the vessel is in or at the loading port, the owners are entitled at any time to terminate the charter party and claim damages for any losses thereby enacted.'* The 'payable day by day' in the Gencon '76, is often deleted and the rider clauses stipulate that it is payable with settlement of accounts and balance of freight, which brings it into line with other charter parties and standard practice. However for small charterers with whom owners have never 'fixed' before, it may be sensible for owners to consider this clause in the light of the likelihood of demurrage occurring.

DESPATCH

It is the reward and incentive to the charterer for loading or discharging the ship within the laytime stipulated. It is paid by the owner to the charterer and is typically charged at half the demurrage rate. It is found in almost all charter parties except the Gencon, but even then it is often inserted as a specific agreement.

The wording most often used is that it is paid on **'laytime saved'** or **'working time saved'**. This is to avoid the disputes that have arisen when the words 'time saved' are used without further specification. In case 'working time' is used it is probably better to say 'actual working time' to be even more specific.

The time honoured reason for paying despatch at half the demurrage rate is that although unexpected earlier readiness is a potential gain for the owner it is less of a gain than the potential loss if he were unexpectedly delayed and missed his next cargo or is in danger of being cancelled thereafter after ballasting to a load port.

LAYTIME EXCEPTIONS/STRIKES/FORCE MAJEURE

The expression 'force majeure' is a French phrase and is often referred to in Charter Parties as '**Exceptions**'. It covers events which are unforeseeable and outside the control of either party. If an obligation is not carried out because of something outside the control of a party (i.e. force majeure circumstances), failure to carry it out is not the fault of the party normally responsible. Thus, failure to deliver the cargo by owners, for example, a primary obligation of the owners, because of events beyond their control, is therefore excepted. Similarly, a failure to provide the cargo at the loading port by charterers, for example, a primary obligation on their part, because of events beyond their control is also therefore excepted.

The clause in the Amwelsh '79 (Clause 4) concerning the loading port includes *'riots, strikes, lockouts, disputes between masters and men, occasioning a stoppage of hands connected with the working or delivery of the coal for which the vessel is stemmed, or by reason of accidents to mines or machinery, obstructions, embargo or delay on the railway or in the dock, or by reason of fire, floods, frosts, fogs, storms or any cause whatsoever beyond the control of the charterers affecting mining, transportation, delivery and or loading of coal not to be computed as part of the loading time (unless any cargo be actually loaded during such time).'* It goes on to stipulate that if it continues for 6 days the charter becomes void.

The Gencon strike clause allows the owner to cancel the charter if there is a strike or lockout affecting the loading of the cargo unless the charterer agrees to *'reckon the laydays as if there was no strike or lockout.'* If part of the cargo has been loaded before the strike, the owner must proceed with the cargo loaded, receiving freight for only such loaded cargo but having the liberty to complete with other cargo. At the discharging port, however, if the strike has not been settled within 48 hours after the vessel's arrival, the receiver can keep her waiting paying half demurrage after expiration of time provided for discharging or order the vessel to another port. This clause is often incorporated into other charter parties such as the Riodoceore. Although the incidence of these strike situations is, in general, fairly low, the damages caused when they do occur are very high. Because the wordings are subject to varying interpretations in specific cases, there have been many arbitrations and court cases concerning these clauses.

The Amwelsh '79 says that at the discharge port, if there are *'strikes, lockouts, civil commotions, or any other accidents beyond the control of the consignee which prevent or delay the discharging'*, then time dos not count except if already on demurrage.

The Amwelsh '93's strike clause (9) is written in clear, modern English and covers the usual Force Majeure events but in another revolutionary change, instead of providing that time does not count, provides that *'half the laytime shall count during such periods'*. The Centrocon strike clause has been much criticised as obscure in its meaning and badly drafted. It should therefore probably be avoided.

In situations where cargo has been loaded and an excepted item happens, it is difficult to draft a clause which covers every eventuality and is fair and equitable to both parties. What is probably most usually agreed is that the vessel has the option either to stay until loading is completed or to sail and load a completion cargo en route.

The Riodoceore clause 30, 'Exceptions clause' states, '*Time lost by reason of force majeure, war, insurrection, civil commotion, political disturbances, floods, landslides, frost, stoppage on railway, whether partial or total, on river, canal, quay, wharf, jetty, rope or cable way, at loading or discharging plants and equipment, lack of trucks, stoppage of miners or workmen or other hands connected with the mining or handling of the cargo, breakdowns of machinery at the mines, whether partial or general, or by reason of any cause whatsoever kind or nature beyond the control of the charterers or their agents, supplying, leading, discharging or conveying the cargo from the mines to the vessel, shall not be computed in the loading or discharging time unless the vessel is already under demurrage. If a case such as the above should last longer than 72 hours, clause 38 (Gencon strike clause) comes into force'*. This is an example of a clause where a charterer is protecting himself from the perils of getting his cargo to the port under the term 'Force Majeure'.

But an Exception or Force Majeure clause protects owners as well. The BFC Exceptions clause. (Clause 37) says, *'It is also mutually agreed that the carrier shall not be liable for loss or damage occasioned by causes beyond his control, by perils of the sea or other waters, by fire from any cause whatsoever occurring by barratry of the master or crew, by enemies, pirates or robbers, by arrests and restraint of princes, rulers or people, by explosion, bursting of boilers, breakage of shafts or any latent defect in hull machinery or appertenances, by collisions, stranding or other accidents of navigation of whatsoever kind, (even when occasioned by the negligence, default or error in judgement, of the pilot, master, mariners or other servants of the ship owner, not resulting, however, in any case from want of due diligence by the owners of the ship or any of them by the ship's husband or manager'*.

This obviously has implications as to seaworthiness, discussed earlier in the chapter. The Norgrain '73 (Clause 35), Norgrain '89 (Clause 36) and Amwelsh '93 (Clause 8) entitled 'Exceptions' commences with the owners having *'to exercise due diligence to make the ship seaworthy'* which refers to the provisions of the Carriage of Goods by Sea Act. It continues to exempt both parties from liability for events beyond their control. The Norgrain states,*'And neither the vessel, her master or owners nor the charterers or receivers shall unless otherwise in this charter party expressly provided be responsible for loss or damage or delay or the failure to supply, load, discharge or deliver the cargo arising or resulting from; act of God, act of war, act of public enemies, pirates or assailing thieves; arrest or restraint of princes, rulers or people, seizure under local process, provided bond is promptly furnished to release the vessel or cargo; floods; fires; blockade; riots; insurrection; civic commotions; earthquakes; explosions. No exception afforded the charterers or receivers under this clause shall release the charterers of or diminish their obligations for payment of any sums due to the owners under provisions of the charter party'*.

The Amwelsh '53 (Clause 7) and Amwelsh '79 (Clause 8) cover the same ground. Exceptions or 'strikes' in the '93 version are covered separately but the Amwelsh '79 specifically includes in the 'Exceptions' clause, the words '*charterer not answerable for any negligence, default or error in judgement of trimmers or stevedores employed in loading or discharging the cargo*'. This really refers to the different matter of **stevedore damage** dealt with separately in this Chapter. By including it in the 'Exceptions' clause it implies that stevedores are outside the control of the charterers, and therefore an exception. Even though the stevedores are likely to be employed by the charterers, it suggests that damage caused by the stevedores is an unforseeable event occurring outside the charterer's control. In fact, logically of course, it is outside of his control, but should it be outside of his responsibility? (See Stevedore Damage).

The common theme in all these rather different clauses is that charterers are attempting to limit the damage to themselves in the form of payments of demurrage by unforseen circumstances outside their control while getting the cargo to the ship or from the ship. The owners are at the same time limiting the damage to themselves in the form of claims by the charterers by unforeseen circumstances out of their control.

However, if a Force Majeure situation does develop it would normally be wise to seek legal guidance. The exact circumstances could alter what appears to be a clear case. To give a very simple example, an **'Act of God',** which means an event without human intervention preventing one party from fully carrying out his obligations, may well cover unexpected very high winds preventing loading and causing damage. Yet, if these winds were a regular feature of the port in certain months of the year the courts may not give the same meaning if it could be said that extra precautions could have been taken such as additional fenders, standby tugs etc..

A real and recent example is from 1998 when the Panama Canal draft was reduced significantly due to the effects of 'El Nino'. Arbitrations resulted in attempting to execute freight contracts that had been fixed on the assumption that the Canal draft was fairly constant. The question before the arbitrators boiled down to, 'Was 'El Nino' an Act of God or a forseeable commercial risk?' It is rare that Force Majeure situations are straightforward. Professional legal guidance is usually therefore worthwhile.

DEVIATION CLAUSE

Article 1V Rule 4 of the **Hague Visby Rules** states, 'Any deviation in saving or attempting to save life or property at sea, or any reasonable deviation shall not be deemed to be an infringement or breach of these rules or of the contract of carriage, and the carrier shall not be liable for any loss or damage resulting therefrom'. Charter parties follow this rule but occasionally they give owners wider liberties.

The Amwelsh '79 Exceptions clause also says, *'The vessel has liberty to call at any ports in any order, to sail without pilots, to tow and assist vessels in distress, and to deviate for the purpose of saving life or property, and to bunker'*. This would include what the Hague Visby Rules state as 'reasonable'. The deviation clause in the Gencon (Clause 3 in Gencon '94) however, adds, *'in any order for any purpose'*. This permission to deviate is very liberal indeed but is taken to mean, ports that will be passed en route. Many charter parties include the P and I Bunkering Clause, giving the right to deviate for bunkers on or off the direct or customary route. (See Chapter Eight).

The Amwelsh '93, having changed the Exceptions clause in previous Amwelsh charter parties has a Deviation clause which is the same as the Norgrain '73 and '89 Deviation clause which reads exactly as per the Hague Visby Rules above but adding; *'provided, however that if the deviation is for the purpose of loading or unloading cargo or passengers, it shall prima facie, be regarded as unreasonable.'* A reasonable deviation would also be the refusal of a Master to enter his ship into a dangerous and warlike area. When preparing pro formas, charterers should make sure the deviation clause, P and I Bunkering clause and a Paramount clause which incorporates the Hague Visby Rules broadly offer the same restrictions and are complementary.

ARBITRATION

Although the last thing in the party's mind when fixing and drawing up the charter party is a dispute, there must be a clear procedure to resolve any difficulties that do arise. The 1996 Arbitration Act states, 'The object of arbitration is to obtain the fair resolution of disputes by an impartial tribunal without unnecessary delay or expense'. The aim is to achieve this without the more academic, time consuming and expensive approach of the Courts and to proceed without legal representation in order that practical and commercial people experienced in the industry or trade concerned can resolve the dispute. In short, since **the charter party is a commercial document, disputes should be settled by commercial arbitration.**

Most charter parties contain an arbitration clause providing for any disputes arising under the charter party to be referred to arbitration. The Gencons until the 1994 revision and CORE7 printed forms, however, do not and one has to be inserted in rider clauses. If one is not inserted, the assumption is that disputes should be settled where the charter party is drawn up. This is defined at the top of any charter party after 'place'.

The wording of an Arbitration clause should be clear and precise. Wording such as, 'Arbitration in London in the usual manner', should be avoided. The procedure is usually that each party appoints an arbitrator and if they cannot agree then those two appoint a third. Whether they are defined as 'commercial' or 'shipping men' or 'members of the Baltic Exchange' is a variable. However, arbitration is not intended to be a situation of advocacy where one arbitrator represents the 'plaintiff', one the 'defendant', and the third being the 'judge and jury'. All three are, in effect, 'judge and jury', their purpose being to give a verdict based on their professional experience and knowledge of the trade. However, should the arbitrators make an award which is considered incorrect on a matter of law, it can be appealed. It is then necessary to involve lawyers to handle the application for leave to appeal, and if leave is granted, the subsequent appeal proceedings in court. That is how the huge body of case law on shipping matters has grown up.

The charter party should define the place of arbitration and the law under which disputes shall be conducted. The Norgrain charter parties offer a London or New York alternative. The 'Ferticon' describes that the place of arbitration as London but fails to mention that it should be conducted under English law although this will be presumed. The 'Sovietwood' charter is even worse saying, *'Any dispute arising under this charter shall be referred to arbitration in the country of the respondent in accordance with the arbitration law and procedure prevailing in the country'*. It does not take much imagination to see that this kind of loose wording could lead to an untold number of disputes and should be avoided. Furthermore, the wording must be practical. A few years ago I encountered a Singaporean shipping lawyer desperately trying to find 'three practising shipbrokers at the place of arbitration and members of the Baltic Exchange', in Singapore where arbitration had been agreed. It was obviously impossible at that time to scrape together three members of the Baltic Exchange who were practising shipbrokers in Singapore. It was a clear case of the parties agreeing to change the location of arbitration from London to Singapore on the charter party pro forma they were negotiating, no doubt because owners, charterers and their brokers were located in the East, but forgetting to change the qualification of the potential arbitrators. All the parties, but especially the brokers, should have been alert to this. Changing the clause after a dispute has arisen is the equivalent of shutting the door after the horse has bolted.

The Centrocon Arbitration clause has a three month time limit. *'Any claim must be made in writing and claimant's arbitrator appointed within three months of final discharge and where this provision is not complied with, the claim shall be deemed to be waived and absolutely barred'*. However, this has been held void if the charter-party incorporates the Clause Paramount as it conflicts with the one year time bar in the Hague Visby Rules.

A few owners and charterers are beginning to be concerned, however, about the nature of arbitration itself, as more arbitrations are appealed on a matter of law and thus taken to court. Some of them have sought to eliminate this by specifying a clause which sends the dispute directly to the High Court. It reads as follows; 'This charter party shall be governed by English Law and any dispute arising out of or in connection with this charter shall be submitted to the exclusive jurisdiction of the High Court of Justice of England and Wales. Owners and charterers irrevocably appoint their respective brokers to accept service in respect of any and all proceedings commenced in the High Court of Justice of England and Wales.' It goes on to exclude disputes where the claim is less than US$ 50,000 which are to be settled according to the small claims procedures (SCP) of the LMMA.

In fact, many charter parties now have a rider clause added to take account of the **London Maritime Arbitrators Association (LMMA)** small claims procedure for the resolution of claims not exceeding U.S.$ 50,000. Some charterers are also introducing time bars. The Sugar '99 has the LMMA clause included in its main body and the Norgrain '89 and Amwelsh '93 have it (Clause 45 and 3 respectively) with New York and London alternatives. It may also be suitable for larger claims where a single issue is at stake. Legal costs are capped, it is quick and excludes the right of appeal. It is therefore becoming increasingly popular to make such a sensible addition to whatever arbitration clause is being used in the charter party.

STEVEDORES AND THE LOADING/DISCHARGING CLAUSE

The Riodoceore states that the cargo should be *'loaded and well trimmed by the loading conveyor belts'* and the Amwelsh, that the cargo should be *'loaded, dumped and spout trimmed'*. Towards the end of loading a cargo of bulk material it is usually trimmed by the loading conveyor or spout. This means pushing the cargo into the corners and sides to prevent the cargo shifting en route and thereby causing the vessel to list or sink. If these words are included it implies that any extra trimming required by the Master is at owner's time and cost. Sometimes these words are expressly added to the terms.

The difference between FIO (and FIOST and FIOSpT) and berth terms or gross load are that with FIO, the owner does not pay for the costs of loading but does pay port charges. These will include such miscellaneous items as light dues, pilotage, towage, tug charges, line handling, garbage disposal and perhaps most importantly wharfage or berth charges. The owner will also pay the agency fee. Under FIO he will not pay for the stevedores and the costs of loading and discharging. Therefore if a ship self loads or self discharges using the crew to drive the ship's gear it is not FIO.

The Riodoceore reflects modern FIO usage in that the costs of loading and discharging are clearly the responsibility of the charterer and says, *'free of any risk, liability and expense whatsoever to the owners'*. The Amwelsh '79 clause 6 says, *'at the tariff rate of the Port at Vessel's expense'*. This reflects 'berth terms' and is normally deleted to reflect standard FIO terms. The Gencon '76 (Clause 5) and Norgrain (Clause 10) have gross terms and FIO alternatives and the Gencon, further additions for geared and gearless ships. The Synacomex '90 says crisply, *'Stowage shall be under master's direction and responsibility'*. The Norgrain '73 has diluted this obligation with the additional words that *'stevedores shall be deemed servants of the owners and shall work under the supervision of the master.'* The Amwelsh '93 says, *'Should the stevedores refuse to follow his instructions, the Master shall protest to them in writing and shall advise the charterers immediately thereof'*.

These words concern one of the most debated subjects in chartering, the extent of the Master's supervision and responsibility for loading. This is an important subject and the object of innumerable arbitrations. It is sometimes complicated by the form of the Clause Paramount. A fuller discussion on the subject will be found in Chapter Seven under 'Loading /Stowing/Discharging' and in Chapter Eight under 'Clause Paramount'. See also "Seaworthiness" earlier in this Chapter.

The Gencon '94 (Clause 5) has updated the wording of the stevedore clause in a much more satisfactory way. Part (a) of clause 5 clearly states that cargo is to be, *'loaded and or trimmed, tallied and or secured and taken from the holds and discharged by the charterers, free of any risk, liability and expense to the owners'*. It continues in (b), *'The owners shall throughout the duration of loading/discharging give free use of the vessel's cargo handling gear and of sufficient motive power to operate all such cargo handling gear. All such equipment to be in good working order. Unless caused by negligence of the stevedores, time lost by breakdown of the vessel's cargo handling gear or motive power - pro rata the total number of cranes/winches required at the time for the loading/discharging of cargo under this charter party - shall not count as laytime or time on demurrage. On request the owners shall provide free of charge cranemen/winchmen from the crew to operate vessel's cargo handling gear, unless local regulations prohibit this, in which latter event labourers shall be for the account of the charterers. Cranemen / winchmen shall be under the charterer's risk and responsibility and stevedores to be deemed as their servants but shall always work under the supervision of the Master'*.

This is a comprehensive clause encompassing all the issues involved with gear and stevedores, including who drives the ship's cranes, the allocation of cost and where responsibility lies for loading. For ships using their own cranes, who operates them is an important issue. In some ports, local regulations demand that shore labour is employed. In other cases the vessel's crew are permitted to do so. It is usually necessary, however, that the charterer or the port arranges payloaders or bulldozers to assist in completing discharge. This part of the Gencon clause 5, entitled 'Loading/Discharging', is sandwiched between 'Costs/Risks' and 'Stevedore Damage' which is logical but a rare pooling of similar and related issues in one comprehensive clause. The Norgrain '73's gear clause says, *'Time lost on account of breakdown of vessel's gear essential to the loading or discharging of this cargo is not to count as laytime or time on demurrage and if this charter party calls for charterers/receivers to pay for cost of loading or discharge any stevedore standby time charges incurred thereby shall be for owner's account'*. The Amwelsh and iron ore charter parties do not have references to gear as the trades rarely involve loading or discharging by gear and where they do they tend to be added as separate clauses.

Sometimes added to the stevedore clause is the stipulation that the owner is to supply full lights for night work in the holds and on deck. At other times it is inserted randomly but it is an important obligation of the owner and rarely contentious.

STEVEDORE DAMAGE

Bulk cargoes are typically discharged by grabs, continuous ship unloaders or, in the case of grain, vacuvators. Most large ports employ grabs and some charter parties specify that the ship has to be suitable for grab discharge. It should be noted that some of these grabs weigh 40 tons and can lift another 40 tons of cargo. While most ports employ well trained and experienced crane operators, occasionally a misdirected grab can cause considerable damage to the ship's holds and hatch coamings. Although environmentalists tend to favour continuous ship unloaders which, they say, cause less dust and spillage, bulk cargo handlers themselves, in the main dispute this and favour what many of them consider is the more reliable grab unloaders. When one considers the loading of steel, logs, pipes, scrap and other potentially damaging cargo, it is clear that the issue of stevedore damage is one that is important and has to be dealt with in a charter party.

Stevedore damage clauses fall into two main categories; those that deny that the charterer has any responsibility at all and those that under certain circumstances allow for the charterer's responsibility. The former has the attraction of simplicity and in the main are accepted by owners carrying bulk cargoes to and from well known, large, sophisticated ports. The latter must go into detail about which circumstances are covered and which are not, what kind of repairs are needed and when they will be made. Which type of clause is used is often dependent on the port and type of cargo. It is rare that such a clause will be necessary with a grain voyage with spout loading and vacuvator discharge. Furthermore continuous self unloaders are less likely to cause damage than a poorly operated grab, for example.

The Amwelsh mentions stevedore damage in the Force Majeure clause, *'Charterer not answerable for any negligence, default or error in judgement of trimmers or stevedores employed in loading or discharging the cargo'* (Clause 7 in Amwelsh '53, Clause 8 in Amwelsh '79) thereby claiming that it is something outside the control of the charterer and unforeseeable. But again, the Amwelsh '93 breaks with Amwelsh tradition in having a separate clause (19) which states, *'Any damage caused by stevedores shall be settled directly between the owners and the stevedores',* but then adds an optional clause which can be deleted or not according to the result of the negotiation. It states, *'In case owners are unsuccessful in obtaining compensation from the stevedores for damage for which they are legally liable, then the charterers shall indemnify the owners for any sums so due and unpaid.'* Here is another reason why charterers will be in no hurry to adopt this charter party, sticking with their older amended and mutilated forms.

Both the Sugar '77 and '99 state, *'damage by grabs (if any) to be settled directly between owners and stevedores, charterers incurring no responsibility therefore'*. The Riodoceore puts the **Repairs of Damage** Clause (24) curiously between 'Bad weather' and 'Lighterage' and it simply states '*Time reasonably required to complete repairs of loading and/or discharge damage, if any, for which the vessel is not responsible, shall count as laytime used in loading or discharging as the case may be.'*

Some charter parties require deeptanks, tunnels and other divisions within the vessel's holds to be protected against damage by stevedores' cranes, grabs and other equipment. If this is not done sufficiently it will affect any potential claims.

The Orevoy (Clause 10) and Gencon (Clause 5) incorporates wording arising from disputes concerned with apparent stevedore damage not immediately discovered and repairs which cannot be repaired immediately which is often the subject of rider clauses in other charter parties. The Gencon '94 puts responsibility on the charterers and continues, *'Such damage shall be notified as soon as reasonably possible by the Master to the charterers or their agents and to their stevedores, failing which the charterers shall not be held responsible. The Master shall endeavour to obtain stevedores' written acknowledgement of liability. The charterers are obliged to repair any stevedore damage prior to completion of the voyage, but must repair stevedore damage affecting the vessel's seaworthiness or class before the vessel sails from the port where such damage was caused or found. All additional expenses incurred shall be for the account of and shall be paid to the owners by the charterers at the demurrage rate'*.

The Orevoy wording is similar but also states, '*The charterers have the right to perform repairs of stevedore damage at any moment prior to or before the completion of the voyage, but must repair stevedore damage affecting the*

Vessel's seaworthiness before the vessel sails from the port where such damage was caused'.

It is sometimes disputed when the damage should be notified. 'At the time of occurrence' was often required by charterers but many owners have sought to replace this with, 'at the time of discovery', to cover damages hidden by cargo covering the damage immediately after it occurred. Charterers then have sought to set a time limit but the Gencon '94 wording, *'as soon as reasonably possible'* is probably the best compromise of a difficult issue if liability is to be admitted by charterers at all. Rider clauses can sometimes be long drawn out affairs which go on to stipulate that if it is impossible to repair at the port of discharge where and when she will repair. Charterers are usually very reluctant to get into these clauses as they fear the longer owners have to repair the longer the file is open and the more it will eventually cost them.

INSPECTIONS

Whatever cargo is loaded, the condition of the ship's holds is a legitimate area of concern since one of the fundamental obligations of the owner is to deliver the cargo in the same condition as when it was loaded. The Sugar '77 and '99 charter parties have such a clause of fairly standard wording. The '99 version sates, *'Ship's holds to be odourless and free from insects, properly swept, cleaned and dried to the satisfaction of shipper' and/or charterers' agents before loading. Ship's holds to be washed down only if cargo injurious to sugar carried previously, and if done, holds to be completely dry before tendering notice of readiness. Charterers have the right to arrange a condition survey and/or hose test prior to commencement of loading which to be at charterer's expense for which purpose a Lloyds Agent or Salvage Association Surveyor will be used where possible, failing which a mutually agreed Surveyor shall be used'.*

Other cargoes such as steel, which will need dry holds to prevent rusting (and possibly specific provisions about dunnaging) may require a similar clause but if so it will usually be dealt with in the rider clauses. Coal and iron ore obviously do not normally need such stringent terms. Grain, however, is a cargo where the cleanlines of the holds is especially important but there is one more reason for inspection when grain is loaded.

Among bulk cargoes, grain is the most free flowing and thus has a tendency to move at sea. **The Safety of Life at Sea Convention (SOLAS 1974)** is an international convention governing the loading and carriage of grain and is implemented in many country's domestic legislation. A ship loading grain must have a **'Grain Inspector's Certificate**', otherwise it may not be allowed to load. This is referred to in lines 23/28 of the BFC and clause 3 of the Norgrain '73 and '89 which says, *'Vessel to load under inspection of National Cargo Bureau, Inc. in USA ports or of the Port Warden in Canadian ports. Vessel is also to load under the inspection of a Grain Inspector licensed, authorised by the United States department of Agriculture as required by the appropriate authorities. Vessel is to comply with the rules of such authorities, and shall load cargo not exceeding what she can reasonably stow and carry. Cost of such inspection shall be borne by the Owners'.*

Clause 17 (d) in the Norgrain '73 and clause 18 (e) of the Norgrain '89 states that the Master's Notice of Readiness shall be accompanied by the National Cargo Bureau's pass and the USDA's Grain Inspector's Certificate of readiness to load. If the ship does not possess them, then she will not actually be *'ready to load'* and therefore will delay the commencement of laytime. It is usual to add that time lost due to vessel failing inspection until vessel is passed is not to count as laytime, although clause 17(b)/18(b) states there is a four hour grace period. This generous provision is usually deleted. Indeed, some charterers will try to insist that if she has lost her 'turn' due to another ship berthing while she was undergoing another inspection, that time will only count from when she is actually re-berthed for loading.

ROTATION AND SAFE OR SEAWORTHY TRIM

Although it is rarely in the main body of the charter, if there is more than one berth or port involved, owners will ask for multiple load and discharge ports to be in 'geographical rotation' since that is the most economical and practical way. It is also standard to state that the vessel to be left in *'safe and seaworthy trim to the satisfaction of the Master'* between them. The trim of the vessel is the difference in draft between fore and aft. If it is the same, it is said to be **'on an even keel',** or if the same or lower at the stern to a safe margin it is said to be **'in trim'**. It is in the charterer's interest that the vessel safely delivers their cargo and thus is rarely a cause of dispute. It is especially catered for in the Norgrain '79 (Clause 22) and '89 (Clause 23) where complex multiple berth and port options are common and in the Sugar '77 and '99 (Clause 27). However, a coal charterer has pointed out to me yet another serious problem in the Amwelsh '93 which unlike previous Amwelshes or indeed the Norgrains or Sugar charter parties, specifically puts seaworthy trim responsibility on the charterer. It reads, *'Charterers shall leave the vessel in seaworthy trim and with cargo on board safely stowed to master's satisfaction between loading berths/ports and between discharging berths/ports respectively: any expenses resulting therefrom shall be from charterer's account and any time shall be used to count.'*

Quite apart from whether one is or represents a charterer or owner, consider the absurdity, illogicality and impracticality of this. How can a coal supplier, for example, who charters a ship to discharge at two ports for two different receivers, be responsible for how the ship is trimmed between discharging ports? It runs totally contrary to the fact that the safety and navigation of the ship is entirely and solely the Master's responsibility and to the meaning of the usual Lien and Cesser Clause (which the Amwelsh '93, clause 21, has side stepped neatly saying, *'liability shall cease except for all other matters provided for in this is charter party')*. Yet safe trim, from a purely practical point of view, must be the responsibility of the Master.

What happens in practice is that when the ship is fixed, the charterer tells the owner that he has, for example, three grades with the approximate quantities and that if they are going to different ports to specify this and ask the owner how he will load them, bearing in mind that all the grades will have to be loaded separately. The owner will suggest a stowage plan which accommodates the charterer's quantities, allows the ship to load each in turn and discharge one grade at the first port and another two grades at the second port. The owner will suggest this only after checking with the port captain in the office or the Master on the ship himself. The ship usually has a computer on board which simulates how the ship is loaded and in particular, the sequence of loading the different grades. Certain loading sequences may set up strains in the hull of the ship which cause the ship to "hog" and "sag" (See Chapter One - Terminology - Materials and Management Issues) which could be detrimental to its safety and even cause it to break. The Master will try alternatives until he finds one which is safe. The stowage plan will be communicated to the charterer. It may take a dialogue of various alternatives before one that is found that is both satisfactory for the charterer's business and for the safety of the ship. This is the normal and practical sequence of events and makes a nonsense of this new clause. The safety of the vessel is at all times, quite rightly, the responsibility of the Master. As will be seen in Chapter Seven, time charter clauses time and again, emphasise this very fundamental point which owners passionately defend.

COMBINATION PORTS

This is mainly a requirement for Mississippi grain loading berths and Japanese grain discharging ports. A normal clause regarding the Mississippi would be, '1-2 safe berth(s) 1 safe port United States Gulf. Mississippi River not north of but including Baton Rouge counting as one port'. Mobile is often excluded because the port is inefficient in delivery of cargo to the vessel and consequently expensive in respect of wharfage/dockage costs.

It is standard for panamax grain shipments into Japan for charterers to request and owners to allow the use of up to three discharge ports in Japan and that one of these is a combination port. Each charterer has its special wording and terms. Each is slightly different and owners evaluate them differently. The Japanese combination ports are Tokyo Bay (Tokyo, Yokohama, Yokosuka, Kawasaki and Chiba), Ise Bay (Nagoya, Yokkaiichi, Kinuura and Toyohashi), Kanmon (Moji-Shimonoseki) and Kagoshima-Shibushi. The issues when negotiating are which costs are for which party. Should the owner pay for all port charges in a so-called combination port where there are different port jurisdictions? If the vessel discharges at what are normally considered different ports but for the purposes of this charter party are considered as one port, the vessel may be assessed for port entry fees or tonnage dues twice. If there are three berths within a combination port they could be widely spaced apart. In this case who pays for the shifting time and expenses? Will they count as laytime or not? Wharfage, pilotage, line handling, tuggage are also negotiable points at all of or sometimes just the 3rd berth. Fortunately, most owners engaged in this trade are experts and are able to cost each charterer's requirement. However, for the uninitiated it is a minefield and a grain specialist shipbroker's advice essential.

A typical loading and discharging wording for a main terms agreement of a grain charter incorporating Mississippi loading and Japan discharging which would be incorporated into the charter party, might be as follows:

"Loading. One to two safe berths, one safe port U.S.Gulf, excluding Brownsville and Mobile, one to three safe berths or anchorages Mississippi River not above but including Baton Rouge to count as one port. Maximum one set of port charges for owner's account.

In the Mississippi River the vessel to load to a safe bar draft as recommended by the Bar Pilot Association unless required by the Master for Panama Canal reason and owners to pay for full port expenses

Discharge port(s). One–two safe berths each One-two-three safe ports Kushiro/Kobe range or in charterer's option. One-two safe berths each one-two-three safe ports Kashima/Kagoshima range including Hakata and/or Shibushi and/or Yatsushiro or in charterer's option one-two safe berths each one-two-three safe ports Otaru/Kobe range or in charterer's option one-two safe berths each one-two-three safe ports Hachinoe/Shibushi range.

Owners guarantee vessel not to arrive with a draft exceeding 11.9 metres at the first discharge port. Owners will pay full port expenses. Rotation of discharge port(s) to be North/South or South/North in geographical rotation in charterer's option. Maximum 5 berths in total at 3 discharge ports. Combination ports are Tokyo Bay (Kawasaki/Yokohama/Chiba) counting as one port and Ise Bay (Nagoya/Yokkaaichi/Kinuura/ Toyohashi) counting as one port. Charterers are only allowed to use one combination port.

All shifting expenses including wharfage, agency, bunkers and time between first and second discharge berths to be for owner's account.

Charterers to have the option of using a third berth in combination port or not, in which case shifting from second to third berth to be for charterer's account and time used to count as laytime. Wharfage and bunkers always to be for owner's account. Charterers to have the option of using a fourth berth in Ise Bay with shifting expenses and time from third berth to fourth berth to be for charterer's account and time used to count as laytime, but charterers to finish discharge of the entire cargo at Ise Bay".

It can be seen that the allocation of costs within the discharging range, especially the combination port is very complex and detailed but necessarily so as anything less will lead to misunderstandings and disputes.

CESSER CLAUSE

In its original form it is a curious clause which seeks to eliminate the charterer's liability at the time of shipment and transfer responsibility of the fulfilment of the charter to the receivers who may not be the charterers. The BFC 1963 Cesser clause is simplicity itself. It states, *'Charterer's liability under this charter shall cease on cargo being shipped'*. It has been recognised for years, however, that the charterer's liability ends only if an alternative remedy in the form of a lien on the cargo, is given to the owner for accrued liabilities, notably freight. Even the 1896 Welsh Coal Charter party gave a lien for freight, demurrage and average. Typically, the lien will apply to the vital matters of freight payment, if later than on signing and releasing Bills of Lading and demurrage at load and discharge port. In other words, in its purest form, the clause does not mean what it appears to say. Yet it was often left unchanged in charter parties as its meaning appeared to be established in law.

In most modern charter parties, however, to clarify the meaning and each party's responsibilities, it is often either qualified by or replaced with a Lien

Clause. Thus, the Gencon '94 has a **Lien Clause** stating, *'The owners shall have a lien on the cargo and all sub freights payable in respect of cargo for freight, deadfreight and demurrage, claims for damages and for all other amounts due under this charter party including costs of recovering same'.* The Amwelsh '93 (Clause 21) is entitled **'Lien and Cesser'** and states, *'The charterer's liability under this charter party shall cease on cargo being shipped, except for payment of freight, deadfreight and demurrage and except for all other matters provided for in this charter party where the charterer's responsibility is specified, the owners shall have a lien on the cargo for freight, deadfreight and demurrage and general average contribution due to them under this charter party.'*

What is a lien? A lien gives the owner the right to retain possession of the cargo should the charterers fail to pay the freight, deadfreight or demurrage. Usually when an owner exercises a lien, it is done by refusing to discharge the cargo or part of that cargo or by discharging into a secure bonded warehouse, if there is one, where the cargo will be held to the owner's order. This will usually secure payment for the money due. There may be a clause giving the owner the right to take it to another port and sell it as an alternative. This is fine in theory but difficult in practice as an alternative receiver or port may not exist, or alternative receivers may not want that cargo or quality of cargo. In fact, the owners could try to exercise the lien after discharge. But this has also practical and legal difficulties. Practical, because once a bulk cargo has gone onto a stockpile how does one monitor what is being done to it? Legally, it is probable that the charter party and Bill of Lading will be subject to English or U.S. Law. If so, discharge ports or places accepting those laws should be relatively straightforward. If the cargo is discharged, however, at a place not recognising English or U.S. law, they may not be prepared to enforce it. If an owner finds himself having to exercise a lien, he will be doing so with specialist legal advice.

Thus, whilst exercising a lien on shore may seem simple in theory, as a matter of practice it is not. An owner will therefore usually refuse to discharge the cargo if the charterer has failed to pay freight. With an unscrupulous charterer this might result in very unfortunate or unexpected actions. It is also an unfortunate but inevitable fact of shipping life that some charterers are poor at paying on time and some, however well intentioned, get into financial difficulties and may be unable to pay. The warnings explained in Chapter Four about checking the viability of the charterer could come into sharp relief when faced with situations like this.

One unfortunate and continuing effect of what might be termed the "Cesser clause mentality" is that although good charter parties allocate risks, responsibilities and costs between owners and charterers, some allocate them to third parties. The Amwelsh '53 gives responsibility, for example, for paying demurrage at the discharge port to the consignees (receivers). The Norgrain '89 has numerous references to receivers as an option instead of owners or charterers in the paying of demurrage, shifting etc.. The Sugar '77 and '99 have references to Shippers/Receivers peppered all through the documents. The problem with all this is that although there may be a contractual relationship between the Shippers/Receivers and the owner through the Bill of Lading, when negotiating the charter party, the owner will take the view that this is too remote or uncertain and will require the charterers to remain responsible. If the charterer does not, for instance, pay demurrage, how does the owner get the receiver to pay it? He may not know who the shipper or receiver is. What happens in most charter parties is that these costs, such as demurrage, are for the charterer's account. In this way, the owners have recourse to their counter party for payment. At the same time the charterer will have a contract with the shipper(s) or receiver(s), in which he gets paid. The charterer is therefore protected in a back to back arrangement. Such allocation to third parties would therefore seem to be unnecessary.

LIGHTERAGE/LIGHTENING

The 'safe port' provisions require that the ship be ordered to a port into which it can enter and discharge. But if it is ordered to a port which it cannot enter without reducing its draft, some of the cargo has to be taken off, or the ship 'lightened'. For some ports, such as Chalna or Chittagong this is customary.

The Riodoceore states simply, *'Lighterage, if required by the Charterers, shall be for their account and time used shall count'*. The Amwelsh '79 puts the responsibility on to the consignees (receivers) but clause 16 of the Amwelsh '93 has a similar clause to the Norgrain. The Norgrain '73 (Clause 23) and Norgrain '89 (Clause 24) commences with a warranty on the draft and only then goes on to state, *'Should the vessel be ordered to discharge at a place to which there is not sufficient water for her to get to first tide after arrival without lightening, and lie always afloat, laytime to count as per clause 17 (NOR and commencement of laytime clause) at a safe anchorage for similar vessels bound for such a place and any lighterage expenses incurred to enable her to reach the place of discharge is to be at the risk and expense of the cargo any custom of the port or place notwithstanding, but time occupied in proceeding from the anchorage to the discharge berth is not to count as laytime or time on demurrage'*.

Unless loading and/or discharging ports are named in this charter party, the responsibility for providing safe berths and/or safe ports of loading and or discharging lies with the charterers/receivers provided the owners have complied with the maximum arrival limitations. This goes back to the safe port/safe berth provisions at the beginning of the charter party and the earlier explanation of a berth charter party compared to a port charter party.

This does not mean that the owner can load his ship to over the draft prevailing at the discharge port. If the discharge port has a 13 metre draft limitation and the owner loads the ship to 15 metres, he clearly cannot fulfil his obligations to proceed to the port and discharge his cargo as he is required to do in the preamble to the charter party. But if the charterer orders the ship to discharge at a place where there is insufficient water for the vessel to reach, then time should count and lighterage expenses be for the charterer's account.

AGENTS

This clause simply defines whose agents are used at loading and discharging port. Owners pay the agency charges. The Gencon '94 states it is the owner's agents, while the Amwelsh, Orevoy, Riodoceore and Norgrain leave the space blank. The issue of whose agents are to be used is usually brought up in the main term negotiations. Charterers tend to like to chose the agents mainly because on frequently used trades and ports, the agents will know exactly the charterer's business and what is expected of them and to a lesser extent, the charterers may negotiate a rebate with an agency company.

Owners will seek the authority to appoint agents in order to try and negotiate the fees and protect their interests. If they have to concede 'charterer's agents', they may appoint their own agents simply to look after their interests. In this case they will be called 'protective agents'. In the grain trades, some charterers try to prohibit owners from appointing protective agents because the owners would use them in respect of signing and release of original Bills of Lading. In their view there is then a danger that time would be wasted and/or result in disputes causing charterers to lose considerable interest on the value of the commodity.

OVERTIME

The usual clause is, *'Overtime is to be for the account of party ordering same. However, if ordered by port authorities, same is for charterer's account.'* It is an uncontentious clause but may occasionally be altered by a rider clause in special circumstances.

SHIFTING

The issues in shifting the vessel from anchorage to berth or from first berth to second or subsequent berths, or in some cases from the berth to anchorage while waiting for the subsequent berth, are the cost and whether they are included or excluded from the laytime. It is usually but not always specifically excluded in a rider clause and therefore one of the few exceptions to the 'Once on demurrage, always on demurrage' rule. However, if the charter party is silent on the issue then the 'Once on demurrage' rule will prevail. These issues are regularly negotiated and most modern charter parties specifically deal with this as a separate clause. The Norgrain '73 (Clause 20) and '89 (Clause 21) goes into them in detail as it is more likely to be an issue in grain voyages, especially where combination ports are involved. Due to the shifting nature of advantages in the market place, this charter party has an owner/charterer alternative, one of which should be deleted.

In general, bulk coal and ore voyages are more likely to go to one berth. The port of discharge under the Amwelsh '79 thus has one line on it only, *'Shifting time from anchorage place to loading or discharging berth is not to count even if vessel is already on demurrage'*. There is rarely more than one berth at steel mills or power station ports, so owners rarely argue about this clause. Nevertheless the Amwelsh '93 has for some reason decided on shifting the advantage again from charterers to owners. This is yet another small disincentive for charterers to use this form. It reads, *'If more than one berth of loading and discharging has been agreed, and used, costs of shifting, including cost of bunkers used, shall be for the charterer's account'*. This is also the usual clause in the Riodoceore. The Sugar '99 says, *'Time proceeding from customary waiting place to loading berth/anchorage not to count as laytime'* The Gencon does not have a specific 'shifting clause' and therefore should be covered in the rider clauses if used.

OPENING/CLOSING OF HATCHES

It is rarely a point of contention. However, if covered at all, such as in the Norgrain, the clause will state that the cost of first opening and last closing of hatches shall be for either the charterer's or owner's account. It is normally for owner's account and where not covered in the standard form, inserted as a rider clause. Charterers require that the vessel is to be *'ready in all respects'* to load and discharge the cargo and this is taken to mean by charterers that the hatches should be open. Some charterers prefer to spell it out in a rider clause.

SEPARATIONS

This mainly concerns grain and break bulk cargoes. It is, however, not covered in the Gencon as regards cost and if applicable has to be added as a rider clause. The Norgrain '73 and '89 (Clause 14), however, states, *'Cost of cargo separations, including labour used for laying same, to be for charterer's account unless required by owners, in which case all resultant expenses shall be borne by owners. Separations ordered by charterers shall be made to master's satisfaction.'* It is a common sense clause and rarely contentious.

SECURING

This is for grain charter parties and covers measures to stop the cargo shifting and thus affecting the vessel's trim in non self trimming ships, especially tweendeckers and short sea box hold ships. Cargoes may be secured by shifting boards, straps or by placing bags of grain on top of the bulk cargo. This clause usually simply allocates the cost. The Norgrain '73 and '89 has provision for the cost to be either for owners or charterers, one of which to be deleted. When for the owner's account it states, *'Any securing (bagging or strapping etc.) required by Master, National Cargo Bureau or Port Warden for safe trim/stowage to be supplied and paid for by owners, and time so used not to count as laytime or time on demurrage. Bleeding of bags, if any, at discharging port(s) to be at owner's expense and time actually lost is not to count'* .

CAR DECKS

For grain charters only, this deals with any extra time and expense in loading, discharging and cleaning for vessels fitted with car decks. This was inserted mainly for vessels with cardecks which used to load in Japan and discharge in the USA and then return with cargoes of American grain for Japan. This car trade in carbulkers has completely been replaced by specialised PCC's (Pure Car Carriers) and thus is superfluous, but is often retained.

WING SPACES

Also a grain charter clause dealing with charterers who require grain to be loaded in wing tanks and dealing once again with allocation of time and expense . The Norgrain '73 and '89 (Clause 12) states, *'Cargo may be loaded into wing spaces if the cargo can bleed into centreholds. Wing spaces are to be spout trimmed; any further trimming in wing spaces and any additional expenses in discharging are to be for owners' account and additional time so used is not to count as laytime or time on demurrage'.* In fact most charterers do not want grain loaded in wing tanks as they tend to be dirty and are very slow to discharge.

EXTRA INSURANCE

The usual clause in most charter parties states, *'Extra insurance, if any, due to vessel's age, flag, classification or ownership, shall be for owner's account.'* This means that extra insurance is being charged by the charterer's insurers because of perceived extra risks of a vessel's age. Amendments to this that might be negotiated are;

1. Clarification of whether extra insurance applies for over 15 or 20 year old ships which often depends whether the cargo is being insured in America or Europe.

2. Owners will sometimes request, and be granted, a maximum limit so they may cost it into their voyage calculation more exactly. Charterers are usually happy to do this as they will receive the extra insurance invoice, know what is likely to be and will not want owners to over compensate the anticipated cost by increasing the freight unnecessarily.

3. A clause may be added specifying that the extra insurance payment be deducted from freight and that charterers are to furnish evidence in the form of supporting vouchers or documentation. This is in the Amwelsh '93 but usually has to be added in rider clauses in older forms.

There is also the case of the owner's hull insurance which may be increased by the nature of charterers trading to war zones or outside IWL, for example. Extra insurance due to the load or discharge ports being in a war zone as classified at Lloyds or by the Owner's P and I Club is usually treated as a separate issue as it is not common and thus not normally in the printed form of the charter parties. It often appeared or was required during conflicts in the Arabian Gulf. It is usual and logical that the charterer pays for this extra insurance since they are requiring the cargo to be carried there. The additional issue here is the 'crew war bonus'. Some charterers might agree to pay this but usually it is a contractual matter between owner and his crew/employees and should be paid for by owners.

SUBLET

Some charter parties include the provision that the charterer may sublet the charter party but remain responsible for the due fulfilment of it. This can be found, for example, in the Norgrain, BFC, Sugar '77 and '99 and reflects that in the sugar and grain trades cargoes can be sold on the water.

SUBSTITUTION

The Riodoceore has a clause (34) which permits substitution of the vessel for another one of the same class, conditions, size and type on the same laydays/cancelling. The reason that this charter party has it and other charter parties do not is due to the fact that the ore trade from Brazil to the main consuming areas is, more than most trades, fixed on contracts of affreightment. Substitution is thus very common and desirable which permits the owner's flexibility while maintaining the shipper's and receiver's pre-arranged schedule.

ADDRESS COMMISSION

In some charter party agreements there is a provision for an address commission. This is in effect a commission payable to the charterer's in house chartering department.

BROKERAGE/COMMISSION

This clause states that a commission, the remuneration for the broker's time and efforts in negotiating and arranging the contract, is payable by the owner on the freight, deadfreight and demurrage. It is only payable if there is performance. The name of the broker is inserted. The following variations should be noted;

1. The Riodoceore, Orevoy and Gencons except for the 1994 version do not allow for commission on demurrage. If it is to be brought up to the standard practice it needs to be inserted.

2. The Amwelsh '79 says that the commission *'is due on payment'* and the Amwelsh '93 is even more specific specifying that the brokerage should be paid *'at the time of the owners receiving these payments*'.

3. The Gencon and Orevoy have the following clause. *'In case of non execution 1/3 of the brokerage on the estimated amount of freight to be paid by the party responsible for such non execution to the Brokers as indemnity for the latter's expenses and work. In case of more voyages the amount of indemnity to be agreed.'* Enforcement of this provision is not easy nor necessarily commercially desirable.

The commission clause is very important for brokers as that is their sole means of remuneration and delays in payment can mean hardship especially in low markets. Until the end of 1999 they had very little power to force payment of commission as the broker is not a party to the contract and therefore could not sue under it. It is, however, a binding term of the agreement and if the owner refuses to pay or delays payment, the broker has been able to request the charterer to sue the owners on the broker's behalf to secure payment. It is not something that brokers like doing, nor do many charterers want the extra responsibility and trouble. Some charter parties, such as the 'Richards Bay Coal Charter Party' specify that brokerage is deductable from the freight by the charterer. It is not usual, but not uncommon, for the charterers to deduct it but should normally be specified.

Alternatively a side letter to the charter party is sometimes agreed between brokers and owners that commission is payable. This will secure a contract directly between broker and owner rather than simply being a third party to the charter party. Most owners, however, pay brokerage promptly and properly as a matter of good business practice. In the last resort anyone who does not, risks losing the market information that is a vital part of the brokerage service. Nevertheless it is not a comfortable position for a broker since not all owners are of the same mind about 'good business practice'!

The situation under English Law altered on 11th November 1999 with the passing of the Contracts (Rights of Third Parties) Act 1999. The Act applies to contracts entered into six months after that date and gives a person who is not a party to the contract the right to enforce a term of that contract if it "purports to confer a benefit on him". This description applies to a shipbroker seeking to enforce a commission clause. The third party must be indentifiable. This will mean that in future the manner in which charter party commission clasues are completed will become important. It will not be advisable for brokers to allow clauses to be worded "for division". All brokers in the transaction should be named and their commission allocation set out.

The act does not apply to a "contract for the carriage of goods by sea" but this is defined as a contract evidenced by a Bill of Lading, seaway bill or for which there is given an undertaking which is contained in the ship's delivery order. The definition, therefore, does not include charter parties which fall within the ambit of the Act.

The Act does not amend the current practice of commission being payable only on performance of the charter party. In the circumstances brokers are advised to insure their commission on high value long-term time charters.

RIDER CLAUSES

As earlier discussed, when most early charter party forms were issued no rider clauses were intended. There are plenty of examples of charter parties executed as late as the mid 1950's and in some cases later, with no additions or rider clauses at all. Many now adorn the walls of shipping offices. However, as ship owning and trading became more precise, specialist, competitive, even scientific and the subject of more arbitrations and disputes, extra clauses were added to be more specific on each of the issues. The result is that many issues are dealt with, in great detail, in rider clauses if either party feels that an issue is either not dealt with sufficiently comprehensively or not dealt with at all in the standard clauses. Furthermore there may be issues specific to that particular trade or voyage or events at that particular time that needs to be dealt with. In the case of clarifications of existing issues, these have been dealt with above. For issues that are not dealt with, the following is a brief guide to some of the issues common in rider clauses.

Grain charters in the late 1990's and early twenty first century tended to have an **Asian Gypsy Moth** clause reflecting concern over examples of infestations of cargo by this insect. It reads something like, 'Owners confirm that the vessel has not called at Soviet Far East ports from Posyet to Olga Bay including Vladivostock, Nahodka and Vostochny during the months of June, July and August and that there is no danger of the vessel being rejected entry and/or delayed by the U.S./Canadian authorities. However, in case this does occur, charterers have the option to cancel charter party or to instruct the vessel to clean and re-present with all time and expense till the vessel is accepted being for owner's account.'

Some grain charterers have a **fumigation clause** which necessitates fumigation as a matter of course which in turn means the crew has to leave the ship. Normally it is only done if there are rats or other vermin on board or there is infestation of the cargo. In any case, all vessels must be in possession of a 'deratisation certificate'.

Another grain clause often added as a rider is if the charterer wants to carry **different grains stowing differently** on the same ship. The owner has fixed the freight on a per ton basis calculated on the basis of a specified grade of cargo. Therefore, such a clause might read, 'If the charterers use their option to load agricultural products, then freight for the hold in which the agricultural products are stowed to be calculated by dividing that hold's cubic feet by 48.5 and multiplying that sum by the relative freight rate of this charter party. However, if the vessel has excess cubic and completes loading with slack hold(s) or vessel loads the maximum tonnage permitted by charter party restrictions (including Panama Canal draft) the freight to be paid on actual tonnage irrespective of stowage factor'.

Another grain clause sometimes used concerns '**carrying charges**' in the United States Gulf ports which are transferred from the charterer to the owner if the vessel misses her cancelling date but is accepted by the charterer. It is usually 20 cents per metric ton per day.

If front end loaders are used at the end of discharging a hold in order to push the bulk cargo together to be collected by the grab, owners will ask that the weight of the front end loaders be in accordance with tank top strengths. Similarly, if **mobile cranes** on deck are required during discharging, which is often the case for grain in Taiwan, a clause specifying the deck strength and often the nature of the mobile crane's wheels is inserted. (See rider clauses also in Chapter Seven).

On panamax and capesize trades a **'gas free certificate'** clause will be included for combination carriers that may have gas residue in the holds after an oil voyage. Owners sometimes request the **option of bunkering during loading/discharging.** Provided that it does not interfere with the charterer's operations, they will usually agree. Some charterers insert a **confidentiality clause**. The Sugar '77 and '99 are two of the only charter parties to have one (Clause 35) written in the standard form. Sometimes charterers will require that the vessel will not be sold for scrap after the voyage. This is to ensure that reasonable maintenance of the ship will continue.

Soft landing clauses will usually be incorporated when scrap is to be loaded especially if it is intended to load motor blocks or other heavy scrap. This means that a protective layer of softer scrap is loaded over the ship's tanktops prior to speeding up loading. If motor blocks or other heavy scrap are simply dropped straight onto the tanktops, they could easily be punctured resulting in very serious damage affecting seaworthiness and necessitating immediate repair and lead to expensive claims against the stevedores or charterers. When owners do permit the loading of scrap, they tend to prefer 'heavy handy deadweight', shredded or proler scrap which exclude the heaviest pieces.

An **alternate hold loading clause** is sometimes required by charterers for iron ore and is because of its low stowage factor of iron ore. It can be loaded in only 4 out of 7 holds in a panamax or 5 out of 9 in a capesize. It is for the benefit of receivers who can discharge the cargo quicker. Some classification societies think this is a risk with the strains that are set up in the ship. Some differentiate between pellets and fines.

Another possible rider clause for iron ore concerns water often loaded with wet iron ore, the drainage that occurs during passage and the effects that has on how freight is calculated. Often called the '**free water drainage clause**', it requires the Master to measure the daily bilge tanks prior to pumping and record the tonnage estimates of free water extracted.

A more common clause introduced in the '90's is the **Drug and Alcohol Policy Clause'.** It is fairly standard and reads, 'Owners guarantee that they have a policy on drug and alcohol abuse applicable to the performing vessel which meets or exceeds the standards of the Oil Companies International Marine Forum guidelines for the control of drugs and alcohol on board ships. An objective of the policy shall be frequent testing routine of crew and be adequate to act as an effective abuse deterrent. The policy will remain effective during the term of the contract and the owners shall exercise due diligence to ensure compliance with the policy'.

SPECIAL CLAUSES FOR CONTRACTS OF AFFREIGHTMENT

The object of a COA from both the owner's and charterer's point of view is to lock in a freight rate with which they are both comfortable. However, on long contracts it is often usual to have a bunker escalation/de-escalation clause and occasionally a port charge clause that will modify the fixed nature of the freight.

BUNKER CLAUSE

The price of bunkers have fluctuated wildly over the past 25 years. (See Figure 6.1).

Since it has an important impact on the voyage freight cost, an owner taking a ten year contract, for example, at a time of low bunker prices without a bunker clause will be hugely and adversely exposed if the bunker price escalates. On the other hand, if it reduces, the owners will be favourably positioned and the charterer disadvantaged. It is therefore usual to fix the price of bunkers based on a Platts daily price on the Bill of Lading date at a bunker port of relevance to the contract. A usual clause would specify something like the following. 'Freight rates shall be calculated against the prevailing Platt's Oilgram, 'bunker wire' Free zone price of USD 70-90 for

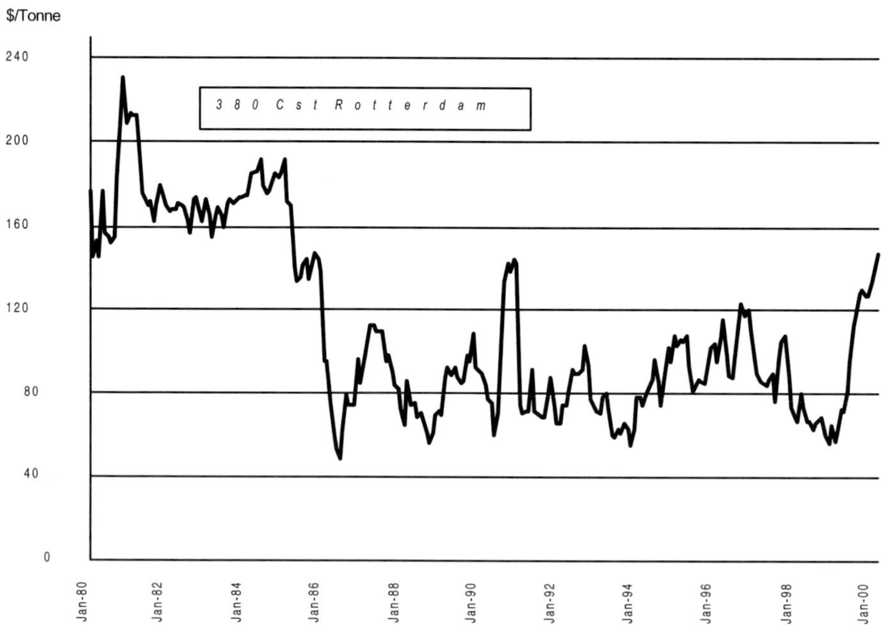

Figure 6.1
The Rotterdam Bunker price over 20 years as measured by Platts

Intermediate Fuel Oil 180 CST at Rotterdam on the date 30 days prior to the Bill of Lading. For every one USD above or below USD 90 respectively USD 70 the freight rate to be increased/decreased by USD 0.015 per metric ton'.

PORT CHARGE CLAUSE

On long contracts, for instance of over 5 years in length, the port charges may also be fixed or capped to allow for changes of port policy charging, inflation or currency changes.

NOMINATION CLAUSE

A nomination clause is needed for a contract or a single cargo charter party which does not provide for a named ship. It will normally provide for a narrowing of the laydays by the charterer and then the nomination of a named ship or substitute by the owner and finally the definite performing vessel. The timing of these nominations will depend on how much flexibility the charterers have in relation to stockpiles and scheduling. A typical clause might read as follows; ‘Charterers are to give owners a minimum of 60 days tentative and 40 days definite notice of a 15 day laycan. Owners are to nominate a vessel or substitute latest within 15 days of charterer’s declaration of laycan. Actual performing vessel to be nominated latest 10 days prior to the first laydays with estimated time of arrival at the load port, expected quantity of cargo and vessel’s P and I Club. Reconfirmation of each nominated vessel or substitute and actual performing vessel by charterers to be given within 24 hours of nomination, Sundays and holidays excluded and same not to be unreasonably withheld’. Reconfirmation of each nominated vessel and the actual performing vessel may be needed usually within one day. This is to ensure the nominated ship is not black listed from the port or at the very least to make sure adequate cargo has been brought forward in case the actual performance vessel is of a different size than the originally nominated and now substituted vessel. This format with negotiated alterations is sufficient to give the shippers adequate notice although sometimes a specified or narrowed loaded quantity is needed with the nomination. In long contracts, it may be that the schedule of liftings is agreed every 3 or 6 months for the period with charterers nominating loadports, discharge ports and quantities well in advance. The option of substitution gives the owners the flexibility to fix another vessel if they can find a cheaper ship or if their intended ship falls out of position. It is normal that the actual performing vessel finally nominated will have to fill in a pre arranged questionnaire as to its description.

7. The Time Charter Party; Words, Phrases and Concepts What is at Stake?

THE TIME CHARTER PARTY BASIC CONCEPT

The main point about time charters is that the owner places the service of the vessel, fully crewed, at the disposal of the charterer. The charterer therefore, decides how to trade the vessel as if he was the owner himself. The owner, is responsible for the crew, insurances, safe navigation, *'same as when trading for their own account'.* Whatever the charter party type, the parties negotiating the printed and rider clauses are attempting to clarify and allocate specific responsibilities and costs within this simple framework.

If something happens that is due to, or is the responsibility of, the vessel, crew or ownership, it is for the owner's account. If it happens because of the way the ship is being traded by the charterers, it is the charterer's responsibility and account.

This simple concept sometimes gets forgotten in the morass of some of the more technical additional clauses. The complexity of modern ship owning and management and of trading different types of cargo world wide, has meant that charterers and owners have felt the need to go to great lengths to specify the details of what may happen and who then bears the cost and responsibility. This has led, especially in recent years, to a proliferation of rider clauses. Moreover, a great deal of information is usually required from the owner about the ship in order to put in the description clause.

The main issues in time charters can be dealt with by an examination of the most used of the time charter forms, the NYPE 1946 (New York Produce Exchange) with occasional references to other charter party forms. This may seem perverse given the more up to date versions, ASBATIME 1981 and NYPE 1993. The fact is, however, that very few charterers use them, despite the fact that the NYPE '93 at least is in every respect a far more user friendly document in the way it is set out. The reasons for this have been briefly outlined in Chapter Five. The '93 is, however, beginning to be used as a base for long term time charter periods. The Baltime or Linertime will be referred to occasionally but they are little used these days and for reasons that will become apparent this author would not normally recommend their use.

Reference will also be made to the 'Gentime', a BIMCO charter party issued in September 1999 which is an attempt to offer an alternative to the NYPE. It is obviously too early to tell if the industry will begin to use it widely. It will almost certainly take some time due to the inertia of the industry and charterer's present comfort with their existing pro formas based on the NYPE '46. In general, however, it is a much better document than the NYPE '93 with a more equitable division of responsibilities and liabilities, more thoughtful and better worded. But it is a much different form in construction, with new terminology in areas where older terminology has been well tested by court decisions. The references to it will help to elaborate certain normal time charter issues and how the charter parties deal with them.

Some issues such as safe ports and arbitration, for example, are common to time charter and voyage charter parties and have been dealt with in the previous chapter. It is not intended to repeat the issues which are the same for both.

THE SHIP'S DESCRIPTION

Since the charterers are hiring the whole vessel rather than just utilising the carrying capacity, they have to know as much about it as possible that is relevant for that particular trip or period. It is therefore normal that the ship's description in time charter parties is longer than that for a voyage fixture. The main features of the ship are inserted into this section; the ownership, year of build, class, flag, deadweight, cubic capacity, draft, registered tonnage, speed and fuel consumption. However, it is usual to add a rider clause with a much more detailed description, especially for period charters, as the charterer aims to be as fully conversant with the ship as the original owners. Thus, major technical information such as each hold's cubic capacity, the deadweights on various key drafts, hatch cover types and dimensions, between deck heights if appropriate etc. are inserted. A rider clause requiring the owners to provide the charterers with a GA plan, capacity plan, a deadweight scale and copies of current approved grain loading plan and trimming scales is sometimes inserted. Warranties may also be given as to the cleanliness of the ship's holds, watertight hatch covers, suitability for the carriage of grain, for the use of bulldozers in vessel's holds or for grab discharge. If hatch covers are found defective a clause may be inserted that this is to be rectified at the owner's time and expense to class surveyors satisfaction They may even be subject to a hose test to prove they are water tight.

A clause detailing the requirement of the possession of necessary trading certificates or the requirement to establish financial security in respect of oil or other pollution damage is either part of the description clause or the subject of separate rider clauses. Information such as the vessel's constants in order to be more accurate on the likely intake of cargo and the exact bunker capacity of the tanks for accurate planning of bunkering operations is also given for certain trips, if needed. Further information may be required for communicating with the crew such as the Master's name, the call sign and radio station that the vessel must listen to and communicate with, the fax and Inmarsat numbers etc., that the Master and the key members of the crew speak English and if there are any implications in trading to various countries because of the nationality of the crew.

Some owners who argue about the meaning of 'self trimming bulk carrier' (See Chapter One, Section B) will not agree to this description but add a clause typically worded something like; 'The upper and lower portions of the vessel's holds are sloped transversely and longitudinally and the vessel could, therefore, be construed as a self trimming bulk carrier for the loading of bulk grain and similar hard surface and free flowing bulk cargoes, but for transverse trimming purposes only'.

It may be thought by owners that too much information is now demanded of them but the industry is far more precise these days than it was in the past and the charterer's questionnaire often forms part of their internal Quality Control Systems. The following description, for example, is taken from an offer for a simple 25 day trip with grain on a gearless bulk carrier incorporating all the information the charterers required in the form of a questionnaire.

MV..............
Panamax Bulk Carrier
Built 1984 Cyprus Flag ITF OK
Dwat 63,920 mt on 13.084 m, LOA 225m, Beam 32.2 m, TPI 162 m
7hoha steel Macgregor hatch covers, side rolling
2,782,435 cuft grain CO2 fitted
about 13 knots on about 30.5 tons IFO 180 CST plus 2 tons mdo
port consumption 2.5 tons mdo daily
Vessel's M/E under pilots/ manouvering / in-out of ports /canals /straights /rivers /shallow waters consumes MDO
Constants about 500 tons excluding fresh water

GRT/NRT 35,808/22,199
55,300 mt Dwat basis 12 metres draft
all figures 'about'
1.Name –
2.Self trimming bulk carrier – yes
3.When/where built- Copenhagen 1984
4.Flag Cyprus
5.Registry Limassol Cyprus
6.Class ABS
7.GRT/NRT as above
8.No of holds and hatches 7/7
9.Hatch sizes- all hatches 14.4 x 15 m
10.Type of hatch covers side rolling steel Mcgregor hatch covers
11.Dwat on summer draft and TPC 13.084m / 63.75 mt
12.Dwat on 11. 25 summer draft 52,100 mt/62.65 mt
13.Loa 225 m
14.Beam 32.24 m
15.Hold cubic capacity grain in Cubic ft
1- 360,210
2- 407530
3- 397,640
4- 397,640
5- 409,650
6- 409,650
7- 400,115
16.Speed/cons –laden as above
17.Speed/consumption – ballast- as above
18.In port consumption- as above
19.IFO/MDO/FW capacity 2300/350/550
20.Call sign V4MS7
21.Does vessel have a telex on board –Yes Inmarsat No 420900941 via

Satelite station 00582
22.Engine B and W
23.Fresh water daily cons/prod 16/16 mt
24.Holds free of obstructions- yes
25.Hold ventilation –no
26.CO2 in holds – yes
27.Vessel has approved grain loading untrimmed ends –yes
28.P and I club-A. Bilbrough and Co. Ltd London
29.H and M value USD 15 million
30.Last dry dock Sept 1996
31.Height from tank tops to hatch coaming 18.6 m
32.Distance from ship side to hatch coaming 8.6 m
33.Distance from waterline to top hatches in ballast condition including no 4 hold ballasted 14.2 m
34.Distance water line to highest point (top of mast) in ballast condition 40.3m
35.When vessel last called at...........
All figures 'about'
Vessel to be a SDSTBC fully ITF and Australian WWF hold ladders fitted

Vessel suitable to load bulk grain according SOLAS regulations with dispensation for untrimmed ends
Vessel not called Cuba for the last 6 months
Owners confirm vessel not called CIS Pacific ports between 40-60 degrees North between July and September in last 2 years- Gypsy moth clause to apply
Vessel to fully comply with ISM code

An offer for an even more simple 25 day trip with iron ore included the following enormous description.

MV ....
Bahamas flag
Built September 1977
Gearless bulk carrier
Owners -Pitcairn Shipping Corp
71,730 mt dwt on 14.026 m SSW
3,090,358 cu.ft. grain in unobstructed main holds
8hoha
LOA/Beam 228/32.2 m
About 12 knots on about 35 tons laden/ballast IFO 180 RME 25 plus about 2.5 MDO DMB (all long tons) up to Beaufort Scale 4
Port consumption about 1/1.5 lt IFO plus about 2.5 LT mdo
Vessel have fore aft folding McGregor hatchcovers
Hatch sizes 1 – 9.15 x 10.07 2/3/5/7/8 each 12.6 x 15.12 m 4/6 each 14.4 x 15.12
Vessel fully ITF
Constants about 350 mt excluding FW
DWAT on 9.5m FW about 41,300
DWAT on 22' FW 24,900 mt
23' FW 26,700 mt
32' BW 43,100 mt Salinity 1015
36' BW 51,700 mt ‘’
37' BW 53,000 mt ‘’
40' BW 58,000 mt ‘’
36' FW 52,100 mt
41' FW 61,600 mt
TPC 65.2 on full draft
Vessel classed Lloyds Register +100 A1 / SS passed November 1995
Cubics including hatches 1/8 cum
5356.9/11428.5/13427.2/11174.1/13068.4/11401.0/10847.0
distance keel to hatch coaming 21.9 m at no 1 hold at no 2 21.36 holds

3-8 21.25m

distance keel to top of mast 44.6

draft with heavy ballast and no 5 flooded 7.44 m

draft with light ballast 5.51 m

GT/NT 38412/25263

Bunker capacity Mdo 259 MT and IFO 2600 mt 98 percent full

INMARSAT TLX No 1305743 Fax 1305744

Call Sign C6LT8

No GA last 3 years

Mooring lines

6 polyprop fore

6 polyprop aft

2 springwires fore

2 springwires aft

plus spares on board

H and M value 8 million

1. Vessel is a single deck self trimming bulk carrier classed Lloyds 100 A1
2. Vessel is in every respect suitable for charterers trading Australia/ China and carry cargo of iron ore in bulk only
3. Vessel is P and I covered during the whole charter period. P and I club is Standard Club of Bermuda
4. Vessel is ITF fitted, does not have AHL therefore owners to be fully responsible for any and all costs/expenses/delays due to vessel's lack of AHL at loading port

Please advise following

1 Owners/disponent owners full style

2 Vessel's manager's full style

3 Vessel' s P and I club

4 H and M value

5 Vessel's class and owners to confirm it will remain fully classed during the currency of this charter party

6 Vessels itinerary and last 3 cargoes
7 Vessel's FO/ DO/ FW tank capacities
8 WLTHC in ballasted and fully laden condition
9 TPI/TPC and constants
10 GRT/NRT
11 Grain capacity breakdown
12 Hatch sizes
13 Max alternative speeds/consumptions
14 Vessel classed for alternate hold loading
15 Inmarsat and telex numbers
16 Max time for deballasting
17 Dwat on 11 and 11.8 m SSW
18 Constants

In addition to all this, some clauses require the owner to fax to the charterer copies of the ship's certificates such as the P and I entry Certificate, International Tonnage Certificate, Gear and Tackle Certificate and ISM Entry Certificate. It is also now usual to include the ISM Certificate number and its validity.

A Ro-Ro would have a charter party description which would also include all the relevant information that the charterer would need to know to evaluate it for its specific needs. For example:

MV..
Built 1975 NIS flag
Trailer vessel Classed DNV+1A1 RoRo EO Ice A
3947 dwt on 5.9 m draft
2311 GRT .848 NRT
LOA 118.4 m Breadth moulded 16m

Capacity	LM	FH	TEUS	TRAILERS (40X8FT)	AXLE LOAD
TANK TOP	170	3.6		28	10T
MAIN DECK	426	6.0	128	34	50T
SHELETER DECK	222		50	17	11T
TOTAL	818		206	51	

Stern ramp; length 8.5 m plus flaps 1.5 m/max weight 200 tons/max axle load 50 t

Stern gate- free height 6m/free width 8m
Elevators ; main deck/shelter deck - 16 x 3/35T
Main deck/tank top - 7.5 x 2.8/20T

Air changes(based on dimensions from ships drawings, compartments and fan capacities) main hold 15 changes per hour (30 with full cargo)
Lower hold 22 hour changes per hour
2 Wartsila/Sulzer Main engines type 9ZH 40/48 4500 BHP 410 RPM
2x KAMEWA Stainless steel reversible pitch propellers
Speed about 16/17 knots on about 22.5 t IFO 40
Bowthruster Brunvoll type FU 63 LTC- 1750 (new 1990) 736 KW
Auxilliaries 2 x Wartsila type 524 TS 750 BHP 750 RPM
1 x Caterpillar (new 1990) type 35/12A 990 BHP 1500RPM
Consumption Auxilliary diesel engines
At sea 2.5 MT (with reefer containers 2.7 MT)
Generators 2 x NESS type WAB 995/8-F 625 KVA 3x 380 V 50 HZ 1500 RPM
In port with lifts working 2.5MT/Domestic use only 1.5MT
Accomodation (including crew) 38 berths in;
7 cabins bridge plus hospital/ 22 cabins shelter deck/ 2 cabins boat deck
all details 'about' and without guarantee

SPEED AND CONSUMPTION

Particular attention should, however, be given to the **speed and consumption** clause. While the earning capacity of the ship depends on the deadweight, draft, cubics and to some extent the length (LOA) and other measurements, one of the most important is the speed and consumption. But unlike the other measurements, which are reasonably precise, albeit covered by the words **'about'**, the speed and consumption is only given as an **'about' figure with certain qualifications**.

The NYPE says that the vessel should be *'capable of steaming, fully laden, under good weather conditions about....... knots on a consumption of about..... tons'*. The Baltime '74 goes further so that the condition includes *'good weather and smooth water'*. Since good weather and smooth water are rarely encountered and certainly not for the duration of a typical voyage, if literally interpreted (and the law does just that), it makes the speed and consumption warranty meaningless. The owners probably only have to show that the ship made the speed and consumption for a day or two. It is true that Clause 9 says that the Master shall prosecute the voyages with the utmost despatch but Clause 13 excludes liability for delay even if caused by the fault or neglect by the owner's servants. It is no doubt one of the main factors why the Baltime is now seldom the choice of charterers as a pro forma and thus seldom used.

The issue in the NYPE wording is nevertheless similar in that the wording tells the charterer some important information but leaves him with equally important questions. If the consumption is based when laden, what is the consumption in ballast? Thus, usually both the laden and ballast speeds are inserted if the vessel is to perform in ballast as well as laden, for example in a round voyage where the first leg is in ballast to the load port or for a longer period where there may be a number of ballast voyages. For period charters and sometimes single trip charters, various alternative speeds and consumptions for both laden and ballast are also inserted.

Both the speed and the consumption are qualified by the word **'about'**. What does 'about', when used in this clause, mean?

The problem is that this type of charter party dates from 1913 when the type of vessels were about 5/10,000 tons deadweight, coal burning and sailed at 9-10 knots. These vessels had no radar or radio. The Master therefore could not route his ship according to the latest weather information. The quality of bunker coals varied. Spare parts could not be sent out by plane. In consequence almost everything in the charter party had to be fudged by the word 'about'. It was not a scientific business. But today, all is different. The necessity to have the word 'about', has to a large extent gone. It is true that the owner still has considerable weather risk. But in today's world of instant global communications, weather monitoring and forecasting, engineering precision and risk management, the risk of the voyage should lie more with the owners as they alone know and operate the ships, not with the charterers who cannot properly calculate the likely performance of the ship if the margin of tolerance is too wide.

One arbitration in 1988 began to recognise this changing world and fixed the tolerance of the word 'about', in the circumstances of the case, at a quarter of a knot rather than half a knot as had been the general interpretation previously. Another arbitration has held that the allowance must be tailored to the ship's configuration, size, draft etc. It is therefore difficult today for ship owners and charterers to predict what allowance will be given in arbitration. However, if both the speed and consumption figures are subject to the 'about' tolerance, the charterer may feel he cannot properly calculate the likely performance nor, if she fails to perform adequately, prove it satisfactorily to an Arbitrator. This is especially the case when it is anyway qualified, '*under good weather'*, and thus is likely to deteriorate under worse weather and sea conditions. It is therefore often agreed that only one 'about' is used and that 'good weather' is qualified as 'up to and including Beaufort 4'. **The Beaufort Scale** is a wind scale and sea disturbance table which grades the force of winds and height of waves. Sometimes the relevant Sea State Scale is also inserted. The NYPE '93 and Gentime incorporate a Beaufort wind scale wording into its main body rather than having it as a rider clause as is necessary when using the usual NYPE '46.

These consumption figures are often qualified by 'at sea', as vessels also consume bunkers in port. Port consumption is usually stated separately and it is standard to add the following, 'Vessel to have the liberty to use diesel oil in port and in confined waters for manoeuvring and for engine room purposes'.

The importance of speed and consumption varies depending on the market. In a high market the party that controls the ships will want the ship to perform at the highest possible speed to complete the voyage so as to start another earning voyage as soon as possible. The cost of the fuel or bunkers will be of a lesser concern. In a low market, however, the cost of the bunkers will be of greater significance. It may well be that performing the voyage at a slower and more economical speed will save bunkers and make the overall result of the voyage much better. This will also depend on the price of bunkers. Over the past few years the Rotterdam bunker price, for example, for IFO 380 CST has fluctuated between around U.S.$ 50 to $ 140 per ton and in the years following the second oil shock in the late 1970's and early to mid 1980's, a price of $ 150-180 was more common. (See Figure 6.1) However, it is important to a charterer who takes the ship for a period to know exactly what he can do with the ship in terms of the slowest and highest speeds, even if that involves the fitting of different nozzles and the varying consumptions at those speeds. The charterer needs to be able to calculate as close as possible to a fixed speed and consumption.

The owner, on the other hand, while wishing to be competitive will be as anxious as possible not to warrant a speed and consumption which is unobtainable in, for example, strong currents and thus leave himself open to under-performance claims from the charterers.

Due to past cases of the supply of poor quality bunkers, which is the charterer's responsibility under time charter, owners will often be willing to be more specific on the vessel's speed and consumption provided that quality standards on bunkers are agreed by the charterers. Thus after the description of the Fuel Oil Viscosity it is not at all unusual these days to agree 'ISO 8217, 1996' or a similar quality standard.

A rider clause is sometimes added that requires the charterer to supply bunkers within a maximum viscosity. Independent analysis is permitted by an appropriate organisation and owners have a certain time limit to advise charterers of bunker related problems after which they are not allowed to make a claim on a bunker quality issue.

It can be seen from the above that it is now standard to modify every word in this clause to such an extent that when drawing up the charter party, the preamble and description is filled in an addition which will read 'see clause......'. This particular rider clause will be a thorough description, which could be typically anything from half a page to three pages depending on the trip, duration and the complexity of the vessel.

However, the issue of speed and consumption is still sometimes further investigated. The evidence of the weather and sea state in the past has only been known to the particular vessel in question at sea and as recorded by the Master in his log. But the Master is employed by the ship owner, not the charterer. It is known therefore, that some log extracts from some ships could be somewhat questionable in the exaggeration of weather conditions encountered en route. It is for this reason that **weather routing companies** started to be employed by charterers to monitor weather conditions on ship's routes, both to check the validity of the Master's reports but also to advise him on routing in the light of meteorological forecasts. It is therefore not unusual to see a weather routing clause added as a rider clause in a charter party.

An example would be as follows, 'In order to maximise the vessel's performance the Master is to follow 'Ocean Routes' suggestions concerning navigation, but Master at his reasonable discretion may not follow the suggested route, in which case he is to detail in the log book the reason for departing from those suggestions. If the Master uses his discretion unreasonably, the charterers can claim for the eventual under performance. For these purposes evidence of weather conditions are to be taken from the vessel's deck log and Ocean Route's report. If there is consistent discrepancy between the deck log and Ocean Routes Report, the Ocean Route report shall be taken as ruling.'

This emphasises the point made earlier about the more precise and scientific approach now taken than was available when the charter parties were originally conceived. However, one important point should be made. In the example of the weather route clause above, the suggestion that an exercise of discretion which is 'unreasonable' may lead to a claim, may serve to concentrate the mind of the Master if he does deviate from advice which will obviously be well founded and given in good faith. But it is really only an expression of hope from the charterers. The safety of the ship, is entirely the Master's responsibility and all factors concerning this, including routing, is his decision. I once fixed a ship from Vancouver to Korea where the Master was advised by the weather routing company to go further north than was usual to avoid severe storms on the usual route. He did not follow this advice and what should have been a 15 day trip turned into a 22 day trip. The charterers were understandably furious at the delay and extra expense. But even if he had made an error of judgement, the responsibility of the ship's safety rests upon him. Clause 26 specifically says, *'Owners remain responsible for the navigation of the vessel'*.

The following weather routing clause accepts this and while charterers get to monitor the ship's performance closely, the owners and Master have more leeway. 'Charterers to provide Ocean Routes assistance to the Master, during each voyage specified by the charterers. The Master to comply with the reporting procedure or the routing service. However, routing of the vessel always at Master's discretion and Ocean Routes' routing always to be understood as a recommendation only. The vessel shall be capable, at all times during the currency of this charter party of steaming as per description clause. For the purpose of this charter party, 'good weather conditions' are to be defined as weather conditions in wind speeds not exceeding Beaufort Force 4 and Sea State Douglas 3. Evidence of weather conditions to be taken from the vessel's deck logs. Evaluation of vessel's performance has to compensate for any difference arising from better or under performance on all voyages during the duration of this charter party, corrections be made and balanced against each other'.

It can be seen that in such ways have the speed and consumption clauses in time charter parties been gradually amended and are now almost as rigorous as tanker time charters which contain a performance clause requiring the owner to warrant a minimum speed in weather conditions defined by a specific Beaufort Scale force. The SBT tanker charter party, for example, warrants that the vessel shall maintain throughout the period a guaranteed average speed and fuel consumption under all weather conditions and others provide for an adjustment of hire in the event of under-performance. While the standard time charter agreements in dry cargo do not go that far, the additional wording usually added to the standard NYPE wording does allow the charterer to calculate and assess the ships properly and fairly, reflect modern conditions and provide a fairer balance between the owner and charterer than that provided by the standard wording of the NYPE alone, which was more appropriate for an earlier age.

'IN EVERY WAY FITTED FOR THE SERVICE'

Line 22 of the NYPE '46 reads that vessel *'on her delivery to be ready to receive cargo with clean swept holds, tight, staunch, strong and in every way fitted for the service'*. This mirrors the normal voyage charter party wording, *'in every way fitted for the voyage*'. This wording, along with the words in line 5, *'with hull, machinery and equipment in a thoroughly efficient state'*, constitute an absolute warranty of **seaworthiness.** However, as discussed in the previous chapter, just as in the voyage charter party, this absolute warranty of seaworthiness may be diluted by other clauses in the charter party. Specifically the inclusion of the U.S. Carriage of Goods by Sea Act by Clause 24 (the Paramount clause), will mean that only due diligence has to be exercised by the ship owner to make the ship seaworthy before delivery. (See Chapter Eight- Clause Paramount) The Asbatime's Paramount clause incorporates this Act into the Bills of Lading only and its seaworthiness obligations are therefore higher than the NYPE '46. The charterers are entitled to cancel the vessel if (a) she misses her cancelling date, (b) she is not in a seaworthy condition and in every way fit for the service, or (c) she is not delivered in a condition described in the charter party.

If the ship is accepted by the charterers in circumstances in which they would have been entitled to refuse to accept delivery, for instance if she has not got *'clean swept holds'* on delivery, such acceptance is no waiver of that right. An addition is often inserted as follows. 'Acceptance of delivery does not constitute any waiver of owner's obligations'.

The warranty of seaworthiness in the NYPE '46 continues with wording about winches with sufficient power. It is often deleted and if the ship has cranes, is dealt with in a rider clause. However, even for a gearless ship, winches for opening hatches need to be in working order and this needs to be covered somewhere. The Gentime gives the charterers the option to accept a delay due to a breakdown of gear against a reduction of hire or to work with shore gear, the owners paying such costs. The wording about the ship having to have a full complement of officers is retained. Rider clauses may be included which adds extra wording to these phrases. A typical one may read, 'The owners shall maintain the vessel's class and keep her in a thoroughly efficient state in hull, machinery, hatch covers and equipment, with all certificates (including tonnage and measurement certificates and all certificates relating to officers and crew) necessary to comply with requirements at ports of call, canals and waterways, for and during the service and with all governmental regulations of the nation of the vessel's flag, failing which the owners will be responsible for actual time lost and related expenses thereby incurred'. It is implied in the words **'in every way fitted for the service'** anyway, but many charterers now find they want to detail the exact requirements. Another rider clause giving more detail to "in every eay fitted for the service" is as follows, 'The vessel is suitable for discharge by grabs and/or vacuvators and is able to load a full cargo of grain and/or grain products in bulk without trimming/levelling and without securing of cargo. The vessel has grain approval for 'filled holds with untrimmed ends' and is approved for grain loading under the rules of the 1960 SOLAS Convention and amendments thereto, having all the necessary certificates on board'. Of course, the 'in every way fitted for the service' on time charter, could include many different kinds of cargo or trading area, thus the exact wording of the additional clause that charterers now try to specifically cover can be of an almost endless variety.

It might be thought the above additional clauses would be more than sufficient. But the maintenance part of this clause, '*with hull, machinery and equipment in a thoroughly efficient state',* under English law has been interpreted that owners have the obligation to make good any deficiencies after they manifest themselves. This may be one reason why, along with the increasing amount of legislation that owners have to comply with in this increasingly precise age, clauses have been introduced which try to cover every eventuality in a much more defined way. This is particularly true of **necessary certificates.** One way of approaching this is to specify that the vessel should have certificates for "all ports and places within trading limits".

Certificates that some rider clauses prefer to specify that are on board the ship rather than rely on the words, *'in every way fitted for the service'* or "for all ports and places within trading limits" are spelled out in the following example of a very specific clause; '(a) the Australian Maritime Safety Authority loading and unloading safety measure regulations, including their Navigation (Orders) Regulations Section 32 which refers to cargo gear, cranes/hold ladders; (b) valid and approved cargo gear register with certificates; (c) SOLAS 1974 (pertaining to loading grain cargoes and the vessel's approved grain loading plan should refer to untrimmed hold ends). Vessel to have on board an approved grain loading certificate from the vessel's country of registry; (d) ILA Convention Number 32 which statutory in the USA under Public Law 85- 742 part 9- Safety and Health Regulations for Longshoring; (e) the United States Department Labour Safety and Health Regulations including as set forth in Part 111 of the Federal Register; (f) International Tonnage Certificate Rules 1969; (g) a United States Coast Guard Certificate of Financial Responsibility as required under the U.S. Water Quality Act of 1970 and any amendments thereto and any further certificates as may be required during the currency of this charter party. If the stevedores, longshoremen or other workmen are not permitted to work due to failure of Master and/or owners to provide the required certificates/

documents, hire shall cease until vessel is in a position to comply with the aforementioned regulations and owners to pay all extra expenses incurred if and/or incidental to and resulting from such failure'.

There is often an additional clause which requires the ship to be in possession of valid necessary certificates during the currency of the charter to comply with current regulations and requirements of the Panama and Suez Canals.

These examples go back to how the ship is managed and compliance with various conventions and regulations detailed in Chapter One, Section B. Other rider clauses require the ship to comply with all safety and health regulations, failing which costs, expenses and loss of time to be for owner's account. Owners are also often required to agree to comply with governmental regulations, carry **Certificates of Financial Responsibility** and establish and maintain financial security in respect of **oil or other pollution damage**.

In the aftermath of the **U.S.Oil Pollution Act 1990 (OPA),** a number of oil pollution clauses were drafted in charter parties. Most of them try to impose on ship owners, as the U.S. Oil Pollution Act is intended, obligations of certification and insurance of liabilities for oil pollution. Owners who trade to the U.S. do carry such certification and insurances. But there is the problem knowing how the various states will legislate in respect of oil pollution, especially if they will impose a wider liability than OPA '90. Owners have to be careful not to accept warranties that go beyond the cover available. In a longer term time charter, a charterer will naturally need to know that the ship owner will comply with pollution requirements, perhaps as yet, unforeseen. After all, the ship has to be *'in every way fitted for the service.'*

A clause they may be asked to accept is that the vessel has to supply various relevant certificates. These may include,

> "Certificates issued pursuant to the Civil Liberty Convention 1965 (CLC), certificates issued pursuant to Section 311 (p) of the U.S. Federal Water Pollution Control Act, as amended (title 33 US Code Section 1321 (p), certificates which may be required by US Federal legislation at any time during the currency of this charter party, provided always that such legislation incorporates the CLC as amended by the 1984 Protocol thereto or contains provisions thereto; notwithstanding anything whether printed or typed herein to the contrary; save as required for compliance with paragraph one as above, owners shall not be required to establish or maintain financial security or responsibility in respect of oil or other pollution damage to enable the vessel lawfully to enter, remain in, or leave port, place territorial or contiguous waters of any country, state or territory in performance of this charter party. Charterers shall indemnify owners and hold them harmless in respect of any loss, damage, liability or expense (including but not limited to the cost of any damage incurred by the vessel to give alterrnative voyage orders) whatsoever and howsoever arising which owners may sustain by reason of the vessel's inability to perform as aforesaid. Owners shall not be liable for any loss, damage, liability or expense whatsoever and however arising which charterers and or the holders of any Bill of Lading issues pursuant to this charter party may sustain by reason of the vessel's inability to perform as aforesaid. Charterers warrant that the terms of this clause will be incorporated effectively into any Bill of Lading issued pursuant to this charter party."

Another issue covered by necessary certificates is the **deratting** certificate. A rider clause will sometimes be specific on this too with a clause something like,

> "The vessel shall be delivered with a valid deratting certificate or deratting exemption certificate. If such certificate does not cover the whole period of the charter, cost of renewal of certificate and any required fumigation for obtaining such certificate, if necessary, shall be for the owner's account, any detention and extra expenses incurred thereby shall be also for the owner's account."

Just as in voyage charters, it is now usual to have an **ISM clause**. The BIMCO clause can be used. Alternatively something with the following is usual.

> "During the currency of this charter party, the owners shall procure that the vessel and the company (as defined by the ISM Code) shall comply with the requirements of the ISM Code. Upon request the owners shall provide a copy of the relevant document of compliance (DOC) and Safety Management Certificate (SMC) to the charterers. Except as otherwise provided in this charter party, loss, damage, expenses or delay caused by failure on the part of the company to comply with the ISM Code shall be for the owner's account".

DELIVERY/REDELIVERY

Delivery time is usually qualified with 'ATDNSHINC' or '*any time day or night Sundays and holidays included'*. The delivery place provisions are deleted and whatever the parties have agreed is inserted, typically **'Arrival Pilot Station'** (APS) or **'Arrival First Sea Pilot Station'** (AFSPS) of the loadport, **'Dropping Outward Pilot'** (DOP) or **'Dropping Last Outward Sea Pilot'** (DLOSP) of the last port of call of the vessel, **'when where ready'** (WWR) or passing a certain point or latitude. As has been pointed out earlier, it is common to insert here, 'Acceptance of delivery by charterers shall not constitute any waiver of owner's obligations hereunder.'

The Sea Pilot is referred to because some ports have more than one pilot, for example, in some circumstances there may be one from the berth to a channel, another within that channel and yet another 'sea pilot' between the channel and the sea pilot station.

If the vessel misses her cancelling, under the NYPE '46 (4pm on the cancelling date but often amended in negotiations to 2400 hours), she still has to present her NOR at the delivery place. The Baltime has what is commonly known in the chartering industry, as the 'Baltime cancellation clause'. Under this, if the vessel cannot be delivered by the cancelling date, *'the charterers, if required, are to declare within 48 hours after receiving notice thereof, whether they cancel or take delivery of the vessel'.* Perhaps surprisingly the NYPE '93 has a similar clause, the authors of which seem to have a more than passing aquantaince with the authors of the Amwelsh '93. *'If the owners warrant that, despite the exercise of due diligence by them, the vessel will not be ready for delivery by the cancelling date, and provided owners are able to state with reasonable certainty the date on which the vessel will be ready, they may at the earliest seven days before the vessel is expected to sail for the port or place of delivery, require the charterers to declare whether or not they will cancel the charter party. Should the charterers elect not to cancel, or should they fail to reply within 2 days or by the cancelling date, whichever shall occur first, then the seventh day after the expected date of readiness for delivery as notified by the owners shall replace the original cancelling date. Should the vessel be further delayed, the owners shall be entitled to require further declarations of the charterers in accordance with this clause'.* This goes beyond the Baltime's provisions in requiring the charterer's repeated declarations. This certainly seems a most generous provision. So much so, that few if any charterers have adopted the charter party as a whole for time charter trips.

The Gentime has restricted the right of owners to require the charterers to declare whether they will cancel or not (interpellate) to one only. BIMCO's Special Circular (September 1999) introducing the Gentime states, '..... realising that the right to interpellate could introduce some owners not to do their utmost in trying to reach the place of delivery within the time agreed should a more lucrative fixture appear, the right of interpellation applies only once'. This argument, at a stroke, destroys the raison d'etre of the repeated declaration wording of the Amwelsh '93 and NYPE '93. But more than that, this argument is in itself very dubious. How many times, in the circumstances described by BIMCO above, would an owner most likely exercise this option? Surely not more than once unless in the most exceptional circumstances.

This 'interpellation' clause, unless specifically inserted for reasons pertaining to the particular circumstances of a fixture, is a sledge hammer solution to crack a peanut of a problem. Indeed, what problem? There is no clamour from owners protesting about the unfairness of the traditional clause, nor is there constant abuse of it from charterers. When ships are delayed it is always dealt with in a practical and commercial way. It is quite common for vessels to get delayed by port delays, congestion and bad weather but it is very uncommon indeed for a charterer to instruct a ship to ballast to the loading port, knowing it will miss the cancelling date and knowing he has another remedy for the problem, only then to tell the vessel when it gives Notice of Readiness that he is cancelled. It would serve no purpose for the charterer and anyway would damage his reputation. This kind of clause is one of the major barriers to these new charter party's being adopted by charterers. The issues are also discussed in Chapter Six under 'Laycan'.

Redelivery is dealt with in clause 4 of the NYPE '46 after 'Hire' and the same kind of conditions as on delivery are agreed. For instance, if the last discharge port is in the eastern Mediterranean, the redelivery place might be argued by charterers and owners during negotiations, owners wanting redelivery 'passing Gibralter' and charterers wanting 'passing Cape Passero', the southern tip of Sicily. For the owners it is not only that they get paid for extra sailing time, it is that they come off hire and are re-delivered nearer the probable next loading port.

Sufficient notices should be given for both delivery and redelivery so that the charterer / owner has time to arrange employment for the ship. Thus a typical clause will state that the 'Owners/Charterers are to give charterers/owners not less than 20/15 days approximate notice with probable port and 10/5 days definite notice of vessels expected date of delivery / redelivery and definite port'. The days are negotiable, as is whether the redelivery place is a 'probable port' or 'definite port' or a range such as 'Hamburg – Gibralter range'.

To equalise advantages and disadvantages of timing when delivery is in one time zone and redelivery in another, a rider clause is sometimes inserted making all delivery and redelivery times subject to the same one, typically Greenwich Mean Time (GMT). If such a clause is not inserted, it is the local times that dictate the delivery and redelivery times. The NYPE '93 actually states in the printed form that all times of delivery/redelivery shall be adjusted to GMT. The Gentime states, "All calculations of hire shall be made by reference to UTC (Universal Time Coordinated)".

It is usual to hold an **'on hire survey'** and an **'off hire survey'** to quantify the amount of bunkers on delivery and redelivery, the condition of the vessel, her equipment and cargo compartments. They are usually conducted by a mutually appointed surveyor, at the port of delivery but if delivery is passing a point or latitude at sea it would be carried out at the next port of call. The costs and time being shared between owners and charterers or more likely charterers pay one and owners the other. The Gentime, however, states that on/off hire should be conducted "without loss of time". In practice these surveys are simple and not time consuming but they are important. For instance, if the ship has been chartered for a trip with petroleum coke or HBI, very dirty cargoes, and the charter party stipulation is that redelivery is with 'clean swept holds', the surveyor should be able to confirm the actual condition of the holds.

HOLD CLEANLINESS ON DELIVERY/REDELIVERY

As noted above, the NYPE states, *'Vessel on her delivery to be ready to receive cargo with clean swept holds'* and that her redelivery should be in *'like good order and condition wear and tear excepted'*. Indeed, all the time charter forms state the same thing. The delivery condition requirement may be expanded if the anticipated first cargo requires more than 'clean swept' and has to pass independent inspections for grain, for example. (See also Chapter Six- Inspections). The Gentime differs in that the obligation to deliver the vessel's holds in a clean condition applies not on delivery but on arrival at the first port of loading. If delivery is prior to the first load port, this is normal, usual and sensible.

If *'redelivery with clean swept holds'*, or *'in same condition as on delivery'*, is agreed, it is common practice to agree a lumpsum **in lieu of hold cleaning**. The charterers therefore redeliver the ship at the earliest moment and the crew will then clean the holds ready for the next cargo. Main terms will specify it in the following shorthand; 'USD 3000 **ILOHC**' (in lieu of hold cleaning). The owners may specify different sums for different last cargoes. Petcoke would take longer to clean and thus cost more than grain for example. A full rider clause might read as follows, 'Vessel's holds to be clean swept, washed down by fresh water and dried, free from rust, insects and odour on delivery. The vessel on arrival at first loadport to be in all respects ready to load and carry charterer's intended cargo including grain, and pass all inspections and surveys required. If the vessel fails, then it is to be placed off hire from the time of failure and all bunkers consumed and any extra expenses to be for owner's account until the vessel has re passed inspection. The vessel to be redelivered with clean swept holds, however, the charterers have the option to redeliver the vessel without cleaning against payment of lumpsum USD 3000 in lieu of hold cleaning'. Such a clause could also include provision for charterers to cancel if, on delivery it fails inspection and it cannot be cleaned within 72 hours thereafter, with the owners indemnifying the charterers against all losses and costs resulting from such a termination. It would be a tough addition and would not be accepted by all owners, but has been agreed on many occasions.

In time charters lasting more than one voyage the charterers may also request the crew to clean holds between cargoes. The time and cost will depend on the last and next cargo. If the previous cargo has been dirty and the next cargo is grain, for example, the charterers will need the full cooperation of the officers and crew. It is therefore usual to insert an **'intermediate hold cleaning clause'** if this is necessary and goes beyond what the crew would be expected to do according to their normal terms and conditions. In this case a clause along the following lines is fairly normal. 'Crew to perform Intermediate hold cleaning after discharging any cargo and prior arrival next load port weather/time permitting if so required by charterers, cleaning holds to the standard as if vessel is in owner's service, to enable vessel to tender for loading next cargo, charterers paying owners USD 3500 or USD 500 per hold for sweeping and washing. Owners cannot be responsible for any failure of hold inspection'. Sometimes different amounts are specified for different cargoes reflecting the extra difficulties, time and expense of cleaning after dirty cargoes. Occasionally, such a clause will also specify that 'any dunnage, debris or lashing material should be removed at charterer's time and expense prior to redelivery and any chemicals and additional fresh water over an above that produced by vessel's evaporator also to be for charterer's account.'

'REDELIVERY IN LIKE GOOD ORDER AND CONDITION'

Lines 54/55 state *'redelivery in like good order and condition, ordinary wear and tear excepted'*. The owners have obligations in lines 37/38 to *'maintain the ship in an efficient state'*. Under the maintenance clauses, as has been discussed above, *'in every way fitted for the service',* owners are obliged to repair damages which occur during the charter period, the charterers being liable to pay for the cost of repair of damages caused by any breach of the charter party. Charterer's obligations relate to damage for which they are responsible. It is usually considered unnecessary, therefore, to have a stevedore damage clause. Nevertheless, some charterers insert one as a rider clause and the NYPE '93 and Gentime have one as standard. (Clause 35).

MARGIN OF PERIOD

The word 'about' in line 14 of the NYPE '46 is now generally deleted for the same general reasons stated in 'Speed and consumption' above when discussing the inability to satisfactorily define the word 'about'. A more precise wording is inserted. The NYPE '93 clause does not include the word 'about' reflecting how the NYPE '46 has been adapted. In period charters, for example, it is usual to agree a minimum and maximum period. This might be, for example, 12 months, one month more or less in charterer's option, or for example, minimum 150 maximum 230 days. Sometimes it is normal to have a minimum but where the spread is two months or less, an "about maximum" where "about" is defined as 10 or 15 days.

Where a maximum period is agreed and the last voyage under the period exceeds the maximum period, the charterer has broken an obligation. The Baltime and Linertime state that in this case the market rate will apply. Under an NYPE if the vessel is sent by the charterer on a last voyage which could reasonably be expected to be completed by the end of the period but is delayed for reasons outside the control of either party, the charter is presumed to continue in operation until the end of the voyage, even if it extends beyond the charter period, the hire being payable at the charter party rate. The circumstances in which such a case will arise will usually be when the market rate is higher than the charter rate and the charterer wants to squeeze in as much profitable trading as possible.

If the charterer, on the other hand, gives an order for a voyage that cannot reasonably expected to be completed by the end of the charter period then the owner is entitled to refuse the order and call for a legitimate last voyage. If no such order is forthcoming, the owner may treat the charter at an end, seek other employment and claim damages. If they accept the order, they will be entitled to hire at the charter rate up to the end of the charter period and where the market rate has risen above the charter rate, the market rate until redelivery. The Gentime, for the first time, explicitly states this in Clause 4(d).

On the other hand if a ship is redelivered to the owner earlier that the stated period the question arises whether the owner can refuse to accept redelivery and continue to claim hire. In fact he will find it hard to do this, so the general rule is that where there has been such a **repudiation**, the owner has to claim damages. The alternative is that the charterer has to keep the ship and pay hire until the earliest possible redelivery.

Some charters are still agreed even when everything else is getting more precise, for an 'about period', for instance, 'duration about 4/6 months'. In this case, what is a reasonable margin should be determined in the light of each individual case. For instance, the period could be described as 'three transatlantic round voyages, about three to four months'. The duration may be actually more than the maximum due to unforeseen port congestion. It is therefore better to add at the end, the words, 'without guarantee' or 'all going well, without guarantee'. The obligation is then for three round voyages. The duration is only guidance from the charterer to the owner.

TRADING EXCLUSIONS OR LIMITS

Lines 27 to 31 are usually deleted to take account of what has actually been agreed. The usual wording is, *'in such lawful trades, between safe port and/or ports, berths and anchorages, trading within Institute Warranty Limits excluding..........'* and then goes on to list the countries to which the charterer is not allowed to send the vessel. The NYPE '93, however, specifies not only *'safe berths'* but *'provided vessel can enter, lie and depart always afloat at any time of tide'*. This is a curious addition as it would exclude numerous ports where ships customarily wait for the high tide to sail. Indeed, it is so peculiar and unnecessarily restrictive that it cannot really mean what it says! Sensibly, the Gentime has not repeated the mistake.

However, reference is made to **Institute Warranty Limits or (IWL) .** What are they?

They are trading limits set by the Institute of London Underwriter's Institute Warranty Committee for reason of extreme conditions, usually associated with ice or other extreme weather. It is therefore usual to exclude areas outside IWL in time charters as it affects the owner's hull and machinery insurance policy releasing the underwriter from liability in case of a breach. There may be exceptions that are required by the charterer that the owner will be able to agree with his underwriter. One is the northern limit of the North Pacific IWL in winter where a northerly route from Canada to Japan or Korea may be recommended by weather routing companies to avoid storms to the south, but may breach IWL for a few days. Some ports are permanently outside IWL and if needed by the charterer will need to be negotiated with the owner against paying an additional insurance premium.

The following clause might deal with the issues as follows. 'Charterers have the privilege of breaching IWL during the currency of the charter party, they paying for any additional insurance premia on hull and machinery actually paid by owners for breaching IWL based on vessel's hull and machinery value of....... Such additional premia is not to exceed that for minimum coverage under the London Underwriter's minimum scale'.

Other countries that may be excluded from the trading limits may be countries that are very ITF minded for vessels with a flag of convenience if that is the flag of the vessel to be fixed. It may exclude likely war zones where there is civil war or countries that are embargoed by the United Nations or important trading countries. It may include ports that have been identified as the origins of the Asian Gypsy moth or politically difficult countries such as Cuba, as there are difficulties thereafter calling at USA ports, or North Korea as there are difficulties thereafter calling at South Korean ports. It may include countries that are not at war but are potentially unstable such as, at the time of writing, Haiiti, Nicaragua, Georgia, North and South Yemen, Ethiopia, Somalia, Albania, Angola, Cambodia, Libya or the former Yugoslavia excluding Slovenia. These will normally be requested by the owner and agreed by the charterer if they do not unduly limit his ability to trade the vessel. For long period charters, it is sensible to provide for the possibility of political change with a clause which says that should the political situation change for the better, charterers are allowed to trade after obtaining the owner's consent, and if for the worse are allowed to ask for the area to be added to the exclusions and these requests are not to be unreasonably withheld. Some owners may not permit trading where the vessel will go aground, such as the River Plate or, while not normal or envisaged, may go aground such as in the Orinoco or Lake Maracaibo.

A clause dealing with war areas will deal with the extra insurances. Owners may also request one which will deal with the practicalities of permissions and permits. Such a clause may read as follows. 'If the vessel is directed to trade in an area which necessitates additional war premium, the charterers warrant that prior to the vessel's entry into the additional premium area, all necessary permissions and permits have been obtained from the relevant government, armed forces, port authority or any other relevant authority or de facto authority. Charterers further warrant that the vessel calling at these ports is not in breach of a United Nations, European Community , NATO or national embargo'.

In addition to the owners limiting the trading area they will often be required to guarantee that the vessel is not black listed by any country. This mainly concerns the Arab blacklist of ships trading to Israel, still in existence but in the improving political climate of the Middle East, more theoretical than real. It may concern the USA taking exception to ships calling at Cuba or a particularly badly maintained ship having already caused problems and therefore having been singled out and blacklisted by the particular port affected. Charter parties usually also exclude ports in countries subject to a United Nations embargo. They are also often asked to guarantee that the vessel has full bunkering privileges in the United States. It is also normal to add that if the vessel is boycotted or delayed that all time, risk and expenses are for the owner's account.

The Master may refuse an order from the charterers to proceed outside the trading limits and may refuse to sign Bills of Lading which names a discharging port outside the trading limits. He is perfectly entitled to do so.

For a simple time charter trip much of the complexity of the above clauses, more relevant to period charters where the charterer is given the right to trade the ship over a wide area, can be avoided by specifying exactly where the owners can trade. For instance, 'one time charter trip via Brazil to Japan with iron ore only', limits the ship to countries and even cargo as if she were doing a voyage charter between specified ports for a specified commodity.

Trading in 'difficult' areas leads to the question of **insurance** and which party is responsible for which ones. The usual expedient is for the owner to be responsible for the basic insurance and any caused by the charterer directing the ship to trade in unusual places, such as war risk areas, for example, are to be for charterer's account. Such a clause might read as follows. 'Basic insurance premia on account of vessel's ownership to be for owner's account. Extra insurance on cargo due to the vessel's age, class, flag or nationality to be for owner's account'. The owners may not accept this, however, since they would argue that the charterers are taking the ship as described including its age, flag etc.. A more normal addition which could readily be agreed is, 'All additional premiums as a result of vessel's trading is for charterer's account. Charterers to pay extra war risk insurance as per invoices including blocking and trapping insurance, crew war risk bonus and/or extra crew war risk insurance'. Many charterers argue that the crew war risk bonus is one expense too far since this is the ship owner's matter. The result will usually depend on the exact circumstances but demonstrates what issues will be at stake.

CARGO

'Lawful merchandise' is usually qualified either in a time charter trip by specifying the cargo or cargoes that are allowed or in a time charter period by inserting a long list of exceptions. These exceptions will be negotiated and will be a compromise between what the owner does not want to carry and what the charterer needs. The owners will usually try to exclude cargoes on three grounds; (1) those that are potentially injurious to the holds in certain circumstances, (2) those that pose a potential health hazard or (3) those that are just dirty and dusty commodities making cleaning of holds difficult and

time consuming thereafter. The following is a typical list of cargo exceptions with explanations in brackets as to why the owners do not like them, if it is not immediately obvious.

> "Acids, ammonium nitrate, ammonium sulphate, ammunition, arms, asbestos (dust dangerous to health), asphalt (liable to melt or combust if heated), bagged cargo (for bulk carriers) black powder, blasting caps, bombs, bones, bulk borax, bulk cargoes listed in the IMO code of practice for solid bulk cargoes 1991 which cannot be certified by shipper as harmless and/or having a history of shipment without problems, byrites, calcium carbide, calcium hypochloride, caustic soda, cement, (with moisture contact liable to solidify) cement clinker (same) charcoal, china clay, concentrates, containers (in bulk carriers), copra (very smelly, liable to taint other cargoes, encourages infestation of the copra bug and liable to spontaneous combustion), copper, cotton (easily damaged and liable to spontaneous combustion), creosoted goods, deck cargo (on bulk carriers when there are no fittings for deck cargo), direct reduced iron ore pellets, (liable to spontaneous combustion) dynamite, explosives, ferro-silicon (emits toxic and inflammable gases), fishmeal, (depending on the type, difficult temperature and moisture requirements, smelly and liable to taint other cargoes) granite blocks (very heavy thus a damage and stowage issue), hazardous cargo, hides (emit offensive smell, liable to taint other cargoes and liable themselves to get damaged), HBI, (hot briqueted iron-dirty and difficult to clean for next cargo) injurious inflammable, dangerous cargo, kaolin (requires exceptionally clean and dry holds in order not to damage it), livestock, (except for livestock carriers), logs, (potential damage to vessel and inadequate hatch strengths) macoya expellers and/or pellets (liable to spontaneous combustion), marble blocks (same as granite blocks), metal borings and cuttings, motor spirit, naptha, nitrates, nuclear fuel materials and waste, oil cakes, palm kernels (spontaneous combustion), potatoes (needs electric ventilation with air at

least 25 air changes, similar to the needs of onions), passengers, petcoke (oily residue a cleanliness issue) petroleum, petroleum products, pig iron, pitch in bulk (liable to melt or combust), pond coal (liable to spontaneous combustion), radio active materials, and waste, radio isotopes, salt (corrosive if in contact with water; if carried holds should usually be whitewashed or painted prior to loading) saltpetre, scrap (potential damage and combustable if oily), motor blocks, turnings, (damage issues especially for motor blocks loading, occasionally a cleanliness issue) shavings, silica sand, soda ash, sunflower seed expellers (accepted by owners if the vessel is CO_2 fitted, as with other grain derivatives), sponge iron, steel (liable to rust causing ruinous cargo claims as this will seriously affect its value), sulphur, (corrosive when mixed with water), tar (liable to melt or combust if heated), TNT, turpentine, war materials (embargo issues), wool (spontaneous combustion), yellow phosphorous, any cargo for which CO2 fitted tonnage is required as per IMO recommendations, charterers undertake to load vessel in accordance with IMO Code of Safe Practice for Bulk Cargoes, also in accordance with load regulations".

The International Maritime Organisation (IMO), constantly referred to above, is an agency of the United Nations whose charter is one directed at the safety of life at sea. It has produced the Code, for the carriage of dangerous goods which recognises nine broad classes and the conditions necessary to handle them. It is constantly under review in the light of new experience and changing cargo and ship types. The purpose of the Code is to inform ship's Masters of the precautions to be considered or needed to prevent problems when carrying certain cargoes. For instance, while coal is generally considered a safe cargo, it is liable, under certain circumstances, to spontaneously combust or to emit methane gas. High sulphur coals may, in contact with moisture, cause sulphuric acid to form, which can erode holds. Different types of coal behave differently and require different cargo management procedures. Coal should always therefore be loaded according to IMO recommendations and charter parties for the carriage of coal will be worded accordingly. There are many types of cargo that need special handling and need to be included under IMO recommendations.

Some of the above list of cargoes are excluded because the vessel may not be suitable. Others are exceptional such as explosives and nuclear materials. Many more are just not preferred as they require more careful and often specialised handling. This is not to say that these cargoes are not carried in certain circumstances. The owner will, in many cases, need advance warning, further financial incentive and higher insurance cover to persuade him to carry some.

Charterers hiring a vessel for a period and without a pre arranged dedicated trade require the widest options. Thus owners usually permit them to load some of these cargoes. A usual clause might read that the charterer has the option to load, for instance, two cargoes of petcoke or HBI. The intermediate hold cleaning rider clause will be important here. Owners might also allow a potentially corrosive cargo as well if needed. If salt is allowed it is usual to have a lime-washing clause along the following lines. 'If salt is loaded and if requested by owners, charterers shall arrange lime washing for the holds at their time and expense before loading and remove same, washing down with fresh water after discharging to Master's satisfaction at their time and expense. Charterers to have the option of painting holds instead of lime washing. Salt not to be the last cargo before redelivery'. Owners would also rather not have sulphur or bulk cement as the last cargo prior to redelivery due to the onerous nature of cleaning the holds and the possible effects on the cleanliness of the holds for the next cargo.

'OWNERS/CHARTERERS SHALL PROVIDE AND PAY FOR'

These clauses (1 and 2) detail what owners and charterers are each responsible for providing in the time charter. They are non contentious and simply explain what is at the heart of the time charter. Clause 1 specifies for owners, *'all provisions, wages, consular shipping and discharging fees of the Crew, shall pay for the insurance of the vessel also for all cabin, engine room and other necessary stores including boiler water and maintain her class and keep the vessel in a thoroughly efficient state in hull, machinery and equipment for and during the service.'* This obligation supplements the warranty of seaworthiness. Typical insertions here may include 'drinking water, lubricating oil, garbage dues' and 'with Inspection Certificates necessary to comply with current requirements at ports of call and canals'. The NYPE '93 adds, *'a full complement of officers and crew'*. The Gentime's Clause 11 neatly lists owner's obligations under the headings, Wages, Stores, Insurance on the vessel, crew's assistance in:, documentation, deratisation and fines for smuggling.

For charterers, the NYPE '46 specifies that *'Charterers shall provide and pay for all the fuel except as otherwise agreed, Port charges, Pilotages, Agencies, Commissions, Consular Charges*'. In other words the charterers must pay for all the items specific for the trading of the vessel, which of course, charterers are responsible for. Thus, if she loads cargo where fumigation is needed, the charterers must pay. This issue is addressed in the NYPE '93 (Clause 7). *'Fumigations ordered because of illness of the crew shall be for the owner's account. Fumigation ordered because of cargoes carried or ports visited while the vessel is employed under this charter party shall be for charterer's account. All other fumigations shall be for the charter's account after the vessel has been on charter for a continuous period of six months or more'*. Under the same principle, if she loads steel and generals, for example, where substantial dunnage is necessary, charterers must pay. This is also specifically mentioned in the NYPE '93. The Gentime's different construction lists, in Clause 13, six obligations of charterers; Voyage expenses, Bunker-fuel, Agency costs, Stevedoreing, Advances to Master and Contraband.

One possible contentious issue is customary, but not compulsory, pilots. Charterers do not like to pay for what they consider unnecessary expenses and some non compulsory pilots, such as English Channel or Dover Strait pilots, come under this heading. The word 'compulsory' is therefore sometimes inserted before 'pilotages'. The NYPE '93 ignores this issue but does specify *'compulsory watchmen and cargo watchmen and compulsory garbage disposal'* under *'port charges'*. 'Canal and river tolls' and 'all taxes and/or dues on the vessel and/or cargo and freight' are also often inserted here. The NYPE '93 also specifies that the charterers should pay for extra fittings for special trades or unusual cargoes and dunnage.

The Charterers normally have to pay for radio messages sent on their behalf, for instance for notices, for meals and gratuities supplied to charterer's representatives, port and customs employees. The NYPE '46 caters for this in terms of a certain amount of money per meal. However it is often deleted and a lump sum agreed for 'all cables, entertainment and victualling' or C/E/V as it is termed in the main terms negotiations. A short clause such as the following may be inserted. 'Charterers to pay owners a lump sum of USD 800 per 30 days or pro rata to cover the cost of extra meals/cables/telexes and other communications, entertainment and representation on behalf of charterers to pilot/stevedores/agents etc'. The Gentime states, *"the owners shall permit the charterers use of Vessel's communications facilities at cost"*.

It should be noted that the Baltime clause 4 makes the charterers liable to pay for fuel even while the ship is off hire but this seems obviously unfair and in the NYPE it is expressly stated in clause 20 that this is for the owner's account.

FUEL/BUNKERS

Clause 3 says that charterers on delivery and owners on redelivery shall take over and pay for all *'fuel remaining on board at the current prices in the respective port, the vessel to be delivered with not less than........'*

This is a very important clause and therefore dealt with here in detail. Clause 3 is often deleted and reference to a much more detailed rider clause indicated. Often an estimate of the amount of bunkers on delivery will be included. Where the estimate is expressed as, 'expected about ....tons', the owners must present an honest estimate based on information they have or ought to have.

The easiest way of dealing with bunkers is that neither owner nor charterer intends making money out of it or to take advantage of the other. That is the position of most parties in such negotiations. The typical way to do this would be that on delivery, the owner delivers with and the charterer takes over the fuel remaining on board (Bunkers ROB) and that on redelivery the charterers redeliver and the owners take over about the same quantities as on delivery. The prices would be the same both on delivery and redelivery or **'both ends'** as it is referred to. Occasionally the owner will arrange with the charterer to redeliver the vessel with a greater quantity of bunkers than originally agreed upon, for example, if the vessel can replenish bunkers en route cheaply without shutting out cargo. In a long term time charter the fairest way of dealing with this is often perceived to be not at the same price but at the actual 'Platts Oilgram' price prevailing at the port of delivery and redelivery.

Normally the payment for bunkers is made with the first hire payment on delivery. The owner on redelivery must pay that back. This is normally effected by an equivalent deduction from the last or penultimate hire payments from the charterer. If this is the case, then the charterer will need to replenish the vessel's bunkers either en route or at the last port.

It may be that the owner may wish to have more bunkers on board on redelivery. For example, it may be that bunkers on delivery and redelivery are agreed at about 1000 tons fuel oil and about 100 tons of marine diesel oil. But the owner now envisages a long trip after redelivery and can pick up cheap bunkers in the area of redelivery. They may well ask for a clause which allows them to bunker the vessel for their own account at the last discharge port, providing this does not interfere with the charterer's discharging operations.

Occasionally the quantities on delivery and redelivery will be different and prices may be different. In this case owners and charterers will need to carefully assess the balance of advantages, disadvantages and risks in this scenario.

If the time charter is of a very short duration, the mechanism that the charterer pays for bunkers on delivery, the owner having to pay it back shortly thereafter, does not work, or at least, is unnecessarily complex. It is then usual for the charterer just to pay for the estimated bunker consumption for the short trip, or perhaps supply bunkers necessary just for the trip. Any balances will be settled on completion of the trip.

As has been mentioned in the description clause, warranties on bunker specifications are sometimes needed and the NYPE '93 has a clause which covers the subject of many rider clauses added to the NYPE '46. *'The owners reserve their right to make a claim against the charterers for any damage to the main engines or the auxiliaries causes by the use of unsuitable fuels or fuels not complying with the agreed specifications.'* If the charterers do supply unsuitable bunkers which *'do not conform with the mutually agreed specifications or otherwise prove unsuitable for burning in the vessel's engines or auxiliaries, the owners shall not be held responsible for any reduction in the vessel's speed performance and/or increases consumption, nor for any time lost and any other consequences'.* This is a rather loose clause as although it deals with the important and topical issue of bunker quality, the words *'otherwise prove unsuitable for burning in the vessel's engines..'*, must cause charterers some worry as it could lead to more disputes than problems it might solve.

Recent rider clauses on this issue agree the specifications, typically,

"RMG 35 –IFO 380 CST
RME IFO 180 CST
Marine diesel oil –DMB
Marine Gas Oil - DMA
Quality of supplied fuel oil to be within Minimum/Maximum limits of ISO 8217 ; 1996. The product must be homogeneous, must exclude polypropylene, must exclude wasted oils and lubricating oils, must exclude any other chemical or substances which can damage marine engines, marine boilers and associated equipment. To maintain the right to claim against suppliers for possible sub standard fuels, vessel to take samples of the fuel during bunkering by automatic drip sampling device (if installed) or by proper drip sampling at the manifold throughout the bunkering period. Any complaints regarding bunker quality must be presented within 30 days after bunkering and documented with proper analysis based on a sample taken as described above".

The Gentime has a much more comprehensive and satisfactory clause than the NYPE '93.

"(d) Bunkering - The Charterers shall supply fuel of the specifications and grades stated in Box 23. The fuels shall be of a stable and homogeneous

nature and unless otherwise agreed in writing, shall comply with ISO standard 8217: 1996 or any subsequent amendments thereof as well as with the relevant provisions of Marpol. The Chief Engineer shall cooperate with the Charterers' bunkering agents and fuel suppliers and comply with their requirements during bunkering, including but not limited to checking, verifying and acknowledgeing sampling, readings or soundings, meters etc. before, during and/or after delivery of fuels. During delivery four representative samples of all fuels shall be taken at a point as close as possible to the vessel's bunker manifold. The samples shall be labelled and sealed and signed by suppliers, Chief Engineer and the Charterers or their agents. Two samples shall be retained by the suppliers and one each by the vessel and the Charterers. If any claim should arise in respect of the quality or specification or grades of the fuels supplied, the samples of the fuels retained as aforesaid shall be analysed by a qualified and independent laboratory.

(e) Liability- The Charterers shall be liable for any loss or damage to the owners caused by the supply of unsuitable fuels or fuels which do not comply with the specifications and grades set out in Box 23 and the owners shall not be held liable for any reduction in the vessel's speed performance and/or increased bunker consumption nor for any time lost and any other consequences arising as a result of such supply"

This clause details the proper sampling procedure and requires the Chief Engineer's active cooperation. Sub clause (e) places full liability on the charterers for any loss or damage to the owners caused by the supply of unsuitable fuel. However, the burden of proof rests with the owners to prove that unsuitable fuel was the cause of loss or damage and hence the importance of proper sampling procedures.

DOMESTIC FUEL

Clause 20 of the NYPE '46 says '*Fuel used for cooking, condensing water or for grates and stoves to be agreed and the cost of replacing same to be allowed by owners'*. This causes more problems and waste of time in negotiations than any other clause as *'grates and stoves'* are historical anachronisms and the cost of fuel for cooking is minor compared with that used for actually driving the ship. English courts have decided that in the light of modern conditions this clause should mean that all domestic fuel, whether for cooking, heating or otherwise should be for the owner's account. The Asbatime, unhelpfully, states that the charterers should provide and pay for all fuel except as otherwise agreed. To make the outdated wording clear it is usual to delete the clause and insert a wording agreeing that fuel used for cooking and heating are for the owner's account. Clause 20, anyway permits the charter to deduct the costs of fuel used for domestic consumption.

HIRE

The term used is for the payment for the agreed period. The NYPE printed form states it is paid 'per calendar month'. Usually this is deleted as hire is usually expressed in dollars per day. Unites States Dollars is the international currency most widely used. Occasionally other currencies can be used. Recently, because Japanese shipyards quote prices in Yen, some long term charters have been concluded fully or partly in Yen to give the charterer the benefit of low interest rates and the elimination of the Yen/Dollar risk margin for the owners. The charterers then have to assume this risk. Some short sea charterers in Europe are beginning to be concluded in Euros having previously been fixed in local currencies. Hire is *'to continue until the hour of the day of her redelivery in like good order and condition, ordinary wear and tear excepted.'* Hire is usually paid *'including overtime'*. This refers to officer's and crew's overtime. Hire is very occasionally, but much less now than hitherto, expressed in dollars per deadweight, per calendar month. In this case, for example, a 160,000 dwt at USD 3.00 is calculated as USD 3.00 multiplied by 160,000 divided by 30.4375 (average days in a month) which equals USD 15,770 per day.

Sometimes if a vessel delivers at the port of loading but the market custom is to calculate and pay for the ballast leg, it then may be agreed to pay a **ballast bonus.** It is usually calculated as follows (Daily hire plus daily bunker cost) x days in ballast. However, this is a guide. The actual amount will depend on the market and if weak, it may well be much less. Since it is in lieu of hire, however, it is only fair to the broker that commission is paid on it, but it must be stipulated in the charter party otherwise the owners have no obligation to pay it. If commission is payable it is termed **'gross ballast bonus'** and if not, **'net ballast bonus'.**

Hire is normally suspended if the vessel puts into any place or port other than those instructed by the Master by reason of accident, breakdown or landing sick crew members. This time is known as **off hire** (See deductions below). Hire is resumed when she is in the same or equidistant position or again at the disposition of the charterer. Often a rider clause is agreed whereby if the vessel is off hire for thirty continuous days, charterers have the right to terminate the charter party provided the vessel has no cargo on board. Other clauses sometimes say that charterers have the option of adding such off hire period to the stipulated period to give charterers the use of the vessel for the period for which she was contracted.

Payment

Clause 5 states payment is, *'in cash in United States currency semi-monthly in advance.'* 'Cash' is interpreted in the context of modern commercial practice and a rider clause will contain details of the owner's bank account and sometimes instructions of how to transfer it. By mutual agreement semi-monthly may be changed to monthly, 30 or 15 days. The latter is most common and it is this that is reflected in the NYPE '93 and Gentime.

The basic principle is that each payment of hire (gross) must be made by the charterers *'in advance'* and received in the owner's designated account by the due date. If that falls on a Sunday, receipt is due on the Friday prior to the Sunday, as the last banking day. Receipt on the following Monday would be late payment. The obligation to pay on or before the date is absolute. Problems sometimes arise because payments are made from and to banks in different time zones with different closing hours and banking holidays. Rider clauses often not only state the owner's bank but precise instructions of how to pay, codes and reference numbers to use, etc..

Right of withdrawal

If the charterer fails to make a punctual payment of an instalment of hire, the owners are entitled to withdraw the ship. This is designed to protect owners if charterers get into difficulties by giving them the power to take the vessel back without having to go through any legal proceedings. Some years ago, a charterer who had a ship on period charter at a much lower rate than the market, paid a number of hires a few days late and on the last occasion the owner withdrew the ship. The charterer was one of the largest shipping companies in the world and there was no chance that the company was in any danger of going bankrupt. The owners, however, took advantage of the market situation and the charterer's lack of care in making payments on time. The charterer, by having the ship withdrawn, missed making money out of a cheap ship on a sharply rising market. In such cases, charterers must be extra diligent in making sure that they make *'punctual'* hire payments or they risk having the ship withdrawn. This withdrawal is final. The owners do not have a right to temporarily withdraw the ship.

But especially on a rising market it is obvious and natural that owners will watch out for delays. Yet, the clause was not designed for owners to try and catch charterers out on a technicality. Lord Denning in a case in 1976 explained the dilemma in the plain English and good sense for which he was famous. 'You take a time charter with hire to be paid through a bank; and the usual clause which enables the shipowner to withdraw the vessel failing punctual and regular payment of hire. During the charter period, the freight market rises. The shipowner is on the lookout for a default. He knows, on the authority of the House of Lords, that the charterer must, at his peril, make payment of hire on the due date. Payment a day or two late, or a minute or two late, will not do. So the shipowner says to himself; 'If only the charterer slips up and is the least little bit late, I shall be able to withdraw the vessel'. Then by some mischance, the charterer does slip up. It may be that hire falls due on a Saturday or Sunday when the banks are closed. The charterer thinks that it will be sufficient if he pays on the Monday. But the shipowner says; 'That wont do, you should have paid last Friday'. He gives notice of withdrawal. Or the charterer's accountants or bankers may have got an hour too late in transmitting the hire to the bank in New York or vice versa. All owing to six hours time difference, the shipowner, who has not suffered in the least bit, at once whips in a notice of withdrawal. The charterer is staggered. He has committed himself right and left on the basis that he will have the use of the vessel, but here he is deprived of the use of it. He seeks to find a means of escape. Sometimes he challenges the time of payment. He says he remedied the breach in sufficient time. He relies on a waiver or an estoppel. Only to find himself lost in a maze of technicalities, not only of law but also of banking practice. If he cannot escape from the grip of the ship owner he may turn round on his bankers and say it was their fault. So the game goes on'. The clause, he explained, designed to protect the innocent owner from unscrupulous or insolvent charterers is now used against innocent charterers, 'only on a rising market. On a falling market the charterers have nothing to fear'.

Unites States law is somewhat more lenient on charterers when they have been badly served by their banker's late payment. However, in either case it is now normal to have a rider clause to prevent this kind of situation. It is known as an "anti-technicality clause" or a "Grace Period" and worded something like the following; 'Where there is any failure to make 'punctual and regular payment', due to oversight or negligence or error or omission of charterer's employees, bankers or agents or otherwise for any reason, where there is an absence of intention to fail to make payments, charterers shall be given three (3) working days notice to rectify the failure. Where so rectified the payment shall stand as 'punctual and regular payment'. A similar clause is found in the NYPE '93. (Clause 11 a and b) and in the Gentime (Clause 8c). These kinds of clauses have largely eliminated market inspired, opportunistic withdrawal.

If there has been a number of previous accepted late payments, it may be that the right of withdrawal is lost comletely or at the very least a written notice requiring prompt payment will be required. If a charterer, however, ceases to pay hire because of financial difficulties this is a "Fundamental breach". The owner therefore has the right of withdrawal, as the charterer is considered to have **repudiated** the charter, and claim damages.

Deductions and Offhire

Deductions are allowed, however, if covered under clause 15 *('loss of time from deficiency of men or stores, fire, breakdown or damages to hull, machinery or equipment or grounding detention by average accidents to ship or cargo, dry docking for the purpose of examination or painting bottom, or by any other cause preventing the full working of the vessel, payment of hire shall cease for the time thereby lost and if upon the voyage the speed is reduced by defect or breakdown of any part of her hull, machinery or equipment, the time so lost and the cost of any extra fuel consumed in consequence thereof and all extra expenses shall be deducted from the hire*) and lines 65/66 (*'Cash for vessels ordinary disbursements at any port may be advanced as required by the Captain, by the Charterers or their Agents, subject to a 2.5 % commission and such advance shall be deducted from hire'*). Clause 15 would apply for example, if the vessel has to put into a port other than instructed by charterers, due to breakdown or to land injured seamen. The port charges, pilotages, bunker consumption and loss of time involved would be for the owner's account and could be deducted. It is therefore the exception to the charterer's primary obligation to pay hire continually. The NYPE '93 repeats this obligation except, curiously, if the vessel puts into a port because of *'stress of weather'*, a gloriously imprecise term. Clause 15 would also cover deductions for speed deficiency. Clause 20 permits the charterer to deduct the costs of fuel used for domestic consumption.

However, in practical terms deductions for speed and consumption claims can be a dangerous area as chartrerers may be tempted to act as judge and jury on the question of if a ship is under-performing in speed and /or consumption or not. As for deductions, the burden of proof is on the charterer to show that the deduction or off hire clause operates in the particular circumstances. If one of these incidents listed happens, such as breakdown of machinery, it does not result automatically in a deduction of hire. It has to be shown that charterer has 'a loss of time' as a consequence of that breakdown. Special rider clauses therefore are sometimes added specifically giving the right to deduct or reduce hire and detailing that the evidence necessary is that from the vessel's log and independent weather routing reports for the area. In the event of consistent discrepancy it is a matter of negotiation whether the owner prevails with the log or the charterer wins and manages to get an independent weather routing report as the final arbiter.

A common addition concerning when hire shall resume in case of off hire are the words, 'until the vessel has returned to the **same or equivalent position'**. This is a sensible addition and a result of cases where the ship was again fully efficient but having put back into port and thus some days away from where she was when hire ceased.

In the case of partial efficiency, such as the breakdown of one crane for discharging when other cranes on the vessel could do the job, the question to be asked is; How much earlier would the vessel have discharged and got away from the port if the full number of cranes had been available throughout? A further addition is often made in line 98/99 after, *'any other cause'*, where the word 'whatsoever' is inserted. The purpose of this is to do with a rule of legal construction, known as "eiusdem generis" by which other causes must be of the type previously listed. The word "whatsoever" therefore significantly hardens the clause in its interpretation of the type of incidents of off hire.

If a 'loss of time' incident is caused by the charterer, such as repairs to damage caused by the charterers ordering the ship to an unsafe berth for example, then the ship will remain on hire and the charterer be responsible for bunkers.

As with many questions arising from standard wording such as these, it is quite common for rider clauses to be inserted to clarify the specifics. The NYPE '93 and Gentime, however, have fairly detailed Off Hire clauses. A comprehensive example would be an off hire clause worded as follows. This is a compilation of different clauses taken from many charter party rider-clauses.

"In the event of delay to the vessel arising from one or more of the following reasons; deficiency of officers/crew or stores; breakdown partial or otherwise, damage to hull, machinery, equipment; detention by average incidents to ship/cargo including collision/stranding; repairs/dry docking or other necessary measures to maintain the efficiency of the vessel; failure to be in possession of valid certificates or other documentation for the vessel, officers and crew; breakdown partial or otherwise, non conformity or disablement of one or any/all winches/cranes/grabs or any other part of vessel's equipment for loading/discharging cargo preventing full operation of the vessel; insufficient power to operate all winches, cranes, grabs at the same time if required; residue of cargo(es) carried prior to delivery under this charter party and/or rust scale and/or loose rust in the holds, the vessel to be off hire for any/all time thereby lost and owners to pay all expenses incurred, together with the cost of any fuel and diesel oil consumed in consequence thereof including but not limited to stevedores standby time, if any, and which shall all be deducted from the hire. In the event of breakdown of cranes by reason of disablement or insufficient power, the hire to be reduced pro rata for the period of insufficiency in proportion to the number of cranes that were available at the time of breakdown of equipment. If charterers elect to continue to work on hatches affected by breakdown by hiring shore appliances, owners are to pay for shore appliances, but in such case charterers are to pay full hire for all time the shore appliances are working. Any stevedoring and or labour charges additionally occurring due to breakdown of vessel's equipment including costs for standby stevedores' labour to be for owner's account".

Another example, sometimes specifically identified, is the arrest of the vessel, her Master, officers or crew for any reason whatsoever as a result of a party purporting to have a claim. All this time while the vessel is not available for charterers, is specified as 'off hire'. The Gentime specifically mentions it. In cases such as these it may be also required that other expenses be reimbursed by the Owner, although the Gentime clause omits any references to extra costs caused by off hire.

Sometimes a rider clause specifies that although normal quarantine time and expenses for the vessel's entering port shall be for charterer's account, 'any time of detention and expenses for quarantine due to pestilence, epidemics and illness of the Master, officers and crew, shall be for owner's account."

Owners are usually required to warrant that the officers and crew are covered by an ITF agreement or a Bona Fide Trade Union agreement and that any loss of time because of non compliance will be considered as off hire and the extra expenses to be for owner's account.

The Gentime has a provision for off hire in case of "Requisition", a very infrequent occurrance.

In long period time charters **drydocking** is usually performed by mutual agreement but for short periods or trips it is usual to have a clause stating, 'No dry docking during this time charter, except in case of emergency'. If the owner knows that a drydock is due, during the period contemplated, he should alert the other party and try to work out a satisfactory mechanism for giving notices. It goes without saying that such period is off hire as per clause 15 and the provision that it recommences on hire only when in the *'same or equivalent position'* should apply if specified. The NYPE '93 has a totally unsatisfactory printed clause which is apparently there to cover the issues rather than solve them as it has alternatives for and against dry docking, depending on the length of time charter and what was agreed.

In practical terms this is often a complex matter. The owners will want to dry dock in a cost effective place. What if the charterer's business is not in that area or that the market is better in another area altogether? With good will and imagination these things can be worked out but I have come across complex clauses which actually give examples with calculations if a vessel discharges in one area and has to ballast for dry docking and how to calculate the loss of time. It may clarify, but it comes within the usual meaning of, *'or equivalent position'*, which still seems perfectly adequate.

There is often a clause whereby the charterer has the option or right to add any off hire time to the charter period.

The last hire payment will not always be a full payment because of imminent redelivery but it may underestimate the time to redelivery. The NYPE states, 'S*hould same not cover the actual time, hire is to be paid for the balance day by day, as it becomes due, if so required by Owners, unless bank guarantee or deposit is made by the Charterers, otherwise failing the punctual and regular payment of the hire, or bank guarantee, or any break of this charter party, the Owners shall be at liberty to withdraw the vessel from the service of the Charterers, without prejudice to any claim they may otherwise have on the Charterers'.* This is a normal, non contentious clause although in practical terms an owner is not going to withdraw a few days away from redelivery with cargo on board even if the charterer does pay the last few days irregularly. Under the Baltime, the full hire payment should be paid and if not fully used reclaimed from owners. A rider clause also usually spells out that the charterer has the liberty to withhold money from the last sufficient hire payments to cover the value of estimated bunkers remaining on board at the time of redelivery which were paid on delivery as well as any advances and fines. The NYPE '93 has incorporated what has been a standard rider clause into its main body (clause 11 c) but instead of charterer's deduction, it stipulates that *'payment(s) is (are) to be made for such a length* *of time as the owners and charterers may agree upon as being the estimated time necessary to complete the voyage and taking into account the bunkers actually on board'.* That an owner and charterer will always agree these calculations is somewhat optimistic. Again the Gentime's wording appears more elegant and practical. The sub clause 8(e) is entitled "Redelivery Adjustment". It reads, *"Should the vessel be on her voyage towards the port or place of redelivery at the time of payment of hire becomes due, said payment shall be made for the estimated time necessary to complete the voyage, less the estimated value of the fuels remaining on board at redelivery. When the vessel is redelivered to the owners any difference shall be refunded to or paid by the charterers as appropriate but not later than thirty days after redelivery of the vessel".*

FRUSTRATION

Clause 16 of the NYPE (and Baltime) provide for a cesssation of hire if the ship is lost and hire paid in advance and not earned, returned to charterers. **'Lost'** means a total loss, constructive total loss, or the commercial destruction of the ship under time charter such as requisition, indefinite detention or the time charter becomes illegal. In this case, the contract is terminated by law if the effect is to destroy the identity of the charterer to make it a totally different thing. This is **frustration** which 'occurs whenever the law recognises that without default of either party a contractual obligation has become incapable of being performed because the circumstances in which performance is called for would render it a thing radically different from that which was undertaken by the contract'.

TRADING/OPERATIONS/NAVIGATION

Clauses 6-12 concern the trading and operation of the ship and more detailed references appear in other parts of the charter party. With one exception, (see Loading/stowing etc. below) these are rarely contentious clauses. They include provisions for trading always afloat for which an insertion can be made for 'customarily safe aground' if mutually agreed. There is a provision for the carriage of passengers under certain conditions but this is normally deleted. There is a mechanism for changing crew in case of charterer's dissatisfaction, a daily charge for Supercargo and providing meals for tally clerks, stevedores etc. which is sometimes negotiated although to simplify the operations it is normal these days to agree a lumpsum per month for all communications, victualling, entertaining and representation in a rider clause and the separate amounts deleted. When one considers all the people, operations and accounting involved in billing a five dollar meal it will be seen that this is a sensible alteration. The Master has the obligation to keep a daily log and exercise due diligence in caring for the ventilation of the cargo. The daily log of course is of vital importance if the speed and consumption becomes contentious.

It also states the obligation of the captain (Master) to *'prosecute his voyages with the utmost despatch'* but goes on to say that the captain *'shall be under the orders and directions of the charterers as regards employment,'* which negates this if the charterer directs him to slow steam. The NYPE '93 and Gentime thus changes *'utmost despatch'* to *'due despatch'*. As to matters of navigation clause 26 reaffirms this remains with the owner and Master. *'The owners to remain responsible for the navigation of the vessel, insurance, crew and all other matters, same as when trading for their own account'*. An insertion is sometimes made here to make it clear that the owner is also responsible for acts of pilots and tugboats. This may appear to be unfair but the law is that the Master is always ultimately responsible for the safety and navigation of the ship. It is the same principle that was mentioned under 'speed and consumption' when discussing weather routing and safe trim between the berths and ports in Chapter Six.

'Same as when trading for their own account', also seems comprehensive. Nevertheless some charterers have deemed it necessary to list all the vessel's services in rider clauses. Sometimes there will simply be a clause specifying that the crew is to be responsible for opening and closing of hatch covers in preparation for loading and discharging. This goes back to the voyage charter party obligation that the vessel should be in all respects ready to load. There are clauses specifying the crew should supervise control of cargo handling, which goes back to line 78, act as watchmen in cargo compartments and assist in docking, undocking, shifting and bunkering.

A particularly comprehensive clause is as follows:

> "The following services are included in the hire and shall be rendered by the Master, officers and crew without charterers paying any additional money.
>
> 1. Raising and lowering of cranes and/or gangways in preparation for loading and discharging.
> 2. Opening and closing of hatches in connection with loading and discharging.
> 3. Closing and opening of hatches in the event of weather which may adversely affect the condition of the cargo carried on board during loading and discharging.
> 4. Supervision for loading and discharging and everything related hereto.
> 5. Maintaining sufficient electric power on all cranes whilst loading and discharging as on board.
> 6. Shifting vessels during loading and discharging and shifting berth.
> 7. Docking and undocking in connection with loading and discharging cargo or bunkering.
> 8. Necessary assistance in the vessel's bunkering operation.
> 9. Officers and crew to shape up vessel's hatches and cranes, grabs and grab connecting devices, if any, as much as possible prior to arrival at

loading and/or discharging places so as to immediately commence loading and/or discharging operations.

10. Vessel's crew to drive cranes when required by the charterers during self loading or self discharging operations. Charterers to pay USD 5.00 per hour per crew member for such work. In such a case, the crew crane drivers are deemed to be charterer's servants, thus owners are not to be responsible for any delays, damages and losses incurred during such operations when crew is involved. Owners/Master/Vessel will not be liable for any delays, damages. Losses whatsoever during self loading or self discharging operation where vessels crew are required to drive cranes. Any damage or losses to ship's holds/fittings as result of this operation will be repaired/replaced by charterers at charterer's time and cost. The actual deployment of crew to operate cranes to be at the discretion of the Master.
11. Limewashing. Vessel's crew to limewash the vessel's holds if required by the charterers and the charterers to pay USD 300 per hold directly to the performing crew members. The cost of lime to be for charterer's account.

The above services shall be considered as a minimum and shall in no way be construed as an alternative to or reduction in the services to be rendered by officers and crew in accordance with the maritime code of the country under whose flag the vessel sails or in accordance with what is customary practice in the trade. In such case, the crew's crane drivers are deemed to be charterer's servants, thus owners not to be responsible for any delays, damages and loses incurred during such operations when crew is involved."

LOADING/STOWING/DISCHARGING

The NYPE reads *'The charterers are to load, stow and trim the cargo at their expense under the supervision of the captain, who is to sign Bills of Lading for cargo as presented, in conformity with Mate's or tally Clerk's receipts'.* This line 78 of the NYPE is a very well known old chestnut with market brokers. Apart from a few normal amendments such as the addition of 'and discharge' after 'load stow and trim,' the biggest source of argument is the request from charterers to add '**and responsibility**' after the words, *'under the supervision of the Captain.'*

The Baltime clearly transfers all responsibilities with regard loading, stowing and unloading operations to the charterers. The NYPE which has the words, *'under the supervision of the Captain,'* means that at first sight it is ambiguous as to where responsibility lies. Courts have found that responsibility for stowage lies with the charterers as Clause 2 states that they are to *'provide and pay for all other usual expenses except those before stated'.* Thus, stevedoring expenses are usually borne by the charterers and there is a strong case for interpreting this as transferring the duty and the obligation to the charterer. To what extent is still a familiar subject of dispute. The position under English law depends on the extent that the Master intervenes in the operation of stowage and the extent that damage is suffered as a result. Some voyage charterers seek to define where the responsibility lies. (See Chapter Six - Stevedores and the Loading/Discharging Clause and Chapter Eight - Clause Paramount).

The Master anyway has a responsibility for seaworthiness and that must include ensuring that the cargo will not be loaded in such a way that it may shift during passage. The stowage plan, often drawn up by the chief officer or presented by the shipper/charterer, is always subject to the Master's scrutiny. The owner also has the fundamental duty to deliver the cargo in the same condition as when it was loaded. That must mean that the Master must ensure that the cargo will not be loaded in a way that will damage it, for example, by the absence of dunnage and separations or being placed near to the cargo or a part of the ship liable to cause damage. He must also load holds in sequences not liable to cause undue stress on the hull. Many charter parties therefore, use the words, 'the stevedores although appointed by the charterers, are to be the servants of the owners and remain under the supervision and direction of the Master'. Does this not imply some responsibility? Where does supervision end and responsibility begin? Should they be responsible for a process they do not fully control?

Charterers often seek both to clarify the ambiguity and shift responsibility, not only for the mechanical process of handling the ship's gear and cargo but also as to matters of stevedore negligence in the strategic planning of loading and discharging of the cargo. It is often fiercely resisted by owners, although if the loading is under the supervision of the Master what is the point if it implies no element of responsibility? Furthermore, the Master is, as we have seen, responsible for safe navigation and therefore that the cargo is safely stowed. Much will depend on the exact situation pertaining at the load and discharge ports and the exact role the charterer takes in the process of loading and discharging. If the charterer's stowage plan overrides the Master's and is subsequently found to be the cause of cargo damage, this obviously changes the situation drastically.

The NYPE '93, however, has not dodged the issue with ambiguous words but has come down firmly on the side of the owners and the lack of any responsibility of the Master. It says, *'Charterers shall perform all cargo handling, including but not limited to loading, stowing trimming, lashing securing, dunnaging unlashing, discharging and tallying, at their risk and expense, under the supervision of the Master'*. The word 'responsibility' is not mentioned but the key word is 'risk', which is charterer's. The Gentime

(Clause 12) has a more elegant wording. *"The Master shall be conversant with the English language and, although appointed by the owners, shall at all times during the currency of this Charter Party be under the orders and directions of the Charterers as regards employment, agency or other arrangements. The Master shall prosecute all voyages with due dispatch and supervise loading and discharging operations to ensure that the seaworthiness of the vessel is not affected. The Charterers recognise the principles stated in IMO Resolution A443 (xi) as regards maritime safety and protection of the marine environment and shall not prevent the Master from taking any decision in this respect which in his professional judegment is necessary"*. It may be a more up to date, elegant and satisfactory wording but the dilemma is the same. Where does supervision end and responsibility begin? The question remains unanswered.

What than are the consequences of adding these two words, 'and responsibility', to line 78 of the NYPE?

The answer is that under the NYPE, cargo claims are usually settled in accordance with the **NYPE Interclub Agreement,** the latest amendments of which are from 1996 (See Appendix 2). It was first introduced in 1970 by P and I Clubs in an attempt to simplify settlement for cargo damage claims due to the previous difficulty of determining liability for cargo claims under the NYPE. A rider clause or in the case of the NYPE '93, a printed main body clause, will specify that this is the case. But if it is not in the charter party then it is not binding. It specifies a very simple formula and while it should be read in full, essentially it says the following; In claims for loss, damage and shortages to cargo that have occurred after commencement of loading of cargo and prior to discharge, if the loss has occurred because of unseaworthiness, error or fault in navigation or management of the vessel it is 100 percent owner's responsibility and cost. But if it arises because of the loading, stowing, lashing, discharge and storage of the cargo, it is deemed to be 100 percent the charterer's responsibilty, unless the words 'and responsibility' are added in line 78. In this case the apportionment is 50/50 (See Appendix 2 to read the document in full).

The Gentime departs from this in its drafting by having a "Responsibilites Clause" (18) which takes the place of the Interclub Agreement. It sets out the definition of a cargo claim and the owner's and charterer's liability while it makes owners liable for *"failure...... properly and carefully to carry, keep and care for the cargo while on board"*. It does not mention loading. Thus, this charter party, like its predecessors, may well be, if widely adopted, as famous for its disputes on line 575 as the NYPE is for line 78. But by being specific, Clause 18 may be unjust on the charterers where a Master has insisted on an unsafe stowage plan or loading sequence. New wordings will no doubt be tested in court before long.

DEVIATION

Lines 105/106 state that the vessel can deviate for the purpose of saving life and property. This is standard and is the provision of the Hague Rules and Carriage of Goods by Sea Act. See also Chapters Six and Eight.

ARBITRATION

This has been dealt with in the previous chapter. It is usual to delete the printed words and re-word it more precisely in one of the rider clauses described in Chapter Six.

LIENS

Liens were dealt with in the previous chapter but complications arise in time charters (NYPE 110/113) where hire is overdue and in consequence owners instruct the Master not to discharge the cargo until hire is paid. However, in case the cargo owner/Bill of Lading holder is not the charterer and has paid for his cargo, he is being denied it through no fault of his own. The Bills of Lading may incorporate the terms of the time charter party in which case it is arguable that the lien can be enforced against the cargo owners. If they are not, then the position is open to considerable doubt. The Bill of Lading holder pays no more than shown on the Bills of Lading. The Bill of Lading is not subject to any hire payment, of which he will no doubt be unaware, being up to date. Is the lien for hire, therefore, effective against the third party holder of a Bill of Lading who is not a party to the charter party? There are conflicting decisions on this issue, but it does say that the owners have a lien on 'all cargoes' and the most recent decisions seem to accept this at face value. However, many commentators dislike it as it offends the doctrine of privity of contract.

In practical terms the receiver will put pressure on the party with whom he is contracted which will usually be the charterer of the vessel. After 'sub freight' in line 110, the word 'sub hires' is often added to cover situations where there is a long time charter chain. In such a chain an owner may call on charterer's agent to collect freight as owner's agents and pay it to him. As the previous chapter explained, a lien on cargo is not in practical terms, necessarily a simple exercise but at least when it is exercised, it is usually done so when in the carrier's possession. A lien on sub freight is more difficult because the carrier cannot control or possess it. It is therefore exercisable by the owner giving notice to the sub charterer or, more often his agent, requiring him to pay sub freight or sub hire to him directly. The exact circumstances will determine how this will work in practice but it is of great importance where a charterer gets into financial difficulties. Where the market is volatile and the charterer has positioned himself wrongly, this does happen, especially where the cargo has been sublet in a chain.

COMMISSIONS

General issues about commissions were dealt with in Chapter Six, however, it is worth detailing how the different time charter forms deal with it. The NYPE '46 (Clause 27) simply says, *'A commission of 2½ % is payable by the Vessel and owners to..... on hire earned and paid under this Charter, and also upon any continuation or extension of this Charter'*. The wording is repeated in the NYPE '93 except the amount is left blank. the Gentime repeats this but adds, *'If the full hire is not paid owing to breach of Charter Party by either of the parties the party liable therefore shall indemnify the brokers against their loss of commission. Should the parties agree to cancel this Charter Party, the owners shall indemnify the Brokers against any loss of commission but in such case the commission shall not exceed the brokerage on one year's hire. In signing this Charter Party the owners acknowledge their agreement with the brokers to pay commissions described in this clause'*. The provision for remuneration in case of mutual cancellation will be welcomed by brokers and the latter provision for owner's acknowledgement was inserted before the Contracts (Rights of Third Parties) Act was passed but will be welcomed anyway if the jurisdiction governing the charter does not have such protection by statute.

RIDER CLAUSES

As with voyage charter parties the number of rider clauses has increased as specialist, practical and modern legal experience has led both parties to tighten up and fully explain older wording that was once deemed sufficient in itself, especially concerning each parties obligations.

One usual clause, especially for panamaxes trading grain to certain ports in Taiwan for instance, is a **mobile crane clause.** It permits this method of discharging under certain conditions. 'Charterers shall have the option of placing sufficient mobile cranes or vacuvators on vessel's main deck to facilitate loading or discharge where same is customary at intended port, provided always (a) that the weight of mobile crane(s)/vacuvators do not exceed vessel's deck strength (b) welding to secure mobile cranes/vacuvators not permitted (c) adequate dunnage to be provided to Master's satisfaction and removed at charterer's expense (d) charterers to have the right to make temporary modifications to hatch covers, stoppers and hatch rails to be rolled to the same side only if detailed plans are submitted to owners and approved by them in advance (e) no modifications shall cause permanent change to the vessel (f) all such work to be made good upon completion of the loading/discharging operation to owner's and Master's satisfaction at charterer's expense, vessel always remaining fully on hire.'

Another rider clause may cover **'loading on deck'**. The issues are usually covered in a clause such as, 'Charterers have the option to load cargo on deck and hatch covers at charterer's risk, time and expense to the Master's satisfaction and fully in accordance with the vessel's specifications as to trim, stability and permissable strength. All Bill(s) of Lading issued for such cargo to be marked, 'Carried on deck without liability for any loss and or damage howsoever caused'. Any damage to the vessel by on deck/hatch loading shall be repaired by charterers at their time and expense'.

Occasionally if a vessel stays in a port over a protracted period of time, especially in warm waters, owners will be concerned at growth on her hull, thereby slowing her speed. They sometimes will ask to insert a clause, if they think this is likely, that either exempts them from the speed/consumption clause if the vessel is stuck in the port for more than a specified period of time or requires the charterers to bottom clean the ship. It should be remembered that this is the result of how the charterer has traded the ship. Thus a clause to cover this may be, 'In case of bottom fouling due to charterers ordering the vessel to stay in port for a minimum period of 35 days, owners will carry out the bottom cleaning (underwater cleaning by divers) at charterer's time and cost prior to vessel sailing from the port, if such facilities are available, otherwise at the next port'.

An **insurance** clause will include the owner's P and I Club name, that charterers have the benefit of the owner's P and I Club as far as the rules permit (though the validity and enforceability of this clause is questionable) and that Owners are to remain responsible for all personal injury claims resulting from Owner's operations. **A War risk clause** will detail that the annual war risk premium is for owner's account but any additional premium for trading to areas in breach of the war risk warranties is for charterer's account. There is sometimes a drug clause for trading to the United States, **a stevedore damage clause, charterer's colours,** giving the charterers the right to fly his company flag and paint their markings on the funnel and hull, and **stowaway clauses**, all of which are found as standard in the NYPE '93 and Gentime. However it seems unlikely that the NYPE '93 will become popular except perhaps as a long period charter, as most charterers want to specify their own clauses for their own trading requirements and need the very simplest of base forms on which to attach them. Moreover, unlike it successor, the Gentime, there are too many one sided clauses. A charterer sent me a rare executed copy of an NYPE '93 recently, on which to base a charter and it had 59 extra rider clauses. The idea of getting the extra clauses standardised in the main body does not seem to have worked especially since there seems to be just as many deletions in the main body as with the '46.

Under the **U.S. Trade Drug Clause**, the charterer warrants, *'the highest degree of care and diligence in preventing unmanifested narcotic drugs and marijuana to be loaded or concealed on board'*, and holds owners *'harmless with all costs for charterer's account with the vessel remaining on hire if time lost'*. This wording in the NYPE '93 has been preceded in rider clauses of earlier charter parties, usually with the reasonable addition that this applies unless the delay and detention is directly attributable to the owners, Master or crew. It is a strange omission in the NYPE '93 and seems to give the clause a very one sided meaning and appears to be a dangerous wording for charterers, despite a later 'smuggling' clause (Clause 42) . The Gentime's wording is more even handed.

Other clauses on the same topic relate not to smuggling but to the crew's **abuse of drugs or alcohol**. For example; 'The owners warrant that they have guidelines on drug and alcohol applicable to the vessel with the object that no seafarer will navigate a ship or operate its on board equipment while impaired by drugs or alcohol and that no seafarer will have the use, possession of or the opportunity to sell, distribute, transport or use illicit or non prescribed drugs on board the vessel'.

Over the last ten years there are an increasing number of anchorages where cargo is loaded either from ship to ship or barge to ship either by the ship's own gear or by an offshore floating crane or a transhipment vessel. It is therefore becoming more frequent to insert a **'double banking clause'** which permits the charterers to undertake such an operation but gives the Master the right to refuse if unsafe. To a large extent this is an unnecessary clause since this is the law anyway. A typical one for ship to barge transfer, however, would read,

> "Charterers, if necessary, have the right to load/discharge the cargo from/to **lighters/barges** etc. If so required by the port authorities or when such operation is customary carried out at the port, charterers to supply at their time and expense fendering to Masters's satisfaction, which shall not be unreasonably withheld. However, it is understood that the Master has the right to order the vessel, lighters, barges or remove his vessel in his opinion for the safety of the vessel. Master always to render full cooperation for the operation. Charterers to indemnify owners for any

damages to the vessel and or loss of hire resulting from unsafe operation. All necessary fendering to be for charterer's account".

Where **floating cranes or transhippers** are involved, loading and discharging large volumes on a regular basis, such a cautious clause is probably not justified. It is necessary simply to say that the charterer will provide and pay for assistance such as sufficiently fendered tugs, barges and floating cranes. The Master always has the right to stop loading or unloading if he feels it unsafe. This is equally true of bad weather at a berth as at a floating transhipment station.

In long term time charters, owners will sometimes request that they have the option to change flag, name or even ownership of the vessel during the course of the charter. This is usually agreed subject to the charterer's prior consent which should not be unreasonably witheld.

8. Bills of Lading, Average and Protective Clauses

BILLS OF LADING

There are many clauses in charter parties, whether in the main body or in the rider clauses that concern Bills of Lading. This is because the role Bills of Lading play is crucial. An understanding of them is therefore essential when negotiating charter parties. Before looking at these various clauses it is necessary to examine their function.

The Bill of Lading has three characteristics;

1. It is a receipt for the cargo prepared by the supplier (usually called the 'shipper') and signed by the carrier to prove he has received the cargo from the shipper.

2. It is a 'document of title' to the cargo; that is, proof of who owns the cargo and therefore to whom the carrier should deliver it.

3. It provides evidence of the terms and conditions of the contract of carriage.

How does this work in practice?

When the cargo is loaded, a document is issued by the carrier describing its condition and quantity. Initially, this is the **'mate's receipt'**. It is issued by the first officer of the ship, the officer responsible for the cargo. He would have issued it, in case of break bulk cargo, after the cargo was 'tallied' into the ship by the tally clerks, or after a draft survey in the case of bulk cargo. This is usually undertaken by an independent surveyor. The mate's receipt may then be exchanged for the 'Bill of Lading'.

Its initial purpose is as a receipt for the goods loaded. At the port of discharge, the holder of the Bill of Lading is the receiver (consignee). Unlike the mate's receipt, therefore the Bill of Lading is the 'document of title' proving ownership. It actually represents the goods, especially as regards third parties, which is why it is so important. The Master therefore releases the cargo at the discharge port to the Bill of Lading holder.

How does this work in detail?

The Bill of Lading is drawn up on a printed form, often relating to a specific trade or in connection with a specific charter party. It shows the quantity and condition of the cargo loaded as well as distinguishing marks and numbers. The names of the ship, shipper and receiver, the loading port, date of loading, the destination and details of freight payment. The latter might say, **'Freight prepaid'** or **'Freight payable as per charter party'.**

The shipper (or supplier) will probably request a **'full set'** of **'original'** Bills of Lading. It is customary to issue more than one, usually three sets, as they are used for a variety of purposes. All Bills of Lading will be signed by the Master or the agent in the agent's capacity as servant of the ship owner who appointed him.

On completion of loading, the Bill of Lading will be **'released'** by the Master or the agents to the shippers. They should obviously not be released if marked 'freight prepaid' and if freight has indeed, not been paid. Many letters of credit call for **'clean Bills of Lading'.** 'Clean' means that the cargo is described as **'in apparent good order and condition'**. If it is not, then the Master may **'clause'** the Bill of Lading. If he did not do so and a receiver at the discharge port receives defective or damaged cargo he has the right to claim against the owner. As was made clear in Chapters Six and Seven, the primary obligation of the owner is to safely carry the cargo and deliver it in the same condition as when loaded. If the cargo was damaged and the Bills of Lading do not reflect that, the owner leaves himself open for a potentially large claim. In practice, the shipper will press for clean Bills of Lading to be signed because most trade is conducted on letters of credit, which invariably call for "clean" Bills of Lading. If there is a problem, however, it will have to be solved by a survey report of the cargo, which will be given to the receiver. Occasionally clean Bills of Lading are issued against a **Letter of Indemnity**, indemnifying the carrier or owner against a claim, especially where the receiver is aware of the condition of the cargo.

At the discharge port the cargo is delivered to the party who produces an original Bill of Lading covering the cargo. The port agent will examine it and when satisfied will stamp it "accomplished", sign and date it on the Master's behalf and release the cargo or issue a **delivery order** in exchange for the Bill of Lading. The receiver presents the delivery order to the stevedores and claims the cargo. If for some reason the Bills of Lading are not at the discharge port, a different **Letter of Indemnity** should be issued though great care has to be taken in this situation. If the cargo is delivered without presentation of a Bill of Lading and later another person appears with an original Bill of Lading evidencing his title to the goods, the carrier is liable for wrongful delivery. The wording of the Letter of Indemnity is therefore of great importance and normally dictated by the owner's P and I Club.

Misunderstandings occur over the Bill of Lading because it involves the shippers and receivers who may have no knowledge of the terms of the charter party. The charterer of the ship, of course, may be neither the shipper or the receiver. It seems confusing when the whole ship is being chartered, that there is a document other than the charter party with obligations and responsibilities with which it may not be entirely compatible.

Therefore, many standard Bill of Lading forms are used with complementary charter party forms. For example, the 'Congenbill' with the 'Gencon', the 'North American Grain Bill' with the 'Norgrain' and the 'Orevoybill' with the Orevoy. The reasons for coupling the Bill of Lading and charter party like this is to incorporate the charter party terms into the Bill of Lading. Thus, the normal Bill of Lading freight clause will state 'freight payable as per charter party dated........'. The confusion occurs because the receiver may not have seen the charter party. He is therefore bound by terms he may not have seen. Much will depend on how the charter party incorporation clause is worded. For example, if the loading and stowing clause in the charter party is worded in such a way as not to make the Master responsible for loading and stowing, the receiver may not be able to claim against the ship owners for damage to the cargo. In the case of a ship owner exercising a lien for deadfreight where the charterer does not pay it, the third party Bill of Lading holder may have to pay, even though it is not his responsibility under the charter party. Thus, chartering affects not only the ship owner and charterer but other parties such as the shipper and receiver and some care must be taken by charterers when writing their pro forma charter parties to cover these points.

When shipping a small cargo, perhaps a single container, there is no charter party. The Bill of Lading therefore becomes not only the receipt and document of title but the evidence of terms and conditions of the contract, indeed possibly the contract itself, as there is no charter party, the terms and conditions of the contract being printed on the reverse. Where, however, the parties concerned in a Bill of Lading have agreed to accept the provisions of the charter party, then the Bill of Lading is subservient to the charter party because, in this case, the Bill of Lading is not a contract itself. Most charter parties and Bills of Lading will contain a clause stating that the Bill of Lading is subject to the provisions of the charter party. Thus, those involved in chartering are mainly concerned with the Bill of Lading only as a 'receipt' and 'document of title'.

The Bill of Lading in international trade is of vital importance because when cargoes are bought and sold FOB or CIF, the ownership changes hands. The Master must deliver the goods at the discharge port to the person or company producing the Bill of Lading. But it is a negotiable document because ownership of the cargo is transferable from one party to another by **endorsement.** It is therefore the key document under which title of ownership of cargoes is transferred in letter of credit transactions. It is also the key document in many cases of fraud which again highlights just how important the subject of 'Investigating the Principal' is, which was discussed in Chapter Four.

One of the easiest frauds to perpetrate is for a company to fix a cargo, then time charter a ship to lift it. It is necessary to pay the first 15 days in advance and a minimal amount of bunkers remaining on board. The Master then signs pre paid Bills of Lading as presented. The charterer then collects the freight on the cargo and disappears. The owner is left to honour the pre paid Bills of Lading and carry out what is probably a long voyage and discharge the cargo, having been paid only a tiny part of their hire. To add insult to injury, the owner probably has to bunker the ship for his own account.

In tanker chartering freight is sometimes paid on completion of discharge which eliminates this problem. However, complications arise in this trade, as there is usually a discharge range rather than specified ports and ownership of the cargo can, and is changed at sea more often than in dry cargo, and therefore instructions can be given to discharge cargo at a different port to that named in the Bill of Lading.

CHARTER PARTY CLAUSES DEALING WITH THE BILL OF LADING

Because of the importance of the Bill of Lading, it follows that a number of charter party clauses deal with or refer to them. The Gencon '76 states (Clause 9), *'The captain to sign Bills of Lading at such rate of freight as presented without prejudice to this charter party but should the freight by Bill of Lading amount to less than the total chartered freight the difference to be paid to the captain in cash on signing Bills of Lading'*. The words from *'but should the freight'* to the end are often deleted as being old fashioned and impractical.

The addition that is often added is that the Bill of Lading can also be presented to the owner's agents. For example The Norgrain states that the Bill of Lading should be the 'North American Grain Bill of Lading' and that, *'if the master elects to delegate the signing of the Bills of Lading to his Agents, he shall give them such power of attorney in writing, copy of which is to be furnished to charterers'*

The Amwelsh '79 says that the Bills of Lading *'shall be prepared in accordance with the dock or railway weight'*. This is usually deleted to reflect that it is prepared according to the draft survey. It also prudently stipulates that the Bills of Lading are *'to be signed at the charterer's or shipper's office within 24 hours after the vessel is loaded'*.

The NYPE '46 stipulates that the Captain *'is to sign Bills of Lading for cargo as presented in conformity with the Mate's or tally clerk's receipts'*. The practice of leaving it to charterers or their agents to prepare and sign Bills of Lading binds the owner in the same way as if the Master had signed them himself. However, *'as presented'* leads to the issue of under what circumstances the Master may refuse to sign. It is a breach of charter for the charterer to require the Master to sign a Bill of Lading imposing on the owner a greater liability than he has accepted under the charter party. For example, the Master has a right and duty not to sign a Bill of Lading which names a port of discharge outside the trading limits. Some time charters stipulate that Bills of Lading are to be signed *'without prejudice to the charter party'*. In this case, notwithstanding anything in the Bill of Lading, the charter party will remain unaltered.

The ASBATIME extends this clause to reflect common practice where the Master delegates his signing powers to the charterers or their agents and provides for an indemnity as follows, *'However, at charterer's option the charterers or their agents may sign Bills of Lading on behalf of the captain always in conformity with mate's or tally clerk's receipts. All Bills of Lading shall be without prejudice to this charter and the charterers shall indemnify the owners against all consequences or liabilities which may arise from any inconsistency between this charter and any bills of lading or waybills signed by the charterers or by their agents or by the captain at their request'*. The Baltime (Clause 9) also provides an indemnity.

The Gentime extends the type of document the Master shall sign. *'The Master shall sign Bills of Lading or waybills as presented in conformity with mate's receipts. If requested, the owners may authorise the Charterers and/or their agents in writing to sign Bills of Lading or multimodal Bills of Lading (herein collecitvely referred to as Contracts of Carriage) on the Owner's and or Master's behalf in conformity with mate's receipts without prejudice to the terms and conditions of the Charter Party.'*

This new provision is to cater for 'door to door' movements of cargo. However, this has insurance implications for the owner where loss or damage takes place beyond the carriage on board the vessel, thus the Gentime continues to make clear that if the owners have authorised the charterers to issue through or multimodal transport Bills of Lading, extending the owner's responsibility for the cargo beyond the period it is on board their vessel, the charterers shall indemnify the owners for any loss, damage or expense which may result.

A number of extra issues may arise. Charterers sometimes may require that Bills of Lading are signed marked **"Freight Prepaid'**, when actually the freight has not been paid. The Orevoy (Clause 22) specifically says, *'Neither the owners nor their servants shall be required to sign or endorse bills of lading showing freight prepaid unless and until the freight due to the owners has actually been paid.'* It is obvious that if the Bill of Lading is signed showing that freight has been paid, the charterers are relieved of paying more. Owners will often agree, but will require a **Letter of Indemnity** drawn on their P and I Club's standard wording and if there are any doubts about the charterer's standing or intentions, or if the owners are simply cautious they may also demand a bank guarantee from a bank acceptable to them. A standard P and I Club Letter of Indemnity would be worded as follows;

Quote
STANDARD FORM LETTER OF INDEMNITY TO BE GIVEN IN RETURN FOR DELIVERING CARGO WITHOUT PRODUCTION OF THE ORIGINAL BILLS OF LADING
To (insert name of owners)
Dear Sirs,
Ship (insert name of ship)
Voyage (insert load and discharge port as stated in the Bill of Lading)
Cargo (insert description of the cargo)
Bill(s) of Lading(insert identification number, date, place of issue)

The above cargo was shipped on the above vessel by (shipper) and consignee (name of consignee) for delivery at the port (name of discharging port as in the Bills of Lading) but the Bills of Lading have not arrived and we (party requesting delivery) hereby request you to give delivery of the said cargo (name of party to whom the delivery should now be made) without production of the original Bill(s) of Lading.

In consideration of your complying with our above request, we hereby agree as follows;

1. To indemnify you, your servants and agents and to hold all of you harmless in respect of any liability, loss, damage or expenses of whatsoever nature which you may sustain by reason of delivering the cargo in accordance with our request.

2. In the event of any proceedings being commenced against you or any of your servants or agents in connection with the delivery of the cargo as aforesaid to provide you or them on demand with sufficient funds to defend the same.

3. If, in connection with the delivery of the cargo aforesaid, the ship or any other ship or property belonging to you should be arrested or detained or if the arrest or detention thereof should be threatened to provide on demand such bail or other security as may be requested to prevent such arrest or detention or to secure the release of such ship or property and to indemnify you in respect of any liability, loss, damage or expense caused by such arrest or detention or threatened arrest or detention whether or not such arrest or detention or threatened, arrest or detention may be justified.

4. As soon as all original Bills of Lading for the above cargo shall have come into our possession to deliver the same to you, whereupon the liability hereunder shall cease.

5. The liability of each and every person under this indemnity shall be joint and several and shall not be conditional upon your proceding first against any person, whether or not such person is party to or liable under this indemnity.

6. The liability of each and every person under this indemnity shall in no circumstance exceed 200% of the CIF value of the above cargo.

7. This indemnity shall be governed by and construed in accordance with English law and each and every person liable under this indemnity shall at your request submit to the jurisdiction of the High Court of Justice of England.

Yours faithfully

For and on behalf of	For and on behalf of
Requestor	Bank
Signatures	Signatures

Unquote

A similar Letter of Indemnity form is necessary if the discharge port is changed.

It must be signed by an authorised official of the charterers with his name and position clearly printed and usually witnessed.

Quote

To Owners

Dear Sirs,

Name of ship

Voyage –Load and Discharge port as in Bill of Lading

Cargo - Description

B/L - Number/date/place of issue

The above named ship under charter dated........has loaded a cargo of..at the port(s) off......or delivery at and Bills of Lading have been issued accordingly.

In consequence of a change in our arrangements we request that you send orders to the Master of the ship at.........to proceed to the port(s) of........ and there deliver the said cargo to his or their order instead of proceeding to and delivering the same at the ports named in the Bills of Lading.

In consideration of you complying with our request as above, we hereby guarantee and undertake to hold you and or the Master and/or agent of the ship, free from and fully protected and indemnified against, any and all claims for loss, costs, damages and/or expenses whatsoever description that arise in consequence of such a change of destination and which may be made and enforced against you and/or the said Master or agent by the owners of the cargo or by any persons interested or claiming to be interested in the cargo.

We also guarantee and undertake to deliver up to you, duly discharged, all of the Bills of Lading for this cargo signed by the captain or by his and or your authority.

This indemnity shall be construed in accordance with English law and each and every person liable under this indemnity shall at your request submit to the jurisdiction of the High Court of Justice of England.

Full style of charterers- Signature.

Witnessed..

Unquote

A rider clause that is beginning to appear is the **US Trade-Unique Bill of Lading Identifier Clause**, which is designed to prevent the delivery of the cargo to the wrong receiver. It typically states something like the following.

'The charterers warrant that each transport document accompanying a shipment of cargo destined to a part or place in the United States of America shall have been endorsed with a unique Bill of Lading identifier as required by US Customs Regulations (19 CFR part 4- Section 4.7A) including subsequent changes, amendments or modifications thereto, no later than the first port of call.
Non compliance with the provisions of this clause shall amount to a breach of warranty for the consequences of which the charterers shall be liable and shall hold the owners harmless and shall keep them indemnified against all claims whatsoever which may arise and made against them. Furthermore all time lost and all expenses incurred including fines as a result of the charterer's breach of the provisions of this clause shall be for the charterer's account.'

It may also state that, 'it is agreed that no unique Bill of Lading reference number shall be duplicated within three years of the initial use of each number'.

PROTECTIVE CLAUSES

Protective clauses are so called because they protect the owner. In the case of the Clause Paramount, General Average and Both to Blame Collision Clause, they protect him even if he or his servants are negligent. In the War Risk Clause and Ice Clause they protect the owner against potential danger and in the P and I Club Bunkering Clause they protect him against the charterer using the provisions of the deviation clause in case of deviation for bunkering.

The Clause Paramount

This makes the charter party subject to **the Hague Visby Rules.** These are internationally agreed standard conditions which apply to contracts of carriage of goods by sea when the contracts are covered by a Bill of Lading issued under a charter party or complying with a charter party. They allocate, define and limit the liabilities and responsibilities of the carrier. The Rules have been given the force of national law in a number of countries under the name of **'Carriage of Goods by Sea Act.'** If it is not part of the law of the country the ship calls at, it can still be applicable by inserting the Clause Paramount into the charter party. As was noted in Chapters Six and Seven, under this Act, the carrier is required to exercise due diligence, before and at the beginning of each voyage, to make the ship seaworthy and to take proper care of the cargo. The NYPE does not contain any provision dealing with the liability of cargo claims except for the exception clause (16) which exempts, *'the act of God, enemies, fire, restraint of princes, rulers and people and all dangers and accidents of seas, rivers, machinery, boilers and steam navigation and errors of navigation throughout this charter'.*

Paramount Clauses vary. They may also require that all Bills of Lading issued under the charter party must contain the Paramount clause. For example, the Norgrain '89 (clause 37) says, *'If the vessel loads in the USA, the USA Clause Paramount shall be incorporated in all Bills of Lading'.* For voyages involving Canada, a Canadian Clause Paramount should be incorporated.

Most owner's P and I Clubs require their members to incorporate a Clause Paramount in the charter party and Bill of Lading and thus, if deleted, will generally not cover any loss. P and I Club Rules limit cargo liability to the level provided by the Hague Visby Rules.

One complication is that the NYPE (Clause 24) states that the charter party is subject to the Harter Act of 1893 and by the Clause Paramount, that is, to the Carriage of Goods by Sea Act. It is not clear whether it is supposed to apply to the charter party only or the Bill of Lading as well, since even though it is part of a charter party it starts off, *'This bill of lading shall have effect..'*, or from and to all ports or just those that begin and end in the USA. To avoid confusions it is usually deleted.

If the Paramount Clause is incorporated into the charter party then the time bar of the Hague Rules (one year) will also apply. This is for the first time given specific mention in a charter party, in the Sugar '99.

The Hague-Visby Rules were also designed to improve the position of the holder of the Bill of Lading. Some exporting countries, however, felt that it was the shipper that needed more protection. UNCTAD (the United Nations Conference on Trade and Development) gave expression to this, finding in a 1971 report that the Hague Visby Rules were unduly favourable to shipowners and unfair to cargo interests. Although damage or loss suffered by cargo interests could be insured against, it was felt that this was wasteful and uneconomic. The alternative was that shipowners could obtain higher cover at a higher cost from the P and I Clubs. They therefore developed the **Hamburg Rules**. An appropriate Clause is necessary to incorporate them into the provisions of a charter party but in this case the Hague Visby Rules cannot also be incorporated.

The difference between the Hague Visby rules and the Hamburg Rules are that under the former, the carrier is not liable unless he fails to exercise due diligence to make the ship seaworthy. In the Hamburg Rules, on the other hand, the onus is on the carrier to prove that he is not responsible for loss, damage or delay in delivery. He must show that all reasonable measures were taken to avoid the damage, loss or delay the carrier will be liable for unseaworthiness throughout the voyage, not only before and at the beginning of the voyage. Owners are unhappy about accepting the Hamburg Rules where not compulsory and will seek to negotiate them out of the charter party if they can. A standard wording they will try to insert is;

> 'Neither charterers nor their agents shall permit the issue of any Bill of Lading, waybill or other document evidencing a contract of carriage (whether or not signed on behalf of owners or on the charterer's behalf or on behalf of any sub charterers) incorporating, where not wholly compulsory applicable the Hamburg Rules or any other legislation giving effect to the Hamburg Rules or any other legislation imposing liabilities in excess of the Hague or Hague Visby Rules. Charterers shall indemnify owners against any liability, loss or damage which may result from any breach of the foregoing provisions of this clause'.

A similarly worded clause is in the Gentime (Clause 17(a)(iii)).

A carrier may even be successful in getting the **Himalaya Bill of Lading Clause**;

> 'It is hereby expressly agreed that no servant or agent of the carrier (including every independent contractor from time to time employed by the carrier) shall in any circumstances whatsoever be under any liability whatsoever to the shipper, consignee or owner of the goods or to any holder of this Bill of Lading for any loss, damage or delay of whatsoever kind arising or resulting directly or indirectly from any act, neglect or default on this part while acting in the course of or in connection with his employment and, but without prejudice to the generality of the foregoing provisions in this clause, every exemption from liability, defence and immunity of whatsoever nature applicable to the carrier or to which the carrier is entitled hereunder shall also be available and shall extend to protect every such servant or agent of the carrier acting as aforesaid and for the purpose of all the foregoing provisions of this clause the carrier is or shall be deemed to be acting as agent or trustee on behalf of and for the benefit of all persons who are or might be his servants or agents from time to time (including independent contractors as aforesaid) and all such persons shall to this extent be or be deemed to be parties to the contract in or evidenced by the Bill of Lading.'

General Average

What is General Average? The idea of general average is of ancient origin and derived from Rhodian Law. (The ancient city state had one of the first maritime trading fleets). It originates as a matter of fairness and practicality and was adopted in all countries in maritime trade but with differencies in law and practice. **The York Antwerp Rules** of 1877 were the attempt to achieve uniformity over many different national laws giving practical effect to the principle that **when a sacrifice is made to save the interests of all the**

parties involved in a voyage, the party making the sacrifice must be compensated by all the parties who stand to benefit from the sacrifice.

Rule A of the York Antwerp Rules 1990 states,

> 'There is a general average act when and only when, any extraordinary sacrifice or expenditure is intentionally and reasonably made or incurred, for the common safety of the purpose of preserving from peril the property involved in a common maritime adventure'.

This expenditure or loss is to be made up by the contribution of all the parties concerned. The York Antwerp Rules are now generally incorporated into charter parties, Bills of Lading and maritime insurance policies.

Where ship and cargo is exposed to a danger and part of the cargo or ship is intentionally sacrificed to avert the danger, this loss by the cargo interest will be subject to General Average contributions and be apportioned between ship, cargo and freight in proportion to the saved value.

The usual clause is, *'In case of average, the same is to be settled in London (or New York) according to York Antwerp Rules 1974 as amended 1994 and any subsequent amendments'*. It often further states that should the vessel be damaged or put into any port leaky or with damage then owners or Master must inform the charterers immediately. It is an uncontentious clause but older forms of charter parties sometimes do not specify where the adjustment should be drawn up and sometimes charter parties are drawn up without co-ordination between the place of adjustment of General Average, the place of arbitration and the applicable law. This is something the parties should make sure is co-ordinated.

There is no need to go into the imperatives and details of the Rules when studying chartering, but it is necessary to know that charter parties explicitly lay down that it is adjusted according to the York Antwerp Rules. The rules of adjustment are complex and carried out by **'average adjusters'**.

Even more protective for the ship owner, since it says that the ship owner can recover General Average contributions from the cargo interests even if the General Average event can be attributed to the owner's negligence, is the **New Jason Clause**. It is inserted into charter parties and Bills of Lading if the carriage has some connection with the USA. It is therefore found in the Amwelshes and grain charters dealing with grain exports from North America.

Both to Blame Collision Clause

This is found in both voyage and time charter parties and in the Bill of Lading. A typical clause can state, *'If the ship comes into collision with another ship as a result of negligence of the other ship and any act, neglect or default of the Master, mariner, pilot or the servants of the carrier in the navigation or in the management of the ship, the owners of the goods carried hereunder will indemnify the carrier against all loss or liability to the other or non carrying ship, or her owners in so far as such loss or liability represents loss of, or damage to, or any claim whatsoever of the owners of the said goods, paid or payable by the other or non carrying ship or her owners to the owners of said goods and set off, recouped or recovered by the other non carrying ship or her owners as part of their claim against the carrying ship or carrier'.*

The effect of the clause is to require the cargo interest to indemnify the carrying vessel for any compensation she may have to pay the non carrying vessel in respect of damage or claims relating to the cargo carried. Charterer's liability insurance should cover the charterers against this risk.

War Risks Clauses

Most charter parties have a war risk clause. Many charter parties used to have the **Chamber of Shipping War Risk Clauses 1 and 2** incorporated. The first says that the Bill of Lading should be signed for blockaded ports and if it becomes blockaded then the cargo should be discharged at another port as ordered by the charterer and that the owner will be entitled to freight. The second says that the ship has liberty to comply with orders given by the nation under whose flag the ship sails. It does not, however, cover the case of an outbreak of war prior to, or during the vessel's voyage to the loadport. Most charter parties which used to have this clause have now therefore changed to the **Voywar clause**, the first version of which was 1950. The most modern one is from 1993 and if it is not in the main body of the charter party it is usually added in the rider clauses. It states that if before the vessel starts loading it appears that the voyage may expose the vessel to war risks, the owner may cancel the voyage and if at any stage of the voyage a war risk may arise, the owner may change the route and may receive additional freight. The full clause may be read in most modern voyage charter parties. The **Conwartime** or the War Clause in the NYPE '93 which cover the same issues is the most suitable for time charter parties. The Conwartime clause is included in the Gentime and the Voywar 1993 forms part of the Appendix to be included in contracts of carriage issued under the time charter. It should be noted that the Conwartime makes the crew war bonus payable by the charterers. (See also Chapter Seven - "Trading Exclusions - IWL").

There is usually a rider clause in most charter parties quite outside the protective clauses, with fairly standard wording which states that in the event of war or war-like operations involving vessels of the flag country and the main economic powers and trading countries, typically the USA, UK, CIS, China, Germany, or France, seriously affecting the fulfilment of the charter, then the owners or charterers have the right to cancel the charter party. Other countries can be added especially if they form part of the regular trading pattern envisaged. It will often specify that this clause means direct war, not local hostilities or civil war. Such a clause (excluding this last provision) is found in the NYPE '93 as standard.

General Ice Clause

The purpose of an Ice Clause is to prevent an owner having to fulfil a contractual obligation to proceed to a port irrespective of potentially dangerous ice conditions that may cause damage to a ship or cargo. If a ship is 'frozen in', ice can cause considerable damage. As was seen in Chapter Six, it is usually the responsibility of the charterer to send the ship to a 'safe port'.

A port which is ice bound or in which ice conditions may cause damage to the ship, will probably not be deemed 'safe'. Ice clauses vary but the BIMCO recommended Ice Clause is used fairly regularly and is in the Gencon as the 'Gencon General Ice Clause'.

The clause covers a situation in which the vessel is unable to load on her contracted voyage because of inaccessibility because of ice. It gives the Master liberty to leave for fear of being frozen in and other liabilities to deal with specific situations reasonably. In case ice should prevent the vessel from reaching the port of discharge the charterers have the option of keeping the vessel waiting until the re opening of navigation and paying demurrage to discharge at an alternative port. Ice clauses are also important in time charters. The NYPE '46 (Clause 25) states, *'The vessel shall not be required to enter any ice bound port or any port where lights or light ships have been or about to be withdrawn or to get out after having completed loading or discharging'*. Protective Ice clauses are often supplemented with additional clauses which are often inserted which say that the vessel should not force ice.

P and I Bunkering Clause

This allows the ship to deviate without breaching the charter party in order to bunker, without a claim from the charterers. The usual deviation clause (See Chapter Six) gives the owner the liberty to deviate only for saving life or property at sea in his primary obligation to carry the charterers cargo to their destination. This clause extends that liberty to bunker the ship at a bunkering port.

> *'The vessel shall have the liberty as part of the contract voyage to proceed to any port or ports at which bunker fuel is available for the purpose of bunkering at any stage of the voyage whatsoever and whether such ports are on or off the direct or customary route or routes between any of the ports of loading or discharge named in this charter party and may take bunkers in any quantity in the discretion of the owners, even to the full capacity of the fuel tanks and deep tanks and any other compartment in which fuel can be carried whether such amount is or is not required for the chartered voyage'.*

Owners' P and I Clubs recommend their members to insist on this clause. It is rarely resisted by the charterers anyway. The delay to the arrival of a cargo at the discharge port by a ship bunkering is unlikely to be more than a day or so as the ship will have no incentive to make a substantial deviation. Besides, if the owners are allowed the liberty to take the cheapest bunkers, they are more likely to be able to offer cheaper freight rates in general.

Appendix One

GLOSSARY OF COMMON ABBREVIATIONS USED IN CHARTERING

AA	ALWAYS AFLOAT
AAAA	ALWAYS AFLOAT ALWAYS ACCESSIBLE
ABS	AMERICAN BUREAU OF SHIPPING
ABT	ABOUT
A/C	AIR CHANGES
A/D/A	ALL DETAILS ABOUT
ADCOM	ADDRESS COMMISSION
A/E	ACCEPT EXCEPT
AFCSPS	ARRIVAL FIRST COMPULSORY SEA PILOT STATION
AFMT	AFTER FIXING MAIN TERMS
AFSPS	ARRIVAL FIRST SEA PILOT STATION
AG	ARABIAN GULF
AGW	ALL GOING WELL
AGW WP	ALL GOING WELL WEATHER PERMITTING
AH	ANTWERP HAMBURG RANGE
AHL	AUSTRALIAN HOLD LADDERS
AOB	AS ON BOARD
AMWELSH	AMERICANISED WELSH COAL CHARTER PARTY
AP	ALL PURPOSES
AP	ADDITIONAL PREMIUM
APS	ARRIVAL PILOT STATION
ARA	ANTWERP – ROTTERDAM – AMSTERDAM
ARAZ	ANTWERP - ROTTERDAM – AMSTERDAM - ZEEBRUGGE
ARB	ARBITRATION

ATS	ALL TIME SAVED
ATUTC	ACTUAL TIME USED TO COUNT
AWRI	ADDITIONAL WAR RISK INSURANCE
BAF	BUNKER ADJUSTMENT FACTOR
BA/BB	BUENOS AIRES/BAHIA BLANCA RANGE
BB	BALLAST BONUS
BB	BARE BOAT
BB CGO	BREAK BULK CARGO –IE GENERAL CARGO
BBB	BEFORE BREAKING BULK (IE BEFORE DISCHARGING)
BC	BULK CARRIER
BCI	BALTIC CAPE INDEX
BENDS	BOTH ENDS (IE AT LOAD AND DISCHARGE PORT)
BFI	BALTIC FREIGHT INDEX
B/G	BANK GUARANTEE
BIFFEX	BALTIC INTERNATIONAL FREIGHT FUTURES INDEX
BIMCO	BALTIC AND INTERNATIONAL MARITIME COUNCIL
B/L	BILL OF LADING
BOD	BUNKERS ON DELIVERY
BOD APP	BOARD OF DIRECTORS APPROVAL
BOR	BUNKERS ON REDELIVERY
BPI	BALTIC PANAMAX INDEX
B TO B	BOTH TO BLAME COLLISION CLAUSE
BW	BRACKISH WATER
BWAD	BRACKISH WATER ARRIVAL DRAFT (IE DENSITY BETWEEN FRESH WATER (1000KGS/CUM) AND SALT WATER (1025)
CBFT	CUBIC FEET
CBM	CUBIC METRES

C/E/V	COMMUNICATION/ENTERTAINMENT/VICTUALLING
CFR	COST AND FREIGHT
CHABE	CHARTERERS AGENTS BOTH ENDS
CHOPT	CHARTERER'S OPTION (AS OPPOSEDTO OWNER'S OPTION)
CHTS	CHARTERERS
CIF	COST INSURANCE FREIGHT
CKD	CARS KNOCKED DOWN
COA	CONTRACT OF AFFREIGHTMENT
COB	CLOSE OF BUSINESS
COGSA	CARRIAGE OF GOODS BY SEA ACT
COMBO	COMBINATION CARRIER
CONCS	CONCENTRATES
COP	CUSTOM OF THE PORT
C/P	CHARTER PARTY
CQD	CUSTOMARY QUICK DESPATCH
CRC	COLD ROLLED COILS
CST	CENTISTOKES
CUFT	CUBIC FEET
CUM	CUBIC METERS
C/V	CONSECUTIVE VOYAGES
DAP	DAYS PURPOSES
DAP	DIAMONIUM PHOSPHATE
DD	DRY DOCK
DEM	DEMURRAGE
DES	DESPATCH
DES	DELIVERED EX SHIP
DFD	DEMURRAGE FREE DESPATCH
DHD	DEMURRAGE/HALF DESPATCH

DHDLTSBENDS	DEMURRAGE 1/2 DES ON LAYTIME SAVED BOTH ENDS
DHDWTSBENDS	AS ABOVE BUT ON WORKING TIME
DISPORT	DISCHARGE PORT
DLOP	DROPPING LAST OUTWARD PILOT
DLSOP	DROPPING LAST OUTWARD SEA PILOT
DO	DIESEL OIL
DOC	DOCUMENT OF COMPLIANCE
DOP	DROPPING OUWARD PILOT
DWAT	DEADWEIGHT ALL TOLD
DWCC	DEADWEIGHT CARGO CAPACITY
DWT	DEADWEIGHT
E/B AFT	ENGINE AND BRIDGE AFT
ELVENT	ELECTRIC VENTILATION
EIU	EVEN IF USED
ETA	ESTIMATED TIME OF ARRIVAL
ETC	ESTIMATED TIME OF COMPLETION OF LOADING
ETD	ESTIMATED TIME OF DEPARTURE
ETS	ESTIMATED TIME OF SAILING
EXC	EXCEPT
EXCL	EXCLUDING / EXCLUDED
EXPLOAD	EXPECTED TO LOAD
FAC	FAST AS CAN
FAS	FREE ALONGSIDE
FCC	FIRST CLASS CHARTERER
FD	FREE DESPATCH
FDEOSSAOCLONL	FREIGHT DEEMED EARNED ON SHIPMENT SHIP AND OR CARGO LOST OR NOT LOST
FEU	40 FT EQUIVALENT UNIT-OUTSIDE LENGTH OF CONTAINER

FFA	FORWARD FREIGHT AGREEMENT
FHEX	FRIDAYS AND HOLIDAYS EXCEPTED
FHINC	FRIDAYS AND HOLIDAYS INCLUDED
FILO	FREE IN LINER OUT
FIO	FREE IN AND OUT
FIOS	FREE IN AND OUT STOWED
FIOST	FREE IN AND OUT STOWED AND TRIMMED
FIOSpT	FREE IN AND OUT SPOUT TRIMMED
FIOT	FREE IN AND OUT TRIMMED
FIOSLSD	FREE IN & OUT STOWED LASHED SECURED & DUNNAGED
FO	FUEL OIL
FOB	FREE ON BOARD
FOW	FIRST OPEN WATER (After ice in Baltic or St Lawrence. Great Lakes trading needs FOW in St Lawrence for example)
FONASBA	FEDERATION OF NATIONAL ASSOCIATIONS OF SHIPBROKERS AND AGENTS
FP	FREE PRATIQUE
FRT	FREIGHT
FW	FRESH WATER
FWAD	FRESH WATER ARRIVAL DRAFT
FWD	FORWARD (OPPOSITE OF AFT)
FYG	FOR YOUR GUIDANCE
FYPG	FOR YOUR PRIVATE GUIDANCE
FYVPG	FOR YOUR VERY PRIVATE GUIDANCE
FXTR	FIXTURE
GA	GENERAL AVERAGE
GA PLAN	GENERAL ARRANGEMENT PLAN
GEOG ROT	GEOGRAPHICAL ROTATION
GO	GAS OIL

GLESS	GEARLESS
GT	GROSS TONNAGE
GRT	GROSS REGISTERED TONNAGE
HBI	HOT BRIQUETTED IRON
H AND M	HULL AND MACHINERY
HOHA	HOLDS/HATCHES
HHDWS	HEAVY HANDY DEADWEIGHT SCRAP (scrap stowing deadweight i.e. about 40-50 cuft per ton)
HRC	HOT ROLLED COILS
HSS	HEAVY SORGHUMS AND SOYAS
HTUTC	HALF TIME USED TO COUNT
H/V	HAGUE VISBY RULES
IACS	INTERNATIONAL ASSOCIATION OF CLASSIFICATION SOCIETIES
IFO	INTERMEDIATE FUEL OIL
IGS	INSERT GAS SYSTEM
ILOW	IN LIEU OF WEIGHING
IMCO	INTERGOVERNMENTAL MARITIME CONSULTITIVE ORGANISATION
IMO	INTERNATIONAL MARITIME ORGANISATION
INS	INSURANCE
ISM	INTERNATIONAL SAFETY MANAGEMENT (CODE)
ISO	INTERNATIONAL STANDARDS ORGANISATION
IWL	INSTITUTE WARRANTY LIMITS
ITF	INTERNATIONAL TRANSPORT WORKERS FEDERATION
ITWF	INTERNATIONAL TRANSPORT WORKERS FEDERATION
KTS	KNOTS

LAYCAN	LAYDAYS/CANCELLING
L/C	LETTER OF CREDIT
LIFO	LINER IN FREE OUT
L/I	LETTER OF INDEMNITY
LMMA	LONDON MARITIME ARBITRATORS ASSOCIATION
LO/LO	LIFT ON / LIFT OFF
LOA	LENGTH OVER ALL
LOW	LAST OPEN WATER
LR	LLOYDS REGISTER OF SHIPPING
L/S	LUMPSUM
LT	LONG TONS
LWT	LIGHTWEIGHT
MDO	MARINE DIESEL OIL
M/E	MAIN ENGINE
MGO	MARINE GAS OIL
M/M	MINIMUM / MAXIMUM
MOLCHOP	MORE OR LESS IN CHARTERER'S OPTION
MOLCO	MORE OR LESS IN CHARTERER'S OPTION
MOLOO	MORE OR LESS IN OWNER'S OPTION
MOP	MURIATE OF POTASH
MPP	MULTI PURPOSE VESSEL
MV	MOTOR VESSEL
MT	METRIC TONS
NAABSA	NOT ALWAYS AFLOAT BUT SAFE AGROUND
NB	NEW BUILDING
NEGOS	NEGOTIATIONS
NIS	NORWEGIAN INTERNATIONAL SHIP REGISTRY
NRT	NET REGISTERED TONNAGE
NOM	NOMINATION
NON REV	NON REVERSIBLE LAYTIME

NOR	NOTICE OF READINESS
NYPE	NEW YORK PRODUCE EXCHANGE CHARTER PARTY
O/A	OVERAGED
OBO	ORE BULK OIL CARRIER
O/O	ORE OIL CARRIER
OO	OWNERS OPTION
OPT	OPTION
OWNS	OWNERS
P AND I	PROTECTION AND INDEMNITY
PG	PERSIAN GULF
PC	PORT CONSUMPTION
P/C	PART CARGO
PCC	PURE CAR CARRIER
PCTC	PURE CAR AND TRUCK CARRIER
PDM	PUNTA DE MADEIRA
PF	PRO FORMA
PHD	PER HATCH DAY
PICO	PORT IN CHARTERER'S OPTION
POPS	PURCHASE OPTIONS
PPT	PROMPT
PMT	PER METRIC TON
PLT	PER LONG TON
PST	PER SHORT TON
PR	PRO RATA
PROBO	COMBINED PRODUCTS AND BULK CARRIER
PWH	PER WORKABLE HATCH
PWHD	PER WORKABLE HATCH DAY
QWT	QUAY WEIGHT AND TONNAGE DUES

REV	REVERSIBLE (AS IN LAYTIME)
ROCKPHOS	PHOSPHATE ROCK
ROB	REMAINING ON BOARD
RORO	ROLL ON ROLL OFF
ROTT	ROTTERDAM
S AND P	SALE AND PURCHASE
SA	SAFE ANCHORAGE
SATSHEX	SATURDAYS, SUNDAYS AND HOLIDAYS EXCLUDED
SSHEX	SATURDAYS, SUNDAYS AND HOLIDAYS EXCLUDED
SATPMSHEX	SATURDAY PM SUNDAYS AND HOLIDAYS EXCLUDED
SB	SAFE BERTH
SEP	SEPETIBA
SF	STOWAGE FACTOR
SFA	SECURITIES AND FUTURES AUTHORITY
SG	SPECIFIC GRAVITY
SHEX	SUNDAYS AND HOLIDAYS EXCLUDED
SHINC	SUNDAYS AND HOLIDAYS INCLUDED
SMC	SAFETY MANAGEMENT CERTIFICATE
SOF	STATEMENT OF FACTS
SOLAS	SAFETY OF LIFE AT SEA (CONVENTION)
SP	SAFE PORT
SP/CON	SPEED AND CONSUMPTION
SPOT	SPOT –(IE VESSEL READY IMMEDIATELY)
S/R B/L	SIGNING AND RELEASING BILLS OF LADING
SS	SPECIAL SURVEY
SSHEX	SATURDAYS SUNDAYS AND HOLIDAYS EXCLUDED
SSINC	SATURDAYS AND SUNDAYS INCLUDED
SSW	SUMMER SALT WATER
SUBS	SUBJECTS

SUB	SUBSTITUTE / SUBJECT
SW	SALT WATER
SWL	SAFE WORKING LOAD
SWAD	SALT WATER ARRIVAL DRAFT
TBN	TO BE NOMINATED/TO BE NAMED
TBRN	TO BE RE-NAMED
T/C	TIME CHARTER
TCT	TIME CHARTER TRIP
TEU	TWENTY FOOT EQUIVALENT UNIT- CONTAINER
TFW	TROPICAL FRESH WATER
TIP	TAKING INWARD PILOT
TUB	TUBARAO
TPC	TONS PER CENTIMETER
TPI	TONS PER INCH
TTBE	TURN TIME BOTH ENDS
TTL	TOTAL
TT	TURN TIME
TSP	TRIPLE SUPER PHOSPHATE
UU	UNLESS USED
UUATUTC	UNLESS USED WHICH CASE ACTUAL TIME USED TO COUNT
USAC	UNITED STATES ATLANTIC COAST
USC	UNLESS SOONER COMMENCED
USEC	UNITED STATES EAST COAST
USD	UNITED STATES DOLLARS
USG	UNITED STATES GULF
USNH	UNITED STATES NORTH OF HATTERAS
USWC	UNITED STATES WEST COAST
VLBC	VERY LARGE BULK CARRIER

WECON	WHETHER ENTERED CUSTOMS OR NOT
WCCON	WHETHER CUSTOMS CLEARED OR NOT
WCYO	WHAT CAN YOU OFFER?
WCYP	WHAT CAN YOU PROPOSE?
WIBON	WHETHER IN BERTH OR NOT
WIFPON	WHETHER IN FREE PRATIQUE OR NOT
WIPON	WHETHER IN PORT OR NOT
WSNP	WEATHER AND SAFE NAVIGATION PERMITTING
WVNS	WITHIN VESSEL'S NATURAL SEGREGATIONS
WW	WORLD WIDE
WW	WEATHER WORKING
WWD	WEATHER WORKING DAY
WWF	WATERSIDE WORKERS FEDERATION
WOG	WITHOUT GUARANTEE
WRIC	WIRE ROD IN COILS
WP	WEATHER PERMITTING
WTS	WORKING TIME SAVED
W/TS	WING TANKS
WWR	WHEN WHERE READY
WWWW	WIBON / WIPON / WIFPON / WCCON
4 X W	WIBON / WIPON / WIFPON / WCCON
Y/A RULES	YORK ANTWERP RULES

Appendix Two

INTER-CLUB NEW YORK PRODUCE EXCHANGE AGREEMENT 1996

This Agreement is made on the 1st of September 1996 between the P&I Clubs being members of The International Group of P&I Associations listed below (hereafter referred to as "the Clubs").

This Agreement replaces the Inter Club Agreement 1984 in respect of all charterparties specified in clause (1) hereof and shall continue in force until varied or terminated. Any variation to be effective must be approved in writing by all the Clubs but it is open to any Club to withdraw from the Agreement on giving to all the other Clubs not less than three months' written notice thereof, such withdrawal to take effect at the expiration of that period. After the expiry of such notice the Agreement shall nevertheless continue as between all the Clubs, other than the Club giving such notice who shall remain bound by and be entitled to the benefit of this Agreement in respect of all Cargo Claims arising out of charterparties commenced prior to the expiration of such notice.

The Clubs will recommend to their Members without qualification that their Members adopt this Agreement for the purpose of apportioning liability for claims in respect of cargo which arise under, out of or in connection with all charterparties on the New York Product Exchange Form 1946 or 1993 or Asbatime Form 1981 (or any subsequent amendment of such Forms), whether or not this Agreement has been incorporated into such charterparties.

SCOPE OF APPLICATION

1. This Agreement applies to any charterparty which

is entered into after the date hereof on the New York Produce Exchange Form 1946 or 1993 or Asbatime Form 1981 (or any subsequent amendment of such Forms).

2. The terms of this Agreement shall apply notwithstanding anything to the contrary in any other provision of the charterparty; in particular the provisions of clause (6) (time bar) shall apply notwithstanding any provision of the charterparty or rule of law to the contrary.

3. For the purposes of this Agreement, cargo Claim(s) mean claims for loss, damage, shortage (including slackage, ullage or pilferage), overcarriage or or delay to cargo including customs dues or fines in respect of such loss, damage, shortage, overcarriage or delay and include

   (a) any legal costs claimed by the original person making any such claim;
   (b) any interest claimed by the original person making any such claim;
   (c) all legal, Club correspondents' and experts' costs reasonably incurred in the defence of or in the settlement of the claim made by the original person, shall not include any costs of whatsoever nature incurred in making a claim under this Agreement or in seeking an indemnity under the charterparty.

4. Apportionment under this Agreement shall only be applied to Cargo Claims where:
   (a) the claim was made under a contract of carriage, whatever its form,
      (i) which was authorised under the charterparty;
      or
      (ii) which would have been authorised under the charterparty but for the inclusion in that contract of carriage of Through

but for the inclusion in that contract of carriage of Through Transport or Combined Transport provision,

provided that

(iii) in the case of contracts of carriage containing Through Transport or Combined Transport provisions (whether falling within (i) or (ii) above) the loss, damage, shortage, overcarriage or delay occurred after commencement of the loading of the cargo onto the chartered vessel and prior to completion of its discharge from that vessel (the burden of proof being on the Charterer to establish that the loss, damage, shortage, overcarriage or delay did or did not so occur); and

(iv) the contract of carriage (or that part of the transit that comprised carriage on the chartered vessel) incorporated terms no less favourable to the carrier than the Hague or Hague Visby Rules, or, when compulsorily applicable by operation of law to the contract of carriage, the Hamburg Rules or any national law giving effect thereto

and

(b) the cargo responsibility clauses in the charterparty have not been materially amended. A material amendment is one which makes the liability, as between Owners adn Charterers, for Cargo Claims clear. In particular, it is agreed solely for the purposes of this Agreement:

(i) that the addition of the words "and responsibility" in clause 8 of the new York Produce Exchange Form 1946 or 1993 or clause 8 of the Asbatime Form 1981, or any similar amendment of the charterparty making the Master responsible for cargo handling, is not a material amendment; and

(ii) that if the words "cargo claims" are added to the second sentence of clause 26 of the New York Produce Exchange Form 1946 or 1993 or clause 25 of the Asbatime Form 1981, apportionment under this Agreement shall not be applied under any circumstances even if the charterparty is made subject to terms of this Agreement;

and

(c) the claim has been properly settled or compromised and paid.

5. This Agreement applies regardless of legal forum or place of arbitration specified in the charterparty and regardless of any incorporation of the Hague, Hague Visby Rules or Hamburg Rules therein.

TIME BAR

6. Recovery under this Agreement by an Owner or Charterer shall be deemed to be waived and absolutely barred unless written notification of the Cargo Claim has been given to the other party to the charterparty within 24 months of the date delivery of the cargo or the date the cargo should have been delivered, save that, where the Hamburg Rules or any national legislation giving effect thereto are compulsorily applicable by operation of law to the contract of carriage or to that part of the transit that comprised carriage on the chartered vessel, the period shall be 36 months. Such notification shall if possible include details of the contract of carriage, the nature of the claim and the amount claimed.

THE APPORTIONMENT

7. The amount of any Cargo Claim to be apportioned under this Agreement shall be the amount in fact borne by the party to the charterparty seeking apportionment, regardless of whether that claim

may be or has been apportioned by application of this Agreement to another charterparty.

8. Cargo Claims shall be apportioned as follows:

(a) Claims in fact arising out of unseaworthiness and/or error or fault in navigation or management of the vessel

100% Owners

save where the Owner proves that the unseaworthiness was caused by the loading, stowage, lashing, discharge or other handling of the cargo, in which case the claim shall be apportioned under sub-clause (b).

(b) Claims in fact arising out of loading, stowage, lashing, discharge, storage or other handling of cargo:
100% Charterers
unless the words "and responsibility" are added in clause 8 or there is a similar amendment making the Master responsible for cargo handling in which case:
50% Charterers
50% Owners
save where the Charterer proves that the failure properly to load, stow, lash, discharge or handle the cargo was caused by the unseaworthiness of the vessel in which case:
100% Owners

(c) Subject to (a) and (b) above, claims for shortage or overcarriage:
50% Charterers
50% Owners
unless there is clear and irrefutable evidence that the claim arose out of pilferage or act or neglect by one or the other (including

their servants or sub-contractors) in which case that party shall then bear 100% of the claim.

(d) All other cargo claims whatsoever (including claims for delay to cargo):

50% Charterers

50% Owners

unless there is clear and irrefutable evidence that the claim arose out of the act or neglect of the one or the other (including their servants or sub-contractors) in which case that party shall then bear 100% of the claim.

GOVERNING LAW

9. This Agreement shall be subject to English Law and Jurisdiction, unless it is incorporated into the charterparty (or the settlement of claims in respect of cargo under the charterparty is made subject to this Agreement), in which case it shall be subject to the law and jurisdiction provisions governing the charterparty.

Appendix Three

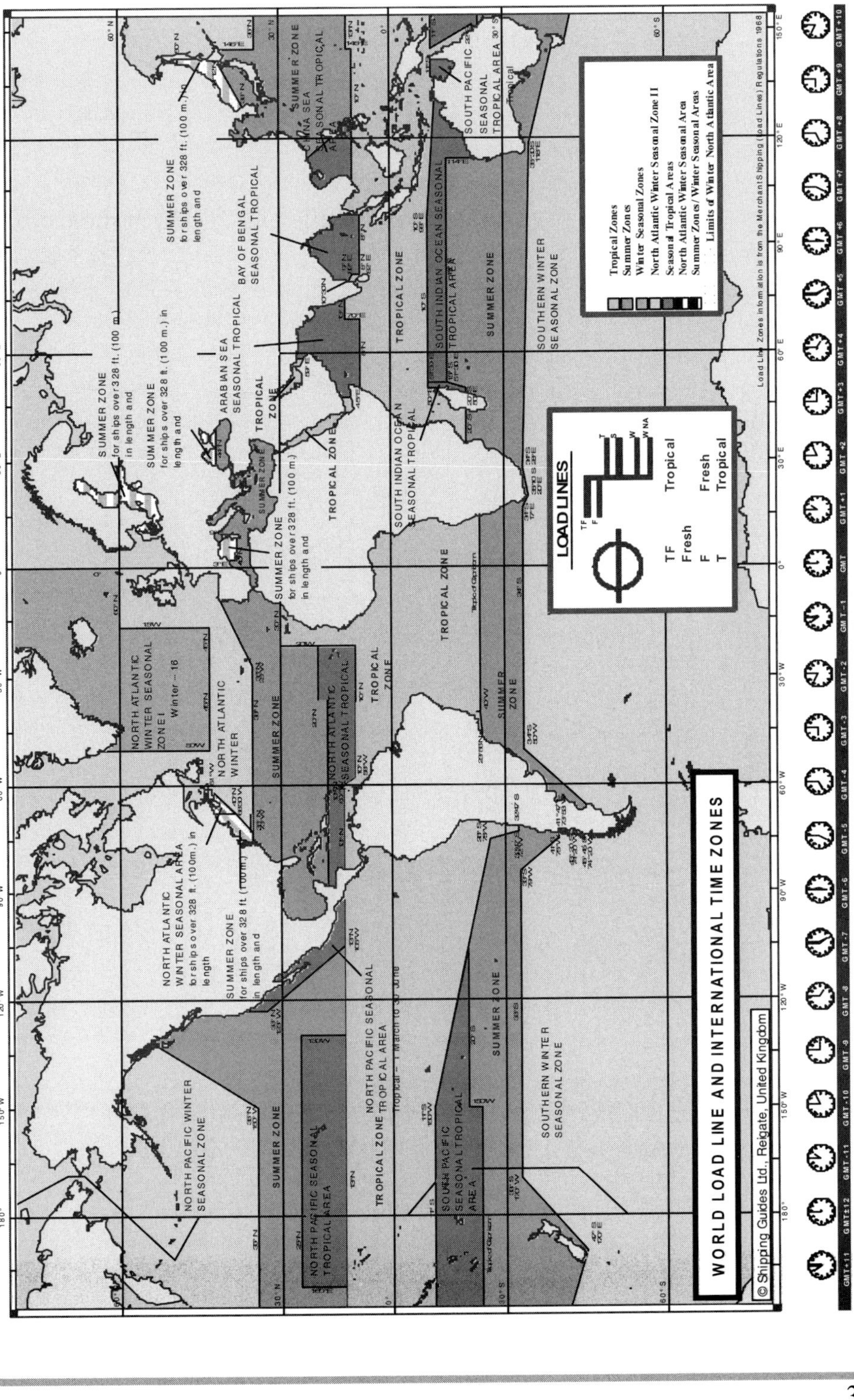

Appendix Four

SOME COMMONLY USED CHARTER PARTY FORMS

Voyage Charter Parties

1. Gencon '76
2. Gencon '94
3. Orevoy
4. Amwelsh '79
5. Amwelsh '93
6. Norgrain '89
7. Sugar '77
8. Sugar '99

Time Charter Parties

1. NYPE '46
2. NYPE '93
3. Gentime

Adopted by
the Documentary Committee of the General
Council of British Shipping, London
and the Documentary Committee of The Japan
Shipping Exchange, Inc., Tokyo

RECOMMENDED
THE BALTIC AND INTERNATIONAL MARITIME CONFERENCE
UNIFORM GENERAL CHARTER (AS REVISED 1922 and 1976)
INCLUDING "F.I.O." ALTERNATIVE, ETC.
(To be used for trades for which no approved form is in force)
CODE NAME: "GENCON"

Part I

1. Shipbroker	2. Place and date
3. Owners/Place of business (Cl. 1)	4. Charterers/Place of business (Cl. 1)
5. Vessel's name (Cl. 1)	6. GRT/NRT (Cl. 1)
7. Deadweight cargo carrying capacity in tons (abt.) (Cl. 1)	8. Present position (Cl. 1)
9. Expected ready to load (abt.) (Cl. 1)	
10. Loading port or place (Cl. 1)	11. Discharging port or place (Cl. 1)
12. Cargo (also state quantity and margin in Owners' option, if agreed; if full and complete cargo not agreed state "part cargo") (Cl. 1)	
13. Freight rate (also state if payable on delivered or intaken quantity) (Cl. 1)	14. Freight payment (state currency and method of payment; also beneficiary and bank account) (Cl. 4)
15. Loading and discharging costs (state alternative (a) or (b) of Cl. 5; also indicate if vessel is gearless)	16. Laytime (if separate laytime for load. and disch. is agreed, fill in a) and b). If total laytime for load. and disch., fill in c) only) (Cl. 6)
	a) Laytime for loading
17. Shippers (state name and address) (Cl. 6)	b) Laytime for discharging
	c) Total laytime for loading and discharging
18. Demurrage rate (loading and discharging) (Cl. 7)	19. Cancelling date (Cl. 10)
20. Brokerage commission and to whom payable (Cl. 14)	
21. Additional clauses covering special provisions, if agreed.	

It is mutually agreed that this Contract shall be performed subject to the conditions contained in this Charter which shall include Part I as well as Part II. In the event of a conflict of conditions, the provisions of Part I shall prevail over those of Part II to the extent of such conflict.

Signature (Owners)	Signature (Charterers)

Printed and sold by Fr. G. Knudtzon Ltd., 55, Toldbodgade, Copenhagen, by authority of The Baltic and International Maritime Conference (BIMCO), Copenhagen.

PART II

"Gencon" Charter (As Revised 1922 and 1976)

Including "F.I.O." Alternative, etc.

1. It is agreed between the party mentioned in Box 3 as Owners of the steamer or motor-vessel named in Box 5, of the gross/nett Register tons indicated in Box 6 and carrying about the number of tons of deadweight cargo stated in Box 7, now in position as stated in Box 8 and expected ready to load under this Charter about the date indicated in Box 9, and the party mentioned as Charterers in Box 4 that:
The said vessel shall proceed to the loading port or place stated in Box 10 or so near thereto as she may safely get and lie always afloat, and there load a full and complete cargo (if shipment of deck cargo agreed same to be at Charterers' risk) as stated in Box 12 (Charterers to provide all mats and/or wood for dunnage and any separations required, the Owners allowing the use of any dunnage wood on board if required) which the Charterers bind themselves to ship, and being so loaded the vessel shall proceed to the discharging port or place stated in Box 11 as ordered on signing Bills of Lading or so near thereto as she may safely get and lie always afloat and there deliver the cargo on being paid freight on delivered or intaken quantity as indicated in Box 13 at the rate stated in Box 13.

2. Owners' Responsibility Clause
Owners are to be responsible for loss of or damage to the goods or for delay in delivery of the goods only in case the loss, damage or delay has been caused by the improper or negligent stowage of the goods (unless stowage performed by shippers/Charterers or their stevedores or servants) or by personal want of due diligence on the part of the Owners or their Manager to make the vessel in all respects seaworthy and to secure that she is properly manned, equipped and supplied or by the personal act or default of the Owners or their Manager.
And the Owners are responsible for no loss or damage or delay arising from any other cause whatsoever, even from the neglect or default of the Captain or crew or some other person employed by the Owners on board or ashore for whose acts they would, but for this clause, be responsible, or from unseaworthiness of the vessel on loading or commencement of the voyage or at any time whatsoever. Damage caused by contact with or leakage, smell or evaporation from other goods or by the inflammable or explosive nature or insufficient package of other goods not to be considered as caused by improper or negligent stowage, even if in fact so caused.

3. Deviation Clause
The vessel has liberty to call at any port or ports in any order, for any purpose, to sail without pilots, to tow and/or assist vessels in all situations, and also to deviate for the purpose of saving life and/or property.

4. Payment of Freight
The freight to be paid in the manner prescribed in Box 14 in cash without discount on delivery of the cargo at mean rate of exchange ruling on day or days of payment, the receivers of the cargo being bound to pay freight on account during delivery, if required by Captain or Owners.
Cash for vessel's ordinary disbursements at port of loading to be advanced by Charterers if required at highest current rate of exchange, subject to two per cent. to cover insurance and other expenses.

5. Loading/Discharging Costs
** (a) Gross Terms*
The cargo to be brought alongside in such a manner as to enable vessel to take the goods with her own tackle. Charterers to procure and pay the necessary men on shore or on board the lighters to do the work there, vessel only heaving the cargo on board.
If the loading takes place by elevator, cargo to be put free in vessel's holds, Owners only paying trimming expenses.
Any pieces and/or packages of cargo over two tons weight, shall be loaded, stowed and discharged by Charterers at their risk and expense.
The cargo to be received by Merchants at their risk and expense alongside the vessel not beyond the reach of her tackle.
** (b) F.i.o. and free stowed/trimmed*
The cargo shall be brought into the holds, loaded, stowed and/or trimmed and taken from the holds and discharged by the Charterers or their Agents, free of any risk, liability and expense whatsoever to the Owners.
The Owners shall provide winches, motive power and winchmen from the Crew if requested and permitted; if not, the Charterers shall provide and pay for winchmen from shore and/or cranes, if any. (This provision shall not apply if vessel is gearless and stated as such in Box 15).
** indicate alternative (a) or (b), as agreed, in Box 15.*

6. Laytime
** (a) Separate laytime for loading and discharging*
The cargo shall be loaded within the number of running hours as indicated in Box 16, weather permitting, Sundays and holidays excepted, unless used, in which event time actually used shall count.
The cargo shall be discharged within the number of running hours as indicated in Box 16, weather permitting, Sundays and holidays excepted, unless used, in which event time actually used shall count.
** (b) Total laytime for loading and discharging*
The cargo shall be loaded and discharged within the number of total running hours as indicated in Box 16, weather permitting, Sundays and holidays excepted, unless used, in which event time actually used shall count.
(c) Commencement of laytime (loading and discharging)
Laytime for loading and discharging shall commence at 1 p.m. if notice of readiness is given before noon, and at 6 a.m. next working day if notice given during office hours after noon. Notice at loading port to be given to the Shippers named in Box 17.
Time actually used before commencement of laytime shall count.
Time lost in waiting for berth to count as loading or discharging time, as the case may be.
** indicate alternative (a) or (b) as agreed, in Box 16.*

7. Demurrage
Ten running days on demurrage at the rate stated in Box 18 per day or pro rata for any part of a day, payable day by day, to be allowed Merchants altogether at ports of loading and discharging.

8. Lien Clause
Owners shall have a lien on the cargo for freight, dead-freight, demurrage and damages for detention. Charterers shall remain responsible for dead-freight and demurrage (including damages for detention), incurred at port of loading. Charterers shall also remain responsible for freight and demurrage (including damages for detention) incurred at port of discharge, but only to such extent as the Owners have been unable to obtain payment thereof by exercising the lien on the cargo.

9. Bills of Lading
The Captain to sign Bills of Lading at such rate of freight as presented without prejudice to this Charterparty, but should the freight by Bills of Lading amount to less than the total chartered freight the difference to be paid to the Captain in cash on signing Bills of Lading.

10. Cancelling Clause
Should the vessel not be ready to load (whether in berth or not) on or before the date indicated in Box 19, Charterers have the option of cancelling this contract, such option to be declared, if demanded, at least 48 hours before vessel's expected arrival at port of loading. Should the vessel be delayed on account of average or otherwise, Charterers to be informed as soon as possible, and if the vessel is delayed for more than 10 days after the day she is stated to be expected ready to load, Charterers have the option of cancelling this contract, unless a cancelling date has been agreed upon.

11. General Average
General average to be settled according to York-Antwerp Rules, 1974. Proprietors of cargo to pay the cargo's share in the general expenses even if same have been necessitated through neglect or default of the Owners' servants (see clause 2).

12. Indemnity
Indemnity for non-performance of this Charterparty, proved damages, not exceeding estimated amount of freight.

13. Agency
In every case the Owners shall appoint his own Broker or Agent both at the port of loading and the port of discharge.

14. Brokerage
A brokerage commission at the rate stated in Box 20 on the freight earned is due to the party mentioned in Box 20.
In case of non-execution at least 1/3 of the brokerage on the estimated amount of freight and dead-freight to be paid by the Owners to the Brokers as indemnity for the latter's expenses and work. In case of more voyages the amount of indemnity to be mutually agreed.

15. GENERAL STRIKE CLAUSE
Neither Charterers nor Owners shall be responsible for the consequences of any strikes or lock-outs preventing or delaying the fulfilment of any obligations under this contract.
If there is a strike or lock-out affecting the loading of the cargo, or any part of it, when vessel is ready to proceed from her last port or at any time during the voyage to the port or ports of loading or after her arrival there, Captain or Owners may ask Charterers to declare, that they agree to reckon the laydays as if there were no strike or lock-out. Unless Charterers have given such declaration in writing (by telegram, if necessary) within 24 hours, Owners shall have the option of cancelling this contract. If part cargo has already been loaded, Owners must proceed with same, (freight payable on loaded quantity only) having liberty to complete with other cargo on the way for their own account.
If there is a strike or lock-out affecting the discharge of the cargo on or after vessel's arrival at or off port of discharge and same has not been settled within 48 hours, Receivers shall have the option of keeping vessel waiting until such strike or lock-out is at an end against paying half demurrage after expiration of the time provided for discharging, or of ordering the vessel to a safe port where she can safely discharge without risk of being detained by strike or lock-out. Such orders to be given within 48 hours after Captain or Owners have given notice to Charterers of the strike or lock-out affecting the discharge. On delivery of the cargo at such port, all conditions of this Charterparty and of the Bill of Lading shall apply and vessel shall receive the same freight as if she had discharged at the original port of destination, except that if the distance of the substituted port exceeds 100 nautical miles, the freight on the cargo delivered at the substituted port to be increased in proportion.

16. War Risks ("Voywar 1950")
(1) In these clauses "War Risks" shall include any blockade or any action which is announced as a blockade by any Government or by any belligerent or by any organized body, sabotage, piracy, and any actual or threatened war, hostilities, warlike operations, civil war, civil commotion, or revolution.
(2) If at any time before the Vessel commences loading, it appears that performance of the contract will subject the Vessel or her Master and crew or her cargo to war risks at any stage of the adventure, the Owners shall be entitled by letter or telegram despatched to the Charterers, to cancel this Charter.
(3) The Master shall not be required to load cargo or to continue loading or to proceed on or to sign Bill(s) of Lading for any adventure on which or any port at which it appears that the Vessel, her Master and crew or her cargo will be subjected to war risks. In the event of the exercise by the Master of his right under this Clause after part or full cargo has been loaded, the Master shall be at liberty either to discharge such cargo at the loading port or to proceed therewith. In the latter case the Vessel shall have liberty to carry other cargo for Owners' benefit and accordingly to proceed to and load or discharge such other cargo at any other port or ports whatsoever, backwards or forwards, although in a contrary direction to or out of or beyond the ordinary route. In the event of the Master electing to proceed with part cargo under this Clause freight shall in any case be payable on the quantity delivered.
(4) If at the time the Master elects to proceed with part or full cargo under Clause 3, or after the Vessel has left the loading port, or the

PART II

"Gencon" Charter (As Revised 1922 and 1976)

Including "F.I.O." Alternative, etc.

last of the loading ports, if more than one, it appears that further performance of the contract will subject the Vessel, her Master and crew or her cargo, to war risks, the cargo shall be discharged, or if the discharge has been commenced shall be completed, at any safe port in vicinity of the port of discharge as may be ordered by the Charterers. If no such orders shall be received from the Charterers within 48 hours after the Owners have despatched a request by telegram to the Charterers for the nomination of a substitute discharging port, the Owners shall be at liberty to discharge the cargo at any safe port which they may, in their discretion, decide on and such discharge shall be deemed to be due fulfilment of the contract of affreightment. In the event of cargo being discharged at any such other port, the Owners shall be entitled to freight as if the discharge had been effected at the port or ports named in the Bill(s) of Lading or to which the Vessel may have been ordered pursuant thereto.

(5) (a) The Vessel shall have liberty to comply with any directions or recommendations as to loading, departure, arrival, routes, ports of call, stoppages, destination, zones, waters, discharge, delivery or in any other wise whatsoever (including any direction or recommendation not to go to the port of destination or to delay proceeding thereto or to proceed to some other port) given by any Government or by any belligerent or by any organized body engaged in civil war, hostilities or warlike operations or by any person or body acting or purporting to act as or with the authority of any Government or belligerent or of any such organized body or by any committee or person having under the terms of the war risks insurance on the Vessel, the right to give any such directions or recommendations. If, by reason of or in compliance with any such direction or recommendation, anything is done or is not done, such shall not be deemed a deviation.

(b) If, by reason of or in compliance with any such directions or recommendations, the Vessel does not proceed to the port or ports named in the Bill(s) of Lading or to which she may have been ordered pursuant thereto, the Vessel may proceed to any port as directed or recommended or to any safe port which the Owners in their discretion may decide on and there discharge the cargo. Such discharge shall be deemed to be due fulfilment of the contract of affreightment and the Owners shall be entitled to freight as if discharge had been effected at the port or ports named in the Bill(s) of Lading or to which the Vessel may have been ordered pursuant thereto.

(6) All extra expenses (including insurance costs) involved in discharging cargo at the loading port or in reaching or discharging the cargo at any port as provided in Clauses 4 and 5 (b) hereof shall be paid by the Charterers and/or cargo owners, and the Owners shall have a lien on the cargo for all moneys due under these Clauses.

17. GENERAL ICE CLAUSE

Port of loading

(a) In the event of the loading port being inaccessible by reason of ice when vessel is ready to proceed from her last port or at any time during the voyage or on vessel's arrival or in case frost sets in after vessel's arrival, the Captain for fear of being frozen in is at liberty to leave without cargo, and this Charter shall be null and void.

(b) If during loading the Captain, for fear of vessel being frozen in, deems it advisable to leave, he has liberty to do so with what cargo he has on board and to proceed to any other port or ports with option of completing cargo for Owners' benefit for any port or ports including port of discharge. Any part cargo thus loaded under this Charter to be forwarded to destination at vessel's expense but against payment of freight, provided that no extra expenses be thereby caused to the Receivers, freight being paid on quantity delivered (in proportion if lumpsum), all other conditions as per Charter.

(c) In case of more than one loading port, and if one or more of the ports are closed by ice, the Captain or Owners to be at liberty either to load the part cargo at the open port and fillup elsewhere for their own account as under section (b) or to declare the Charter null and void unless Charterers agree to load full cargo at the open port.

(d) This Ice Clause not to apply in the Spring.

Port of discharge

(a) Should ice (except in the Spring) prevent vessel from reaching port of discharge Receivers shall have the option of keeping vessel waiting until the re-opening of navigation and paying demurrage, or of ordering the vessel to a safe and immediately accessible port where she can safely discharge without risk of detention by ice. Such orders to be given within 48 hours after Captain or Owners have given notice to Charterers of the impossibility of reaching port of destination.

(b) If during discharging the Captain for fear of vessel being frozen in deems it advisable to leave, he has liberty to do so with what cargo he has on board and to proceed to the nearest accessible port where she can safely discharge.

(c) On delivery of the cargo at such port, all conditions of the Bill of Lading shall apply and vessel shall receive the same freight as if she had discharged at the original port of destination, except that if the distance of the substituted port exceeds 100 nautical miles, the freight on the cargo delivered at the substituted port to be increased in proportion.

RECOMMENDED
THE BALTIC AND INTERNATIONAL MARITIME COUNCIL
UNIFORM GENERAL CHARTER (AS REVISED 1922, 1976 and 1994)
(To be used for trades for which no specially approved form is in force)
CODE NAME: "GENCON"

Part I

1. Shipbroker	2. Place and date
3. Owners/Place of business (Cl. 1)	4. Charterers/Place of business (Cl. 1)
5. Vessel's name (Cl. 1)	6. GT/NT (Cl. 1)
7. DWT all told on summer load line in metric tons (abt.) (Cl. 1)	8. Present position (Cl. 1)
9. Expected ready to load (abt.) (Cl. 1)	
10. Loading port or place (Cl. 1)	11. Discharging port or place (Cl. 1)
12. Cargo (also state quantity and margin in Owners' option, if agreed; if full and complete cargo not agreed state "part cargo" (Cl. 1)	
13. Freight rate (also state whether freight prepaid or payable on delivery) (Cl. 4)	14. Freight payment (state currency and method of payment; also beneficiary and bank account) (Cl. 4)
15. State if vessel's cargo handling gear shall not be used (Cl. 5)	16. Laytime (if separate laytime for load. and disch. is agreed, fill in a) and b). If total laytime for load. and disch., fill in c) only) (Cl. 6)
17. Shippers/Place of business (Cl. 6)	(a) Laytime for loading
18. Agents (loading) (Cl. 6)	(b) Laytime for discharging
19. Agents (discharging) (Cl. 6)	(c) Total laytime for loading and discharging
20. Demurrage rate and manner payable (loading and discharging) (Cl. 7)	21. Cancelling date (Cl. 9)
	22. General Average to be adjusted at (Cl. 12)
23. Freight Tax (state if for the Owners' account (Cl .13 (c))	24. Brokerage commission and to whom payable (Cl. 15)
25. Law and Arbitration (state 19 (a), 19 (b) or 19 (c) of Cl. 19; if 19 (c) agreed also state Place of Arbitration) (if not filled in 19 (a) shall apply) (Cl. 19)	
(a) State maximum amount for small claims/shortened arbitration (Cl. 19)	26. Additional clauses covering special provisions, if agreed

It is mutually agreed that this Contract shall be performed subject to the conditions contained in this Charter Party which shall include Part I as well as Part II. In the event of a conflict of conditions, the provisions of Part I shall prevail over those of Part II to the extent of such conflict.

Signature (Owners)	Signature (Charterers)

Printed and sold by Fr. G. Knudtzons Bogtrykkeri A/S, 61 Vallensbækvej, DK-2625 Vallensbæk,
Telefax +45 43 66 07 08 by authority of The Baltic and International Maritime Council (BIMCO), Copenhagen

PART II

"Gencon" Charter (As Revised 1922, 1976 and 1994)

1. It is agreed between the party mentioned in Box 3 as the Owners of the Vessel named in Box 5, of the GT/NT indicated in Box 6 and carrying about the number of metric tons of deadweight capacity all told on summer loadline stated in Box 7, now in position as stated in Box 8 and expected ready to load under this Charter Party about the date indicated in Box 9, and the party mentioned as the Charterers in Box 4 that:

The said Vessel shall, as soon as her prior commitments have been completed, proceed to the loading port(s) or place(s) stated in Box 10 or so near thereto as she may safely get and lie always afloat, and there load a full and complete cargo (if shipment of deck cargo agreed same to be at the Charterers' risk and responsibility) as stated in Box 12, which the Charterers bind themselves to ship, and being so loaded the Vessel shall proceed to the discharging port(s) or place(s) stated in Box 11 as ordered on signing Bills of Lading, or so near thereto as she may safely get and lie always afloat, and there deliver the cargo.

2. **Owners' Responsibility Clause**

The Owners are to be responsible for loss of or damage to the goods or for delay in delivery of the goods only in case the loss, damage or delay has been caused by personal want of due diligence on the part of the Owners or their Manager to make the Vessel in all respects seaworthy and to secure that she is properly manned, equipped and supplied, or by the personal act or default of the Owners or their Manager.

And the Owners are not responsible for loss, damage or delay arising from any other cause whatsoever, even from the neglect or default of the Master or crew or some other person employed by the Owners on board or ashore for whose acts they would, but for this Clause, be responsible, or from unseaworthiness of the Vessel on loading or commencement of the voyage or at any time whatsoever.

3. **Deviation Clause**

The Vessel has liberty to call at any port or ports in any order, for any purpose, to sail without pilots, to tow and/or assist Vessels in all situations, and also to deviate for the purpose of saving life and/or property.

4. **Payment of Freight**

(a) The freight at the rate stated in Box 13 shall be paid in cash calculated on the intaken quantity of cargo.

(b) Prepaid. If according to Box 13 freight is to be paid on shipment, it shall be deemed earned and non-returnable, Vessel and/or cargo lost or not lost.

Neither the Owners nor their agents shall be required to sign or endorse bills of lading showing freight prepaid unless the freight due to the Owners has actually been paid.

(c) On delivery. If according to Box 13 freight, or part thereof, is payable at destination it shall not be deemed earned until the cargo is thus delivered. Notwithstanding the provisions under (a), if freight or part thereof is payable on delivery of the cargo the Charterers shall have the option of paying the freight on delivered weight/quantity provided such option is declared before breaking bulk and the weight/quantity can be ascertained by official weighing machine, joint draft survey or tally.

Cash for Vessel's ordinary disbursements at the port of loading to be advanced by the Charterers, if required, at highest current rate of exchange, subject to two (2) per cent to cover insurance and other expenses.

5. **Loading/Discharging**

(a) Costs/Risks

The cargo shall be brought into the holds, loaded, stowed and/or trimmed, tallied, lashed and/or secured and taken from the holds and discharged by the Charterers, free of any risk, liability and expense whatsoever to the Owners. The Charterers shall provide and lay all dunnage material as required for the proper stowage and protection of the cargo on board, the Owners allowing the use of all dunnage available on board. The Charterers shall be responsible for and pay the cost of removing their dunnage after discharge of the cargo under this Charter Party and time to count until dunnage has been removed.

(b) Cargo Handling Gear

Unless the Vessel is gearless or unless it has been agreed between the parties that the Vessel's gear shall not be used and stated as such in Box 15, the Owners shall throughout the duration of loading/discharging give free use of the Vessel's cargo handling gear and of sufficient motive power to operate all such cargo handling gear. All such equipment to be in good working order. Unless caused by negligence of the stevedores, time lost by breakdown of the Vessel's cargo handling gear or motive power – pro rata the total number of cranes/winches required at that time for the loading/discharging of cargo under this Charter Party – shall not count as laytime or time on demurrage.

On request the Owners shall provide free of charge cranemen/winchmen from the crew to operate the Vessel's cargo handling gear, unless local regulations prohibit this, in which latter event shore labourers shall be for the account of the Charterers. Cranemen/winchmen shall be under the Charterers' risk and responsibility and as stevedores to be deemed as their servants but shall always work under the supervision of the Master.

(c) Stevedore Damage

The Charterers shall be responsible for damage (beyond ordinary wear and tear) to any part of the Vessel caused by Stevedores. Such damage shall be notified as soon as reasonably possible by the Master to the Charterers or their agents and to their Stevedores, failing which the Charterers shall not be held responsible. The Master shall endeavour to obtain the Stevedores' written acknowledgement of liability.

The Charterers are obliged to repair any stevedore damage prior to completion of the voyage, but must repair stevedore damage affecting the Vessel's seaworthiness or class before the Vessel sails from the port where such damage was caused or found. All additional expenses incurred shall be for the account of the Charterers and any time lost shall be for the account of and shall be paid to the Owners by the Charterers at the demurrage rate.

6. **Laytime**

* *(a) Separate laytime for loading and discharging*

The cargo shall be loaded within the number of running days/hours as indicated in Box 16, weather permitting, Sundays and holidays excepted, unless used, in which event time used shall count.

The cargo shall be discharged within the number of running days/hours as indicated in Box 16, weather permitting, Sundays and holidays excepted, unless used, in which event time used shall count.

* *(b) Total laytime for loading and discharging*

The cargo shall be loaded and discharged within the number of total running days/hours as indicated in Box 16, weather permitting, Sundays and holidays excepted, unless used, in which event time used shall count.

(c) Commencement of laytime (loading and discharging)

Laytime for loading and discharging shall commence at 13.00 hours, if notice of readiness is given up to and including 12.00 hours, and at 06.00 hours next working day if notice given during office hours after 12.00 hours. Notice of readiness at loading port to be given to the Shippers named in Box 17 or if not named, to the Charterers or their agents named in Box 18. Notice of readiness at the discharging port to be given to the Receivers or, if not known, to the Charterers or their agents named in Box 19.

If the loading/discharging berth is not available on the Vessel's arrival at or off the port of loading/discharging, the Vessel shall be entitled to give notice of readiness within ordinary office hours on arrival there, whether in free pratique or not, whether customs cleared or not. Laytime or time on demurrage shall then count as if she were in berth and in all respects ready for loading/discharging provided that the Master warrants that she is in fact ready in all respects. Time used in moving from the place of waiting to the loading/discharging berth shall not count as laytime.

If, after inspection, the Vessel is found not to be ready in all respects to load/discharge time lost after the discovery thereof until the Vessel is again ready to load/discharge shall not count as laytime.

Time used before commencement of laytime shall count.

* *Indicate alternative (a) or (b) as agreed, in Box 16.*

7. **Demurrage**

Demurrage at the loading and discharging port is payable by the Charterers at the rate stated in Box 20 in the manner stated in Box 20 per day or pro rata for any part of a day. Demurrage shall fall due day by day and shall be payable upon receipt of the Owners' invoice.

In the event the demurrage is not paid in accordance with the above, the Owners shall give the Charterers 96 running hours written notice to rectify the failure. If the demurrage is not paid at the expiration of this time limit and if the vessel is in or at the loading port, the Owners are entitled at any time to terminate the Charter Party and claim damages for any losses caused thereby.

8. **Lien Clause**

The Owners shall have a lien on the cargo and on all sub-freights payable in respect of the cargo, for freight, deadfreight, demurrage, claims for damages and for all other amounts due under this Charter Party including costs of recovering same.

9. **Cancelling Clause**

(a) Should the Vessel not be ready to load (whether in berth or not) on the cancelling date indicated in Box 21, the Charterers shall have the option of cancelling this Charter Party.

(b) Should the Owners anticipate that, despite the exercise of due diligence, the Vessel will not be ready to load by the cancelling date, they shall notify the Charterers thereof without delay stating the expected date of the Vessel's readiness to load and asking whether the Charterers will exercise their option of cancelling the Charter Party, or agree to a new cancelling date.

Such option must be declared by the Charterers within 48 running hours after the receipt of the Owners' notice. If the Charterers do not exercise their option of cancelling, then this Charter Party shall be deemed to be amended such that the seventh day after the new readiness date stated in the Owners' notification to the Charterers shall be the new cancelling date.

The provisions of sub-clause (b) of this Clause shall operate only once, and in case of the Vessel's further delay, the Charterers shall have the option of cancelling the Charter Party as per sub-clause (a) of this Clause.

10. **Bills of Lading**

Bills of Lading shall be presented and signed by the Master as per the "Congenbill" Bill of Lading form, Edition 1994, without prejudice to this Charter Party, or by the Owners' agents provided written authority has been given by Owners to the agents, a copy of which is to be furnished to the Charterers. The Charterers shall indemnify the Owners against all consequences or liabilities that may arise from the signing of bills of lading as presented to the extent that the terms or contents of such bills of lading impose or result in the imposition of more onerous liabilities upon the Owners than those assumed by the Owners under this Charter Party.

11. **Both-to-Blame Collision Clause**

If the Vessel comes into collision with another vessel as a result of the negligence of the other vessel and any act, neglect or default of the Master, Mariner, Pilot or the servants of the Owners in the navigation or in the management of the Vessel, the owners of the cargo carried hereunder will indemnify the Owners against all loss or liability to the other or non-carrying vessel or her owners in so far as such loss or liability represents loss of, or damage to, or any claim whatsoever of the owners of said cargo, paid or payable by the other or non-carrying vessel or her owners to the owners of said cargo and set-off, recouped or recovered by the other or non-carrying vessel or her owners as part of their claim against the carrying Vessel or the Owners.

The foregoing provisions shall also apply where the owners, operators or those in charge of any vessel or vessels or objects other than, or in addition to, the colliding vessels or objects are at fault in respect of a collision or contact.

12. **General Average and New Jason Clause**

General Average shall be adjusted in London unless otherwise agreed in Box 22 according to York-Antwerp Rules 1994 and any subsequent modification thereof. Proprietors of cargo to pay the cargo's share in the general expenses even if same have been necessitated through neglect or default of the Owners' servants (see Clause 2).

If General Average is to be adjusted in accordance with the law and practice of the United States of America, the following Clause shall apply: "In the event of accident, danger, damage or disaster before or after the commencement of the voyage, resulting from any cause whatsoever, whether due to negligence or not, for which, or for the consequence of which, the Owners are not responsible, by statute, contract or otherwise, the cargo shippers, consignees or the owners of the cargo shall contribute with the Owners in General Average to the payment of any sacrifices, losses or expenses of a General Average nature that may be made or incurred and shall pay salvage and special charges incurred in respect of the cargo. If a salving vessel is owned or operated by the Owners, salvage shall be paid for as fully as if the said salving vessel or vessels belonged to strangers. Such deposit as the Owners, or their agents, may deem sufficient to cover the estimated contribution of the goods and any salvage and special charges thereon shall, if required, be made by the cargo, shippers, consignees or owners of the goods to the Owners before delivery.".

13. **Taxes and Dues Clause**

(a) On Vessel -The Owners shall pay all dues, charges and taxes customarily levied on the Vessel, howsoever the amount thereof may be assessed.

(b) On cargo -The Charterers shall pay all dues, charges, duties and taxes customarily levied on the cargo, howsoever the amount thereof may be assessed.

(c) On freight -Unless otherwise agreed in Box 23, taxes levied on the freight shall be for the Charterers' account.

PART II
"Gencon" Charter (As Revised 1922, 1976 and 1994)

14. Agency

In every case the Owners shall appoint their own Agent both at the port of loading and the port of discharge.

15. Brokerage

A brokerage commission at the rate stated in Box 24 on the freight, dead-freight and demurrage earned is due to the party mentioned in Box 24.

In case of non-execution 1/3 of the brokerage on the estimated amount of freight to be paid by the party responsible for such non-execution to the Brokers as indemnity for the latter's expenses and work. In case of more voyages the amount of indemnity to be agreed.

16. General Strike Clause

(a) If there is a strike or lock-out affecting or preventing the actual loading of the cargo, or any part of it, when the Vessel is ready to proceed from her last port or at any time during the voyage to the port or ports of loading or after her arrival there, the Master or the Owners may ask the Charterers to declare, that they agree to reckon the laydays as if there were no strike or lock-out. Unless the Charterers have given such declaration in writing (by telegram, if necessary) within 24 hours, the Owners shall have the option of cancelling this Charter Party. If part cargo has already been loaded, the Owners must proceed with same, (freight payable on loaded quantity only) having liberty to complete with other cargo on the way for their own account.

(b) If there is a strike or lock-out affecting or preventing the actual discharging of the cargo on or after the Vessel's arrival at or off port of discharge and same has not been settled within 48 hours, the Charterers shall have the option of keeping the Vessel waiting until such strike or lock-out is at an end against paying half demurrage after expiration of the time provided for discharging until the strike or lock-out terminates and thereafter full demurrage shall be payable until the completion of discharging, or of ordering the Vessel to a safe port where she can safely discharge without risk of being detained by strike or lock-out. Such orders to be given within 48 hours after the Master or the Owners have given notice to the Charterers of the strike or lock-out affecting the discharge. On delivery of the cargo at such port, all conditions of this Charter Party and of the Bill of Lading shall apply and the Vessel shall receive the same freight as if she had discharged at the original port of destination, except that if the distance to the substituted port exceeds 100 nautical miles, the freight on the cargo delivered at the substituted port to be increased in proportion.

(c) Except for the obligations described above, neither the Charterers nor the Owners shall be responsible for the consequences of any strikes or lock-outs preventing or affecting the actual loading or discharging of the cargo.

17. War Risks ("Voywar 1993")

(1) For the purpose of this Clause, the words:

(a) The "Owners" shall include the shipowners, bareboat charterers, disponent owners, managers or other operators who are charged with the management of the Vessel, and the Master; and

(b) "War Risks" shall include any war (whether actual or threatened), act of war, civil war, hostilities, revolution, rebellion, civil commotion, warlike operations, the laying of mines (whether actual or reported), acts of piracy, acts of terrorists, acts of hostility or malicious damage, blockades (whether imposed against all Vessels or imposed selectively against Vessels of certain flags or ownership, or against certain cargoes or crews or otherwise howsoever), by any person, body, terrorist or political group, or the Government of any state whatsoever, which, in the reasonable judgement of the Master and/or the Owners, may be dangerous or are likely to be or to become dangerous to the Vessel, her cargo, crew or other persons on board the Vessel.

(2) If at any time before the Vessel commences loading, it appears that, in the reasonable judgement of the Master and/or the Owners, performance of the Contract of Carriage, or any part of it, may expose, or is likely to expose, the Vessel, her cargo, crew or other persons on board the Vessel to War Risks, the Owners may give notice to the Charterers cancelling this Contract of Carriage, or may refuse to perform such part of it as may expose, or may be likely to expose, the Vessel, her cargo, crew or other persons on board the Vessel to War Risks; provided always that if this Contract of Carriage provides that loading or discharging is to take place within a range of ports, and at the port or ports nominated by the Charterers the Vessel, her cargo, crew, or other persons onboard the Vessel may be exposed, or may be likely to be exposed, to War Risks, the Owners shall first require the Charterers to nominate any other safe port which lies within the range for loading or discharging, and may only cancel this Contract of Carriage if the Charterers shall not have nominated such safe port or ports within 48 hours of receipt of notice of such requirement.

(3) The Owners shall not be required to continue to load cargo for any voyage, or to sign Bills of Lading for any port or place, or to proceed or continue on any voyage, or on any part thereof, or to proceed through any canal or waterway, or to proceed to or remain at any port or place whatsoever, where it appears, either after the loading of the cargo commences, or at any stage of the voyage thereafter before the discharge of the cargo is completed, that, in the reasonable judgement of the Master and/or the Owners, the Vessel, her cargo (or any part thereof), crew or other persons on board the Vessel (or any one or more of them) may be, or are likely to be, exposed to War Risks. If it should so appear, the Owners may by notice request the Charterers to nominate a safe port for the discharge of the cargo or any part thereof, and if within 48 hours of the receipt of such notice, the Charterers shall not have nominated such a port, the Owners may discharge the cargo at any safe port of their choice (including the port of loading) in complete fulfilment of the Contract of Carriage. The Owners shall be entitled to recover from the Charterers the extra expenses of such discharge and, if the discharge takes place at any port other than the loading port, to receive the full freight as though the cargo had been carried to the discharging port and if the extra distance exceeds 100 miles, to additional freight which shall be the same percentage of the freight contracted for as the percentage which the extra distance represents to the distance of the normal and customary route, the Owners having a lien on the cargo for such expenses and freight.

(4) If at any stage of the voyage after the loading of the cargo commences, it appears that, in the reasonable judgement of the Master and/or the Owners, the Vessel, her cargo, crew or other persons on board the Vessel may be, or are likely to be, exposed to War Risks on any part of the route (including any canal or waterway) which is normally and customarily used in a voyage of the nature contracted for, and there is another longer route to the discharging port, the Owners shall give notice to the Charterers that this route will be taken. In this event the Owners shall be entitled, if the total extra distance exceeds 100 miles, to additional freight which shall be the same percentage of the freight contracted for as the percentage which the extra distance represents to the distance of the normal and customary route.

(5) The Vessel shall have liberty:-

(a) to comply with all orders, directions, recommendations or advice as to departure, arrival, routes, sailing in convoy, ports of call, stoppages, destinations, discharge of cargo, delivery or in any way whatsoever which are given by the Government of the Nation under whose flag the Vessel sails, or other Government to whose laws the Owners are subject, or any other Government which so requires, or any body or group acting with the power to compel compliance with their orders or directions;

(b) to comply with the orders, directions or recommendations of any war risks underwriters who have the authority to give the same under the terms of the war risks insurance;

(c) to comply with the terms of any resolution of the Security Council of the United Nations, any directives of the European Community, the effective orders of any other Supranational body which has the right to issue and give the same, and with national laws aimed at enforcing the same to which the Owners are subject, and to obey the orders and directions of those who are charged with their enforcement;

(d) to discharge at any other port any cargo or part thereof which may render the Vessel liable to confiscation as a contraband carrier;

(e) to call at any other port to change the crew or any part thereof or other persons on board the Vessel when there is reason to believe that they may be subject to internment, imprisonment or other sanctions;

(f) where cargo has not been loaded or has been discharged by the Owners under any provisions of this Clause, to load other cargo for the Owners' own benefit and carry it to any other port or ports whatsoever, whether backwards or forwards or in a contrary direction to the ordinary or customary route.

(6) If in compliance with any of the provisions of sub-clauses (2) to (5) of this Clause anything is done or not done, such shall not be deemed to be a deviation, but shall be considered as due fulfilment of the Contract of Carriage.

18. General Ice Clause

Port of loading

(a) In the event of the loading port being inaccessible by reason of ice when the Vessel is ready to proceed from her last port or at any time during the voyage or on the Vessel's arrival or in case frost sets in after the Vessel's arrival, the Master for fear of being frozen in is at liberty to leave without cargo, and this Charter Party shall be null and void.

(b) If during loading the Master, for fear of the Vessel being frozen in, deems it advisable to leave, he has liberty to do so with what cargo he has on board and to proceed to any other port or ports with option of completing cargo for the Owners' benefit for any port or ports including port of discharge. Any part cargo thus loaded under this Charter Party to be forwarded to destination at the Vessel's expense but against payment of freight, provided that no extra expenses be thereby caused to the Charterers, freight being paid on quantity delivered (in proportion if lumpsum), all other conditions as per this Charter Party.

(c) In case of more than one loading port, and if one or more of the ports are closed by ice, the Master or the Owners to be at liberty either to load the part cargo at the open port and fill up elsewhere for their own account as under section (b) or to declare the Charter Party null and void unless the Charterers agree to load full cargo at the open port.

Port of discharge

(a) Should ice prevent the Vessel from reaching port of discharge the Charterers shall have the option of keeping the Vessel waiting until the re-opening of navigation and paying demurrage or of ordering the Vessel to a safe and immediately accessible port where she can safely discharge without risk of detention by ice. Such orders to be given within 48 hours after the Master or the Owners have given notice to the Charterers of the impossibility of reaching port of destination.

(b) If during discharging the Master for fear of the Vessel being frozen in deems it advisable to leave, he has liberty to do so with what cargo he has on board and to proceed to the nearest accessible port where she can safely discharge.

(c) On delivery of the cargo at such port, all conditions of the Bill of Lading shall apply and the Vessel shall receive the same freight as if she had discharged at the original port of destination, except that if the distance of the substituted port exceeds 100 nautical miles, the freight on the cargo delivered at the substituted port to be increased in proportion.

19. Law and Arbitration

* (a) This Charter Party shall be governed by and construed in accordance with English law and any dispute arising out of this Charter Party shall be referred to arbitration in London in accordance with the Arbitration Acts 1950 and 1979 or any statutory modification or re-enactment thereof for the time being in force. Unless the parties agree upon a sole arbitrator, one arbitrator shall be appointed by each party and the arbitrators so appointed shall appoint a third arbitrator, the decision of the three-man tribunal thus constituted or any two of them, shall be final. On the receipt by one party of the nomination in writing of the other party's arbitrator, that party shall appoint their arbitrator within fourteen days, failing which the decision of the single arbitrator appointed shall be final.

For disputes where the total amount claimed by either party does not exceed the amount stated in Box 25** the arbitration shall be conducted in accordance with the Small Claims Procedure of the London Maritime Arbitrators Association.

* (b) This Charter Party shall be governed by and construed in accordance with Title 9 of the United States Code and the Maritime Law of the United States and should any dispute arise out of this Charter Party, the matter in dispute shall be referred to three persons at New York, one to be appointed by each of the parties hereto, and the third by the two so chosen; their decision or that of any two of them shall be final, and for purpose of enforcing any award, this agreement may be made a rule of the Court. The proceedings shall be conducted in accordance with the rules of the Society of Maritime Arbitrators, Inc..

For disputes where the total amount claimed by either party does not exceed the amount stated in Box 25** the arbitration shall be conducted in accordance with the Shortened Arbitration Procedure of the Society of Maritime Arbitrators, Inc..

* (c) Any dispute arising out of this Charter Party shall be referred to arbitration at the place indicated in Box 25, subject to the procedures applicable there. The laws of the place indicated in Box 25 shall govern this Charter Party.

(d) If Box 25 in Part I is not filled in, sub-clause (a) of this Clause shall apply.

* *(a), (b) and (c) are alternatives; indicate alternative agreed in Box 25.*

** *Where no figure is supplied in Box 25 in Part I, this provision only shall be void but the other provisions of this Clause shall have full force and remain in effect.*

Agreed with MALMEXPORT AB, Stockholm and ROHSTOFFHANDEL G.m.b.H., Düsseldorf

Adopted by the Documentary Committee of the General Council of British Shipping, London and The Federation of National Associations of Ship Brokers and Agents (FONASBA), London.

THE BALTIC AND INTERNATIONAL MARITIME CONFERENCE
STANDARD ORE CHARTER PARTY
CODE NAME: "OREVOY"

PART I

1. Shipbroker	2. Place and date of Charter Party
3. Owners/Disponent Owners/Time-Chartered Owners (indicate name, address & telex number)	4. Charterers (indicate name, address & telex number)
5. Vessel's name and flag	6. Rate in tons per hour (load.) (Cl. 1.4.)
7. Vessel's particulars, if required (Cl. 1)	8. Present position and prior commitments, if known (Cl. 2.2.)
9. Laydays date (Cl. 2.1.)	10. Expected readiness to load (Cl. 2.2.)
11. Cancelling date (also state if other period of declaration of cancelling agreed) (Cl. 2.3.)	12. Substitution (state "no" if not agreed) (Cl. 4)

13. Cargo (5 per cent. more or less in Owners' option unless other margin agreed) in tons of 1000 kilos (if full and complete cargo not agreed indicate "part cargo") (Cl. 5.1.)

14. Advance notices (load. and disch.) (State number of running days' notice to be given and to whom) (Cl. 6)

15. Loading port(s)/berth(s) (Cl. 7.1.)	16. Discharging port(s)/berth(s) (Cl. 7.2.)
17. Reduced voyage speed (state "no" if not agreed) (Cl. 7.2.)	18. Notice time in running hours (load. and disch.) (only to be filled in if agreed) (Cl. 8.2.1.)
19. Laytime (if separate laytime for load. and disch. is agreed, fill in a) and b); If total laytime for load. and disch., fill in c) only) (Cl. 8.2.5. & 8.2.6.) a) Laytime for loading b) Laytime for discharging c) Total laytime for loading and discharging	20. Laytime exceptions (loading) (Cl. 8.3.1.) 21. Laytime exceptions (discharging) (Cl. 8.3.1.)
22. Demurrage rate (loading) (Cl. 8.5.2.)	23. Demurrage rate (discharging) (Cl. 8.5.2.)
24. Despatch money (load. &/or disch.) (Optional; if agreed indicate rate of despatch money) (Cl. 8.5.3.)	25. Freight tax (state whether for Owners' or Charterers' account) (Cl. 11.3.)
26. Agents at loading port(s) (Cl. 12)	27. Agents at discharging port(s) (Cl. 12)
28. Freight rate per metric ton (state whether fully or partly prepaid) (Cl. 13)	29. Freight payment (currency and when/where payable; also state beneficiary and bank account) (Cl. 13)
30. General average shall be adjusted/settled at (Cl. 20)	31. Law and Arbitration (state 23.1., 23.2. or 23.3. of Cl. 23, as agreed; if 23.3. agreed state place of arbitration) (if not filled in 23.1. shall apply) (Cl. 23)
32. Brokerage commission and to whom payable (Cl. 24)	33. Numbers of additional clauses covering special provisions, if agreed

It is mutually agreed that this Contract shall be performed subject to the conditions contained in the Charter consisting of PART I including additional clauses, if any agreed and stated in Box 33 and PART II. In the event of a conflict of conditions, the provisions of PART I shall prevail over those of PART II to the extent of such conflict but no further.

Signature (Owners)	Signature (Charterers)

Printed and sold by Fr. G. Knudtzon Ltd., 55, Toldbodgade, Copenhagen
by authority of The Baltic and International Maritime Conference (BIMCO), Copenhagen.

PART II
"OREVOY" Charter Party

1. Vessel

The Owners shall

1.1. before and at the beginning of the loaded voyage exercise due diligence to make the Vessel seaworthy and in every way fit for the voyage, with a full complement of Master, officers and crew for a vessel of her type, tonnage and flag;

1.2. ensure that the Vessel and her Master and crew will comply with all safety and health regulations and other statutory rules or regulations and internationally recognized requirements necessary to secure safe and unhindered loading of the cargo, performance of the voyage and discharge of the cargo.

The Vessel shall

1.3. be classed Lloyd's 100 A1 or equivalent unless otherwise agreed in Box 7, the Owners exercising due diligence to maintain that class during the currency of this Charter Party;

1.4. be suitable for mechanical loading of the cargo and capable of receiving the cargo at the rate (if any) specified in Box 6 and be suitable for grab discharge, failing which Clause 8.3.3. shall apply and the Owners shall reimburse the Charterers any actual extra discharge costs;

1.5. be equipped to meet the technical requirements if and as specified in Box 7.

2. Laydays Date, Expected Time of Arrival (E.T.A.) and Cancelling

2.1. Laydays shall not commence before 00.00 hours on the date stated in Box 9. However, notice of readiness may be given before that date and notice time, if provided for in Box 18, shall run forthwith.

2.2. Present position of Vessel as per Box 8.
Commitments prior to commencement of this Charter as per Box 8.
Expected readiness to load as per Box 10.

2.3. The Charterers shall have the option of cancelling the Charter Party if the Vessel be not ready to load on or before twelve midnight (24.00 hours) on the cancelling date stated in Box 11.
If it appears that the Vessel will be delayed beyond the cancelling date stated in Box 11 the Owners shall, as soon as they are in a position to state with reasonable certainty the day on which the Vessel should be ready, give notice thereof to the Charterers asking whether they will exercise their option of cancelling the Charter Party. The option must then be declared within five (5) running days (unless otherwise agreed in Box 11) of the receipt by the Charterers of such notice, but not earlier than twenty (20) running days before the revised date of loadreadiness. If the Charterers do not then exercise their option of cancelling, the seventh (7th) day after the readiness date stated in the Owners' notice shall be regarded as a new cancelling date. This provision shall operate only once, and should the Vessel not be ready to load on the new cancelling date the Charterers shall have the option of cancelling the Charter Party. The Charterers shall in any event declare whether they exercise any option of cancelling under sub-clause 2.3. no later than the time of the Vessel's readiness to load.

3. Subletting, Assigning

The Charterers shall have the liberty of subletting or assigning this Charter Party to any individual or company, but the Charterers shall always remain responsible for the due fulfilment of all the terms and conditions of this Charter Party and shall warrant that any such sublet or assignment will not result in the Vessel being restricted in her future trading.

4. Substitution

The Owners shall have liberty to substitute a Vessel, provided that such substitute Vessel's main particulars and position shall be subject to the Charterers' prior approval, which is not to be unreasonably withheld, but the Owners under this Charter Party shall remain responsible to the Charterers for the due fulfilment of this Charter Party.
This Clause shall not apply if "No" inserted in Box 12.

5. Cargo

5.1. The Charterers warrant that unless otherwise specified in Part I, the cargo referred to in Box 13 is non-hazardous and non-dangerous for carriage according to applicable safety regulations including IMCO Code(s).

5.2. The Charterers shall have the right to ship parcels of different qualities and/or for different receivers in separate holds within the Vessel's natural segregation and suitable for her trim provided that such parcels can be loaded, carried and discharged in accordance with the Vessel's seaworthiness. Other means of separation of different parcels may be specified in Part I.

5.3. Unless otherwise agreed in Part I, all quantities shall be expressed in tons of 1,000 kilograms.

6. Advance Notices

The Owners or the Master shall give notices of expected readiness to load/discharge as specified in Box 14 to the parties named therein and shall keep those parties advised of any alteration in expected readiness.

7. Port of Loading, Voyage, Port of Discharge

7.1. After completion of prior commitments as may be stated in Box 8, the Vessel shall proceed to the loading port(s)/berth(s) as stated in Box 15.

7.2. The Vessel shall carry the cargo with all possible despatch to the port(s)/berth(s) of discharge stated in Box 16. However, unless "No" is inserted in Box 17, the Owners may order the Vessel to proceed at reduced speed solely to conserve fuel.
If the Charterers have the right to order the Vessel to discharge at one or more ports out of several ports named or within a specific range, the Charterers shall declare the actual port(s) of discharge to be inserted in the Bills of Lading prior to the arrival of the Vessel at the port of loading.

7.3. Only when the loading/discharging port(s)/berth(s) are not specifically mentioned herein, the Charterers warrant the safety of port(s)/berth(s) nominated and that the Vessel will be loaded and discharged always afloat.

7.4. The Vessel shall be left in seaworthy trim for shifting between berths and ports.

7.5. Unless otherwise agreed, loading and/or discharging at two or more ports shall be effected in geographical rotation.

8. Notices of Readiness, Laytime, Demurrage/Despatch Money

8.1. _Notice of Readiness_

8.1.1. At each port of loading and discharging notice of readiness shall be given to the Charterers or their Agents when the Vessel is in all respects ready to load/discharge at the loading/discharging berth.

8.1.2. If a loading/discharging berth is not designated or if such designated berth is not available upon the Vessel's arrival at or off the port, notice of readiness may be given upon arrival at the waiting place at or off the port.
However, if the Vessel is at that time prevented from proceeding to the loading/discharging berth due to her inefficiency, weather, tidal conditions, strikes of tugs or pilots or mandatory regulations, notice of readiness may be given only when such hindrance(s) has (have) ceased.

8.1.3. Notice of readiness may be given on any day at any time.

8.2. _Laytime_

8.2.1. The laytime shall commence when notice of readiness has been given and after expiration of notice time, if any, provided for in Box 18.
Should the Vessel arrive at the (first) loading port and be ready to load before the date stated in Box 9, the Charterers shall have the right to start loading. The Charterers shall also have the right to load/discharge before the expiration of notice time. In either event, during such periods only time actually used shall count as laytime or as time on demurrage.

8.2.2. The notice time shall run continuously.

8.2.3. The notice time, if any, shall only apply at first or sole loading and discharging port, respectively.

8.2.4. If total time for loading and discharging has been agreed in Box 19 notice time, if any, at port of discharge shall be applied whether the Vessel be on demurrage or not on sailing from the (last) loading port.

8.2.5. _Separate laytime._ – The cargo shall be loaded within the number of hours/days of 24 consecutive hours or at the average loading rate per day of 24 consecutive hours as stated in Box 19a).
The cargo shall be discharged within the number of hours/days of 24 consecutive hours or at the average discharging rate per day of 24 consecutive hours as stated in Box 19b).

8.2.6. _Total laytime._ – The cargo shall be loaded and discharged within the number of hours/days of 24 consecutive hours stated in Box 19c).

8.2.7. In the case of loading and/or discharging at more than one berth, laytime shall run continuously as if loading/discharging had been effected at one berth only but without prejudice to sub-clause 8.3.

8.3. _Suspension of Laytime_

8.3.1. Unless the Vessel is on demurrage, laytime shall not count

(i) during periods excepted as per Boxes 20 and 21, unless used, in which case only time actually used shall count;

(ii) for the duration of bad weather or sea conditions which actually prevent the Vessel's loading, discharging or the shifting between loading/discharging berths of the Vessel;

(iii) if so provided for in Clause 14.

8.3.2. Time shall not count as laytime or as time on demurrage whilst Vessel actually moving from waiting place whether at or off the port or from a lightening place off the port, until the Vessel is securely moored at the designated loading/discharging berth.

8.3.3. Time lost due to inefficiency or any other cause attributable to the Vessel, her Master, her crew or the Owners shall not count as notice time or as laytime or as time on demurrage to the extent that loading or discharging or the matters covered by sub-clause 8.4.1. are thereby affected.

8.3.4. If pursuant to Clause 9.13. the Vessel has to vacate the loading/discharging berth, notice time or laytime or time on demurrage shall not count from that time until she be in all respects ready to load/discharge and notification has been given to the Charterers accordingly.

8.3.5. If due to the matters referred to in sub-clauses 8.3.3. or 8.3.4., the Vessel loses her turn, time shall count again only as from 24 hours after notification of the Vessel's new readiness has been given to the Charterers or when loading/discharging resumes whichever may be the sooner.

8.4. _Termination of Laytime_

8.4.1. Laytime/Demurrage shall stop counting on completion of:

(a) loading/discharging at the relevant port, (b) cargo documentation and/or draft survey for determination of cargo weight, (c) repairs to stevedore damage under Clause 10.2., whichever may be the later.

8.4.2. If required, the Vessel shall leave the berth as soon as possible within her control on completion of loading/discharging, failing which the Charterers shall be entitled to proved damages provided that if she then has to wait for reasons (b) and/or (c) above, there must be a place available at which she can safely wait, and any extra expenses shall be for the Charterers' account.

8.5. *Demurrage/Despatch Money*

8.5.1. Demurrage accrued under this Charter Party shall be considered as constituting liquidated damages for exceeding the laytime provided for herein. However, if the Vessel has been on demurrage for 15 days or more and no cargo has been loaded, the Owners shall have the option of cancelling this Charter Party. No claim which the Owners may otherwise have against the Charterers shall be prejudiced by the Owners exercising their option of cancelling.

8.5.2. Demurrage shall be due and payable by the Charterers day by day at the rate specified in Boxes 22 and 23 and in the manner provided for in Box 29.

8.5.3. Despatch money, if agreed upon in Box 24, shall be paid promptly by the Owners to the Charterers at half the demurrage rate or as otherwise agreed upon in Box 24 for laytime saved in loading and/or discharging.

9. Loading and Discharging

9.1. The Vessel shall be loaded and discharged as and where ordered by the Charterers.

9.2. If the Charterers have not nominated a suitable loading or discharging berth on the Vessel's arrival off the port, or if such berth should not be available, the Vessel is to wait at a suitable place at or off the port.
The Charterers shall have the right to designate a safe waiting place, otherwise the Master shall choose a waiting place using due diligence to minimize extra shifting costs provided for in sub-clause 9.4.

9.3. The Charterers shall have the right to load and/or discharge at two berths at each port or place subject to sub-clause 9.4.

9.4. *Shifting.* – Costs of moving the Vessel, including bunkers, in excess of those which would have been incurred if the Charterers had nominated a free loading or discharging berth on arrival, provided the Vessel arrives on or after the date stated in Box 9, and/or if all cargo had been loaded or discharged during one operation at the first berth only other than a lightening place off the port, shall be for the Charterers' account unless caused by the Vessel's default. Other costs on board the Vessel including wages and officers' and crew's overtime charges to be for the Owners' account.

9.5. The Owners or the Master shall in due time prior to commencement of loading submit to the Charterers (or their nominees) at the loading port a loading plan which shall be based on a reasonable number of shiftings between hatches and also meet applicable rules and regulations, including IMCO Code(s). The Charterers shall inform the Owners/Master of any special composition of cargo required in sufficient time to permit the Owners/Master to work out and submit such loading plan.

9.6. Prior to loading, the Vessel's holds shall be adequately cleaned for loading the contracted cargo.

9.7. The Charterers shall, always within the capacity of the loading installations, load and trim the cargo as per the loading plan, free of any risk, liability and expense to the Vessel. Any extra trimming and/or levelling required by the Master or Owners shall be performed at the Owners' expense and any time lost thereby shall not count as laytime/demurrage. Discharging, including shovel cleaning, shall be effected by the Charterers free of any risk, liability and expense to the Vessel.

9.8. The Vessel shall move along any one berth, as reasonably required by the Charterers, solely for the purpose of making any hatch or hatches available to the loading/discharging appliances at that berth, and costs on board the Vessel including bunkers, wages and officers' and crew's overtime charges shall be for the Owners' account. However, the costs of any necessary outside services shall be for the Charterers' account. Laytime or time on demurrage shall not be interrupted thereby.

9.9. The Vessel shall work day and night and during any time as may be excepted as per Box 20 and Box 21, as required by the Charterers.

9.10. The Vessel shall, at her own risk and expense, open and close hatches prior to and after loading/discharging and also during loading/discharging as may be required by the Charterers to protect the cargo, provided local shore regulations permit. If same, however, is not permitted by local shore labour regulations, shore labour is to be employed by the Charterers at their risk, liability and expense. The Vessel shall furnish and give free use of sufficient light for deck and holds, as on board.

9.11. The Charterers shall have the right to order the Vessel to leave without having loaded a full cargo, always provided that the Vessel be in seaworthy condition and that the Charterers pay deadfreight according to Clause 13.7.

9.12. Overtime for loading and discharging to be for the account of the party ordering the same. If overtime be ordered by Port Authorities or any other Governmental Agencies, the Charterers to pay any extra expenses incurred. Officers' and crew's overtime charges always to be paid by the Owners.

9.13. In the event of loading/discharging being impossible due to inefficiency or any other cause attributable to the Vessel, her Master, her crew or the Owners and such impossibility continuing for more than three consecutive hours, the Charterers shall have the right to order the Vessel to vacate the berth and shifting from and back to berth shall be at the Owners' expense and time.

10. Stevedore Damage

10.1. The Charterers shall be responsible for damage (beyond ordinary wear and tear) to any part of the Vessel caused by Stevedores at both ends. Such damage, as soon as apparent, shall be notified immediately by the Master to the Charterers or their port agents and to their Stevedores. The Owners/Master shall endeavour to obtain the Stevedores' written acknowledgment of liability and to settle stevedore damage claims direct with the Stevedores.

10.2. The Charterers have the right to perform any repairs of stevedore damage at any moment prior to or before the completion of the voyage, but must repair stevedore damage affecting the Vessel's seaworthiness before the Vessel sails from the port where such damage was caused.

11. Dues, Taxes and Charges, Extra Insurance

11.1. *On the Vessel.* – The Owners shall pay all dues, duties, taxes and other charges customarily levied on the Vessel, howsoever the amount thereof may be assessed.

11.2. *On the cargo.* – The Charterers shall pay all dues, duties, taxes and charges levied on the cargo at the port of loading/discharging, howsoever the amount thereof may be assessed.

11.3. *On the freight.* – Taxes levied on the freight shall be paid by the Owners or the Charterers as agreed in Box 25.

11.4. *Extra Insurance.* – Any extra insurance on cargo actually paid by the Charterers owing to Vessel's age, class, flag or ownership shall be for the Owners' account and may be deducted from the freight. The Charterers shall furnish evidence of payment supporting any such deduction. Unless a maximum amount has been agreed in Part I, such extra insurance shall not exceed the lowest extra premium which would be charged for the Vessel and voyage in the London insurance market.

12. Agents

At the port(s) of loading the Vessel shall be consigned to the Agents as stated in Box 26 and at the port(s) of discharge to the Agents as stipulated in Box 27, the Owners always paying the customary fees.

13. Freight

The freight at the rate stated in Box 28 shall be calculated on intaken quantity.

13.1. *Prepaid.* – If according to Boxes 28 or 29 freight is to be paid on shipment, it shall be deemed earned and non-returnable Vessel and/or cargo lost or not lost.
Bills of Lading showing "Freight prepaid" or the like shall not be released until the freight has been duly paid.

13.2. *After shipment.* – If according to Box 29 freight shall be payable within a number of days after shipment, the freight shall be deemed earned as per sub-clause 13.1.
In such case Bills of Lading shall not be endorsed "Freight prepaid" or the like, unless the freight has been paid.

13.3. *Partly on Delivery.* – If according to Boxes 28 or 29 a percentage of the freight shall be payable as per sub-clauses 13.1. or 13.2. the balance shall be paid as per sub-clause 13.4. However, in such case the total freight shall be deemed earned as per sub-clause 13.1. and the Charterers shall not have the option referred to in sub-clause 13.4.1.

13.4. *On Delivery.* – If according to Boxes 28 or 29 freight is payable at destination or on right and true delivery of the cargo, it shall not be deemed earned until the cargo is thus delivered.

13.4.1. *On Delivered Weight.* – When the freight is payable on delivery of cargo the Charterers shall have the option of paying freight on delivered weight, provided such option be declared in writing before breaking bulk and the weight be ascertained by official weighing machine, otherwise by joint draught survey. The Charterers shall pay all costs incurred in connection with weighing or draught survey. The Owners shall be at liberty to appoint check clerks at their own expense.

13.5. *Deductions.* – The freight shall be paid in cash without discount in the manner described in Box 29. The Charterers shall only be entitled to deduct from the freight any freight advances made as per sub-clause 13.6., despatch money and extra insurance, provided properly documented, as per Clause 11.4.

13.6. *Freight Advances.* – The Owners shall put the Agents at the loading port(s) in funds to cover the Vessel's ordinary disbursements for Owners' account, prior to the Vessel's sailing from the port(s) of loading. Otherwise the amount shall be advanced by Charterers and be endorsed upon Bills of Lading as advance freight, with the addition of 3 per cent. to cover interest, commission and the cost of insurance.

13.7. *Deadfreight.* – If the Charterers fail to supply a cargo as specified in Box 13, deadfreight shall be payable but the Charterers shall not be bound to supply cargo in excess of any quantity stated by the Owners as the Vessel's capacity made available to the Charterers.
The laytime shall be calculated on that quantity.
The Owners/Master shall be entitled to clause Bills of Lading for any deadfreight due.
If the Shippers/Suppliers state in writing that no more cargo will be shipped, the Owners shall not need to have any such statement confirmed by the Charterers.

14. Strikes and Other Hindrances

In the event of any of the causes referred to in Clause 21.2. either preventing or delaying or, being already in existence, threatening to prevent or delay the loading of the cargo intended for the Vessel, or its discharging, the following provisions shall apply:

14.1. *Loading Port.* – When the Vessel is ready to proceed from her last port or at any time during the voyage to the port or ports of loading or after her arrival there, the Owners may ask the Charterers to declare that they agree to count the laytime as if there were to be no such hindrance. Unless the Charterers have given such declaration in writing (by telegram or telex if necessary) on the second business day after receipt of the request, the Owners shall have the option of cancelling this Charter Party. If part cargo has already been loaded the Vessel must carry it to the port of discharge (freight payable on loaded quantity only) having liberty to complete with other cargo on the way for the Owners' own account, but the Owners are entitled to keep the Vessel waiting at the loading port

PART II
"OREVOY" Charter Party

without time counting. In case of more than one loading port and if the causes referred to above do not prevent the loading in all ports, the Charterers are entitled to order the Vessel to proceed to the second or subsequent port and there to load a full cargo; in such event, the Owners are not entitled to cancel the Charter Party as hereabove stipulated.

14.2. *Discharging Port*. – On or after the Vessel's arrival at or off the port of discharge, the Vessel shall wait until any such hindrance is at an end, the Charterers paying half demurrage after expiration of the laytime (unless the Vessel is already on demurrage in which event full demurrage remains payable) full demurrage being payable from the moment when the hindrance is at an end.
The Charterers shall have the option at any time of ordering the Vessel to another safe port within 600 nautical miles' distance where she can safely discharge without being detained by any cause enumerated above. Shifting time shall count as laytime or as full demurrage time as the case may be.
The Charterers shall reimburse the Owners additional port charges including pilotage and canal dues, if any, incurred thereby; however, the Owners shall bear the costs of bunkers consumed. All conditions of this Charter Party and/or of the Bills of Lading issued hereunder shall apply to the delivery of the cargo at the substituted port and the Owners shall receive the same freight as if the cargo had been discharged at the original destination.

15. Ice

Loading Port

15.1. If the Vessel cannot reach the loading port by reason of ice when she is ready to proceed from her last port, or at any time during the voyage, or on her arrival, or if frost sets in after her arrival, the Master – for fear of the Vessel being frozen in – is at liberty to leave without cargo; in such cases this Charter Party shall become null and void.

15.2. If during the loading the Master, for fear of the Vessel being frozen in, deems it advisable to leave, he has liberty to do so with what cargo he has on board and to proceed to any other port with option of completing with cargo for the Owners' own account to any port or ports including the port of discharge. Any part cargo thus loaded under this Charter Party is to be forwarded to destination at the Vessel's expense against payment of the agreed freight, provided that no extra expenses be thereby caused to the Charterers, freight being paid on the quantity delivered (in proportion if lump sum), all other conditions as per Charter Party.

15.3. In the case of more than one loading port, and if one or more of the ports are closed by ice, the Master or Owners are to be at liberty either to load the part cargo at the open port and fill up elsewhere for the Owners' own account as under sub-clause 15.2. or to declare the Charter Party null and void, unless the Charterers agree to load full cargo at the open port.

Voyage and Discharging Port

15.4. Should ice prevent the Vessel from reaching the port of discharge, the Charterers shall have the option of keeping the Vessel waiting until the re-opening of navigation and paying demurrage, or of ordering the Vessel to a safe and immediately accessible port where she can safely discharge without risk of detention by ice. Such orders are to be given within 48 hours after the Owners or Master have given notice to the Charterers of the impossibility of reaching the port of destination.

15.5. If during discharging the Master, for fear of the Vessel being frozen in, deems it advisable to leave, he has liberty to do so with what cargo he has on board and to proceed to the nearest safe and accessible port. Such port to be nominated by the Charterers as soon as possible, but not later than 24 running hours, Sundays and holidays excluded, of receipt of the Owners' request for nomination of a substitute discharging port, failing which the Master will himself choose such port.

15.6. On delivery of the cargo at such port, all conditions of the Bill of Lading shall apply and the Owners shall receive the same freight as if the Vessel had discharged at the original port of destination except that if the distance to the substitute port exceeds 100 nautical miles, the freight on the cargo delivered at that port is to be increased in proportion.

16. War Risks ("Voywar 1950")

16.1. In these Clauses "war risks" shall include any blockade or any action which is announced as a blockade by any Government or by any belligerent or by any organized body, sabotage, piracy, and any actual or threatened war, hostilities, warlike operations, civil war, civil commotion, or revolution.

16.2. If at any time before the Vessel commences loading, it appears that performance of the contract will subject the Vessel or her Master and crew or her cargo to war risks at any stage of the adventure, the Owners shall be entitled by letter or telegram despatched to the Charterers, to cancel this Charter Party.

16.3. The Master shall not be required to load cargo or to continue loading or to proceed on or to sign Bill(s) of Lading for any adventure on which or any port at which it appears that the Vessel, her Master and crew or her cargo will be subjected to war risks. In the event of the exercise by the Master of his right under this Clause after part or full cargo has been loaded, the Master shall be at liberty either to discharge such cargo at the loading port or to proceed therewith. In the latter case the Vessel shall have liberty to carry other cargo for Owners' benefit and accordingly to proceed to and load or discharge such other cargo at any other port or ports whatsoever, backwards or forwards, although in a contrary direction to or out of or beyond the ordinary route. In the event of the Master electing to proceed with part cargo under this Clause freight shall in any case be payable on the quantity delivered.

16.4. If at the time the Master elects to proceed with part or full cargo under Clause 16.3. or after the Vessel has left the loading port, or the last of the loading ports if more than one, it appears that further performance of the Charter Party will subject the Vessel, her Master and crew or her cargo, to war risks, the cargo shall be discharged, or if the discharge has been commenced shall be completed, at any safe port in vicinity of the port of discharge as may be ordered by the Charterers. If no such orders shall be received from the Charterers within 48 hours after the Owners have despatched a request by telegram or telex to the Charterers for the nomination of a substitute discharging port, the Owners shall be at liberty to discharge the cargo at any safe port which they may, in their discretion, decide on and such discharge shall be deemed to be due fulfilment of the Charter Party. In the event of cargo being discharged at any such other port, the Owners shall be entitled to freight as if the discharge had been effected at the port or ports named in the Bill(s) of Lading, or to which the Vessel may have been ordered pursuant thereto.

16.5. (a) The Vessel shall have liberty to comply with any directions or recommendations as to loading, departure, arrival, routes, ports of call, stoppages, destination, zones, waters, discharges, delivery or in any other wise whatsoever (including any direction or recommendation not to go to the port of destination or to delay proceeding thereto or to proceed to some other port) given by any Government or by any belligerent or by any organized body engaged in civil war, hostilities or warlike operations or by any person or body acting or purporting to act as or with the authority of any Government or belligerent or of any such organized body or by any committee or person having under the terms of the war risks insurance on the Vessel, the right to give any such directions or recommendations. If, by reason of or in compliance with any such direction or recommendation, anything is done or is not done, such shall not be deemed a deviation.
(b) If, by reason of or in compliance with any such directions or recommendations, the Vessel does not proceed to the port or ports named in the Bill(s) of Lading or to which she may have been ordered pursuant thereto, the Vessel may proceed to any port as directed or recommended or to any safe port which the Owners in their discretion may decide on and there discharge the cargo. Such discharge shall be deemed to be due fulfilment of the Charter Party and the Owners shall be entitled to freight as if discharge had been effected at the port or ports named in the Bill(s) of Lading or to which the Vessel may have been ordered pursuant thereto.

16.6. All extra expenses (including insurance costs) involved in discharging cargo at the loading port or in reaching or discharging the cargo at any port as provided in Clauses 16.4. and 16.5.(b) hereof shall be paid by the Charterers and/or cargo owners, and the Owners shall have a lien on the cargo for all moneys due under these Clauses.

17. Lien

The Owners shall have a lien on the cargo for freight, deadfreight, demurrage and damages for detention. The Charterers shall remain responsible for deadfreight and demurrage (including damages for detention), incurred at port of loading. The Charterers shall also remain responsible for freight and demurrage (including damages for detention) incurred at port of discharge, but only to such extent as the Owners have been unable to obtain payment thereof by exercising the lien on the cargo.

18. Liberty

The Vessel shall have liberty to sail with or without pilots, to tow or go to the assistance of vessels in distress, to call at any port or place for oil fuel supplies, and to deviate for the purpose of saving life or property, or for any other reasonable purpose whatsoever.

19. Both-to-Blame Collision Clause

If the Vessel comes into collision with another vessel as a result of the negligence of the other vessel and any act, neglect or default of the Master, mariner, pilot or the servants of the Owners in the navigation or in the management of the Vessel, the owners of the cargo carried hereunder will indemnify Owners against all loss or liability to the other or non-carrying vessel or her Owners in so far as such loss or liability represents loss of, or damage to, or any claim whatsoever of the owners of said cargo, paid or payable by the other or non-carrying vessel or her Owners to the owners of said cargo and set-off, recouped or recovered by the other or non-carrying vessel or her Owners as part of their claim against the carrying vessel or Owners.
The foregoing provisions shall also apply where the owners, operators or those in charge of any vessel or vessels or objects other than, or in addition to, the colliding vessels or objects are at fault in respect of a collision or contact.

20. General Average and New Jason Clause

General Average shall be adjusted and settled at the place indicated in Box 30 according to the York/Antwerp Rules, 1974, or any modification thereof, but if, notwithstanding the provisions specified in Box 30, the adjustment is made in accordance with the law and practice of the United States of America, the following clause shall apply:
"In the event of accident, danger, damage or disaster before or after the commencement of the voyage, resulting from any cause whatsoever, whether due to negligence or not, for which, or for the consequence of which, Owners are not responsible, by statute, contract or otherwise, the goods, shippers, consignees or owners of the goods shall contribute with Owners in general average to the payment of any sacrifices, losses or expenses of a general average nature that may be made or incurred and shall pay salvage and special charges incurred in respect of the goods. If a salving Vessel is owned or operated by Owners, salvage shall be paid for as fully as if the said salving Vessel or vessels belonged to strangers. Such deposit as Owners, or their agents, may deem sufficient to cover the estimated contribution of the goods and any salvage and special charges thereon shall, if required, be made by the goods, shippers, consignees or owners of the goods to Owners before delivery".

PART II
"OREVOY" Charter Party

21. Responsibilities and Immunities

21.1.1. The Hague Rules contained in the International Convention for the Unification of certain rules relating to Bills of Lading, dated Brussels the 25th August 1924 as enacted in the country of shipment shall apply to this Contract and to any Bill of Lading issued hereunder.
When no such enactment is in force in the country of shipment, the corresponding legislation of the country of destination shall apply, but in respect of shipments to which no such enactments are compulsorily applicable, the terms of the said Convention shall apply.

21.1.2. In trades where the International Brussels Convention 1924 as amended by the Protocol signed at Brussels on February 23rd, 1968 – The Hague-Visby Rules – apply compulsorily, the provisions of the respective legislation shall apply.

21.1.3. The Owners shall in no case be responsible for loss of or damage to cargo howsoever arising prior to loading into and after discharge from the Vessel or while the goods are in the charge of another owner nor in respect of deck cargo and live animals. This sub-clause shall not detract from the Owners' obligations under Clause 4.

21.2. Save to the extent otherwise in this Charter Party expressly provided, neither party shall be responsible for any loss or damage or delay or failure in performance hereunder resulting from Act of God, war, civil commotion, quarantine, strikes, lockouts, arrest or restraint of princes, rulers and peoples or any other event whatsoever which cannot be avoided or guarded against.

22. Bills of Lading

22.1. Bills of Lading are to be signed as per the "Orevoybill" Bill of Lading without prejudice to this Charter Party, and the Charterers hereby indemnify the Owners against all liabilities that may arise from the signing of Bills of Lading as presented to the extent that the terms of such Bills of Lading impose more onerous liabilities upon the Owners than those assumed by the Owners under the terms of this Charter Party.
Neither the Owners nor their Servants shall be required to sign or endorse Bills of Lading showing freight prepaid unless and until the freight due to the Owners has actually been paid.

22.2. The Master may be required to sign separate Bills of Lading for cargo in different holds or for parcels properly separated upon shipment by the Charterers or their Agents, the Owners not being answerable for separate delivery, nor for the cost of cargo short-delivered (if any) provided all the cargo taken on board is delivered.

23. Law and Arbitration

23.1. Unless otherwise agreed in Box 31, this Charter Party shall be governed by English Law and any dispute arising out of this Charter Party or any Bill of Lading issued thereunder shall be referred to arbitration in London, one arbitrator being appointed by each party, in accordance with the Arbitration Acts 1950 and 1979 or any statutory modification or re-enactment thereof for the time being in force. On the receipt by one party of the notification in writing of the appointment of the other party's arbitrator, that party shall appoint their arbitrator within fourteen days failing which the decision of the single arbitrator appointed shall apply. If two arbitrators properly appointed shall not agree they shall appoint an umpire whose decision shall be final.

23.2. If agreed and stated in Box 31, this Charter Party shall be governed by U.S. Law and all disputes arising out of this Charter Party or any Bill of Lading issued thereunder shall be arbitrated at New York in the following manner:
One arbitrator is to be appointed by each of the parties hereto and a third by the two so chosen. Their decision or that of any two of them shall be final, and for the purpose of enforcing any award, this agreement may be made a rule of the court. The arbitrators shall be commercial men. Such arbitration is to be conducted in accordance with the rules of the Society of Maritime Arbitrators, Inc.
For disputes where the total amount claimed by either party does not exceed U.S. $ 3,500.00, or an amount as mutually agreed, the arbitration may be conducted in accordance with the Simplified Arbitration Procedure of the Society of Maritime Arbitrators Inc. if so desired by both parties.

23.3. If agreed and stated in Box 31, any disputes arising out of this Charter Party or any Bill of Lading issued thereunder shall be referred to arbitration at the place or before the arbitration tribunal indicated in Box 31, subject to the law and procedures applicable there.

24. Brokerage

24.1. The brokerage as stated in Box 32 on freight and deadfreight shall be paid by the Owners and is deemed to be earned by the Brokers upon shipment of cargo.

24.2. In case of cancellation pursuant to Clause 2.3., at least one third of the brokerage on the estimated amount of freight shall be paid by the Owners as indemnity to the Brokers.

AMERICANIZED WELSH COAL CHARTER
APPROVED BY
ASSOCIATION OF SHIP BROKERS & AGENTS (U.S.A.), INC.
NEW YORK--1953; AMENDED 1979.

19

It is this day mutually agreed, BETWEEN

Owner of the Steamship/Motorship

of , built at of

tons net register, or thereabouts, and about tons total deadweight inclusive of bunkers, classed

in length overall beam

draft now

and Charterer;

1. That the said vessel being tight, staunch and strong, and in every way fitted for the voyage, shall, with all possible dispatch, sail and proceed to

and there load, always afloat, in the customary manner from the Charterer, in such dock as may be ordered by him, a full and complete cargo of coal not exceeding tons nor less than tons, quantity at Vessel's option, and not exceeding what she can reasonably stow and carry, over and above her tackle, apparel, provisions and furniture; and being so loaded, shall therewith proceed, with all possible dispatch, to

or so near thereunto as she can safely get, and there deliver her cargo alongside any wharf and/or vessel and/or craft, as ordered, where she can safely deliver, always afloat, on being paid freight at the rate of

U.S. currency per ton of 1,000 kilos on bill of lading quantity. The Owner shall furnish, if required, a statutory declaration by the master and other officers that all cargo received on board has been delivered. The freight is in full of loading, dumping and trimming, and all port charges, pilotages, agency fees and consulages on the vessel. All wharfage dues on the cargo to be paid by the Charterer.

2. The FREIGHT is to be paid

3. Notice of approximate quantity of cargo required and of vessel's expected date of arrival at port of loading to be given to Charterer or his agents at least days in advance.

4. The Cargo to be loaded into vessel

weather working day(s) of 24 consecutive hours, (excluding bunkering time, Sundays, custom house, colliery, legal and/or local holidays, and from noon on Saturday or the day previous to any such holiday to 7 a.m. on Monday or the day after any such holiday, unless used in which event only time actually used in loading cargo to count) commencing 24 hours after vessel tenders and is ready to load, unless sooner worked, whereupon time is to commence and written notice is given of the vessel's being completely discharged of inward cargo and ballast in all her holds and ready to load, such notice to be given between business hours of 9 a.m. and 5 p.m., or 9 a.m. and 1 p.m. on Saturdays. Any time lost through riots, strikes, lockouts, or any dispute between masters and men, occasioning a stoppage of pitmen, trimmers or other hands connected with the working or delivery of the coal for which the vessel is stemmed, or by reason of accidents to mines or machinery, obstructions, embargo or delay on the railway or in the dock; or by reason of fire, floods, frosts, fogs, storms or any cause whatsoever beyond the control of the Charterer affecting mining, transportation, delivery and/or loading of the coal, not to be computed as part of the loading time (unless any cargo be actually loaded during such time). In the event of any stoppage or stoppages arising from any of these causes continuing for the period of six running days from the time of the vessel's being ready to load, this Charter shall become null and void; provided, however, that no cargo shall have been shipped on board the vessel previous to such stoppage or stoppages. In case of partial holiday, or partial stoppage of colliery, collieries or railway from any or either of the aforenamed causes, the lay-days to be extended proportionately to the diminution of output arising from such partial holiday or stoppage. If longer detained, Charterer to pay U.S. Currency per running day (or pro rata for part thereof) demurrage. If sooner dispatched, vessel to pay Charterer or his agents U.S. Currency per day (or pro rata for part thereof) dispatch money for time saved. No deduction of time shall be allowed for stoppage, unless due notice be given at the time to the master or Owner.

5. If any dispute or difference should arise under this Charter, same to be referred to three parties in the City of New York, one to be appointed by each of the parties hereto, the third by the two so chosen, and their decision, or that of any two of them, shall be final and binding, and this agreement may, for enforcing the same, be made a rule of Court. Said three parties to be commercial men.

6. The cargo to be loaded, dumped and trimmed by men appointed by the Charterer at the tariff rate of the port at vessel's expense.

7. The bills of lading shall be prepared in accordance with the dock or railway weight and shall be endorsed by the master, agent or Owner, weight unknown, freight and all conditions as per this Charter, such bills of lading to be signed at the Charterer's or shipper's office within twenty-four hours after the vessel is loaded. Master shall sign a certificate stating that the weight of the cargo loaded is in accordance with railway weight certificate. Charterer is to hold Owner harmless should any shortage occur.

8. The Act of God, the king's enemies, restraints of princes and rulers, and perils of the sea excepted. Also fire, barratry of the master and crew, pirates, collisions, strandings and accidents of navigation, or latent defects in or accidents to, hull and/or machinery and/or boilers always excepted, even when occasioned by the negligence, default or error in judgment of the pilot, master, mariners or other persons employed by the shipowner, or for whose acts he is responsible, not resulting, however, in any case from want of due diligence by the Owner of the ship, or by the ship's husband or manager. Charterer not answerable for any negligence, default, or error in judgment of trimmers or stevedores employed in loading or discharging the cargo. The vessel has liberty to call at any ports in any order, to sail without pilots, to tow and assist vessels in distress, and to deviate for the purpose of saving life or property, and to bunker.

9. The cargo to be discharged by consignee at port of discharge, free of expense and risk to the vessel, at the average rate of tons per day, weather permitting, Sundays and holidays and after noon on Saturdays excepted provided vessel can deliver it at this rate. If longer detained, consignee to pay vessel demurrage at the rate of U.S. currency per running day (or pro rata for part thereof). If sooner dispatched, vessel to pay Charterer or his agents U.S currency per day (or pro rata for part thereof) dispatch money for time saved. Time to commence twenty-four (24) hours, Sundays and holidays excepted, after vessel is ready to unload and written notice given, whether in berth or not, even if vessel is already on demurrage, and the time allowable for discharging to be calculated on the basis of the bill of lading quantity. In case of strikes, lockouts, civil commotions, or any other causes or accidents beyond the control of the consignee which prevent or delay the discharging, such time is not to count unless the vessel is already on demurrage.

10. Notice at port of discharge to be given in writing to consignee's agent on working days between the hours of 9 a.m. and 5 p.m., and 9 a.m. and noon on Saturdays.

11. Shifting time from anchorage place to loading or discharging berth is not to count even if vessel is already on demurrage.

12. Opening and closing of hatches at commencement and completion of loading and discharging shall be for Owner's account and time used is not to count.

13. Lighterage, if any, at discharge port to be at the risk and expense of consignees and time used to count as laytime.

14. In case of average, the same to be settled according to York/Antwerp Rules 1974. Should the vessel put into any port or ports leaky or with damage, the captain or Owner shall, without delay, inform the Charterer thereof. Captain to telegraph Charterer in case of putting in anywhere.

15. Vessel not to tender before 9 a.m. on and if vessel be not ready at loading port as ordered before 9 a.m. on , or if any wilful misrepresentation be made respecting the size, position or state of the vessel, Charterer to have the option of cancelling this Charter, such option to be declared on notice of readiness being given.

16. Vessel to be consigned to agents at port of loading, and to agents at port of discharge.

17. Overtime is to be for account of party ordering same. However, if ordered by port authorities, same is to be for Charterer's account Officers' and crew overtime expenses to be for Owner's account.

18. Extra insurance, if any, due to vessel's age, flag, classification or ownership shall be for Owner's account.

19. No cargo is to be loaded in deeptanks or similar places inaccessible to reach by grabs.

20. Any damage by stevedores shall be settled directly between Owner and stevedores.

21. Owner shall, at his risk and expense, comply with all applicable rules, regulations and laws relevant to water and/or air pollution at ports of loading and discharging. In cases where vessel calls at a U.S. port, Owner warrants to have secured and carry on board the vessel a Certificate of Financial Responsibility as required under U.S. law.

22. All bills of lading shall include the following three clauses:

NEW JASON CLAUSE: In the event of accident, danger, damage or disaster before or after commencement of the voyage, resulting from any cause whatsoever, whether due to negligence or not, for which, or for the consequences of which, the carrier is not responsible, by statute, contract or otherwise, the goods, shippers, consignees or owners of the goods shall contribute with the carrier in general average to the payment of any sacrifices, losses or expenses of a general average nature that may be made or incurred, and shall pay salvage and special charges incurred in respect of the goods.

If a salving ship is owned or operated by the carrier, salvage shall be paid for as fully as if such salving ship or ships belonged to strangers. Such deposit as the carrier or his agents may deem sufficient to cover the estimated contribution of the goods, and any salvage and special charges thereon shall, if required, be made by the goods, shippers, consignees or owners of the goods to the carrier before delivery.

CLAUSE PARAMOUNT: This bill of lading shall have effect subject to the provisions of the Carriage of Goods by Sea Act of the United States, approved April 16th, 1936, which shall be deemed to be incorporated herein, and nothing herein contained shall be deemed a surrender by the carrier of any of its rights or immunities or an increase of any of its responsibilities or liabilities under said Act. If any terms of this bill of lading be repugnant to said Act to any extent, such term shall be void to that extent but no further.

NEW BOTH-TO-BLAME COLLISION CLAUSE: If the ship comes into collision with another ship as a result of the negligence of the other ship and any act, neglect or default of the master, mariner, pilot or the servants of the carrier in the navigation or in the management of the ship, the owners of the goods carried hereunder will indemnify the carrier against all loss or liability to the other or non-carrying ship or her owners in so far as such loss or liability represents loss of, or damage to, or any claim whatsoever of the owners of said goods, paid or payable by the other or non-carrying ship or her owners to the owners of said goods and set off, recouped or recovered by the other or non-carrying ship or her owners as part of their claim against the carrying ship or carrier.

The foregoing provisions shall also apply where the owners, operators or those in charge of any ship or ships or objects other than, or in addition to, the colliding ships or objects are at fault in respect to a collision or contact.

23. PROTECTION & INDEMNITY BUNKERING CLAUSE: The vessel in addition to all other liberties shall have liberty as part of the contract voyage and at any stage thereof to proceed to any port or ports whatsoever whether such ports are on or off

the direct and/or customary route or routes to the ports of loading or discharge named in this Charter and there take oil bunkers in any quantity in the discretion of Owners even to the full capacity of fuel tanks, deep tanks and any other compartment in which oil can be carried whether such amount is or is not required for the chartered voyage.

24. C.S.U.K. WAR RISKS CLAUSES 1 & 2: No bills of lading to be signed for any blockaded port and if the port of discharge be declared blockaded after bills of lading have been signed, or if the port to which the ship has been ordered to discharge either on signing bills of lading or thereafter be one to which the ship is or shall be prohibited from going by the government of the nation under whose flag the ship sails or by any other government, the Owner shall discharge the cargo at any other port covered by this Charter Party as ordered by the Charterers (provided such other port is not a blockaded or prohibited port as above mentioned) and shall be entitled to freight as if the ship had discharged at the port or ports of discharge to which she was originally ordered.

The ship shall have liberty to comply with any orders or directions as to departure, arrival, routes, ports of call, stoppages, destination, delivery or otherwise howsoever given by the government of the nation under whose flag the vessel sails or any department thereof, or any person acting or purporting to act with the authority of such government or of any department thereof, or by any committee or person having, under the terms of the war risks insurance on the ship the right to give such orders or directions and if by reason of and in compliance with any such orders or directions anything is done or is not done, the same shall not be deemed a deviation, and delivery in accordance with such orders or directions shall be a fulfillment of the contract voyage and the freight shall be payable accordingly.

25. Charterer shall have the privilege of transferring part or whole of the Charter Party to others, Charterer guaranteeing to the Owner due fulfillment of this Charter Party.

26. The Charterer's liability shall cease as soon as the cargo is shipped, and the freight, dead freight and demurrage in loading (if any) are paid, the Owner having a lien on the cargo for freight, demurrage and average.

27. Penalty for non-performance of this agreement, proved damages, not exceeding the estimated amount of freight.

28. An address commission of percent on the gross amount of freight, dead freight and demurrage is due by the vessel and Owner to the Charterer on payment of freight.

29. A commission of percent on the gross amount of freight, dead freight and demurrage is due on payment of freight by the vessel and Owner to

Code Name: **"AMWELSH 93"**
Recommended by
The Baltic and International Maritime Council (BIMCO)
The Federation of National Associations of
Ship Brokers and Agents (FONASBA)

AMERICANIZED WELSH COAL CHARTER

Issued by the Association of Ship Brokers and Agents (U.S.A), Inc.
New York - 1953; Amended 1979; Revised 1993

THIS CHARTER PARTY, made and concluded in .... this .... day of .... 19 ....

Between .... **Owners** of the .... (flag) Vessel .... of ...., built .... (year) at .... (where) of .... tons of 1000 kilos total deadweight on summer freeboard, inclusive of bunkers, classed .... in .... and registered at .... under No. .... The Vessel's length overall is .... and beam is .... The Vessel's fully laden draft on summer freeboard is .... now .... and .... **Charterers** .... of the city of ....

1. Loading Port(s)/Discharging Port(s)

That the said Vessel being tight, staunch and strong, and in every way fit for the voyage, shall, with all convenient speed, proceed to .... and there load, always afloat, and in the customary manner from the Charterers, in such safe berth as they shall direct, a full and complete cargo of coal .... tons of 2240 lbs/1000 kilos* .... % more or less in the Owners' option; and being so loaded, shall therefrom proceed, with all convenient speed, to .... or so near thereunto as she can safely get, and there deliver her cargo, as ordered by the Charterers, where she can safely deliver it, always afloat, on having been paid freight at the rate of .... US $ per ton of 2240 lbs/1000 kilos* on bill of lading quantity.

**) Delete as appropriate*

2. Freight Payment

The FREIGHT shall be paid in ....

3. Notices & Loading Port Orders

The Master shall give the Charterers (telegraphic address ".........", Telex No ...., Fax No ....) and .... days notice of the date of the Vessel's expected readiness to load, and approximate quantity of cargo required with the .... day notice. The Charterers shall be kept advised by any form of telecommunication of any alterations in that date, as and when known. The Charterers shall declare first or sole loading port on receipt of the Master's .... day notice, unless declared earlier.

4. Discharging Port Orders

The Master shall apply to the Charterers by any form of telecommunication for declaration of the first or sole discharging port 96 hours before the Vessel is due off/at .... and they are to declare same to the Master not later than 48 hours following receipt of the Master's application.

5. Laydays/Cancelling

Laytime for loading shall not commence before 0800 on the .... day of .... Should the Vessel's notice of readiness not have been tendered in accordance with Clause 6, before 1700 on the .... day of ...., the Charterers shall have the option of cancelling this Charter Party, not later than one hour after the said notice has been tendered. The said cancelling date shall be extended by as many days (rounded to the nearest day) as the Charterers shall have failed to give loading port orders as provided in Clause 3 hereabove, without prejudice to the Owners' claim for detention.

If the Owners warrant that, despite the exercise of due diligence by the Owners, the Vessel will not be ready to tender notice of readiness by the cancelling date, and provided the Owners are able to state with reasonable certainty the date on which the Vessel will be ready, they may, at the earliest seven days before the Vessel is expected to sail for the port or place of loading, require the Charterers to declare whether or not they will cancel the Charter. Should the Charterers elect not to cancel, or should they fail to reply within seven days or by the cancelling date, whichever shall first occur, then the seventh day after the expected date of readiness for loading as notified by the Owners shall replace the original cancelling date. Should the Vessel be further delayed, the Owners shall be entitled to require further declarations of the Charterers in accordance with this Clause.

6. Time Counting

(a) Notice of the Vessel's readiness to load and discharge at the first or sole port shall be tendered in writing to the Charterers between 0800 and 1700 on Mondays to Fridays and between 0800 and 1200 on Saturdays. Following tender of notice of readiness, laytime shall commence 12 hours thereafter, unless the Vessel's loading or discharging has sooner commenced.

Such notice of readiness shall be tendered when the Vessel is in the loading or discharging berth, if available, and is in all respects ready to load or discharge the cargo, unless the berth is not available on the Vessel's arrival, whereupon the Master may tender the said notice from a lay berth or anchorage within the port limits.

(b) If the Vessel is prevented from entering the port limits because the first or sole loading or discharging berth, or a lay berth or anchorage is not available, or on the order of the Charterers or any competent official body or authority, and the Master warrants that the Vessel is physically ready in all respects to load or discharge, he may tender notice, by radio, if desired, from the usual anchorage outside the port limits, whether in free pratique or not, and/or whether customs cleared or not. If after entering the port limits the Vessel is found not to be ready, the time lost from the discovery thereof, until she is ready, shall not count as laytime, or time on demurrage.

(c) Once the loading or discharging berth becomes available laytime or time on demurrage shall cease until the Vessel is in the berth, and shifting expenses shall be for the Owners' account.

(d) *Subsequent Ports* - At second or subsequent ports of loading and/or discharging, laytime or time on demurrage shall resume counting from the Vessel's arrival in loading or discharging berth, if available, or if unavailable, from the arrival time within or outside the port limits, as provided in paragraph (a) supra.

7. Laytime

(a) The Vessel shall be loaded at the average rate of .... tons of 1000 kilos per day, or pro-rata for any part of a day, or within .... running days, both of twenty-four consecutive hours, weather permitting, Sundays and Holidays excepted/included *, and discharged at the average rate of .... tons of 1000 kilos per day, or pro-rata for any part of a day, or within .... running days, both of twenty four consecutive hours, weather permitting, Sundays and Holidays excepted/included*.

Days Purposes

(b) Vessel shall be loaded and discharged within .... days of twenty-four consecutive hours, weather permitting, Sundays and Holidays excepted/included* at loading, and excepted/included* at discharge.

(c) Time used in loading and discharging during excepted periods, if any, shall count as laytime.

Non-reversible laytime

(d) In cases of separate laytime for loading and discharging, laytime shall be non-reversible.

*) *Delete as appropriate*

8. Exceptions

The Owners shall be bound before and at the beginning of the voyage to exercise due diligence to make the Vessel seaworthy, and to have her properly manned, equipped and supplied, and neither the Vessel, nor the Master, or Owners shall be, or shall be held liable for any loss of, or damage, or delay to the cargo for causes excepted by the Hague Rules, or the Hague-Visby Rules, where applicable.
Neither the Vessel, her Master or Owners, nor the Charterers shall, unless otherwise expressly provided in this Charter Party, be responsible for loss or damage to, or failure to supply, load, discharge or deliver the cargo resulting from: Act of God, act of war, act of public enemies, pirates or assailing thieves; arrest or restraint of princes, rulers or people; embargoes; seizure under legal process, provided bond is promptly furnished to release vessel or cargo; floods; frosts; fogs; fires; blockades; riots; insurrections; civil commotions; earthquakes; explosions; collisions; strandings and accidents of navigation; accidents at the mines or to machinery or to loading equipment; or any other causes beyond the Owners' or the Charterers' control; always provided that such events directly affect the loading and/or discharging process of the Vessel, and its performance under this Charter Party.

9. Strikes

In the event of loss of time to the Vessel directly affecting the loading or discharging of this cargo, caused by a strike or lockout of any personnel connected with the production, mining, or any essential inland transport of the cargo to be loaded or discharged into/from this Vessel from point of origin, up to, and including the actual loading and discharging operations, or by any personnel essential to the actual loading and discharging of the cargo, half the laytime shall count during such periods, provided always that none of the aforementioned events did exist at the date of the charter party. If at any time during the continuance of such strikes or lockouts the Vessel goes on demurrage, said demurrage shall be paid at half the rate specified in Clause 10, hereunder, until such time as the strike or lockout terminates; thence full demurrage unless the Vessel was already on demurrage before the strike broke out, in which case full demurrage shall be paid for its entire period.

10. Demurrage/Despatch

Demurrage, if incurred, at loading and/or discharging port(s), shall be paid by the Charterers to the Owners at the rate of .... per day, or pro-rata for part of a day. Despatch money shall be paid by the Owners to the Charterers at half the demurrage rate for all laytime saved.

11. Cost of Loading and Discharging

The cargo shall be loaded, dumped, spout trimmed, and discharged by Charterers'*/Receivers'* stevedores free of risk and expense to the Vessel, under the supervision of the Master. Should the stevedores refuse to follow his instructions, the Master shall protest to them in writing and shall advise the Charterers immediately thereof.

12. Overtime

(a) *Expenses*

(i) All overtime expenses at loading and discharging ports shall be for account of the party ordering same.

(ii) If overtime is ordered by port authorities or the party controlling the loading and/or discharging terminal or facility all overtime expenses shall be equally shared between the Owners and the Charterers* /Receivers*.

(iii) Overtime expenses for the Vessel's officers and crew shall always be for the Owners' account.

(b) *Time Counting*

If overtime work ordered by the Owners be performed during periods excepted from laytime the actual time used shall count; if ordered by the Charterers/Receivers, the actual time used shall not count; if ordered by port authorities or the party controlling the loading and/or discharging terminal or facility half the actual time used shall count.

**) Delete as appropriate*

13. Opening & Closing Hatches

Opening and closing of hatches at commencement and completion of loading and discharging shall be for the Owners' account and time so used is not to count. All other opening and closing of hatches shall be for the Charterers' account and time so used shall count.

14. Seaworthy Trim

Charterers shall leave the Vessel in seaworthy trim and with cargo on board safely stowed to Master's satisfaction between loading berths/ports and between discharging berths/ports, respectively; any expenses resulting therefrom shall be for Charterers' account and any time used shall count.

15. Shifting

If more than one berth of loading and discharging has been agreed, and used, costs of shifting, including cost of bunkers used, shall be for the Charterers' account, time counting.

16. Lighterage

Should the Vessel be ordered to discharge at a place where there is insufficient water for the Vessel to reach it in the first tide after her arrival there, without lightening and lie always afloat, laytime shall count as per Clause 6 at a safe anchorage or lightening place for similar size vessels bound for such a place, and any lighterage expenses incurred to enable her to reach the place of discharge shall be for the Charterers' account, any custom of the port to the contrary notwithstanding. Time occupied in proceeding from the lightening place to the discharging berth shall not count as laytime or time on demurrage.

17. Agents

The Vessel shall be consigned to .... agents at port(s) of loading, and to .... agents at port(s) of discharge.

18. Extra Insurance on Cargo

Any extra insurance on cargo, incurred owing to Vessel's age, class, flag, or ownership to be for Owners' account up to a maximum of .... and may be deducted from the freight in the Charterers' option. The Charterers shall furnish evidence of payment supporting such deduction.

19. Stevedore Damage

(a) Any damage caused by stevedores shall be settled directly between the Owners and the stevedores.

(b) *In case the Owners are unsuccessful in obtaining compensation from the stevedores for damage for which they are legally liable, then the Charterers shall indemnify the Owners for any sums so due and unpaid.

**) Sub-clause (b) is optional and shall apply unless deleted.*

20. Deviation

Should the Vessel deviate to save or attempt to save life or property at sea, or make any reasonable deviation, the said deviation shall not be deemed to be an infringement or breach of this Charter Party, and the Owners shall not be liable for any loss or damage resulting therefrom provided, however, that if the deviation is for the purpose of loading or unloading cargo or passengers, it shall "prima facie", be regarded as unreasonable.

21. Lien and Cesser

The Charterers' liability under this Charter Party shall cease on cargo being shipped, except for payment of freight, deadfreight and demurrage, and except for all other matters provided for in this Charter Party where the Charterers' responsibility is specified. The Owners shall have a lien on the cargo for freight, deadfreight, demurrage and general average contribution due to them under this Charter Party.

22. Bills of Lading

The bills of lading shall be prepared in accordance with the dock or railway weight and shall be endorsed by the Master, agent or Owners, weight unknown, freight and all conditions as per this Charter, such bills of lading to be signed at the Charterers' or shippers' office within twenty four hours after the Vessel is loaded. The Master shall sign a certificate stating that the weight of the cargo loaded is in accordance with railway weight certificate. The Charterers are to hold the Owners harmless should any shortage occur.

23. Grab Discharge

No cargo shall be loaded in any cargo compartment inaccessible to reach by grabs.

24. Protective Clauses

This Charter Party is subject to the following clauses all of which are also to be included in all bills of lading issued hereunder:

(a) "CLAUSE PARAMOUNT: This bill of lading shall have effect subject to the provisions of the Carriage of Goods by Sea Act of the United States, the Hague Rules, or the Hague-Visby Rules, as applicable, or such other similar national legislation as may mandatorily apply by virtue of origin or destination of the bills of lading, which shall be deemed to be incorporated herein and nothing herein contained shall be deemed a surrender by the carrier of any of its rights or immunities or an increase of any of its responsibilities or liabilities under said applicable Act. If any term of this bill of lading be repugnant to said applicable Act to any extent, such term shall be void to that extent, but no further."

and

(b) "NEW BOTH-TO-BLAME COLLISION CLAUSE: If the ship comes into collision with another ship as a result of the negligence of the other ship and any act, neglect or default of the master, mariner, pilot or the servants of the carrier in the navigation or in the management of the ship, the owners of the goods carried hereunder will indemnify the carrier against all loss or liability to the other or non-carrying ship or her owners in so far as such loss or liability represents loss of, or damage to, or any claim whatsoever of the owners of said goods, paid or payable by the other or non-carrying ship or her owners to the owners of said goods and set off, recouped or recovered by the other or non-carrying ship or her owners as part of their claim against the carrying ship or carrier.

The foregoing provisions shall also apply where the owners, operators or those in charge of any ship or ships or objects other than, or in addition to, the colliding ships or objects are at fault in respect to a collision or contact."

and

(c) "NEW JASON CLAUSE: In the event of accident, danger, damage or disaster before or after commencement of the voyage, resulting from any cause whatsoever, whether due to negligence or not, for which, or for the consequences of which, the carrier is not responsible, by statute, contract or otherwise, the goods, shippers, consignees or owners of the goods shall contribute with the carrier in general average to the payment of any sacrifices, losses or expenses of a general average nature that may be made or incurred, and shall pay salvage and special charges incurred in respect of the goods.

If a salving ship is owned or operated by the carrier, salvage shall be paid for as fully as if such salving ship or ships belonged to strangers. Such deposit as the carrier or his agents may deem sufficient to cover the estimated contribution of the goods, and any salvage and special charges thereon shall, if required, be made by the goods, shippers, consignees or owners of the goods to the carrier before delivery."

and

(d) "PROTECTION AND INDEMNITY BUNKERING CLAUSE: The Vessel in addition to all other liberties shall have liberty as part of the contract voyage and at any stage thereof to proceed to any port or ports whatsoever whether such ports are on or off the direct and/or customary route or routes to the ports of loading or discharge named in this Charter and there take oil bunkers in any quantity in the discretion of the Owners even to the full capacity of fuel tanks, deep tanks and any other compartment in which oil can be carried whether such amount is or is not required for the chartered voyage."

25. <u>Ice Clause</u>

Loading Port

(a) If the Vessel cannot reach the loading port by reason of ice when she is ready to proceed from her last port, or at any time during the voyage, or on her arrival, or if frost sets in after her arrival, the Master - for fear of the Vessel being frozen in - is at liberty to leave without cargo; in such cases this Charter Party shall be null and void.

(b) If during loading, the Master, for fear of the Vessel being frozen in, deems it advisable to leave, he has the liberty to do so with what cargo he has on board and to proceed to any other port with option of completing cargo for the Owners' own account to any port or ports including the port of discharge. Any part cargo thus loaded under this Charter Party to be forwarded to destination at the Vessel's expense against payment of the agreed freight, provided that no extra expenses be thereby caused to the Consignees, freight being paid on quantity delivered (in proportion if lump sum), all other conditions as per Charter Party.

(c) In case of more than one loading port, and if one or more of the ports are closed by ice, the Master or Owners to be at liberty either to load the part cargo at the open port and fill up elsewhere for the Owners' own account as under sub-clause (b) or to declare the Charter Party null and void unless the Charterers agree to load full cargo at the open port.

Voyage and Discharging Port

(d) Should ice prevent the Vessel from reaching the port of discharge, the Charterers/Receivers shall have the option of keeping the Vessel waiting until the re-opening of navigation and paying demurrage or of ordering the Vessel to a safe and immediately accessible port where she can safely discharge without risk of detention by ice. Such orders to be given within 48 hours after the Owners or Master have given notice to the Charterers/Receivers of impossibility of reaching port of destination.

(e) If during discharging, the Master, for fear of the Vessel being frozen in, deems it advisable to leave, he has liberty to do so with what cargo he has on board and to proceed to the nearest safe and accessible port. Such port to be nominated by the Charterers/Receivers as soon as possible, but not later than 24 running hours, Sundays and holidays excluded, of receipt of the Owners' request for nomination of a substitute discharging port, failing which the Master will himself choose such port.

(f) On delivery of the cargo at such port, all conditions of the Bill of Lading shall apply and the Owners shall receive the same freight as if the Vessel had discharged at the original port of destination, except that if the distance to the substitute port exceeds 100 nautical miles the freight on the cargo delivered at that port to be increased in proportion.

26. General Average

General average shall be adjusted according to York-Antwerp Rules 1974, as amended 1990, or any subsequent modification thereof, in ...., and settled in .... currency.

27. War Risks

1. The Master shall not be required or bound to sign Bills of Lading for any blockaded port or for any port which the Master or Owners in his or their discretion consider dangerous or impossible to enter or reach.

2. (A) If any port of loading or of discharge named in this Charter Party or to which the Vessel may properly be ordered pursuant to the terms of the Bills of Lading be blockaded, or

(B) If owing to any war, hostilities, warlike operations, civil war, civil commotions, revolutions, or the operation of international law (a) entry to any such port of loading or of discharge or the loading or discharge of cargo at any such port be considered by the Master or Owners in his or their discretion dangerous or (b) it be considered by the Master or Owners in his or their discretion dangerous or impossible for the Vessel to reach any such port of loading or of discharge - the Charterers shall have the right to order the cargo or such part of it as may be affected to be loaded or discharged at any other safe port of loading or of discharge within the range of loading or discharging ports respectively established under the provisions of the Charter Party (provided such other port is not blockaded or that entry thereto or loading or discharge of cargo thereat is not in the Master's or Owners' discretion dangerous or prohibited). If in respect of a port of discharge no orders be received from the Charterers within 48 hours after they or their agents have received from the Owners a request for the nomination of a substitute port, the Owners shall then be at liberty to discharge the cargo at any safe port which they or the Master may in their or his discretion decide on (whether within the range of discharging ports established under the provisions of the Charter Party or not) and such discharge shall be deemed to be due fulfilment of the contract or contracts of affreightment so far as cargo so discharged is concerned. In the event of the cargo being loaded or discharged at any such other port within the respective range of loading or discharging ports established under the provisions of the Charter Party, the Charter Party shall be read in respect of the freight and all other conditions whatsoever as if the voyage performed were that originally designated. In the event, however, that the Vessel discharges the cargo at a port outside the range of discharging ports established under the provisions of the Charter Party, freight shall be paid for as for the voyage originally designated and all extra expenses involved in reaching the actual port of discharge and/or discharging the cargo thereat shall be paid by the Charterers or cargo owners. In this latter event the Owners shall have a lien on the cargo for all such extra expenses.

3. The Vessel shall have liberty to comply with any directions or recommendations as to departure, arrival, routes, ports of call, stoppages, destinations, zones, waters, delivery or in any other wise whatsoever given by the government of the nation under whose flag the Vessel sails or any other government or local authority including any de facto government or local authority or by any person or body acting or purporting to act as or with the authority of any such government or authority or by any committee or person having under the terms of the war risks insurance on the Vessel the right to give any such directions or recommendations. If by reason of or in compliance with any such directions or recommendations, anything is done or is not done such shall not be deemed a deviation.

If by reason of or in compliance with any such directions or recommendations the Vessel does not proceed to the port or ports of discharge originally designated or to which she may have been ordered pursuant to the terms of the Bills of Lading, the Vessel may proceed to any safe port of discharge which the Master or Owners in his or their discretion may decide on and there discharge the cargo. Such discharge shall be deemed to be due fulfilment of the contract or contracts of affreightment and the Owners shall be entitled to freight as if discharge has been effected at the port or ports originally designated or to which the Vessel may have been ordered pursuant to the terms of the Bill of Lading. All extra expenses involved in reaching and discharging the cargo at any such other port of discharge shall be paid by the Charterers and/or cargo owners and the Owners shall have a lien on the cargo for freight and all such expenses.

28. Dues and/or Taxes

....
....
....

29. Transfer

The Charterers shall have the privilege of transferring part or whole of the Charter Party to others, guaranteeing to the Owners due fulfillment of this Charter Party.

30. Address Commission

An address commission of .... % on gross freight, deadfreight, and demurrage is due to the Charterers at the time these are paid, Vessel lost or not lost. The Charterers shall have the right to deduct such commissions from such payments.

31. Brokerage Commission

A brokerage commission of .... % on gross freight, deadfreight and demurrage is payable by the Owners to ....
....
.... at the time of the Owners receiving these payments.

32. Arbitration

(a) *NEW YORK

All disputes arising out of this contract shall be arbitrated at New York in the following manner, and subject to U.S. Law:

One Arbitrator is to be appointed by each of the parties hereto and a third by the two so chosen. Their decision or that of any two of them shall be final, and for the purpose of enforcing any award, this agreement may be made a rule of court. The Arbitrators shall be commercial men, conversant with shipping matters. Such Arbitration is to be conducted in accordance with the rules of the Society of Maritime Arbitrators Inc.

For disputes where the total amount claimed by either party does not exceed US $ .... ** the arbitration shall be conducted in accordance with the Shortened Arbitration Procedure of the Society of Maritime Arbitrators Inc.

(b) *LONDON

All disputes arising out of this contract shall be arbitrated at London and, unless the parties agree forthwith on a single Arbitrator, be referred to the final arbitrament of two Arbitrators carrying on business in London who shall be members of the Baltic Mercantile & Shipping Exchange and engaged in Shipping, one to be appointed by each of the parties, with power to such Arbitrators to appoint an Umpire. No award shall be questioned or invalidated on the ground that any of the Arbitrators is not qualified as above, unless objection to his action be taken before the award is made. Any dispute arising hereunder shall be governed by English Law.

For disputes where the total amount claimed by either party does not exceed US $ .... ** the arbitration shall be conducted in accordance with the Small Claims Procedure of the London Maritime Arbitrators Association.

** Delete (a) or (b) as appropriate*

*** Where no figure is supplied in the blank space this provision only shall be void but the other provisions of this clause shall have full force and remain in effect.*

Code Name: Norgrain 89
RECOMMENDED BY
THE BALTIC AND INTERNATIONAL MARITIME COUNCIL (BIMCO)
THE FEDERATION OF NATIONAL ASSOCIATIONS OF SHIP BROKERS AND AGENTS (FONASBA)

AMENDED MAY 1989

NORTH AMERICAN GRAIN CHARTERPARTY 1973

ISSUED BY THE ASSOCIATION OF SHIP BROKERS AND AGENTS (U.S.A.) INC.

.... 19......

Owners — IT IS THIS DAY MUTUALLY AGREED, between ....

Note: Delete as appropriate — Owners | Disponent Owners | Time-chartered Owners | Chartered Owners |- of the .... SS / M.V. — Self/Non Self Trimming Bulk Carrier / Tween Decker / Tanker .... Call Sign ....

Description of Vessel — Built .... at .... of .... tons of 2,240 lbs. deadweight all told, or thereabouts, and with a grain cubic capacity available for cargo of .... cubic feet (including .... cubic feet in self-bleeding wing spaces)

....

Classification — Classed .... in .... now ....

....

Note: Insert vessel's Itinerary. — ....

....

Charterers — and .... of .... Charterers.

Loading Port(s) — 1. That the said vessel, being tight, staunch strong and in every way fit for the voyage, shall with all convenient speed proceed to ....

.... and there load

at .... safe loading berth(s) in Charterers' option.

Description of Cargo — always afloat, a full and complete*/part* cargo in bulk of

....

....

at Charterers' option .... tons of 2,240 lbs.*/1,000 Kilos.* .... % more or less, quantity at Owners' option.

Notice and Loading Port Orders

2. Owners are to give Charterers (or their Agents) (telegraphic address " .... " telex number: ....) 15 and 7 days notice of vessel's expected readiness to load date, and approximate quantity of cargo required with the 15 days' notice, such quantity to be based on cargo of Heavy Grain, unless the cargo composition has been declared or indicated.

The Charterers are to be kept continuously advised by telegram/telex of any alteration in vessel's readiness to load date.

Master to apply to .... (telegraphic address " .... ") for first or sole loading port orders 144 hours before vessel's expected readiness to load date but not sooner than 144 hours before the laydays in Clause 4 and Charterers or their Agents are to give orders for first or sole loading port within 72 hours of receipt of Master's application, unless given earlier.

Orders for second port of loading, if used, to be given to the Master not later than ....

....

Master is to give Charterers (or their Agents) 72 and 12 hours notice of vessel's estimated time of arrival at first or sole loading port together with vessel's estimated readiness to load date.

Vessel Inspection

3. Vessel is to load under inspection of National Cargo Bureau, Inc in U.S.A. ports or of the Port Warden in Canadian ports. Vessel is also to load under inspection of a Grain Inspector licenced/authorised by the United States Department of Agriculture pursuant to the U.S. Grain Standards Act and/or of a Grain Inspector employed by the Canada Department of Agriculture as required by the appropriate authorities.

If vessel loads at other than U.S. or Canadian ports, she is to load under inspection of such national and/or regulatory bodies as may be required.

Vessel is to comply with the rules of such authorities, and shall load cargo not exceeding what she can reasonably stow and carry over and above her Cabin, Tackle, Apparel, Provisions, Fuel, Furniture and Water. Cost of such inspections shall be borne by Owners.

Laydays/ Cancelling

4. Laytime for loading, if required by Charterers, not to commence before 0800 on the .... day of .... 19 ....

Should the vessel's notice of readiness not be tendered and accepted as per Clause 18 before 1200 on the .... day of .... 19 .... the Charterers have the option of cancelling this Charterparty any time thereafter, but not later than one hour after the tender of notice of readiness as per Clause 18.

Destination

5. On being so loaded, the vessel shall proceed to ....

....

as ordered by Charterers/Receivers*, and deliver the cargo, according to Bills of Lading at .... safe discharging berths in Charterers' option, vessel being always afloat, on being*/having been* paid freight as per Clauses 8 and 9.

Discharging Port Orders

Master to apply by radio to .... (telegraphic address " .... ") for first or sole discharging port order 96 hours before vessel is due off/at* .... and they are to give first or sole discharging port orders by radio within 48 hours of receipt of Master's application unless given earlier. If Master's application is received on a Saturday, the time allowed shall be 52 hours instead of 48 hours.

Orders for second and/or third port(s) of discharge are to be given to the Master not later than vessel's arrival at first or subsequent port.

Master to radio Charterers/Receivers (or their Agents) 72 and 24 hours notice of vessel's estimated time of arrival at first or sole discharging port. Charterers/Receivers (or their Agents) are to be kept continuously advised by radio/telegram/telex of any alterations in such estimated time of arrival.

Bills of

6. The Master is to sign Bills of Lading as presented on the North American Grain Bill of Lading form without prejudice to the terms, conditions and exceptions of this Charterparty. If the Master elects

Lading to delegate the signing of Bills of Lading to his Agents he shall give them authority to do so in writing, copy of which is to be furnished to Charterers if so required.

Rotation of Ports

7. Rotation of loading ports is to be in Owners'*/Charterers'* option.

Rotation of discharging ports is to be in Owners'*/Charterers'* option, but if more than two (2) ports of discharge are used rotation is to be geographic .... of ....

Freight

8. Freight to be paid as follows:

....

....

....

....

per ton of 2,240 lbs./1,000 Kilos.*
Charterers have the option of ordering the vessel to load at ....

....

in which case the rate of freight to be ....

....

....

per ton of 2,240 lbs./1,000 Kilos.*

Charterers/Receivers have the option of ordering the vessel to discharge at ....

....

in which case the rate of freight to be ....

....

....

per ton of 2,240 lbs./1,000 Kilos.*

If more than one port of loading and/or discharging is used, the rate of freight shall be increased by ....

....

.... per ton of 2,240 lbs./1,000 Kilos.* for each additional loading and/or discharging port on the entire cargo.

Freight Payment

9. (a) Freight shall be fully prepaid on surrender of signed Bills of Lading in .... in .... currency to

....

....

on Bill of Lading weight, discountless, not returnable, vessel and/or cargo lost or not lost. Freight shall be deemed earned as cargo is loaded on board.

Once the Bills of Lading have been signed, and Charterers call for surrender of Original Bills of Lading against freight payment above, it will be incumbent upon Owners or their Agents to comply immediately with such call for surrender during office hours, Mondays to Fridays inclusive.

(Other)

(b) ....

....

....

Cost of Loading and Discharging

10. (a)* Cargo is to be loaded and spout trimmed (to Master's satisfaction in respect of seaworthiness) free of expense to the vessel. Cargo is to be discharged free of expense to the vessel (to Master's satisfaction in respect of seaworthiness).

(b)* Cargo is to be loaded and trimmed at Owners' expense. Cargo is to be discharged free of expense to the vessel (to Master's satisfaction in respect of seaworthiness).

Stevedores at Loading Port(s) and Discharging Port(s)

11. Stevedores at loading Port(s) are to be appointed by Charterers*/Owners* and paid by Charterers*/Owners.*

If stevedores are appointed by Owners, they are to be approved by Charterers at loading port(s), and such approval is not to be unreasonably withheld. Stevedores at discharging port(s) are to be appointed and paid for by Charterers/Receivers*.

In all cases, stevedores shall be deemed to be the servants of the Owners and shall work under the supervision of the Master.

Bulk Carrier and Wing Spaces

12. (a) The vessel is warranted to be a self-trimming bulk carrier*/non-self-trimming bulk carrier.*

(b) Cargo may be loaded into wing spaces if the cargo can bleed into centerholds. Wing spaces are to be spout trimmed; any further trimming in wing spaces and any additional expenses in discharging are to be for Owners' account, and additional time so used is not to count as laytime or time on demurrage.

Overtime

13. (a) **Expenses**

(i) All overtime expenses at loading and discharging ports shall be for account of the party ordering same.

(ii) If overtime is ordered by port authorities or the party controlling the loading and/or discharging terminal or facility all overtime expenses are to be equally shared between the Owners and Charterers*/Receivers.*

(iii) Overtime expenses for vessel's officers and crew shall always be for Owners' account.

(b) **Time Counting**

If overtime ordered by Owners be worked during periods excepted from laytime the actual time used shall count; if ordered by Charterers/Receivers, the actual time used shall not count; if ordered by port authorities or the party controlling the loading and/or discharging terminal or facility half the actual time used shall count.

Separations

14. Cost of cargo separations, including labor used for laying same, to be for Charterers' account unless required by Owners, in which case all resultant expenses shall be borne by the Owners. Separations ordered by Charterers shall be made to Master's satisfaction (but not exceeding the requirements of the competent authorities).

Securing

Delete para (a) or (b) as appropriate

15. (a) **For Owners' account**

Any securing required by Master, National Cargo Bureau or Port Warden for safe trim/stowage to be supplied by and paid for by Owners, and time so used not to count as laytime or time on demurrage. Bleeding of bags, if any, at discharge port(s) to be at Owners' expense, and time actually lost is not to count.

(b) **For Charterers' account**

Any securing required by Master, National Cargo Bureau or Port Warden for safe trim/stowage to be supplied by and paid for by Charterers, and time so used to count as laytime or time on demurrage.

Bleeding of bags, if any, at discharge port(s) to be at Charterers'/Receivers' expense.

Fumigation

16. If after loading has commenced, and at any time thereafter until completion of discharge, the cargo is required to be fumigated in vessel's holds, the Owners are to permit same to take place at Charterers' risk and expense, including necessary expenses for accommodating and victualling vessel's personnel ashore.

The Charterers warrant that the fumigants used will not expose the vessel's personnel to any health hazards whatsoever, and will comply with current IMO regulations.

Time lost to the vessel is to count at the demurrage rate.

Opening/ Closing Hatches

17. At each loading and discharging port, cost of first opening and last closing of hatches and removal and replacing of beams, if any, shall be for Owners' account. Cost of all other opening and closing of hatches, removal and replacing of beams shall be for Charterers'/Receivers' account.

18. (a) **Notice of Readiness**
Notification of vessel's readiness to load and discharge at the first or sole loading and discharging port shall be delivered in writing at the office of Charterers/Receivers between O900 and 1700 on all days except Sundays and holidays, and between 0900 and 1200 on Saturdays. Such notice of readiness shall be delivered when the vessel is in the loading or discharging berth if vacant, failing which from a lay berth or anchorage within limits of the port, or otherwise as provided in Clause 18 (b) hereunder.

Time Counting

(b) **Waiting for Berth Outside Port Limits**
If the vessel is prevented from entering the limits of the loading/discharging port(s) because the first or sole loading/discharging berth or a lay berth or anchorage is not available within the port limits, or on the order of the Charterers/Receivers or any competent official body or authority, and the Master warrants that the vessel is physically ready in all respects to load or discharge, the Master may tender vessel's notice of readiness, by radio if desired, from the usual anchorage outside the limits of the port, whether in free pratique or not, whether customs cleared or not. If after entering the limits of the loading port, vessel fails to pass inspections as per Clause 18 (e) any time so lost shall not count as laytime or time on demurrage from the time vessel fails inspections until she is passed, but if this delay in obtaining said passes exceeds 24 running hours shex all time spent waiting outside the limits of the port shall not count.

(c) **Commencement of Laytime**
Following receipt of notice of readiness laytime will commence at 0800 on the next day not excepted from laytime. Time (not excepted from laytime) actually used before commencement of laytime shall count.

(d) **Subsequent Ports**
At second or subsequent port(s) of loading and/or discharging, laytime or time on demurrage shall resume counting from vessel's arrival within the limits of the port or as provided in Clause 18 (b) if applicable.

(e) **Inspection**
Unless the conditions of Clause 18 (b) apply, at first or sole loading port Master's notice of readiness shall be accompanied by pass of the National Cargo Bureau/Port Warden and Grain Inspector's certificate of vessel's readiness in all compartments to be loaded, for the entire cargo covered by the Charterparty as per Clause 3. In the event that vessel loads in subsequent port(s) and is required to re-pass inspections in these ports, any time lost thereat in securing the required certificates shall not count as laytime or time on demurrage.

Laytime

19. (a) Vessel is to be loaded and discharged within .... working days of twenty-four (24) consecutive hours each (weather permitting). Sundays and Holidays excepted.

(b) Vessel is to be loaded within .... working days of twenty-four (24) consecutive hours each (weather permitting). Sundays and Holidays excepted.

Delete para (a), (b) or (c) as appropriate

(c) Vessel is to be discharged at the average rate of .... tons of 2,240 lbs.*/1,000 Kilos.* per working day of twenty-four (24) consecutive hours (weather permitting), Sundays and Holidays excepted on the basis of the Bill of Lading weight.

(d) Notwithstanding any custom of the port to the contrary, Saturdays shall not count as laytime at loading and discharging port or ports where stevedoring labor and/or grain handling facilities are unavailable on Saturdays or available only at overtime and/or premium rates.

In ports where only part of Saturdays is affected by such conditions, as described above, laytime shall count until the expiration of the last straight time period.

Where six or more hours of work are performed at normal rates, Saturday shall count as a full lay day.

(e) In the event that the vessel is waiting for loading or discharging berth, no laytime is to be deducted during such period for reasons of weather unless the vessel occupying the loading or discharging berth in question is actually prevented from working grain due to weather conditions in which case time so lost is not to count.

Demurrage/ Despatch Money

20. Demurrage at loading and/or discharging ports is to be paid at the rate of .... per day or *pro rata* for part of a day and shall be paid by Charterers in respect of loading port(s) and by Charterers/Receivers* in respect of discharging port(s). Despatch money to be paid by Owners at half the demurrage rate for all laytime saved at loading and/or discharging ports.

Any time lost for which Charterers/Receivers are responsible, which is not excepted under this Charterparty, shall count as laytime, until same has expired, thence time on demurrage.

Shifting

21. (a) **Shifting expenses and time**

(i) Cost of shifting between loading berths and cost of shifting between discharging berths, including bunker fuel used, to be for Owners'*/Charterers'/Recievers'* account, time counting.

(ii) If vessel is required to shift from one loading or discharging berth to a lay berth or anchorage due to subsequent loading or discharging berth(s) not being available, all such shifting expenses, as defined above shall be for Owners'*/Charterers'/Receivers'* account, time counting.

(iii) If the vessel shifts from the anchorage or waiting place outside the port limits either directly to the first loading or discharging berth or to a lay berth or anchorage within the port limits the cost of that shifting shall be for Owners' account and time so used shall not count even if vessel is on demurrage.

(iv) Cost of shifting from lay berth or anchorage within the port limits to first loading or first discharging berth to be for Owners' account, time counting.

(b) **Shifting in and out of the same berth**

If vessel is required by Charterers/Receivers* to shift out of the loading berth or the discharging berth and back to the same berth, one berth shall be deemed to have been used, but shifting expenses from and back to the loading or discharging berth so incurred shall be for Charterers'/Receivers'* account and laytime or time on demurrage shall count.

(c) Overtime expenses for vessel's officers and crew shall always be for Owners' account.

Gear and lights

22. If required, the Master is to give free use of vessel's cargo gear, including runners, ropes and slings as on board, and power to operate the same.

Vessel's personnel is to operate the gear if permitted to do so by shore regulations, failing which shore operators are to be used.

Such shore operators are to be for Owners' account at loading port(s) if the provisions of Clause 10 (b) apply, otherwise for Charterers' account at loading and Charterers'*/Receivers'* account at discharging port(s).

Time lost on account of breakdowns of vessel's gear essential to the loading or discharging of this cargo is not to count as laytime or time on demurrage, and if Clause 10 (a) applies any stevedore standby time charges incurred thereby shall be for Owners' account.

If required, Master shall give free use of the vessel's lighting as on board for night work.

Seaworthy Trim

23. If ordered to be loaded or discharged at two or more ports, the vessel is to be left in seaworthy trim to Master's satisfaction (not exceeding the requirements of the Safety of Life at Sea Convention as applied in the country in which such ports are situated) for the passage between ports at Charterers' expense at loading and at Charterers'/Receivers'* expense at discharging ports, and time used for placing vessel in seaworthy trim shall count as laytime or time on demurrage.

Draft/ Lighterage

24. Owners warrant the vessel's deepest salt water draft shall not exceed .... feet .... inches on completion of loading and .... feet .... inches on arrival at first or sole discharging port.

Should the vessel be ordered to discharge at a place in which there is not sufficient water for her to get the first tide after arrival without lightening, and lie always afloat, laytime is to count as per Clause 18 at a safe anchorage for similar vessels bound for such a place and any lighterage expenses incurred to enable her to reach the place of discharge is to be at the expense and risk of the cargo, any custom of the port or place to the contrary notwithstanding, but time occupied in proceeding from the anchorage to the discharging berth is not to count as laytime or time on demurrage.

Unless loading and/or discharging ports are named in this Charterparty, the responsibility for providing safe port of loading and/or discharging lies with the Charterers/Receivers* provided Owners have complied with the maximum draft limitations in Lines 173/174.

Car Decks, etc.

25. It is understood that if this vessel is fitted with car decks, container fittings and/or any other special fittings not connected with the carriage of grain in bulk, any extra expenses incurred in loading and/or discharging as a result of the presence of such car decks, container fittings and/or special fittings are to be for Owners' account. Time so lost shall not count as laytime or time on demurrage.

Dues and/or Taxes

26. ....

....

....

Seaway Tolls 27. All St. Lawrence Seaway and/or Welland Canal tolls on vessel and/or cargo assessed by Canadian and United States Authorities are to be paid and borne by Owners.

Water Pollution 28. Any time lost on account of vessel's non-compliance with Government and/or State and/or Provincial regulations pertaining to water pollution shall not count as laytime or time on demurrage.

Agents 29. Owners*/Charterers* are to appoint agents at loading port(s) and Owners*/Charterers* are to appoint agents at discharging port(s).

In all instances, agency fees shall be for Owners' account but are not to exceed customary applicable fees.

Strikes, Stoppages, etc. 30. If the cargo cannot be loaded by reason of Riots, Civil Commotions or of a Strike or Lock-out of any class of workmen essential to the loading of the cargo, or by reason of obstructions or stoppages beyond the control of the Charterers caused by Riots, Civil Commotions or a Strike or Lock-out on the Railways or in the Docks or other loading places, or if the cargo cannot be discharged by reason of Riots, Civil Commotions, or of a Strike or Lock-out of any class of workmen essential to the discharge, the time for loading or discharging, as the case may be, shall not count during the continuance of such causes, provided that a Strike or Lock-out of Shippers' and/or Receivers' men shall not prevent demurrage accruing if by the use of reasonable diligence they could have obtained other suitable labor at rates current before the Strike or Lock-out. In case of any delay by reason of the before mentioned causes, no claim for damages or demurrage shall be made by the Charterers/Receivers of the cargo or Owners of the vessel. For the purpose, however, of settling despatch rebate accounts, any time lost by the vessel through any of the above causes shall be counted as time used in loading, or discharging, as the case may be.

Ice 31. **Loading Port**

(a) If the Vessel cannot reach the loading port by reason of ice when she is ready to proceed from her last port, or at any time during the voyage, or on her arrival, or if frost sets in after her arrival, the Master - for fear of the Vessel being frozen in - is at liberty to leave without cargo; in such cases this Charterparty shall be null and void.

(b) If during loading, the Master, for fear of Vessel being frozen in, deems it advisable to leave, he has the liberty to do so with what cargo he has on board and to proceed to any other port with option of completing cargo for Owners' own account to any port or ports including the port of discharge. Any part cargo thus loaded under this Charterparty to be forwarded to destination at Vessel's expense against payment of the agreed freight, provided that no extra expenses be thereby caused to the Consignees, freight being paid on quantity delivered (in proportion if lump sum), all other conditions as per Charterparty.

(c) In case of more than one loading port, and if one or more of the ports are closed by ice, the Master or Owners to be at liberty either to load the part cargo at the open port and fill up elsewhere for the Owners' own account as under sub-clause (b) or to declare the Charterparty null and void unless the Charterers agree to load full cargo at the open port.

Voyage and Discharging Port

(d) Should ice prevent the Vessel from reaching the port of discharge, the Charterers/Receivers shall have the option of keeping the Vessel waiting until the re-opening of navigation and paying demurrage or of ordering the vessel to a safe and immediately accessible port where she can safely discharge without risk of detention by ice. Such orders to be given within 48 hours after the Owners or Master have given notice to the Charterers/Receivers of impossibility of reaching port of destination.

(e) If during discharging, the Master, for fear of Vessel being frozen in, deems it advisable to leave, he has liberty to do so with what cargo he has on board and to proceed to the nearest safe and accessible port. Such port to be nominated by Charterers/Receivers as soon as possible, but not later than 24 running hours, Sundays and holidays excluded, of receipt of Owners' request for nomination of a substitute discharging port, failing which the Master will himself choose such port.

(f) On delivery of the cargo at such port, all conditions of the Bill of Lading shall apply and the Owners shall receive the same freight as if the Vessel had discharged at the original port of destination, except that if the distance to the substitute port exceeds 100 nautical miles the freight on the cargo delivered at that port to be increased in proportion.

Extra Insurance 32. Any extra insurance on cargo incurred owing to vessel's age, class, flag or ownership to be for Owners' account up to a maximum of .... and may be deducted from the freight, in Charterers' option. The Charterers shall furnish evidence of payment supporting such deduction.

P. & I. Bunker Clause 33. The vessel shall have the liberty as part of the contract voyage to proceed to any port or ports at which bunker oil is available for the purpose of bunkering at any stage of the voyage whatsoever and whether such ports are on or off the direct and/or customary route or routes, between any of the ports of loading or discharge named in this Charterparty and may there take oil bunkers in any quantity in the discretion of Owners even to the full capacity of bunker tanks and deep tanks and any other compartment in which oil can be carried whether such amount is or is not required for the chartered voyage.

Deviation 34. Any deviation in saving or attempting to save life or property at sea or any reasonable deviation shall not be deemed to be an infringement or breach of this Charterparty and the Owners shall not be liable for any loss or damage resulting therefrom; provided, however, that if the deviation is for the purpose of loading or unloading cargo or passengers it shall, *prima facie*, be regarded as unreasonable.

Lien and Cesser Clause

35. The Owners shall have a lien on the cargo for freight, deadfreight, demurrage, and average contribution due to them under this Charterparty.

Charterers' liability under this Charterparty is to cease on cargo being shipped except for payment of freight, deadfreight, and demurrage at loading, and except for all other matters provided for in this Charterparty where the Charterers' responsibility is specified.

Exceptions

36. Owners shall be bound before and at the beginning of the voyage to exercise due diligence to make the vessel seaworthy and to have her properly manned, equipped and supplied and neither the vessel nor the Master or Owners shall be or shall be held liable for any loss of or damage or delay to the cargo for causes excepted by the U.S. Carriage of Goods by Sea Act, 1936 or the Canadian Carriage of Goods by Water Act, 1970, or any statutory re-enactment thereof.

And neither the vessel, her Master or Owners, nor the Charterers or Receivers shall, unless otherwise in this Charterparty expressly provided, be responsible for loss of or damage or delay to or failure to supply, load, discharge or deliver the cargo arising or resulting from: - Act of God, act of war, act of public enemies, pirates or assailing thieves; arrest or restraint of princes, rulers or people; seizure under legal process, provided bond is promptly furnished to release the vessel or cargo; floods; fires; blockades; riots; insurrections; Civil Commotions; earthquakes; explosions. No exception afforded the Charterers or Receivers under this clause shall relieve the Charterers or Receivers of or diminish their obligations for payment of any sums due to the Owners under provisions of this Charterparty.

U.S.A. Clause Paramount

37. If the vessel loads in the U.S.A. the U.S.A. Clause Paramount shall be incorporated in all Bills of Lading and shall read as follows:

"This Bill of Lading, shall have effect subject to the provisions of the Carriage of Goods by Sea Act of the United States, approved April 16, 1936, or any statutory re-enactment thereof, which shall be deemed to be incorporated herein, and nothing herein contained shall be deemed a surrender by the carrier of any of its rights or immunities or an increase of any of its responsibilities or liabilities under said Act. If any term of this Bill of Lading be repugnant to said Act to any extent, such terms shall be void to that extent but no further."

Canadian Clause Paramount

38. If the vessel loads in Canada the Canadian Clause Paramount shall be incorporated in all Bills of Lading and shall read as follows:

"This Bill of Lading, so far as it relates to the carriage of goods by water, shall have effect, subject to the provisions of the Carriage of Goods by Water Act, 1970. Revised Statutes of Canada, Chapter C-15, enacted by the Parliament of the Dominion of Canada, or any statutory re-enactment thereof, which shall be deemed to be incorporated herein, and nothing herein contained shall be deemed a surrender by the carrier of any of its rights or immunities or an increase of any of its responsibilities or liabilities under the said Act. If any term of this Bill of Lading be repugnant to said Act to any extent, such term shall be void to that extent, but no further."

Both-to-Blame Collision Clause

39. If the liability for any collision in which the vessel is involved while performing this Charterparty falls to be determined in accordance with the laws of the United Slates of America, the following clause shall apply:

"If the vessel comes into collision with another vessel as a result of the negligence of the other vessel and any act, neglect or default of the master, mariner, pilot or the servants of the Carrier in the navigation or in the management of the vessel, the owners of the goods carried hereunder will indemnify the Carrier against all loss or liability to the other or non-carrying vessel or her owners in so far as such loss or liability represents loss of or damage to or any claim whatsoever of the owners of the said goods, paid or payable by the other or non-carrying vessel or her owners to the owners of the said goods and set off, recouped or recovered by the other or non-carrying vessel or her owners as part of their claim against the carrying vessel or Carrier."

The foregoing provisions shall also apply where the Owners, operators or those in charge of any vessel or vessels or objects other than, or in addition to, the colliding vessels or objects are at fault in respect to a collision or contact."

The Charterers shall procure that all Bills of Lading issued under this Charterparty shall contain the same clause.

General Average/ New Jason

40. General Average shall be adjusted according to the York/Antwerp Rules 1974 and shall be settled ....

Where the adjustment is made in accordance with the law and practice of the United States of America, the following clause shall apply:

"In the event of accident, danger, damage or disaster before or after commencement of the voyage, resulting from any cause whatsoever, whether due to negligence or not, for the consequences of which, the Carrier is not responsible, by Statute, contract or otherwise, the goods, shippers, consignees or owners of the goods shall contribute with the Carrier in general average to the payment of any sacrifices, losses or expenses of a general average nature that may be made or incurred and shall pay salvage and special charges incurred in respect of the goods.

If a salving vessel is owned or operated by the Carrier, salvage shall be paid for as fully as if the said salving vessel or vessels belonged to strangers. Such deposit as the Carrier or his agents may deem sufficient to cover the estimated contribution of the goods and any salvage and special charges thereon shall, if required, be made by the goods, shippers, consignees or owners of the goods to the Carrier before delivery."

The Charterers shall procure that all Bills of Lading issued under this Charterparty shall contain the same clause.

War risks

41. 1. The Master shall not be required or bound to sign Bills of Lading for any blockaded port or for any port which the Master or Owners in his or their discretion consider dangerous or impossible to enter or reach.

2. (A) If any port of loading or of discharge named in this Charterparty or to which the vessel may properly be ordered pursuant to the terms of the Bills of Lading be blockaded, or

(B) if owing to any war, hostilities, warlike operations, civil war, civil commotions, revolutions, or the operation of international law (a) entry to any such port of loading or of discharge or the loading or discharge of cargo at any such port be considered by the Master or Owners in his or their discretion dangerous or (b) it be considered by the Master or Owners in his or their discretion dangerous or impossible for the vessel to reach any such port of loading or of discharge - the Charterers shall have the right to order the cargo or such part of it as may be affected to be loaded or discharged at any other safe port of loading or of discharge within the range of loading or discharging ports respectively established under the provisions of the Charterparty (provided such other port is not blockaded or that entry thereto or loading or discharge of cargo thereat is not in the Master's or Owners' discretion dangerous or prohibited). If in respect of a port of discharge no orders be received from the Charterers within 48 hours after they or their agents have received from the Owners a request for the nomination of a substitute port, the Owners shall then be at liberty to discharge the cargo at any safe port which they or the Master may in their or his discretion decide on (whether within the range of discharging ports established under the provisions of the Charterparty or not) and such discharge shall be deemed to be due fulfilment of the contract or contracts of affreightment so far as cargo so discharged is concerned. In the event of the cargo being loaded or discharged at any such other port within the respective range of loading or discharging ports established under the provisions of the Charterparty, the Charterparty shall be read in respect of the freight and all other conditions whatsoever as if the voyage performed were that originally designated. In the event, however, that the vessel discharges the cargo at a port outside the range of discharging ports established under the provisions of the Charterparty, freight shall be paid as for the voyage originally designated and all extra expenses involved in reaching the actual port of discharge and/or discharging the cargo thereat shall be paid by the Charterers or Cargo Owners. In this latter event the Owners shall have a lien on the cargo for all such extra expenses.

3. The vessel shall have liberty to comply with any directions or recommendations as to departure, arrival, routes, ports of call, stoppages, destinations, zones. waters, delivery or in any other wise whatsoever given by the government of the nation under whose flag the vessel sails or any other government or local authority including any de facto government or local authority or by any person or body acting or purporting to act as or with the authority of any such government or authority or by any committee or person having under the terms of the war risks insurance on the vessel the right to give any such directions or recommendations. If by reason of or in compliance with any such directions or recommendations, anything is done or is not done such shall not be deemed a deviation.

If by reason of or in compliance with any such directions or recommendations the vessel does not proceed to the port or ports of discharge originally designated or to which she may have been ordered pursuant to the terms of the Bills of Lading, the vessel may proceed to any safe port of discharge which the Master or Owners in his or their discretion may decide on and there discharge the cargo. Such discharge shall be deemed to be due fulfilment of the contract or contracts of affreightment and the Owners shall be entitled to freight as if discharge has been effected at the port or ports originally designated or to which the vessel may have been ordered pursuant to the terms of the Bills of Lading. All extra expenses involved in reaching and discharging the cargo at any such other port of discharge shall be paid by the Charterers and/or Cargo Owners and the Owners shall have a lien on the cargo for freight and all such expenses.

Address Commission

42. An address commission of .... % on gross freight, deadfreight and demurrage is due to Charterers at time freight and/or demurrage is paid, vessel lost or not lost, Charterers having the right to deduct such commission from payment of freight and/or demurrage.

Brokerage Commission

43. A brokerage commission of .... % on gross freight, deadfreight, and demurrage is payable by Owners to ....

....

at time of receiving freight payment and/or demurrage payment(s), vessel lost or not lost.

Assignment

44. Charterers have the privilege of transferring/assigning/reletting all or part of this Charterparty to others (guaranteeing to the Owners the due fulfilment of this Charterparty).

Arbitration

Delete para (a) or (b) as appropriate

45. (a) **New York.** All disputes arising out of this contract shall be arbitrated at New York in the following manner, and be subject to U.S. Law:
One Arbitrator is to be appointed by each of the parties hereto and a third by the two so chosen. Their decision or that of any two of them shall be final, and for the purpose of enforcing any award, this agreement may be made a rule of the court. The Arbitrators shall be commercial men, conversant with shipping matters. Such Arbitration is to be conducted in accordance with the rules of the Society of Maritime Arbitrators Inc.

For disputes where the total amount claimed by either party does not exceed U.S.$ .... ** the arbitration shall be conducted in accordance with the Shortened Arbitration Procedure of the Society of Maritime Arbitrators Inc.

(b) **London.** All disputes arising out of this contract shall be arbitrated at London and, unless the parties agree forthwith on a single Arbitrator, be referred to the final arbitrament of two Arbitrators carrying on business in London who shall be members of the Baltic Mercantile & Shipping Exchange and engaged in the Shipping and/or Grain Trades. one to be appointed by each of the parties, with power to such Arbitrators to appoint an Umpire. No award shall be questioned or invalidated on the ground that any of the Arbitrators is not qualified as above. unless objection to his action be taken before the award is made. Any dispute arising hereunder shall be governed by English Law.

For disputes where the total amount claimed by either party does not exceed U.S. $ .... ** the arbitration shall be conducted in accordance with the Small Claims Procedure of the London Maritime Arbitrators Association.

* Delete as appropriate.

**Where no figure is supplied in the blank space this provision only shall be void but the other provisions of this clause shall have full force and remain in effect.

Sugar Charter-Party 1969.

(Revised 1977).

.... 19........

It is this day mutually agreed BETWEEN ....

OWNERS

1. Owners of the good motor/steam vessel called the .... highest class .... (and to be of that class for the duration of the voyage), Flag: .... Built: .... Call Sign: ....

DESCRIPTION OF VESSEL

2. N.R.T./G.R.T. .... / .... : Type .... : Summer deadweight (salt water) .... : Fully loaded draft (summer marks) salt water .... : Length O.L. .... : Number of Hatches/Holds .... : Gear .... : Engine located amid/aft. Speed .... : Bale/Grain Cubic (....)

POSITION

3. Now ....
....

CHARTERERS

4. and .... Charterers, that the said Vessel being tight,

LOADING AREA

5. staunch, strong and in every way fitted for the voyage, shall with all convenient speed sail and proceed to ....
.... and there load always afloat, or safe aground where vessels of similar size, are accustomed to lie in safety, at ONE or TWO safe ports,

DESCRIPTION OF CARGO

6. ONE or TWO safe berths each port, as ordered, from the Factors of the said Charterers, a full and complete cargo of Raw and/or White Sugar in Cotton and/or Jute Bags, or in Charterers' option, declarable .... days/hours prior vessel's readiness to load, in Bulk, of .... long/metric tons .... per cent net weight in Master's option, which the said Charterer's bind themselves to ship, not exceeding what the vessel can reasonably stow or carry over and above fuel for bunkers and ships use, her tackle and apparel, provisions and furniture, always under ship's deck in cargo holds only. The said cargo to be brought to and taken from alongside, free of expense and risk to the ship, and being so laden shall proceed with all convenient speed as directed to

DISCHARGING OPTIONS

7. (a) **CASABLANCA and/or TANGIER or CEUTA.**
Peage Dues (if any) in Morocco to be for Receivers account.

(b) **1/2 safe ports ALGERIA or LIBYA.**
Any dues and/or taxes on cargo and/or freight at discharge to be for Receivers account.

(c) **1/2/3 safe ports TUNISIA.**
Any dues and/or taxes on cargo and/or freight in Tunisia to be for Receivers account. In the event of Charterers exercising their option of discharging at more than ONE port, sufficient cargo to be discharged at BIZERTA and/or SFAX to enable vessel to discharge at SUSA or TUNIS, always afloat, and if BIZERTA or SFAX is used as first port, SUSA as second port, and TUNIS as third port, then sufficient cargo to be discharged at SUSA to enable vessel to discharge at TUNIS, always afloat.

(d) **1/2 safe ports WEST ITALY (including Islands), or 1/2 safe ports ITALIAN ADRIATIC.**
RAVENNA, if declared, to be second port of discharge in Adriatic range and sufficient cargo to be discharged at first port to enable vessel to enter RAVENNA, always afloat.

(e) **1/2 safe ports YUGOSLAV ADRIATIC.**

(f) **1/2 safe ports GREECE (including Islands).**

(g) **1/2 safe ports SYRIA/LEBANON Range.**
If required by Receivers, Owners agree Bills of Lading may be claused "Zone Franche".

(h) **1/2 ports out of ALEXANDRIA, PORT SAID or SUEZ.**

(i) **1/2 safe ports HUELVA/BARCELONA Range, or 1/2 safe ports VIGO/PASAJES Range.**
Any dues and/or taxes on cargo and/or freight in Spain for Receivers account. Tonnage Tax Spain (if any), for Owners' account.

(j) **LISBON and/or LEIXOES.** (rotation in Receivers' option).
Time from 5 p.m. Fridays until 8 a.m. Mondays excepted, even if used.
Any dues and/or taxes on cargo and/or freight, including "Gold Dues" (Commercial Maritime Tax) to be for Receivers' account.

(k) **MARSEILLES, or 1/2 safe ports BAYONNE/DUNKIRK Range (including ROUEN).**
Time from 5 p.m. Fridays until 8 a.m. Mondays excepted, even if used.

(l) **1/2 safe ports ANTWERP/HAMBURG Range.**
Time from 5 p.m. Fridays until 8 a.m. Mondays excepted, even if used.
Quay, Weight and Tonnage Dues Germany to be for Receivers' Account.

(m) **1/2 safe ports UNITED KINGDOM.** (Greenock maximum 27' 9").
Time from 5 p.m. Fridays until 8 a.m. Mondays excepted, even if used.
If this option is agreed, then separate Charter-Party to be issued on declaration, terms of which are the subject of special negotiation and agreement.

(n) **1/2 safe ports NORWAY, SWEDEN, FINLAND or DENMARK.** (MALMOE maximum draft 29' brackish water).
Time from 5 p.m. Fridays until 8 a.m. Mondays excepted, even if used.

(o) **1/2 safe ports RED SEA (excluding ISRAEL).**

(p) **1 safe port RED SEA (excluding ISRAEL) and 1 safe port ARABIAN or PERSIAN GULF.**

(q) **1/2 safe ports ARABIAN or PERSIAN GULF.**
If vessel discharges in IRAN, any dues and/or taxes on cargo and/or freight to be for Receivers' account.

(r) **1/2 safe ports EAST AFRICA.**

(s) **1/2 safe ports SRI LANKA.**

Despatch all time saved Sri Lanka. If this option is agreed, then separate Charter-Party to be issued on declaration, terms of which are the subject of special negotiation and agreement.

(t) **1/2 safe ports WEST PAKISTAN.**

(u) **1/2 safe ports BANGLADESH.**

(v) **1/2 safe ports MALAYSIA and/or SINGAPORE.**

(w) **1/2 safe ports INDONESIA.**

(x) **1/2 main ports CHINA.**

(y) **1/2/3 safe ports JAPAN.**

If this option is agreed, then separate Charter-Party to be issued upon declaration, terms of which are the subject of special negotiation and agreement.

or so near thereunto as she may safely get, always afloat or safe aground, where vessels of similar

EXCEPTIONS

8\. size are accustomed to lie in safety, (the Act of God, perils of the sea, fire on board, in hulk or craft, or on shore, barratry of the Master and Crew, enemies, pirates, and thieves, arrests and restraints of princes, rulers and people, collisions, stranding, and other accidents of Navigation excepted, even when occasioned by negligence, default, or error in judgment of the Pilot, Master, mariners or other servants of the Shipowners. Not answerable for any loss or damage arising from explosion, bursting of boilers, breakages of shafts, or any latent defect in the machinery or hull, not resulting from want of due diligence by the Owners of the ship, or any of them, or by the ship's Husband or Manager),

FREIGHT PAYMENT

9\. and there deliver the same in One or Two safe berths each port as ordered, on being paid freight "as per agreement" per ton of 2240 lbs. or 1016 kilos net weight Sugar delivered (Sweepings to be subject to a deduction of 25%), or at Charterers' option, declarable before breaking bulk, per ton of 2240 lbs. or 1016 kilos net Bill of Lading weight less One per cent, being in full of all Port charges, Pilotages, and Harbour dues on the vessel. The freight to be paid in ....

Currency to Owners Bank ....

....

....

....

....

as follows: 80% (Eighty per cent) of the estimated freight less commissions and estimated loading despatch if any, to be paid within seven days of sailing from final loading port, provided that signed clean bills of lading are released immediately to Shippers on completion of loading, unendorsed "Freight Paid" or Freight Prepaid, and the balance on right and true delivery of the cargo and surrender and agreement of timesheets and statements of facts, with Owners' calculations of any demurrage or despatch incurred at loading and discharging ports.

LIEN

10\. It is also agreed that the Owners of the said vessel shall reserve to themselves the right of lien upon the cargo laden on board for the recovery and payment of all freight, deadfreight and demurrage (if any).

CESSOR

11\. Charterers liability to cease when cargo is shipped and Bills of Lading signed, except as regards payment of freight, deadfreight and demurrage (if any).

NOTICES

12\. 20, 14 and 7 days provisional notice, 72 and 24 hours definite notice of E.T.A. at loading range or first loading port is to be sent by Master by cable to ....

.... Owners or Master to keep Charterers fully informed of any change in ship's position prior to loading. Charterers to nominate first (or sole) loading port on receipt of the 72 hours definite notice to Owners or their Agents. Nomination of additional loading port (if any) to be declared 24 hours prior to sailing from previous port, and any nomination given earlier not to be regarded as a final declaration.

Master to send a cable to Charterers (cable address ....

....) on departure from last loading port, giving the gross and net quantities, and number of bags stated on Bills of Lading, also sailing date, and E.T.A. at discharging range, or first discharging port.

LAYDAYS/ CANCELLING

13\. Laydays for loading not to count before the ....

and if the ship is not ready to load by the .... Charterers have the option to cancel this Charter-Party, declarable latest upon vessel's arrival at loading port.

STEVEDORES F.I.O.S.T.

14\. Stevedores for loading, stowing, trimming and discharging to be employed by Charterers or Shippers/Receivers at their expense and under Master's control. Stevedores shall be considered as Owners servants, and the Charterers/Shippers/Receivers are not to be responsible for any negligence of whatsoever nature, default or error in judgment of the stevedores employed.

TALLYMEN

15\. Shore tallymen to be employed by the Vessel at the expense of the Vessel. Quantity stated on Bills of Lading to be conclusive evidence against the ship as to the number of bags of Sugar shipped, errors and obvious fraud excepted. Ship to be responsible for any number of bags short delivered of signed Bill of Lading quantity.

MATE'S RECEIPTS AND BILLS OF LADING

16\. Clean Mate's receipts to be signed for each parcel of sugar when on board, and Master to sign bills of lading in accordance therewith as requested by Charterers or Shippers. Master's right to reject any cargo that would involve the clausing of mate's receipts and/or bills of lading. If bills of lading are issued showing a destination at any time prior to official declaration in accordance with Clause 20, such destination not to constitute a declaration of discharging port(s). If this situation occurs, Owners or their Agents will authorise without reservation or delay, the amendment, addition and/or deletion with regard to destination shown on bills of lading, or, to the signing of new sets of bills of lading, Charterers or their Agents delivering up old sets of bills of lading in exchange.

PREPARATION FOR LOADING AND

17\. Ship's holds to be odourless and free from insects, properly swept, cleaned and dried to the satisfaction of Shippers' or Charterers' Agents before loading. Ship's holds to be washed down only if cargo injurious to sugar carried previously, and if done, holds to be completely dry before tendering

DISCHARGING

notice of readiness.

(a) **BAGGED CARGO.**

Ship to provide and lay sufficient dunnage and mats (or Kraft paper dunnage if agreed by Charterers), and to be so dunnaged and matted so as to effectively protect and prevent the bags coming into contact with the edges of beams and stringer-plates.

If cargo is stowed in refrigerator hatches, alleyways, bunker hatches, deep tanks or other awkward places, Owners shall pay the extra labour costs of loading and/or discharging from such places, and shall allow Charterers additional laytime for such loading and discharging.

Should the ship use paint or other injurious substance for marking the bags, the ship to be responsible for all loss or damage thereby caused.

No bags to be cut for stowage purposes. Ship to be responsible for any loss sustained in the event of bags being cut.

(b) **BULK CARGO.**

No cargo to be loaded in deep tanks or other awkward places.

All cargo battens, tween-deck hatch boards, dunnage and ship's gear and stores, etc., to be removed prior to loading and stowed in compartments not containing sugar. Spare propeller if carried in hold, to be properly boxed in. The removal and replacement of beams, hatch covers, tents and tanktop lids, as and when required by Charterers, to be carried out by ship's crew, at ship's expense at both ends.

Owners consider the vessel suitable for grab discharge. Tanktops, tunnel shaft and exposed pipe lines to be effectively protected by Owners. Bleeding holes in the coamings to be securely covered, and bilge limbers to be sealed.

Damage by grabs (if any) to be settled directly between Owners and Stevedores.

Vessel's holds not to be ventilated during the voyage. All ventilators to be sealed and any access of fresh air to the cargo to be strictly prevented.

At discharging port(s) the collection of sweepings from the holds, and bilges and coamings; to be done by the ship's crew (if local regulations permit), or stevedores at Owners expense, and time used not to count as laytime.

Vessel not to take any fresh or ballast water on board at discharging port(s) until the vessel has completed discharge.

GENERAL

18. Vessel to be in possession of a valid certificate of efficiency for winches and derricks for the duration of this Charter.

Vessel to supply at both ends, at all times, free of charge to Charterers, winches, power, and gear in good working order, including ropes and slings as required for loading and discharging sugar, also full lights for night work on deck and in the holds, if required.

In the event of a breakdown of a winch or winches by reason of disablement or insufficient power, the laytime to be extended pro-rata for the period of such inefficiency in relation to the number of working gangs available. If on demurrage, time lost pro-rata to be deducted from same.

Owners are to pay in addition the cost of labour affected by the breakdown, either stood off or additionally engaged, or as otherwise regulated by the custom of the port. The Shippers and/or Consignees will be permitted to load and discharge outside ordinary working periods, and during excepted periods, the Owners providing free of charge, all vessel's facilities, including services of Officers and Crew.

Understood rates of loading and discharging in the Charter-Party are based on a minimum of five hatches being available at commencement of loading and discharging; if less than five hatches are available, loading and/or discharging rates to be reduced pro-rata. Vessel having less than five hatches, but with any hatch exceeding fifteen metres length (or less in Charterers' discretion) and able to work two gangs simultaneously with ship's gear, shall have such hatch counted as two hatches.

All opening and closing of hatches and tweendeck hatches, including the handling and shifting of beams, at loading and discharging ports is to be done or paid for by the vessel, and time used not to count as laytime.

LOADING LAYTIME

19. At each loading port, laytime for loading to begin at the next regular working period commencing before 3 p.m., after written notice of readiness to receive cargo has been tendered to Agents in ordinary office hours, whether in berth or not, Saturdays after noon, Sundays (or local equivalents) and holidays excepted.

Laydays at the average rate of .... metric tons calculated on gross weight provided vessel can receive at this rate, per weather working day of 24 consecutive hours, time from noon Saturdays to 8 a.m. Mondays (or local equivalents) and from 5 p.m. day preceding a holiday until 8 a.m. next working day excepted, even if used, shall be allowed to the said Charterers, for loading and waiting for orders. Time employed in shifting anchorages or loading places within the same port or its jurisdiction not to count as laytime, and shifting expenses to be for Owners account.

DISCHARGING NOTICES

20. Master to cable ....

.... 7, 4 and 2 days off discharging port or range, giving his E.T.A.

Charterers to declare first (or sole) discharging port to Owners or their Agents upon receipt of Master's 4 days notice. Each additional discharging port (if any) to be declared to Owners or their Agents latest 24 hours prior to sailing from previous port, and any nominations given earlier not to be regarded as a final declaration.

DEVIATION

21. The ship has liberty to call at any port or ports for fuel or other supplies, and to sail without pilots also to tow and assist vessels in distress for Owners benefit, or to be assisted in all situations, and to deviate for the purpose of saving life or property.

DISCHARGING LAYTIME

22. At first (or sole) discharging port, laytime to commence 24 hours after written notice of readiness to deliver cargo has been tendered to Agents in ordinary office hours, whether in berth or not, Saturdays after noon, Sundays (or local equivalents) and holidays excepted. At subsequent discharging ports (if used), time to count from next working period after arrival, whether in berth or not, according to the custom of the port, Saturdays after noon, Sundays (or local equivalents) and

holidays excepted.

Ship to discharge at the average rate of (............................) metric tons calculated on gross weight provided vessel can deliver at this rate per weather working day of 24 consecutive hours, time from Saturdays noon to 8 a.m. Mondays (or local equivalents) and from 5 p.m. day preceding a holiday until 8 a.m. next working day excepted, even if used. Time employed in shifting anchorages or discharging places within the same port or its jurisdiction not to count as laytime, and shifting expenses to be for Owners account.

DEMURRAGE DESPATCH 23. If longer detained in loading and/or discharging ports, demurrage to be paid at the rate of .... per day, or in proportion for any part of a day.

Ship to pay .... per day, or in proportion, despatch money for all working time saved at both ends. Such time lost or saved is to be calculated in accordance with the custom of the port. Laytime to be non-reversible between loading and discharging ports, but may be reversible between the ports of loading or the ports of discharging.

Demurrage or despatch to be settled directly between Owners and Receivers at discharging port(s).

OVERTIME 24. Overtime to be for account of the party ordering it. Officers and Crew overtime always to be for account of the vessel.

EXTRA INSURANCE 25. Any extra insurance for cargo and/or prepaid freight owing to vessel's age and/or class and/or flag and/or Ownership to be for Owners account, and same to be deducted from the first freight payment.

SEAWORTHY TRIM 26. Vessel to be left in seaworthy trim to Master's satisfaction for voyage between discharging ports.

AGENTS 27. Owners to consign the vessel to shippers/receivers nominees at loading/discharging ports, ship paying the customary agency fees.

STRIKES AND FORCE MAJEURE 28. Strikes or lockouts of men, or any accidents or stoppages on Railway and/or Canal and/or River by ice or frost, or any other force majeure causes including Government interferences, occurring beyond the control of the Shippers, or Consignees, which may prevent or delay the loading and discharging the vessel, always excepted.

GENERAL AVERAGE 29. General Average, if any, in London, as per York-Antwerp Rules, 1974.

ARBITRATION 30. Any dispute that may arise under this Charter to be settled by arbitration, each party appointing an Arbitrator, and should they be unable to agree, the decision of an Umpire selected by them to be final. The Arbitrators and Umpires are all to be commercial men and resident in London, and the arbitration to take place there. This submission may be made a rule of the High Court of Justice in England by either party.

NON-PERFORMANCE 31. Penalty for non-performance of this Charter, proved damages not exceeding estimated amount of freight.

SUB-LET 32. Charterers have the option of sub-letting this Charter-Party, they remaining responsible to Owners for payment of freight and due fulfilment of terms of this Charter-Party.

ARAB BLACK LIST 33. Owners guarantee that the vessel fixed under this Charter is not wholly or partially owned by Israeli interests, and will not call at any Israeli ports from date of fixture until completion of discharge of this cargo. Owners further guarantee that this vessel is not on the Arab Black List, and undertake to provide a certificate from Arab Authorities, if so required, and allow bills of lading to be so attested if requested.

PROTECTIVES 34. War Risks Clauses 1 and 2, Both-to-Blame Collision Clause, New Jason Clause and P. & I. Bunkering Clause are deemed to be incorporated in this Charter-Party.

SECRECY 35. Under no circumstances are Owners and Brokers concerned in the fixture of this vessel to divulge any details whatsoever to anyone outside their own organisation.

OWNERS **CHARTERERS**

....

RIDER

CHARTER-PARTY dated in .... the ....

(Not to be attached to Charter-Party)

With reference to Clause 9, "Freight as per agreement",rates of freight are to be set hereunder:

(a) MOROCCO.
(b) ALGERIA/LIBYA.
(c) TUNISIA.
(d) WEST ITALY/ITALIAN ADRIATIC.
(e) YUGOSLAVIA.
(f) GREECE.
(g) SYRIA/LEBANON.
(h) EGYPT.
(i) HUELVA/BARCELONA Range.
VIGO/PASAJES Range.
(j) PORTUGAL.
(k) MARSEILLES.
BAYONNE-DUNKIRK Range.
(l) ANTWERP-HAMBURG Range.
(m) UNITED KINGDOM.
(n) NORWAY,
SWEDEN,
FINLAND,
DENMARK.
(o) RED SEA.
(p) RED SEA and ARABIAN/PERSIAN GULF.
(q) ARABIAN/PERSIAN GULF.
If vessel is to discharge at any port involving transit of the SHATT-EL-ARAB, freight to be increased by ....
(r) EAST AFRICA
(s) SRI LANKA.
(t) WEST PAKISTAN.
(u) BANGLADESH.
(v) MALAYSIA.
(w) INDONESIA.
(x) CHINA.
(y) JAPAN.

BULK SUGAR LOADING MECHANICAL BERTH.
Where Charters are abe to arrange loading rate of .... tons, the rate of freight is to be decreased by .... per long ton on the entire cargo.

ADDITIONAL FREIGHT.
Where Charterers exercise their option of discharging at more than ONE port, extra freight of .... on entire cargo for each additional discharging port used.

FREIGHT PAID BILLS OF LADING.
Owners to authorise Charterers' Agent, once the 80% freight has been received , to mark Bills of Lading "Prepaid" or "Freight Paid".

COMMISSION
OWNERS to pay a commission of 5% to the order of Charterers, and a brokerage of 11/4% to the order of ...., payable on the gross amount of freight, deadfreight and demurrage, due on shipment of cargo, ship lost or not lost.

OWNERS. **CHARTERERS.**

....

Sugar Charter Party 1999

DATE ....

CHARTERERS/ OWNERS

It is this day mutually agreed BETWEEN .... Charterers

1. and Owners .... of the good motor vessel called the .... highest class .... (and to be of that class for the duration of the voyage), Last Special Survey: .... Flag: .... Built: .... Call Sign: ....

DESCRIPTION OF VESSEL

2. G.T./N.T: .... / .... Type: .... Summer deadweight (salt water): .... Fully loaded draught (summer marks) salt water: .... LOA/Beam: .... Engines located amidships/aft: .... Number of Holds/Hatches: .... Hatch Sizes: .... Gear (including vessel's union purchase capacity): .... Tunnel shaft, if any, to be floored over. Speed: .... Bale/Grain Cubic:(....) Last .... cargoes: ....

(a) Owners guarantee that the vessel is fully insured for Hull and Machinery risks. Owners guarantee that the vessel is insured with .... for the amount of USD .... and that the vessel will remain fully covered for the duration of this voyage.

(b) Owners guarantee that the vessel is fully P & 1 covered with .... and that the vessel will remain fully covered for the duration of this voyage.

(c) Owners guarantee that the vessel will not change flag/class/Ownership /Managers /P & 1 Club coverage during the currency of this Charter-Party without Charterer's prior consent.

(d) Owners guarantee:

(i) that the vessel carries and will do so for the duration of the voyage all certificates and other documentation whatsoever required by her flag, state authorities and/or the authorities at any place of call under this Charter-Party, and

(ii) that, from the date of coming into force of the International Safety Management (ISM) Code in relation to the vessel and thereafter during the currency of the voyage both the vessel and "the Company" (as defined by the ISM Code) shall comply with the requirements of the ISM Code. Upon request the Owners shall provide the Charterers with a copy of the relevant document of compliance and Safety Management Certificate. Compliance by the Owners with the provisions of this Clause 2(d) is a condition of this Charter-Party the breach thereof will entitle the Charterers to claim damages for any costs/consequences arising as a result and/or at any time cancel this Charter-Party.

POSITION

3. Now .... that the said vessel being tight, staunch, strong and in every way fitted for the voyage including the fulfilment of all documentary requirements for the service contemplated by this Charter-Party, shall with all Charter-Party speed,

LOADING AREA

4. weather permitting, sail and proceed to .... and there load always afloat, or safe aground where vessels of similar size are accustomed to lie in safety, at ONE or TWO safe ports, ONE or TWO safe loading berths and/or safe loading anchorages each port, as ordered, from the Factors of the said Charterers, a full

DESCRIPTION OF CARGO

5. and complete cargo of .... metric tons .... per cent net weight in Charterer's/Master's option, as sole cargo only, which the said Charterers bind themselves to ship, always under ship's deck in cargo holds only. The said cargo to be brought to and taken from alongside, free of expense and risk to the ship, and being so laden shall proceed with all

DISCHARGING AREA

Charter-Party speed as directed to ....
....
....
....
....
or so near thereunto as she may safely get always afloat or safe aground where vessels of similar size are accustomed to lie in safety, and there deliver the same in ONE or TWO safe discharging berths and/or safe discharging anchorages each port as ordered, on being paid freight "as per agreement".

EXCEPTIONS

6. The Act of God, perils of the sea, fire on board, in hulk or craft, or on shore, crew, enemies, pirates, and thieves, arrests and restraints of princes, rulers and people, collisions, stranding, and other accidents of navigation excepted, even when occasioned by negligence, default, or error in judgement of the Pilot, Master, mariners or other servants of the Shipowners. Not answerable for any loss or damage arising from explosion, bursting of boilers, breakages of shafts, or any latent defect in the machinery or hull, not resulting from want of due diligence by the Owners of the ship, or any of them, or by the ship's Husband or Manager.

AGENTS

7. At port(s) of loading and discharging Owners to appoint, employ and to be solely responsible for Agents, as selected by Charterers without risk or liability to Charterers, for all ship's business, owners paying the agency fees.

TAXES/DUES/ DISBURSEMENTS

8. Except for the taxes and/or dues specified below all taxes and/or dues on vessel and/or freight at load/discharge ports to be for Owners' account and all taxes and/or dues on cargo to be for Shippers' account at load port(s) and Receivers'

account at discharge port(s).

(a) In **BRAZIL**
Brazilian Merchant Marine Renewal Tax, Quota da Provedencia, Contribuicao da Uniao and Port Utilisation Tax to be for Shippers' account. All other customary taxes and/or dues on the vessel to be for Owners' account.

(b) In **GERMANY**
Quay, Weight and Tonnage Dues to be for Shippers' account.

(c) In **MOROCCO**
Peage Dues to be for Receivers' account.

(d) In **SPAIN**
Tonnage Tax to be for Owners' account.

(e) In **PORTUGAL**
Gold Dues (Commercial Maritime Tax) to be for Receivers' account.

(f) In **YEMEN**
Compulsory shore cranage to be for Receivers' account.

(g) In **SRI LANKA**
Sri Lankan Tonnage Dues to be for Owners' account.

(h) In **FINLAND**
Finnish Fairway Dues to be for Owners' account.

(i) In **GHANA**
Ghana Shippers' Council Service charge to be for Owners' account.

At all ports of loading and discharging all customary port charges including pilotage and harbour dues on the vessel to be for Owners' account. Owners to put load and discharge port Agents in funds prior to vessel's arrival. In the event that Owners fail to put Agents in funds prior to vessel's arrival and vessel's berthing/commencement of loading/discharging/sailing is delayed, then Owners to be fully responsible for all/any delays/costs/consequences that may arise either directly or indirectly as a result.

FREIGHT PAYMENT

9. Freight payable per metric ton net Bill of Lading weight being in full of all taxes and/or dues stipulated to be for Owners' account as per Clause 8, Port charges, Pilotages, and Harbour dues on the vessel. The freight is deemed earned upon the safe arrival of the vessel and right and true delivery of the cargo at destination. The freight to be paid in United States Currency to Owners' Bank ....

....

....

....

....

Owners to advise their New York corresponding Bank, otherwise Charterers not to be responsible for late receipt of freight by Owners ....

....

as follows: 90% (Ninety per cent) of the estimated freight less commissions, estimated loading despatch and extra insurance, if any, to be paid within seven days of sailing from final loading port, provided that signed clean bills of lading are released immediately to Shippers on completion of loading, stating 'Freight payable as per Charter-Party'.

The balance of freight, from which load and discharge despatches are to be deducted (allowing for any estimated loading despatch already deducted) or to which load and discharge demurrages are to be added, as applicable, to be paid on right and true delivery of the cargo and surrender and agreement of timesheets and statements of facts and signed notice of readiness, with Owners' calculations of any demurrage or despatch incurred at loading and discharging ports.

Any advance on freight made to Owners in order to obtain 'Freight Prepaid' Bills of Lading is not recoverable from the shipowners if the vessel and/or cargo is lost by reason or as a consequence of any of the excepted perils as listed in Article IV, Rule 2 of the Hague Visby Rules.

LIEN

10. It is also agreed that the Owners of the said vessel shall reserve to themselves the right of lien upon the cargo laden on board for the recovery and payment of all freight, deadfreight and demurrage (if any).

CESSOR

11. Charterers liability to cease when cargo is shipped and Bills of Lading signed, except as regards payment of freight, deadfreight and demurrage (if any).

NOTICES

12. Notice on fixing and 20, 14, 10 and 7 days provisional notice, 72, 48 and 24 hours definite notice of E.T.A. at loading range or first loading port is to be sent by Master by cable/telex to ....
.... Owners or Master to keep Charterers fully informed of any change in ship's position prior to loading. Owners to be responsible for all consequences and damages of whatsoever nature and howsoever arising in the event of Owner's or Master's failure to keep Charterers fully informed of any change in ship's position prior to loading. Owners to advise Charterers whether they intend to bunker prior arrival at loadport and/or their bunkering plans prior to sailing from last load port. Charterers to nominate first (or sole) loading port on receipt of the 72 hours definite notice to Owners or their Agents. Nomination of additional loading port (if any) to be declared 24 hours prior to sailing from previous port, and any nomination given earlier not to be regarded as a final declaration.

Master to send a cable/telex to Charterers (cable/telex address ....
..............................) on departure from last loading port, giving the gross and net quantities, and number of bags stated on Bills of Lading, also sailing date, and E.T.A. at discharging range, or first discharging port. On sailing from final load port Master to cable/telex Charterers every 48 hours vessel's ETA basis intended discharge area or port. Should the vessel be delayed on passage for any reason longer than 24 hours Master to immediately cable/telex Charterers reason for delay with revised ETA and Owners responsible for all consequences and damages of whatsoever nature and howsoever arising in the event of Owners or Master failing to do so.

LAYDAYS/ CANCELLING

13. Laydays for loading not to count before the ....
and if the ship is not ready to load by the .... Charterers have the option to cancel this Charter-Party, declarable latest upon vessel's arrival at loading port.

STEVEDORES

14. Stevedores for loading, stowing, trimming and discharging to be employed by Charterers or Shippers/Receivers at

F.I.O.S.T.

their expense and under Master's control. Stevedores shall be considered as Owners servants, and the Charterers/Shippers/Receivers are not to be responsible for any negligence of whatsoever nature, default or error in judgement of the stevedores employed.

TALLYMEN

15. Shore tallymen to be employed by the Vessel at the expense of the Vessel. Quantity stated on Bills of Lading to be conclusive evidence against the ship as to the number of bags of sugar shipped, errors and obvious fraud excepted. Ship to be responsible for any number of bags short delivered of signed Bill of Lading quantity.

MATE'S RECEIPTS AND BILLS OF LADING

16. Clean Mate's Receipts to be signed for each parcel of sugar when on board, and Master to sign Bills of Lading in accordance therewith as presented by Charterers or Shippers. Master to reject any cargo that would involve the clausing of Mate's Receipts and/or Bills of Lading. If Bills of Lading are issued showing a destination at any time prior to official declaration in accordance with Clause 20, such destination not to constitute a declaration of discharging port(s). If this situation occurs, Owners or their Agents will authorise Charterers or nominated Agents without reservation or delay, the amendment, addition and/or deletion with regard to destination shown on Bills of Lading, or, to the signing of new sets of Bills of Lading, Charterers or their Agents delivering up old sets of Bills of Lading in exchange. Bills of Lading to be released and forwarded to Shippers or their Agents for each parcel immediately on completion of loading such parcel. In the case of a single Bill of Lading covering the entire cargo such Bill of Lading to be released immediately on completion of loading.

PREPARATION FOR LOADING AND DISCHARGING

17. Ship's holds to be odourless and free from insects, properly swept, cleaned and dried to the satisfaction of Shippers' and/or Charterer's Agents before loading. Ship's holds to be washed down only if cargo injurious to sugar carried previously, and if done, holds to be completely dry before tendering notice of readiness. Charterers have the right to arrange a condition survey and/or hose test prior to commencement of loading which to be at Charterer's expense for which purposes a Lloyds Agent or Salvage Association Surveyor will be used where possible, failing which a mutually agreed Surveyor shall be used.

a) BAGGED CARGO.

Ship to provide and lay sufficient dunnage and mats or Kraft paper, and to be so dunnaged so as to effectively protect and prevent the bags coming into contact with the edges of beams and stringer-plates.

If cargo is stowed in refrigerator hatches, alleyways, bunker hatches, deep tanks or other awkward places, Owners shall pay the extra labour costs of loading and/or discharging from such places. The loading and discharging rate shall be half the Charter-Party loading and discharging rate for cargo carried in such places.

No paint or other injurious substance to be used by the ship for marking the bags, the ship to be responsible for all loss or damage caused thereby.

No bags to be cut for stowage purposes. Ship to be responsible for all loss sustained in the event of bags being cut.

(b) BULK CARGO.

No cargo to be loaded in deep tanks or other awkward places.

All cargo battens, tween-deck hatch boards, dunnage and ship's gear and stores, etc., to be removed prior to loading and stowed in compartments not containing sugar. Spare propeller if carried in hold, to be properly boxed in. The removal and replacement of beams, hatch covers, tents and tanktop lids, as and when required by Charterers, to be carried out by ship's crew, at ship's expense at both ends.

Owners consider the vessel suitable for grab discharge. Tanktops, tunnel shaft and exposed pipe lines to be effectively protected by Owners. Bleeding holes in the coamings to be securely covered, and bilge limbers to be sealed.

Damage by grabs (if any) to be settled directly between Owners and Stevedores, Charterers incurring no responsibility therefore.

Vessel's holds not to be ventilated during the voyage. All ventilators to be sealed and any access of fresh air to the cargo to be strictly prevented.

At discharging port(s) the collection of sweepings from the holds, bilges and coamings to be done by the Stevedores at Receivers expense, and time used to count as laytime.

Vessel not to take any fresh or ballast water on board at discharging port(s) until the vessel has completed discharge.

GENERAL

18. Vessel to be in possession of a valid certificate of efficiency for winches and derricks/cranes for the duration of this Charter.

Vessel to supply at both ends, at all times, free of charge to Charterers, winches and derricks/cranes, power, and gear in good working order at all hatches including ropes as required for loading and discharging sugar, also full lights for night work on deck and in the holds, if required.

In the event of a breakdown of a winch and derrick/crane or winches and derricks/cranes by reason of disablement or insufficient power and/or failure of lights, the laytime to be extended pro-rata for the period of such inefficiency in relation to the number of working gangs available. If on demurrage, time lost pro-rata to be deducted from same. Owners are to pay in addition the cost of labour affected by the breakdown, either stood off or additionally engaged including the hire of shore gear, or as otherwise regulated by the custom of the port.

The Shippers and/or Consignees will be permitted to load and discharge outside ordinary working periods and during excepted periods, the Owners providing free of charge all vessel's facilities, including services of Officers and Crew.

Understood rates of loading and discharging in the Charter-Party are based on a minimum of four hatches being available at commencement of loading and discharging; if less than four hatches are available, loading and/or discharging rates to be reduced pro-rata. Vessel having less than four hatches, but with any hatch exceeding fifteen metres length (or less at Charterers' discretion) and able to work two gangs simultaneously with ship's gear, shall have such hatch counted as two hatches.

All opening and closing of hatches and tweendeck hatches, including the handling and shifting of beams, at loading and discharging ports is to be done or paid for by the vessel, and time used not to count as laytime.

LOADING LAYTIME

19. At each loading port, even if loading commences earlier, laytime for loading to begin at 1400 hours if written/cabled/telexed notice of readiness to load is tendered to Agents before noon and at 0800 hours next working day if written/cabled/telexed notice of readiness is tendered to Agents after noon. Notice of readiness to be tendered to Agents in ordinary office hours, Saturdays afternoon, Sundays (or local equivalents) and holidays excepted, whether in berth or not.

Laydays at the average rate of .... metric tons calculated on gross weight provided vessel can receive at this rate, per weather working day of 24 consecutive hours, time from noon Saturdays to 0800 hours. Mondays (or local equivalents) and from 1700 hours day preceding a holiday until 0800 hours next working day excepted, even if used, shall be allowed to the said Charterers, for loading and waiting for orders. Time employed in shifting anchorages and/or loading places within the same port or its jurisdiction not to count as laytime, and shifting expenses to be for Owners account.

At loading port(s) in the event of congestion Master has the right to tender notice of readiness at the customary waiting place in ordinary office hours by cable/telex to Agents whether in berth or not, whether in port or not, whether in free pratique or not, whether customs cleared or not. Time proceeding from customary waiting place to loading berth/anchorage not to count as laytime. If the loadport surveyor is unable to attend the vessel at the customary waiting place and after vessel's arrival at loading berth/anchorage the vessel fails her survey, laytime/demurrage shall cease from such failure until the vessel's holds are passed accordingly.

DISCHARGING NOTICES

20. Master to cable .... 7, 4, 2 days and 24 hours off discharging port or range, giving his E.T.A.

Charterers to declare first (or sole) discharging port to Owners or their Agents upon receipt of Master's 4 days notice. Each additional discharging port (if any) to be declared to Owners or their Agents latest 24 hours prior to sailing from previous port, and any nominations given earlier not to be regarded as a final declaration. Owners to be responsible for all costs, consequences and damages of whatsoever nature and howsoever arising in the event of Owners or Master's failure to keep Charterers fully informed of any change in ship's position prior to arrival at discharging port(s).

DEVIATION

21. The ship has liberty to call at any port or ports on the route for fuel or other supplies, and to sail without pilots also to tow and assist vessels in distress for Owners benefit, or to be assisted in all situations and to deviate for the purpose of saving life or property.

DISCHARGING LAYTIME

22. At each discharging port, even if discharging commences earlier, laytime for discharge to begin at 1400 hours if written/cabled/telexed notice of readiness to discharge is tendered to Agents before noon and at 0800 hours next working day if written/cabled/telexed notice of readiness is tendered to Agents after noon. Master has the right to tender notice of readiness from the customary waiting place in ordinary office hours. Notice of readiness to be tendered to Agents in ordinary office hours Saturdays afternoon, Sundays (or local equivalents) and holidays excepted whether in berth or not.

Ship to discharge at the average rate of (....................................) metric tons calculated on gross weight provided vessel can deliver at this rate, per weather working day of 24 consecutive hours, time from Saturdays noon to 0800 hours Mondays (or local equivalents) and from 1700 hours day preceding a holiday until 0800 hours next working day excepted, even if used. Time employed in shifting anchorages or discharging places within the same port or its jurisdiction not to count as laytime, and shifting expenses to be for Owners' account.

At discharging port(s) in the event of congestion Master has the right to tender his notice of readiness by cable/telex in ordinary office hours to Agents whether in berth or not, whether in port or not, whether in free pratique or not, whether customs cleared or not. Time proceeding from customary waiting place to discharge berth/anchorage not to count as laytime.

DEMURRAGE DESPATCH

23. If longer detained in loading and/or discharging ports, demurrage to be paid at the rate of .... per day, or in proportion for any part of a day.

Ship to pay .... per day, or in proportion, despatch money for all working time saved at both ends. Laytime to be non-reversible between loading and discharging ports, but may be reversible at Charterer's option between the ports of loading or the ports of discharging.

Demurrage or despatch to he settled directly between Owners and Charterers in accordance with the terms, conditions and exceptions of this Charter-Party.

WAITING

24. In the event that Charterers require the vessel to wait at any time prior to arrival at destination, Owners agree to instruct the Master to anchor at any safe place on passage in international waters or in Charterer's option at waiting place at discharge port. In respect of such Charterers are to pay Owners USD .... per day or pro rata inclusive of bunkers but less commission. However, if the vessel waits at a place where the vessel is able to tender her notice of readiness then Charterers may elect to commence laytime as per Charter-Party.

OVERTIME

25. Overtime to be for account of the party ordering it. Officers and Crew overtime always to be for account of the vessel. If ordered by Port Authorities at loading/discharging ports to be for Shippers/Receivers' account.

EXTRA INSURANCE

26. Any extra insurance for cargo and/or prepaid freight owing to vessel's age and/or class and/or flag and/or Ownership to be for Owners account, and same to be deducted without documentation from freight.

SEAWORTHY TRIM

27. Should more than one load or one discharge port be used vessel to be left in seaworthy trim to Master's satisfaction for voyage between ports of loading or ports of discharging.

STRIKES AND FORCE MAJEURE

28. In the event that whilst at or off the loading place or discharging place the loading and/or discharging of the vessel is prevented or delayed by any of the following occurrences: strikes, riots, civil commotions, lockouts of men, accidents and/or breakdowns on railways, stoppages on railway and/or river and/or canal by ice or frost, mechanical breakdowns at mechanical loading plants, government interferences, vessel being inoperative or rendered inoperative due to the terms and conditions of employment of the Officers and Crew, time so lost shall not count as laytime or time on demurrage or detention.

GENERAL AVERAGE

29. General Average, if any, shall be settled in London, as per York-Antwerp Rules 1994 and subsequent amendments.

TIME BAR

30. Either party shall be discharged and released from all liability in respect of any claim or claims which either party may have under this Charter-Party and such claim or claims shall be totally extinguished, unless such claim or claims have been notified in detail to either party in writing within 12 (twelve) months from completion of discharge of the appropriate cargo under this Charter-Party.

ARBITRATION

31. All disputes from time to time arising out of, or in connection with, this Charter-Party shall, unless the parties agree forthwith on a single arbitrator, be referred to the final arbitrament of two arbitrators, one to be appointed by each of the parties, with power to such arbitrators to appoint an umpire. The arbitrators shall be commercial men with knowledge of shipping and freight matters or members of the London Maritime Arbitrators Association. The arbitration to take place in London. If a party fails to appoint an arbitrator within 14 days of being called to do so, the other party may, in order to complete the arbitration tribunal, apply to the President of the LMAA for the appointment of an arbitrator on behalf of that party.

The award of the sole arbitrator, two arbitrators or the umpire (as the case may be) shall be final and binding on both parties. No award shall be questioned or invalidated on the grounds that any of the arbitrators is not qualified as above, unless objection to his acting be taken during appointment.

By mutual agreement the parties also have the option to adopt London Maritime Arbitrators Association Small

Claims Procedure.
This Charter-Party is governed by and construed in accordance with English Law.

ARAB BLACK LIST 32. Owners guarantee that the vessel fixed under this Charter is not wholly or partially owned by Israeli interests, and will not call at any Israeli ports from date of fixture until completion of discharge of this cargo. Owners further guarantee that this vessel is not on the Arab Black List, and undertake to provide a certificate from Arab Authorities, if so required, and allow Bills of Lading to be so attested, if requested.

SUB-LET 33. Charterers have the option of sub-letting this Charter-Party, they remaining responsible to Owners for payment of freight and due fulfilment of terms of this Charter-Party.

SATELLITE TRACKING 34. If required by Charterers/Shippers/Receivers or the cargo underwriters, a satellite tracking device may be placed on the vessel at the port of loading, carried free of charge and removed prior to completion of discharge.

CERTIFICATES 35. If required by Charterers, Owners undertake to issue or otherwise supply any letters or certificates in connection with vessel's classification, registration, age, flag, gear, details of vessel's entry into P and I Club or any other certificates required by Charterers.

BREAKING UP 36. Owners guarantee that this vessel has not already been sold for breaking up nor will be sold for breaking up during the currency of this Charter-Party.

PROTECTIVES 37. War Risks Clauses 1 and 2, Both-to-Blame Collision Clause, New Jason Clause and P & I Bunkering Clause are deemed to be incorporated in this Charter-Party.

SECRECY 38. Under no circumstances are Owners and Brokers concerned in the fixture of this vessel to divulge any details of this fixture whatsoever to anyone outside their own organisation.

OWNERS **CHARTERERS**

Rider

CHARTER-PARTY dated in .... the ....
(This Rider is deemed fully incorporated in but not to be attached to Charter-Party)

With reference to Clause 9, "Freight as per agreement", rates of freight are to be as set hereunder:

FREIGHT PAID BILLS OF LADING
Charterers are authorised, once the 90% freight has been remitted to mark Bills of Lading "Prepaid" or "Freight Paid".

COMMISSION
Owners to pay a commission of 6.25% to the order of Charterers, and a brokerage of 1.25% to order of .... payable on the gross amount of freight,deadfreight and demurrage, due on shipment of cargo, ship lost or not lost and subsequent demurrage at discharge port(s).

OWNERS **CHARTERERS**

Time Charter

GOVERNMENT FORM

Approved by the New York Produce Exchange

November 6th, 1913 - Amended October 20th, 1921; August 6th, 1931; October 3rd, 1946

This Charter Party, made and concluded in .... day of .... 19 ....

Between ....

Owners of the good .... Steamship/Motorship .... of ....

of .... tons gross register, and .... tons net register, having engines of .... indicated horse power

and with hull, machinery and equipment in a thoroughly efficient state, and classed ....

at .... of about .... cubic feet bale capacity, and about .... tons of 2240 lbs. deadweight capacity (cargo and bunkers, including fresh water and stores not exceeding one and one-half percent of ship's deadweight capacity, allowing a minimum of fifty tons) on a draft of .... feet .... inches on .... Summer freeboard, inclusive of permanent bunkers, which are of the capacity of about .... tons of fuel, and capable of steaming, fully laden, under good weather conditions about .... knots on a consumption of about .... tons of best Welsh coal - best grade fuel oil - best grade Diesel oil, now ....

.... and .... Charterers of the City of ....

Witnesseth, That the said Owners agree to let, and the said Charterers agree to hire the said vessel, from the time of delivery, for about ....

.... within below mentioned trading limits.

Charterers to have liberty to sublet the vessel for all or any part of the time covered by this Charter, but Charterers remaining responsible for the fulfillment of this Charter Party.

Vessel to be placed at the disposal of the Charterers, at ....

....

in such dock or at such wharf or place (where she may safely lie, always afloat, at all times of tide, except as otherwise provided in clause No. 6), as the Charterers may direct. If such dock, wharf or place be not available time to count as provided for in clause No. 5. Vessel on her delivery to be ready to receive cargo with clean-swept holds and tight, staunch, strong and in every way fitted for the service, having water ballast, winches and donkey boiler with sufficient steam power, or if not equipped with donkey boiler, then other power sufficient to run all the winches at one and the same time (and with full complement of officers, seamen, engineers and firemen for a vessel of her tonnage), to be employed, in carrying lawful merchandise, including petroleum or its products, in proper containers, excluding ....

(vessel is not to be employed in the carriage of Live Stock, but Charterers are to have the privilege of shipping a small number on deck at their risk, all necessary fittings and other requirements to be for account of Charterers), in such lawful trades, between safe port and/or ports in British North America, and/or United States of America, and/or West Indies, and/or Central America, and/or Caribbean Sea, and/or Gulf of Mexico, and/or Mexico, and/or South America .... and/or Europe and/or Africa, and/or Asia, and/or Australia, and/or Tasmania, and/or New Zealand, but excluding Magdalena River, River St. Lawrence between October 31st and May 15th, Hudson Bay and all unsafe ports; also excluding, when out of season, White Sea, Black Sea and the Baltic,

....

....

....

as the Charterers or their Agents shall direct, on the following conditions:

1. That the Owners shall provide and pay for all provisions, wages and consular shipping and discharging fees of the Crew; shall pay for the insurance of the vessel, also for all the cabin, deck, engine-room and other necessary stores, including boiler water and maintain her class and keep the vessel in a thoroughly efficient state in hull, machinery and equipment for and during the service.

2. That the Charterers shall provide and pay for all the fuel except as otherwise agreed, Port Charges, Pilotages, Agencies, Commissions, Consular Charges (except those pertaining to the Crew), and all other usual expenses except those before stated, but when the vessel puts into a port for causes for which vessel is responsible, then all such charges incurred shall be paid by the Owners. Fumigations ordered because of illness of the crew to be for Owners account. Fumigations ordered because of cargoes carried or ports visited while vessel is employed under this charter to be for Charterers account. All other fumigations to be for Charterers account after vessel has been on charter for a continuous period of six months or more.

Charterers are to provide necessary dunnage and shifting boards, also any extra fittings requisite for a special trade or unusual cargo, but Owners to allow them the use of any dunnage and shifting boards already aboard vessel. Charterers to have the privilege of using shifting boards for dunnage, they making good any damage thereto.

3. That the Charterers, at the port of delivery, and the Owners, at the port of re-delivery, shall take over and pay for all fuel remaining on board the vessel at the current prices in the respective ports, the vessel to be delivered with not less than .... tons and not more than .... tons and to be re-delivered with not less than .... tons and not more than .... tons.

4. That the Charterers shall pay for the use and hire of the said Vessel at the rate of ....

.... United States Currency per ton on vessel's total deadweight carrying capacity, including bunkers and stores, on .... summer freeboard, per Calendar Month, commencing on and from the day of her delivery, as aforesaid, and at and after the same rate for any part of a month; hire to continue until the hour of the day of her re-delivery in like good order and condition, ordinary wear and tear excepted, to the Owners (unless lost) at ....

.... unless otherwise mutually agreed. Charterers are to give Owners not less than .... days notice of vessels expected date of re-delivery, and probable port.

5. Payment of said hire to be made in New York in cash in United States Currency, semi-monthly in advance, and for the last half month or part of same the approximate amount of hire, and should same not cover the actual time, hire is to be paid for the balance day by day, as it becomes

due, if so required by Owners, unless bank guarantee or deposit is made by the Charterers, otherwise failing the punctual and regular payment of the hire, or bank guarantee, or on any breach of this Charter Party, the Owners shall be at liberty to withdraw the vessel from the service of the Charterers, without prejudice to any claim they (the Owners) may otherwise have on the Charterers. Time to count from 7 a.m. on the working day following that on which written notice of readiness has been given to Charterers or their Agents before 4 p.m., but if required by Charterers, they to have the privilege of using vessel at once, such time used to count as hire.

Cash for vessel's ordinary disbursements at any port may be advanced as required by the Captain, by the Charterers or their Agents, subject to 2 1/2% commission and such advances shall be deducted from the hire. The Charterers, however, shall in no way be responsible for the application of such advances.

6. That the cargo or cargoes be laden and/or discharged in any dock or at any wharf or place that Charterers or their Agents may direct, provided the vessel can safely lie always afloat at any time of tide, except at such places where it is customary for similar size vessels to safely lie aground.

7. That the whole reach of the Vessel's Hold, Decks, and usual places of loading (not more than she can reasonably stow and carry), also accommodations for Supercargo, if carried, shall be at the Charterers' disposal, reserving only proper and sufficient space for Ship's officers, crew, tackle, apparel, furniture, provisions, stores and fuel. Charterers have the privilege of passengers as far as accommodations allow, Charterers paying Owners .... per day per passenger for accommodations and meals. However, it is agreed that in case any fines or extra expenses are incurred in the consequences of the carriage of passengers, Charterers are to bear such risk and expense.

8. That the Captain shall prosecute his voyages with the utmost despatch, and shall render all customary assistance with ship's crew and boats. The Captain (although appointed by the Owners), shall be under the orders and directions of the Charterers as regards employment and agency; and Charterers are to load, stow, and trim the cargo at their expense under the supervision of the Captain, who is to sign Bills of Lading for cargo as presented, in conformity with Mate's or Tally Clerk's receipts.

9. That if the Charterers shall have reason to be dissatisfied with the conduct of the Captain, Officers, or Engineers, the Owners shall on receiving particulars of the complaint, investigate the same, and, if necessary, make a change in the appointments.

10. That the Charterers shall have permission to appoint a Supercargo, who shall accompany the vessel and see that voyages are prosecuted with the utmost despatch. He is to be furnished with free accommodation, and same fare as provided for Captain's table, Charterers paying at the rate of $1.00 per day. Owners to victual Pilots and Customs Officers, and also, when authorized by Charterers or their Agents, to victual Tally Clerks, Stevedore's Foreman, etc., Charterers paying at the current rate per meal, for all such victualling.

11. That the Charterers shall furnish the Captain from time to time with all requisite instructions and sailing directions, in writing, and the Captain shall keep a full and correct Log of the voyage or voyages, which are to be patent to the Charterers or their Agents, and furnish the Charterers, their Agents or Supercargo, when required, with a true copy of daily Logs, showing the course of the vessel and distance run and the consumption of fuel.

12. That the Captain shall use diligence in caring for the ventilation of the cargo.

13. That the Charterers shall have the option of continuing this charter for a further period of ....

....

on giving written notice thereof to the Owners or their Agents .... days previous to the expiration of the first-named term, or any declared option.

14. That if required by Charterers, time not to commence before .... and should vessel not have given written notice of readiness on or before .... but not later than 4 p.m. Charterers or their Agents to have the option of cancelling this Charter at any time not later than the day of vessel's readiness.

15. That in the event of the loss of time from deficiency of men or stores, fire, breakdown or damages to hull, machinery or equipment, grounding, detention by average accidents to ship or cargo, drydocking for the purpose of examination or painting bottom, or by any other cause preventing the full working of the vessel, the payment of hire shall cease for the time thereby lost; and if upon the voyage the speed be reduced by defect in or breakdown of any part of her hull, machinery or equipment, the time so lost, and the cost of any extra fuel consumed in consequence thereof, and all extra expenses shall be deducted from the hire.

16. That should the Vessel be lost, money paid in advance and not earned (reckoning from the date of loss or being last heard of) shall be returned to the Charterers at once. The act of God, enemies, fire, restraint of Princes, Rulers and People, and all dangers and accidents of the Seas, Rivers, Machinery, Boilers and Steam Navigation, and errors of Navigation throughout this Charter Party, always mutually excepted.

The vessel shall have the liberty to sail with or without pilots, to tow and to be towed, to assist vessels in distress, and to deviate for the purpose of saving life and property.

17. That should any dispute arise between Owners and the Charterers, the matter in dispute shall be referred to three persons at New York, one to be appointed by each of the parties hereto, and the third by the two so chosen; their decision or that of any two of them, shall be final, and for the purpose of enforcing any award, this agreement may be made a rule of the Court. The Arbitrators shall be commercial men.

18. That the Owners shall have a lien upon all cargoes, and all sub-freights for any amounts due under this Charter, including General Average contributions, and the Charterers to have a lien on the Ship for all monies paid in advance and not earned, and any overpaid hire or excess deposit to be returned at once. Charterers will not suffer, nor permit to be continued, any lien or encumbrance incurred by them or their agents, which might have priority over the title and interest of the owners in the vessel.

19. That all derelicts and salvage shall be for Owners' and Charterers' equal benefit after deducting Owners' and Charterers' expenses and Crew's proportion. General Average shall be adjusted, stated and settled, according to Rules 1 to 15, inclusive, 17 to 22, inclusive, and Rule F of York-Antwerp Rules 1924, at such port or place in the United States as may be selected by the carrier, and as to matters not provided for by these Rules, according to the laws and usages at the port of New York. In such adjustment disbursements in foreign currencies shall be exchanged into United States money at the rate prevailing on the dates made and allowances for damage to cargo claimed in foreign currency shall be converted at the rate prevailing on the last day of discharge at the port or place of final discharge of such damaged cargo from the ship. Average agreement or bond and such additional security, as may be required by the carrier, must be furnished before delivery of the goods. Such cash deposit as the carrier or his agents may deem sufficient as additional security for the contribution of the goods and for any salvage and special charges thereon, shall, if required, be made by the goods, shippers, consignees or owners of the goods to the carrier before delivery. Such deposit shall, at the option of the carrier, be payable in United States money and be remitted to the adjuster. When so remitted the deposit shall be held in a special account at the place of adjustment in the name of the adjuster pending settlement of the General Average and refunds or credit balances, if any, shall be paid in United States money.

In the event of accident, danger, damage, or disaster, before or after commencement of the voyage resulting from any cause whatsoever, whether due to negligence or not, for which, or for the consequence of which, the carrier is not responsible, by statute, contract, or otherwise, the goods, the shipper and the consignee, jointly and severally, shall contribute with the carrier in general average to the payment of any sacrifices, losses, or expenses of a general average nature that may be made or incurred, and shall pay salvage and special charges incurred in respect of the goods. If a salving ship is owned or operated by the carrier, salvage shall be paid for as fully and in the same manner as if such salving ship or ships belonged to strangers.

Provisions as to General Average in accordance with the above are to be included in all bills of lading issued hereunder.

20. Fuel used by the vessel while off hire, also for cooking, condensing water, or for grates and stoves to be agreed to as to quantity, and the cost of replacing same, to be allowed by Owners.

21. That as the vessel may be from time to time employed in tropical waters during the term of this Charter, Vessel is to be docked at a

convenient place, bottom cleaned and painted whenever Charterers and Captain think necessary, at least once in every six months, reckoning from time of last painting, and payment of the hire to be suspended until she is again in proper state for the service.

....

....

22. Owners shall maintain the gear of the ship as fitted, providing gear (for all derricks) capable of handling lifts up to three tons, also providing ropes, falls, slings and blocks. If vessel is fitted with derricks capable of handling heavier lifts, Owners are to provide necessary gear for same, otherwise equipment and gear for heavier lifts shall be for Charterers' account. Owners also to provide on the vessel lanterns and oil for night work, and vessel to give use of electric light when so fitted, but any additional lights over those on board to be at Charterers' expense. The Charterers to have the use of any gear on board the vessel.

23. Vessel to work night and day, if required by Charterers, and all winches to be at Charterers' disposal during loading and discharging; steamer to provide one winchman per hatch to work winches day and night, as required, Charterers agreeing to pay officers, engineers, winchmen, deck hands and donkeymen for overtime work done in accordance with the working hours and rates stated in the ship's articles. If the rules of the port, or labor unions, prevent crew from driving winches, shore Winchmen to be paid by Charterers. In the event of a disabled winch or winches, or insufficient power to operate winches, Owners to pay for shore engine, or engines, in lieu thereof, if required, and pay any loss of time occasioned thereby.

24. It is also mutually agreed that this Charter is subject to all the terms and provisions of and all the exemptions from liability contained in the Act of Congress of the United States approved on the 13th day of February, 1893, and entitled "An Act relating to Navigation of Vessels; etc.," in respect of all cargo shipped under this charter to or from the United States of America. It is further subject to the following clauses, both of which are to be included in all bills of lading issued hereunder:

U. S. A. Clause Paramount

This bill of lading shall have effect subject to the provisions of the Carriage of Goods by Sea Act of the United States, approved April 16, 1936, which shall be deemed to be incorporated herein, and nothing herein contained shall be deemed a surrender by the carrier of any of its rights or immunities or an increase of any of its responsibilities or liabilities under said Act. If any term of this bill of lading be repugnant to said Act to any extent, such term shall be void to that extent, but no further.

Both-to-Blame Collision Clause

If the ship comes into collision with another ship as a result of the negligence of the other ship and any act, neglect or default of the Master, mariner, pilot or the servants of the Carrier in the navigation or in the management of the ship, the owners of the goods carried hereunder will indemnify the Carrier against all loss or liability to the other or non-carrying ship or her owners in so far as such loss or liability represents loss of, or damage to, or any claim whatsoever of the owners of said goods, paid or payable by the other or non-carrying ship or her owners to the owners of said goods and set off, recouped or recovered by the other or non-carrying ship or her owners as part of their claim against the carrying ship or carrier.

25. The vessel shall not be required to enter any ice-bound port, or any port where lights or light-ships have been or are about to be withdrawn by reason of ice, or where there is risk that in the ordinary course of things the vessel will not be able on account of ice to safely enter the port or to get out after having completed loading or discharging.

26. Nothing herein stated is to be construed as a demise of the vessel to the Time Charterers. The owners to remain responsible for the navigation of the vessel, insurance, crew, and all other matters, same as when trading for their own account.

27. A commission of 2 1/2 per cent is payable by the Vessel and Owners to

....

on hire earned and paid under this Charter, and also upon any continuation or extension of this Charter.

28. An address commission of 2 1/2 per cent payable to .... on the hire earned and paid under this Charter.

Code Name: **"NYPE 93"**
Recommended by:
The Baltic and International Maritime Council(BIMCO)
The Federation of National Associations of
Ship Brokers and Agents (FONASBA)

TIME CHARTER©

New York Produce Exchange Form
Issued by the Association of Ship Brokers and Agents (U.S.A.), Inc.

November 6th, 1913 - Amended October 20th, 1921; August 6th, 1931; October 3rd, 1946;
Revised June 12th, 1981; September 14th 1993.

THIS CHARTER PARTY, made and concluded in ....
this .... day of .... 19 ....

Between ....
....
Owners of the Vessel described below, and ....
....
....
Charterers.

Description of Vessel

Name .... Flag .... Built .... (year).
Port and number of Registry ....
Classed .... in ....
Deadweight ....long*/metric* tons (cargo and bunkers, including freshwater and stores not exceeding .... long*/metric* tons) on a salt water draft of .... on summer freeboard.
Capacity .... cubic feet grain .... cubic feet bale space.
Tonnage .... GT/GRT.
Speed about .... knots, fully laden, in good weather conditions up to and including maximum Force .... on the Beaufort wind scale, on a consumption of about .... long*/metric* tons of ....

** Delete as appropriate.*
For further description see Appendix "A" (if applicable)

1. Duration

The Owners agree to let and the Charterers agree to hire the Vessel from the time of delivery for a period of ....
....
....
.... within below mentioned trading limits.

2. Delivery

The Vessel shall be placed at the disposal of the Charterers at ....
....
....
.... The Vessel on her delivery shall be ready to receive cargo with clean-swept holds and tight, staunch, strong and in every way fitted for ordinary cargo service, having water ballast and with sufficient power to operate all cargo-handling gear simultaneously.

The Owners shall give the Charterers not less than .... days notice of expected date of delivery.

3. On-Off Hire Survey

Prior to delivery and redelivery the parties shall, unless otherwise agreed, each appoint surveyors, for their respective accounts, who shall not later than at first loading port/last discharging port respectively, conduct joint on-hire/off-hire surveys, for the purpose of ascertaining quantity of bunkers on board and the condition of the Vessel. A single report shall be prepared on each occasion and signed by each surveyor, without prejudice to his right to file a separate report setting forth items upon which the surveyors cannot agree. If either party fails to have a representative attend the survey and sign the joint survey report, such party shall nevertheless be bound for all purposes by the findings in any report prepared by the other party. On-hire survey shall be on Charterers' time and off-hire survey on Owners' time.

4. Dangerous Cargo/Cargo Exclusions

(a) The Vessel shall be employed in carrying lawful merchandise excluding any goods of a dangerous, injurious, flammable or corrosive nature unless carried in accordance with the requirements or recommendations of the competent authorities of the country of the Vessel's registry and of ports of shipment and discharge and of any intermediate countries or ports through whose waters the Vessel must pass. Without prejudice to the generality of the foregoing, in addition the following are specifically excluded: livestock of any description, arms, ammunition, explosives, nuclear and radioactive materials,
....
....
....
....
....
....
....
....
....
....

(b) If IMO-classified cargo is agreed to be carried, the amount of such cargo shall be limited to .... tons and the Charterers shall provide the Master with any evidence he may reasonably require to show that the cargo is packaged, labelled, loaded and stowed in accordance with IMO regulations, failing which the Master is entitled to refuse such cargo or, if already loaded, to unload it at the Charterers' risk and expense.

5. Trading Limits

The Vessel shall be employed in such lawful trades between safe ports and safe places within ....
.... excluding
....
....
.... as the Charterers shall direct.

6. Owners to Provide

The Owners shall provide and pay for the insurance of the Vessel, except as otherwise provided, and for all provisions, cabin, deck, engine-room and other necessary stores, including boiler water; shall pay for wages, consular shipping and discharging fees of the crew and charges for port services pertaining to the crew; shall maintain the Vessel's class and keep her in a thoroughly efficient state in hull, machinery and equipment for and during the service, and have a full complement of officers and crew.

7. Charterers to Provide

The Charterers, while the Vessel is on hire, shall provide and pay for all the bunkers except as otherwise agreed; shall pay for port charges (including compulsory watchmen and cargo watchmen and compulsory garbage disposal), all communication expenses pertaining to the Charterers' business at cost, pilotages, towages, agencies, commissions, consular charges (except those pertaining to individual crew members or flag of the Vessel), and all other usual expenses except those stated in Clause 6, but when the Vessel puts into a port for causes for which the Vessel is responsible (other than by stress of weather), then all such charges incurred shall be paid by the Owners. Fumigations ordered because of illness of the crew shall be for the Owners' account. Fumigations ordered because of cargoes carried or ports visited while the Vessel is employed under this Charter Party shall be for the Charterers' account. All other fumigations shall be for the Charterers' account after the Vessel has been on charter for a continuous period of six months or more.

The Charterers shall provide and pay for necessary dunnage and also any extra fittings requisite for a special trade or unusual cargo, but the Owners shall allow them the use of any dunnage already aboard the Vessel. Prior to redelivery the Charterers shall remove their dunnage and fittings at their cost and in their time.

8. Performance of Voyages

(a) The Master shall perform the voyages with due despatch, and shall render all customary assistance with the Vessel's crew. The Master shall be conversant with the English language and (although appointed by the Owners) shall be under the orders and directions of the Charterers as regards employment and agency; and the Charterers shall perform all cargo handling, including but not limited to loading, stowing, trimming, lashing, securing, dunnaging, unlashing, discharging, and tallying, at their risk and expense, under the supervision of the Master.

(b) If the Charterers shall have reasonable cause to be dissatisfied with the conduct of the Master or officers, the Owners shall, on receiving particulars of the complaint, investigate the same, and, if necessary, make a change in the appointments.

9. Bunkers

(a) The Charterers on delivery, and the Owners on redelivery, shall take over and pay for all fuel and diesel oil remaining on board the Vessel as hereunder. The Vessel shall be delivered with: .... long*/metric* tons of fuel oil at the price of .... per ton; .... tons of diesel oil at the price of .... per ton. The vessel shall be redelivered with: .... tons of fuel oil at the price of .... per ton; .... tons of diesel oil at the price of .... per ton.

** Same tons apply throughout this clause.*

(b) The Charterers shall supply bunkers of a quality suitable for burning in the Vessel's engines and auxiliaries and which conform to the specification(s) as set out in Appendix A.

The Owners reserve their right to make a claim against the Charterers for any damage to the main engines or the auxiliaries caused by the use of unsuitable fuels or fuels not complying with the agreed specification(s). Additionally, if bunker fuels supplied do not conform with the mutually agreed specification(s) or otherwise prove unsuitable for burning in the Vessel's engines or auxiliaries, the Owners shall not be held responsible for any reduction in the Vessel's speed performance and/or increased bunker consumption, nor for any time lost and any other consequences.

10. Rate of Hire/Redelivery Areas and Notices

The Charterers shall pay for the use and hire of the said Vessel at the rate of $ .... U.S. currency, daily, **or** $ .... U.S. currency per ton on the Vessel's total deadweight carrying capacity, including bunkers and stores, on .... summer freeboard, per 30 days, commencing on and from the day of her delivery, as aforesaid, and at and after the same rate for any part of a month; hire shall continue until the hour of the day of her redelivery in like good order and condition, ordinary wear and tear excepted, to the Owners (unless Vessel lost) at .... unless otherwise mutually agreed.

The Charterers shall give the Owners not less than .... days notice of the Vessel's expected date and probable port of redelivery.

For the purpose of hire calculations, the times of delivery, redelivery or termination of charter shall be adjusted to GMT.

11. Hire Payment

(a) *Payment*

Payment of Hire shall be made so as to be received by the Owners or their designated payee in ...., viz .... in .... currency, or in United States Currency, in funds available to the Owners on the due date, 15 days in advance, and for the last month or part of same the approximate amount of hire, and should same not cover the actual time, hire shall be paid for the balance day by day as it becomes due, if so required by the Owners. Failing the punctual and regular payment of the hire, or on any fundamental breach whatsoever of this Charter Party, the Owners shall be at liberty to withdraw the Vessel from the service of the Charterers without prejudice to any claims they (the Owners) may otherwise have on the Charterers.

At any time after the expiry of the grace period provided in Sub-clause 11 (b) hereunder and while the hire is outstanding, the Owners shall, without prejudice to the liberty to withdraw, be entitled to withhold the performance of any and all of their obligations hereunder and shall have no responsibility whatsoever for any consequences thereof, in respect of which the Charterers hereby indemnify the Owners, and hire shall continue to accrue and any extra expenses resulting from such withholding shall be for the Charterers' account.

(b) *Grace Period*

Where there is failure to make punctual and regular payment of hire due to oversight, negligence, errors or omissions on the part of the Charterers or their bankers, the Charterers shall be given by the Owners .... clear banking days (as recognized at the agreed place of payment) written notice to rectify the failure, and when so rectified within those .... days following the Owners' notice, the payment shall stand as regular and punctual.

Failure by the Charterers to pay the hire within .... days of their receiving the Owners' notice as provided herein, shall entitle the Owners to withdraw as set forth in Sub-clause 11 (a) above.

(c) *Last Hire Payment*

Should the Vessel be on her voyage towards port of redelivery at the time the last and/or the penultimate payment of hire is/are due, said payment(s) is/are to be made for such length of time as the Owners and the Charterers may agree upon as being the estimated time necessary to complete the voyage, and taking into account bunkers actually on board, to be taken over by the Owners and estimated disbursements for the Owners' account before redelivery. Should same not cover the actual time, hire is to be paid for the balance, day by day, as it becomes due. When the Vessel has been redelivered, any difference is to be refunded by the Owners or paid by the Charterers, as the case may be.

(d) *Cash Advances*

Cash for the Vessel's ordinary disbursements at any port may be advanced by the Charterers, as required by the Owners, subject to 2 1/2 percent commission and such advances shall be deducted from the hire. The Charterers, however, shall in no way be responsible for the application of such advances.

12. Berths

The Vessel shall be loaded and discharged in any safe dock or at any safe berth or safe place that Charterers or their agents may direct, provided the Vessel can safely enter, lie and depart always afloat at any time of tide.

13. Spaces Available

(a) The whole reach of the Vessel's holds, decks, and other cargo spaces (not more than she can reasonably and safely stow and carry), also accommodations for supercargo, if carried, shall be at the Charterers' disposal, reserving only proper and sufficient space for the Vessel's officers, crew, tackle, apparel, furniture, provisions, stores and fuel.

(b) In the event of deck cargo being carried, the Owners are to be and are hereby indemnified by the Charterers for any loss and/or damage and/or liability of whatsoever nature caused to the Vessel as a result of the carriage of deck cargo and which would not have arisen had deck cargo not been loaded.

14. Supercargo and Meals

The Charterers are entitled to appoint a supercargo, who shall accompany the Vessel at the Charterers' risk and see that voyages are performed with due despatch. He is to be furnished with free accommodation and same fare as provided for the Master's table, the Charterers paying at the rate of .... per day. The Owners shall victual pilots and customs officers, and also, when authorized by the Charterers or their agents, shall victual tally clerks, stevedore's foreman, etc., Charterers paying at the rate of .... per meal for all such victualling.

15. Sailing Orders and Logs

The Charterers shall furnish the Master from time to time with all requisite instructions and sailing directions, in writing, in the Enqlish language, and the Master shall keep full and correct deck and engine logs of the voyage or voyages, which are to be patent to the Charterers or their agents, and furnish the Charterers, their agents or supercargo, when required, with a true copy of such deck and engine logs, showing the course of the Vessel, distance run and the consumption of bunkers. Any log extracts required by the Charterers shall be in the English language.

16. Delivery/Cancelling

If required by the Charterers, time shall not commence before .... and should the Vessel not be ready for delivery on or before .... but not later than .... hours, the Charterers shall have the option of cancelling this Charter Party.

Extension of Cancelling

If the Owners warrant that, despite the exercise of due diligence by them, the Vessel will not be ready for delivery by the cancelling date, and provided the Owners are able to state with reasonable certainty the date on which the Vessel will be ready, they may, at the earliest seven days before the Vessel is expected to sail for the port or place of delivery, require the Charterers to declare whether or not they will cancel the Charter Party. Should the Charterers elect not to cancel, or should they fail to reply within two days or by the cancelling date, whichever shall first occur, then the seventh day after the expected date of readiness for delivery as notified by the Owners shall replace the original cancelling date. Should the Vessel be further delayed, the Owners shall be entitled to require further declarations of the Charterers in accordance with this Clause.

17. Off Hire

In the event of loss of time from deficiency and/or default and/or strike of officers or crew, or deficiency of stores, fire, breakdown of, or damages to hull, machinery or equipment, grounding, detention by the arrest of the Vessel, (unless such arrest is caused by events for which the Charterers, their servants, agents or subcontractors are responsible), or detention by average accidents to the Vessel or cargo unless resulting from inherent vice, quality or defect of the cargo, drydocking for the purpose of examination or painting bottom, or by any other similar cause preventing the full working of the Vessel, the payment of hire and overtime, if any, shall cease for the time thereby lost. Should the Vessel deviate or put back during a voyage, contrary to the orders or directions of the Charterers, for any reason other than accident to the cargo or where permitted in lines 257 to 258 hereunder, the hire is to be suspended from the time of her deviating or putting back until she is again in the same or equidistant position from the destination and the voyage resumed therefrom. All bunkers used by the Vessel while off hire shall be for the Owners' account. In the event of the Vessel being driven into port or to anchorage through stress of weather, trading to shallow harbors or to rivers or ports with bars, any detention of the Vessel and/or expenses resulting from such detention shall be for the Charterers' account. If upon the voyage the speed be reduced by defect in, or breakdown of, any part of her hull, machinery or equipment, the time so lost, and the cost of any extra bunkers consumed in consequence thereof, and all extra proven expenses may be deducted from the hire.

18. Sublet

Unless otherwise agreed, the Charterers shall have the liberty to sublet the Vessel for all or any part of the time covered by this Charter Party, but the Charterers remain responsible for the fulfillment of this Charter Party.

19. Drydocking

The Vessel was last drydocked ....

*(a) The Owners shall have the option to place the Vessel in drydock during the currency of this Charter at a convenient time and place, to be mutually agreed upon between the Owners and the Charterers, for bottom cleaning and painting and/or repair as required by class or dictated by circumstances.

*(b) Except in case of emergency no drydocking shall take place during the currency of this Charter Party.

** Delete as appropriate*

20. Total Loss

Should the Vessel be lost, money paid in advance and not earned (reckoning from the date of loss or being last heard of) shall be returned to the Charterers at once.

21. Exceptions

The act of God, enemies, fire, restraint of princes, rulers and people, and all dangers and accidents of the seas, rivers, machinery, boilers, and navigation, and errors of navigation throughout this Charter, always mutually excepted.

22. Liberties

The Vessel shall have the liberty to sail with or without pilots, to tow and to be towed, to assist vessels in distress, and to deviate for the purpose of saving life and property.

23. Liens

The Owners shall have a lien upon all cargoes and all sub-freights and/or sub-hire for any amounts due under this Charter Party, including general average contributions, and the Charterers shall have a lien on the Vessel for all monies paid in advance and not earned, and any overpaid hire or excess deposit to be returned at once.

The Charterers will not directly or indirectly suffer, nor permit to be continued, any lien or encumbrance, which might have priority over the title and interest of the Owners in the Vessel. The Charterers undertake that during the period of this Charter Party, they will not procure any supplies or necessaries or services, including any port expenses and bunkers, on the credit of the Owners or in the Owners' time.

24. Salvage

All derelicts and salvage shall be for the Owners' and the Charterers' equal benefit after deducting Owners' and Charterers' expenses and crew's proportion.

25. General Average

General average shall be adjusted according to York-Antwerp Rules 1974, as amended 1990, or any subsequent modification thereof, in .... and settled in .... currency.

The Charterers shall procure that all bills of lading issued during the currency of the Charter Party will contain a provision to the effect that general average shall be adjusted according to York-Antwerp Rules 1974, as amended 1990, or any subsequent modification thereof and will include the "New Jason Clause" as per Clause 31.

Time charter hire shall not contribute to general average.

26. Navigation

Nothing herein stated is to be construed as a demise of the Vessel to the Time Charterers. The Owners shall remain responsible for the navigation of the Vessel, acts of pilots and tug boats, insurance, crew, and all other matters, same as when trading for their own account.

27. Cargo Claims

Cargo claims as between the Owners and the Charterers shall be settled in accordance with the Inter-Club New York Produce Exchange Agreement of February 1970, as amended May, 1984, or any subsequent modification or replacement thereof.

28. Cargo Gear and Lights

The Owners shall maintain the cargo handling gear of the Vessel which is as follows: ....
....
....
....
providing gear (for all derricks or cranes) capable of lifting capacity as described. The Owners shall also provide on the Vessel for night work lights as on board, but all additional lights over those on board shall be at the Charterers' expense. The Charterers shall have the use of any gear on board the Vessel. If required by the Charterers, the Vessel shall work night and day and all cargo handling gear shall be at the Charterers' disposal during loading and discharging. In the event of disabled cargo handling gear, or insufficient power to operate the same, the Vessel is to be considered to be off hire to the extent that time is actually lost to the Charterers and the Owners to pay stevedore stand-by charges occasioned thereby, unless such disablement or insufficiency of power is caused by the Charterers' stevedores. If required by the Charterers, the Owners shall bear the cost of hiring shore gear in lieu thereof, in which case the Vessel shall remain on hire.

29. Crew Overtime

In lieu of any overtime payments to officers and crew for work ordered by the Charterers or their agents, the Charterers shall pay the Owners, concurrently with the hire .... per month or pro rata.

30. Bills of Lading

(a) The Master shall sign the bills of lading or waybills for cargo as presented in conformity with mates or tally clerk's receipts. However, the Charterers may sign bills of lading or waybills on behalf of the Master, with the Owner's prior written authority, always in conformity with mates or tally clerk's receipts.

(b) All bills of lading or waybills shall be without prejudice to this Charter Party and the Charterers shall indemnify the Owners against all consequences or liabilities which may arise from any inconsistency between this Charter Party and any bills of lading or waybills signed by the Charterers or by the Master at their request.

(c) Bills of lading covering deck cargo shall be claused: "Shipped on deck at Charterers', Shippers' and Receivers' risk, expense and responsibility, without liability on the part of the Vessel, or her Owners for any loss, damage, expense or delay howsoever caused."

31. Protective Clauses

This Charter Party is subject to the following clauses all of which are also to be included in all bills of lading or waybills issued hereunder:

(a) CLAUSE PARAMOUNT
"This bill of lading shall have effect subject to the provisions of the Carriage of Goods by Sea Act of the United States, the Hague Rules, or the Hague-Visby Rules, as applicable, or such other similar national legislation as may mandatorily apply by virtue of origin or destination of the bills of lading, which shall be deemed to be incorporated herein and nothing herein contained shall be deemed a surrender by the carrier of any of its rights or immunities or an increase of any of its responsibilities or liabilities under said applicable Act. If any term of this bill of lading be repugnant to said applicable Act to any extent, such term shall be void to that extent, but no further."

and

(b) BOTH-TO-BLAME COLLISION CLAUSE
"If the ship comes into collision with another ship as a result of the negligence of the other ship and any act, neglect or default of the master, mariner, pilot or the servants of the carrier in the navigation or in the management of the ship, the owners of the goods carried hereunder will indemnify the carrier against all loss or liability to the other or non-carrying ship or her owners insofar as such loss or liability represents loss of, or damage to, or any claim whatsoever of the owners of said goods, paid or payable by the other or non-carrying ship or her owners to the owners of said goods and set off, recouped or recovered by the other or non-carrying ship or her owners as part of their claim against the carrying ship or carrier.

The foregoing provisions shall also apply where the owners, operators or those in charge of any ships or objects other than, or in addition to, the colliding ships or objects are at fault in respect to a collision or contact."

and

(c) NEW JASON CLAUSE
"In the event of accident, danger, damage or disaster before or after the commencement of the voyage resulting from any cause whatsoever, whether due to negligence or not, for which, or for the consequences of which, the carrier is not responsible, by statute, contract, or otherwise, the goods, shippers, consignees, or owners of the goods shall contribute with the carrier in general average to the payment of any sacrifices, losses, or expenses of a general average nature that may be made or incurred, and shall pay salvage and special charges incurred in respect of the goods.

If a salving ship is owned or operated by the carrier, salvage shall be paid for as fully as if salving ship or ships belonged to strangers. Such deposit as the carrier or his agents may deem sufficient to cover the estimated contribution of the goods and any salvage and special charges thereon shall, if required, be made by the goods, shippers, consignees or owners of the goods to the carrier before delivery."

and

(d) U.S. TRADE - DRUG CLAUSE
"In pursuance of the provisions of the U.S. Anti Drug Abuse Act 1986 or any re-enactment thereof, the Charterers warrant to exercise the highest degree of care and diligence in preventing unmanifested narcotic drugs and marijuana to be loaded or concealed on board the Vessel.

Non-compliance with the provisions of this clause shall amount to breach of warranty for consequences of which the Charterers shall be liable and shall hold the Owners, the Master and the crew of the Vessel harmless and shall keep them indemnified against all claims whatsoever which may arise and be made against them individually or jointly. Furthermore, all time lost and all expenses incurred, including fines, as a result of the Charterers' breach of the provisions of this clause shall be for the Charterer's account and the Vessel shall remain on hire.

Should the Vessel be arrested as a result of the Charterers' non-compliance with the provisions of this clause, the Charterers shall at their expense take all reasonable steps to secure that within a reasonable time the Vessel is released and at their expense put up the bails to secure release of the Vessel.

The Owners shall remain responsible for all time lost and all expenses incurred, including fines, in the event that unmanifested narcotic drugs and marijuana are found in the possession or effects of the Vessel's personnel."

and

(e) WAR CLAUSES

"(i) No contraband of war shall be shipped. The Vessel shall not be required, without the consent of the Owners, which shall not be unreasonably withheld, to enter any port or zone which is involved in a state of war, warlike operations, or hostilities, civil strife, insurrection or piracy whether there be a declaration of war or not, where the Vessel, cargo or crew might reasonably be expected to be subject to capture, seizure or arrest, or to a hostile act by a belligerent power (the term "power" meaning any de jure or de facto authority or any purported governmental organization maintaining naval, military or air forces).

(ii) If such consent is given by the Owners, the Charterers will pay the provable additional cost of insuring the Vessel against hull war risks in an amount equal to the value under her ordinary hull policy but not exceeding a valuation of .... In addition, the Owners may purchase and the Charterers will pay for war risk insurance on ancillary risks such as loss of hire, freight disbursements, total loss, blocking and trapping, etc. If such insurance is not obtainable commercially or through a government program, the Vessel shall not be required to enter or remain at any such port or zone.

(iii) In the event of the existence of the conditions described in (i) subsequent to the date of this Charter, or while the Vessel is on hire under this Charter, the Charterers shall, in respect of voyages to any such port or zone assume the provable additional cost of wages and insurance properly incurred in connection with master, officers and crew as a consequence of such war, warlike operations or hostilities.

(iv) Any war bonus to officers and crew due to the Vessel's trading or cargo carried shall be for the Charterers' account."

32. War Cancellation

In the event of the outbreak of war (whether there be a declaration of war or not) between any two or more of the following countries: ....
....
....
....
either the Owners or the Charterers may cancel this Charter Party. Whereupon, the Charterers shall redeliver the Vessel to the Owners in accordance with Clause 10; if she has cargo on board, after discharge thereof at destination, or, if debarred under this Clause from reaching or entering it, at a near open and safe port as directed by the Owners; or, if she has no cargo on board, at the port at which she then is; or, if at sea, at a near open and safe port as directed by the Owners. In all cases hire shall continue to be paid in accordance with Clause 11 and except as aforesaid all other provisions of this Charter Party shall apply until redelivery.

33. Ice

The Vessel shall not be required to enter or remain in any icebound port or area, nor any port or area where lights or lightships have been or are about to be withdrawn by reason of ice, nor where there is risk that in the ordinary course of things the Vessel will not be able on account of ice to safely enter and remain in the port or area or to get out after having completed loading or discharging. Subject to the Owners' prior approval the Vessel is to follow ice-breakers when reasonably required with regard to her size, construction and ice class.

34. Requisition

Should the Vessel be requisitioned by the government of the Vessel's flag during the period of this Charter Party, the Vessel shall be deemed to be off hire during the period of such requisition, and any hire paid by the said government in respect of such requisition period shall be retained by the Owners. The period during which the Vessel is on requisition to the said government shall count as part of the period provided for in this Charter Party.

If the period of requisition exceeds .... months, either party shall have the option of cancelling this Charter Party and no consequential claim may be made by either party.

35. Stevedore Damage

Notwithstanding anything contained herein to the contrary, the Charterers shall pay for any and all damage to the Vessel caused by stevedores provided the Master has notified the Charterers and/or their agents in writing as soon as practical but not later than 48 hours after any damage is discovered. Such notice to specify the damage in detail and to invite Charterers to appoint a surveyor to assess the extent of such damage.

(a) In case of any and all damage(s) affecting the Vessel's seaworthiness and/or the safety of the crew and/or affecting the trading capabilities of the Vessel, the Charterers shall immediately arrange for repairs of such damage(s) at their expense and the Vessel is to remain on hire until such repairs are completed and if required passed by the Vessel's classification society.

(b) Any and all damage(s) not described under point (a) above shall be repaired at the Charterers' option, before or after redelivery concurrently with the Owners' work. In such case no hire and/or expenses will be paid to the Owners except and insofar as the time and/or the expenses required for the repairs for which the Charterers are responsible, exceed the time and/or expenses necessary to carry out the Owners' work.

36. Cleaning of Holds

The Charterers shall provide and pay extra for sweeping and/or washing and/or cleaning of holds between voyages and/or between cargoes provided such work can be undertaken by the crew and is permitted by local regulations, at the rate of .... per hold.

In connection with any such operation, the Owners shall not be responsible if the Vessel's holds are not accepted or passed by the port or any other authority. The Charterers shall have the option to re-deliver the Vessel with unclean/unswept holds against a lumpsum payment of .... in lieu of cleaning.

37. Taxes

Charterers to pay all local, State, National taxes and/or dues assessed on the Vessel or the Owners resulting from the Charterers' orders herein, whether assessed during or after the currency of this Charter Party including any taxes and/or dues on cargo and/or freights and/or sub-freights and/or hire (excluding taxes levied by the country of the flag of the Vessel or the Owners).

38. Charterers' Colors

The Charterers shall have the privilege of flying their own house flag and painting the Vessel with their own markings. The Vessel shall be repainted in the Owners' colors before termination of the Charter Party. Cost and time of painting, maintaining and repainting those changes effected by the Charterers shall be for Charterers' account.

39. Laid Up Returns

The Charterers shall have the benefit of any return insurance premium receivable by the Owners from their underwriters as and when received from underwriters by reason of the Vessel being in port for a minimum period of 30 days if on full hire for this period or pro rata for the time actually on hire.

40. Documentation

The Owners shall provide any documentation relating to the Vessel that may be required to permit the Vessel to trade within the agreed trade limits, including, but not limited to certificates of financial responsibility for oil pollution, provided such oil pollution certificates are obtainable from the Owners' P & I club, valid international tonnage certificate, Suez and Panama tonnage certificates, valid certificate of registry and certificates relating to the strength and/or serviceability of the Vessel's gear.

41. Stowaways

(a) (i) The Charterers warrant to exercise due care and diligence in preventing stowaways in gaining access to the Vessel by means of secreting away in the goods and/or containers shipped by the Charterers.

(ii) If, despite the exercise of due care and diligence by the Charterers, stowaways have gained access to the Vessel by means of secreting away in the goods and/or containers shipped by the Charterers, this shall amount to breach of charter for the consequences of which the Charterers shall be liable and shall hold the Owners harmless and shall keep them indemnified against all claims whatsoever which may arise and be made against them. Furthermore, all time lost and all expenses whatsoever and howsoever incurred, including fines, shall be for the Charterers' account and the Vessel shall remain on hire.

(iii) Should the Vessel be arrested as a result of the Charterers' breach of charter according to sub-clause (a)(ii) above, the Charterers shall take all reasonable steps to secure that, within a reasonable time, the Vessel is released and at their expense put up bail to secure release of the Vessel.

(b) (i) If, despite the exercise of due care and diligence by the Owners, stowaways have gained access to the Vessel by means other than secreting away in the goods and/or containers shipped by the Charterers, all time lost and all expenses whatsoever and howsoever incurred, including fines, shall be for the Owners' account and the Vessel shall be off hire.

(ii) Should the Vessel be arrested as a result of stowaways having gained access to the Vessel by means other than secreting away in the goods and/or containers shipped by the Charterers, the Owners shall take all reasonable steps to secure that, within a reasonable time, the Vessel is released and at their expense put up bail to secure release of the Vessel.

42. Smuggling

In the event of smuggling by the Master, Officers and/or crew, the Owners shall bear the cost of any fines, taxes, or imposts levied and the Vessel shall be off hire for any time lost as a result thereof.

43. Commissions

A commission of .... percent is payable by the Vessel and the Owners to ....
....
....
....
on hire earned and paid under this Charter, and also upon any continuation or extension of this Charter.

44. Address Commission

An address commission of .... percent is payable to ....
....
....
.... on hire earned and paid under this Charter.

45. Arbitration

(a) NEW YORK
All disputes arising out of this contract shall be arbitrated at New York in the following manner, and subject to U.S. Law:

One Arbitrator is to be appointed by each of the parties hereto and a third by the two so chosen. Their decision or that of any two of them shall be final, and for the purpose of enforcing any award, this agreement may be made a rule of the court. The Arbitrators shall be commercial men, conversant with shipping matters. Such Arbitration is to be conducted in accordance with the rules of the Society of Maritime Arbitrators Inc.

For disputes where the total amount claimed by either party does not exceed US $ ....**

the arbitration shall be conducted in accordance with the Shortened Arbitration Procedure of the Society of Maritime Arbitrators Inc.

(b) LONDON

All disputes arising out of this contract shall be arbitrated at London and, unless the parties agree forthwith on a single Arbitrator, be referred to the final arbitrament of two Arbitrators carrying on business in London who shall be members of the Baltic Mercantile & Shipping Exchange and engaged in Shipping, one to be appointed by each of the parties, with power to such Arbitrators to appoint an Umpire. No award shall be questioned or invalidated on the ground that any of the Arbitrators is not qualified as above, unless objection to his action be taken before the award is made. Any dispute arising hereunder shall be governed by English Law.

For disputes where the total amount claimed by either party does not exceed US $ ....** the arbitration shall be conducted in accordance with the Small Claims Procedure of the London Maritime Arbitrators Association.

** Delete para (a) or (b) as appropriate*

*** Where no figure is supplied in the blank space this provision only shall be void but the other provisions of this clause shall have full force and remain in effect.*

If mutually agreed, clauses .... to ...., both inclusive, as attached hereto are fully incorporated in this Charter Party.

APPENDIX "A"

To Charter Party dated ……………………………………………………………………
Between …………………………………………………………………… Owners
and …………………………………………………………………… Charterers

Further details of the Vessel: ……………………………………………………………………
……………………………………………………………………

Ship Brokers	THE BALTIC AND INTERNATIONAL MARITIME COUNCIL (BIMCO) GENERAL TIME CHARTER PARTY CODE NAME: "GENTIME" PART I
	1. Place and Date of Charter
2. Owners/Disponent Owners/Place of business (State full name, address, telex and fax. No.)	3. Charterers/Place of business (State full name, address, telex and fax. No.)
4. Vessel's Name	5. Vessel's Description Flag: Year Built: Class: M/tons Deadweight (Summer): GT/NT: Grain/Bale Capacity: Speed capability in knots (about): Consumption in m/tons at above speed (about): (Speed and Consumption on Summer dwt in good weather, max. windspeed 4Bft)
6. Period of Charter (Cl. 1(a))	
6(a). Margin on Final Period (Cl. 1(a))	
7. Optional Period and Notice (Cl. 1(a))	
8. Delivery Port/Place or Range (Cl. 1(b))	
9. Earliest Delivery Date/Time (Cl. 1(c)) / 10. Cancellation Date/Time (Cl. 1(c)(d))	
11. Notices of Delivery (Cl. 1(e)) / 12. Intended First Cargo (Cl. 1(f))	
13. Trading Limits and Excluded Countries (Cl. 2(a))	
14. Excepted Countries (Cl. 2(b))	

(continued overleaf)

15. Excluded Cargoes (Cl. 3(b))			
16. Hazardous Cargo Limit (Cl. 3(c))	17. Redelivery Port/Place or Range (Cl. 4(a))		18. Notices of Redelivery (Cl. 4(c))
19. Fuel Quantity on Delivery (Cl.6(a))	20. Fuel Quantity on Redelivery (Cl. 6(a))	21. Fuel Price on Delivery (Cl. 6(c))	22. Fuel Price on Redelivery (Cl. 6(c))
23. Fuel Specifications (Cl. 6(d))			
24. Hire (Cl. 8(a))	25. Owner's Bank Account (Cl.8(b))		
26. Grace Period (Cl. 8 (c))	27. Max. Period for Requisition (Cl. 9(c))	28. General Average Adjustment (Cl. 14(b))	
29. Supercargo (Cl. 15(f))	30. Victualling (Cl. 15(g))	31. Representation (Cl. 15(h))	32. Hold Cleaning by Crew (Cl. 15(m))
33. Lumpsum for Hold Cleaning on Redelivery (Cl. 15 (m))		34. Vessel's Insured Value (Cl. 20 (a))	
35. Law and Arbitration (state Cl. 22(a), 22(b) or 22(c) of Cl. 22 as agreed; if 22(c) agreed, place of arbitration must be stated (Cl. 22))		36. Commission and to whom payable (Cl. 23)	
37. Additional Clauses			

It is agreed that this Contract shall be performed subject to the conditions contained in this Charter Party consisting of PART I including any additional clauses agreed and stated in Box 37 and PART II as well as Appendix A attached thereto. In the event of any conflict of conditions, the provisions of PART I and Appendix A shall prevail over those of PART II to the extent of such conflict but no further.

Signature (Owners)	Signature (Charterers)

Printed and sold by Fr. G. Knudtzons Bogtrykkeri A/S, Vallensbaekvej 61, DK-2625 Vallensbaek. Fax: +45 4366 0708

"GENTIME" - General Time Charter Party
Index

PART II
"GENTIME" General Time Charter Party

It is agreed on the date shown in Box 1 between the party named in Box 2 as Owners/ Disponent Owners (hereinafter called "the Owners") of the Vessel named in Box 4, of the description stated in Box 5 and the party named in Box 3 as Charterers as follows:

1. Period and Delivery

(a) *Period* - In consideration of the hire stated in Box 24 the Owners let and the Charterers hire the Vessel for the period/trip(s) stated in Box 6.
The Charterers shall have the option to extend the Charter Party by the period(s)/ trip(s) stated in Box 7 which option shall be exercised by giving written notice to the Owners on or before the date(s) stated in Box 7.
Unless otherwise agreed, the Charterers shall have the option to increase or to reduce the final period of the Charter Party by up to the number of days stated in Box 6(a), which shall be applied only to the period finally declared.

(b) *Delivery Place* - The Owners shall deliver the Vessel to the Charterers at the port or place stated in Box 8 or a port or place within the range stated in Box 8.

(c) *Delivery Time* - Delivery shall take place no earlier than the date/time stated in Box 9 and no later than the date/time stated in Box 10. Delivery shall be effected at any time day or night, Saturdays, Sundays and holidays included.

(d) *Cancellation* - Should the Vessel not be delivered by the date/time stated in Box 10 the Charterers shall have the option to cancel the Charter Party without prejudice to any claims the Charterers may otherwise have on the Owners under the Charter Party. If the Owners anticipate that, despite their exercise of due diligence, the Vessel will not be ready for delivery by the date/time stated in Box 10, they may notify the Charterers in writing, stating the anticipated new date of readiness for delivery, proposing a new cancelling date/time and requiring the Charterers to declare whether they will cancel or will take delivery of the Vessel. Should the Charterers elect not to cancel or should they fail to reply within two (2) working days (as applying at the Charterers' place of business) of receipt of such notification, then unless otherwise agreed, the proposed new cancelling date/time will replace the date/time stated in Box 10. This provision shall operate only once and should the Vessel not be ready for delivery at the new cancelling date/time the Charterers shall have the option of cancelling this Charter Party.

(e) *Notice(s)* - The Owners shall give the Charterers not less than the number of days notice stated in Box 11 of the date/time on which the Vessel is expected to be delivered and shall keep the Charterers closely advised of possible changes in the Vessel's expected date/time of delivery. The Owners shall give the Charterers and/or their local agents notice of delivery when the Vessel is in a position to come on hire.

(f) *Vessel's Condition* - On arrival at the first port or place of loading the Vessel's holds shall be clean and in all respects ready to receive the intended cargo identified in Box 12, failing which the Vessel shall be off-hire from the time of rejection until she is deemed ready.

(g) *Charterers' Acceptance* - Acceptance of delivery of the Vessel by the Charterers shall not prejudice their rights against the Owners under this Charter Party.

2. Trading Areas

(a) *Trading Limits* - The Vessel shall be employed in lawful trades within Institute Warranty Limits (IWL) and within the trading limits as stated in Box 13 between safe ports or safe places where she can safely enter, lie always afloat, and depart.

(b) *Excepted Countries* - The Owners warrant that at the time of delivery the Vessel will not have traded to any of the countries listed in Box 14.

(c) *Ice* - The Vessel shall not be required to enter or remain in any icebound port or area, nor any port or area where lights, lightships, markers or buoys have been or are about to be withdrawn by reason of ice, nor where on account of ice there is risk that, in the ordinary course of events, the Vessel will not be able safely to enter and remain in the port or area or to depart after completion of loading or discharging. The Vessel shall not be obliged to force ice but, subject to the Owners' prior approval, may follow ice-breakers when reasonably required, with due regard to her size, construction and class. If, on account of ice, the Master considers it dangerous to remain at the port or place of loading or discharging for fear of the Vessel being frozen in and/or damaged he shall be at liberty to sail to any convenient place and there await the Charterers' new instructions.

3. Cargo - Restrictions and Exclusions

(a) *Lawful Cargoes* - The Vessel shall be employed in carrying lawful cargo. Cargo of a hazardous, injurious, or noxious nature or IMO-classified cargo shall not be carried without the Owners' prior consent in which case it shall be carried only in accordance with the provisions of sub-clause (c) of this Clause.

(b) *Excluded Cargoes* - Without prejudice to the generality of the foregoing, the following cargoes shall be excluded: livestock, arms, ammunition, explosives, nuclear and radioactive material other than radio-isotopes as described in sub-clause (d) of this clause and any other cargoes enumerated in Box 15.

(c) *Hazardous Cargoes* - If the Owners agree that the Charterers may carry hazardous, injurious, noxious or IMO-classified cargo, the amount of such cargo shall be limited to the quantity indicated in Box 16 and the Charterers shall provide the Master with evidence that the cargo has been packed, labelled and documented and shall be loaded and stowed in accordance with IMO regulations, any mandatory local requirements and regulations and/or recommendations of the competent authorities of the country of the Vessel's registry. Failure to observe the foregoing shall entitle the Master to refuse such cargo or, if already loaded, to discharge it in the Charterers' time and at their risk and expense.

(d) *Radio-active Cargoes* - Radio-isotopes, used or intended to be used for industrial, commercial, agricultural, medical or scientific purposes, may be carried subject to prior consent by the Owners and the Master, provided that they are not of such a category as to invalidate the Vessel's P & I cover.

(e) *Containers* - If cargo is carried in ISO-containers such containers shall comply with the International Convention for Safe Containers.

(f) *Deck Cargo* - Subject to the Master's prior approval, which shall not be unreasonably withheld, cargo may be carried on deck in accordance with the provisions of Clauses 17 (c) and 18.

4. Redelivery

(a) *Redelivery Place* - The Charterers shall redeliver the Vessel to the Owners at the port or place stated in Box 17 or a port or place within the range stated in Box 17, in the same order and condition as when the Vessel was delivered, fair wear and tear excepted.

(b) *Acceptance of Redelivery* - Acceptance of redelivery of the Vessel by the Owners shall not prejudice their rights against the Charterers under this Charter Party.

(c) *Notice* - The Charterers shall give the Owners not less than the number of days notice stated in Box 18 indicating the port or place of redelivery and the expected date on which the Vessel is to be ready for redelivery.

(d) *Last Voyage* - The Charterers warrant that they will not order the Vessel to commence a voyage (including any preceding ballast voyage) which cannot reasonably be expected to be completed in time to allow redelivery of the Vessel within the period agreed and declared as per Clause 1(a). If, nevertheless, such an order is given, the Owners shall have the option: (i) to refuse the order and require a substitute order allowing timely redelivery; or (ii) to perform the order without prejudice to their rights to claim damages for breach of charter in case of late redelivery. In any event, for the number of days by which the period agreed and declared as per Clause 1(a) is exceeded, the Charterers shall pay the market rate if this is higher than the rate stated in Box 24.

5. On/Off-hire Surveys

Joint on-hire and off-hire surveys shall be conducted by mutually acceptable surveyors at ports or places to be agreed. The on-hire survey shall be conducted without loss of time to the Charterers, whereas the off-hire survey shall be conducted in the Charterers' time. Survey fees and expenses shall be shared equally between the Owners and the Charterers.
Both surveys shall cover the condition of the Vessel and her equipment as well as quantities of fuels remaining on board. The Owners shall instruct the Master to co-operate with the surveyors in conducting such surveys.

6. Bunkers

(a) *Quantity at Delivery/Redelivery* - The Vessel shall be delivered with about the quantity of fuels stated in Box 19 and, unless indicated to the contrary in Box 20, the Vessel shall be redelivered with about the same quantity, provided that the quantity of fuels at redelivery is at least sufficient to allow the Vessel to safely reach the nearest port at which fuels of the required type or better are available.

(b) *Bunkering prior to Delivery and Redelivery* - Provided that it can be accomplished at scheduled ports, without hindrance to the operation of the Vessel, and by prior arrangement between the parties, the Owners shall allow the Charterers to bunker for the account of the Charterers prior to delivery and the Charterers shall allow the Owners to bunker for the account of the Owners prior to redelivery.

(c) *Purchase Price* - The Charterers shall purchase the fuels on board at delivery at the price stated in Box 21 and the Owners shall purchase the fuels on board at redelivery at the price stated in Box 22. The value of the fuel on delivery shall be paid together with the first instalment of hire.

(d) *Bunkering* - The Charterers shall supply fuel of the specifications and grades stated in Box 23. The fuels shall be of a stable and homogeneous nature and unless otherwise agreed in writing, shall comply with ISO standard 8217: 1996 or any subsequent amendments thereof as well as with the relevant provisions of Marpol. The Chief Engineer shall co-operate with the Charterers' bunkering agents and fuel suppliers and comply with their requirements during bunkering, including but not limited to checking, verifying and acknowledging sampling, readings or soundings, meters etc. before, during and/or after delivery of fuels. During delivery four representative samples of all fuels shall be taken at a point as close as possible to the Vessel's bunker manifold. The samples shall be labelled and sealed and signed by suppliers, Chief Engineer and the Charterers or their agents. Two samples shall be retained by the suppliers and one each by the Vessel and the Charterers. If any claim should arise in respect of the quality or specification or grades of the fuels supplied, the samples of the fuels retained as aforesaid shall be analysed by a qualified and independent laboratory.

(e) *Liability* - The Charterers shall be liable for any loss or damage to the Owners caused by the supply of unsuitable fuels or fuels which do not comply with the specifications and grades set out in Box 23 and the Owners shall not be held liable for any reduction in the Vessel's speed performance and/or increased bunker consumption nor for any time lost and any other consequences arising as a result of such supply.

7. Vessel's Gear and Equipment

(a) *Regulations* - The Vessel's cargo gear, if any, and any other related equipment shall comply with the law and national regulations of the countries to which the Vessel may be employed and the Owners shall ensure that the Vessel is at all times in possession of valid certificates to establish compliance with such regulations. If stevedores are not permitted to work due to failure of the Master and/or the Owners to comply with the aforementioned regulations or because the Vessel is not in possession of such valid certificates, then the Charterers may suspend hire for the time lost thereby and the Owners shall pay all expenses incurred incidental to and resulting from such failure (see Clause 11(d)).

(b) *Breakdown of Vessel's Gear* - All cargo handling gear, including derricks/cranes/ winches if any, shall be kept in good working order and the Owners shall exercise due diligence in maintaining such gear. In the event of loss of time due to a breakdown of derrick(s), crane(s) or winch(es) for any period by reason of disablement or insufficient power, the hire shall be reduced for the actual time lost thereby during loading/discharging unless the lost time is caused by negligence of the Charterers or their servants. If the Charterers continue working by using shore-crane(s) the Owners shall pay the cost of shore craneage, to an amount not exceeding the amount of hire payable to the Owners for such period.

(c) *Suez and Panama Canal* - During the currency of this Charter Party the Vessel shall be equipped with all necessary fittings in good working order for Suez and Panama Canal transit .

(d) *Lighting* - The Owners shall ensure that the Vessel will supply, free of expense to the Charterers, sufficient lighting on deck and in holds to permit 24 hour working.

8. Hire

(a) *Rate* - The Charterers shall pay hire per day or pro rata for any part of a day from the time the Vessel is delivered to the Charterers until her redelivery to the Owners, in the currency and at the rate stated in Box 24. In the event that additional hire is payable in accordance with Clause 9(d) such hire shall be based on the rate applicable at the time of redelivery. All calculation of hire shall be made by reference to UTC (Universal Time Coordinated).

(b) *Payment* - Subject to sub-clause (d) payment of hire shall be made in advance in full, without discount every 15 days to the Owners' bank account designated in Box 25 or to such other account as the Owners may from time to time designate in writing, in funds available to the Owners on the due date.

(c) *Default* - In default of punctual and regular payment of hire the Owners shall have the right to withdraw the Vessel without prejudice to any other claim the Owners may have against the Charterers under this Charter Party.
Where there is a failure to make punctual and regular payment of hire due to oversight, negligence, errors or omissions on the part of the Charterers or their bankers, the Owners shall give the Charterers written notice of the number of clear banking days stated in Box 26 (as recognized at the agreed place of payment) in which to rectify the failure, and when so rectified within such number of days following the Owners' notice, the payment shall stand as regular and punctual. Failure by the Charterers to pay hire within the number of days stated in Box 26 of their receiving the Owners' notice as provided herein, shall entitle the Owners to withdraw the Vessel without further notice and without prejudice to any other claim they may have against the Charterers.
Further, at any time after the period stated in Box 26, as long as hire remains

unpaid, the Owners shall, without prejudice to their right to withdraw, be entitled to suspend the performance of any and all of their obligations hereunder and shall have no responsibility whatsoever for any consequences thereof in respect of which the Charterers hereby agree to indemnify the Owners. Notwithstanding the provisions of Clause 9(a)(ii), hire shall continue to accrue and any extra expenses resulting from such suspension shall be for the Charterers' account.

(d) _Deductions_ - On production of supporting vouchers the Charterers shall be entitled to deduct from the next hire due any expenditure incurred on behalf of the Owners which is for the Owners' account under this Charter Party. If such expenditure is incurred in a currency other than that in which hire is payable, conversion into such currency for the purpose of deduction shall be effected at the rate of exchange prevailing on the date the expenditure was incurred.

(e) _Redelivery Adjustment_ - Should the Vessel be on her voyage towards the port or place of redelivery at the time payment of hire becomes due, said payment shall be made for the estimated time necessary to complete the voyage, less the estimated value of the fuels remaining on board at redelivery. When the Vessel is redelivered to the Owners any difference shall be refunded to or paid by the Charterers as appropriate, but not later than thirty days after redelivery of the Vessel.

9. Off-hire

After delivery in accordance with Clause 1 hereof the Vessel shall remain on hire until redelivered in accordance with Clause 4, except for the following periods:

(a) _Inability to Perform Services_

If the Vessel is unable to comply with the instructions of the Charterers on account of:

(i) any damage, defect, breakdown, deficiency of, or accident to the Vessel's hull, machinery, equipment or repairs or maintenance thereto, including drydocking, excepting those occasions where Clauses 7(b) and 16(b) apply;

(ii) any deficiency of the Master, Officers and/or Crew, including the failure or refusal or inability of the Master, Officers and/or Crew to perform services when required;

(iii) Arrest of the Vessel at the suit of a claimant except where the arrest is caused by, or arises from any act or omission of the Charterers, their servants, agents or sub-contractors;

(iv) the terms of employment of the Master, Officers and/or Crew;

then the Vessel will be off-hire for the time thereby lost.

(b) _Deviation_ - In the event of the Vessel deviating (which expression includes putting back, or putting into any port or place other than that to which she is bound under the instructions of the Charterers) for reasons other than to save life or property the Vessel shall be off-hire from the commencement of such deviation until the time when the Vessel is again ready to resume her service from a position not less favourable to the Charterers than that at which the deviation commenced, provided always that due allowance shall be given for any distance made good towards the Vessel's destination and any bunkers saved. However, should the Vessel alter course to avoid bad weather or be driven into port or anchorage by stress of weather, the Vessel shall remain on hire and all costs thereby incurred shall be for the Charterers' account.

(c) _Requisitions_ - Should the Vessel be requisitioned by any government or governmental authority during the period of this Charter Party, the Owners shall immediately notify the Charterers. The Vessel shall be off-hire during the period of such requisition and any hire or compensation paid by any government or governmental authority in respect of such requisition shall be paid to the Owners. However, if the period of requisition exceeds the number of days stated in Box 27, either party shall have the option of cancelling the balance period of the Charter Party, by giving 14 days notice of cancellation to the other.

(d) _Addition to Charter Period_ - Any time during which the Vessel is off-hire under this Charter Party may be added, at the option of the Charterers, to the charter period as determined in accordance with Clause 1(a). Such option shall be declared in writing not less than one month before the expected date of redelivery, or latest one week after the event if such event occurs less than one month before the expected date of redelivery.

10. Loss of Vessel

This Charter Party shall terminate and hire shall cease at noon on the day the Vessel is lost or becomes a constructive total loss and if missing, at noon on the date when last heard of. Any hire paid in advance and not earned shall be returned to the Charterers and payment of any hire due shall be deferred until the Vessel is reported safe.

11. Owners' Obligations

Except as provided elsewhere in this Charter Party, the Owners shall deliver the Vessel in the Class indicated in Box 5 and in a thoroughly efficient state of hull and machinery and shall exercise due diligence to maintain the Vessel in such Class and in every way fit for the service throughout the period of the Charter Party.

Nothing contained in this Charter Party shall be construed as a demise of the Vessel to the Charterers and the Owners remain at all times responsible for her navigation and for the due performance of related services, including but not limited to pilotage and towage even if paid for by the Charterers.

Unless otherwise agreed, the Owners shall provide and pay for the costs of the following:-

(a) _Wages_ - Master's, Officers' and Crew's wages.

(b) _Stores_ - All provisions, deck and engine-room stores, including lubricants.

(c) _Insurance of the Vessel_: (See Clause 20).

(d) _Crew's assistance_ in:-

(i) preparing the Vessel's cranes, derricks, winches and/or cargo handling gear for use,

(ii) opening and closing any hatches (other than pontoon type hatches), ramps and other means of access to cargo,

(iii) docking, undocking and shifting operations in port,

(iv) bunkering,

(v) maintaining power during loading and discharging operations,

(vi) instructing crane drivers and winchmen in the use of the Vessel's gear,

The above services will be rendered by the crew if required, provided port and local regulations permit; otherwise charges for such services shall be for the Charterers' account.

(e) _Documentation_ - Any documentation relating to the Vessel as required at the commencement of the Charter Party to permit the Vessel to trade within the limits provided in Box 13, including but not limited to international tonnage certificate, Suez and Panama tonnage certificates, certificate of registry, certificates relating to the strength, safety and/or serviceability of the Vessel's gear and certificates of financial responsibility for oil pollution as long as such oil pollution certificates can be obtained by the Owners in the market on ordinary commercial terms.

Such documentation shall be maintained during the currency of the Charter Party as necessary.

(f) _Deratisation_ - A deratisation certificate at the commencement of the Charter Party and any renewal thereof throughout the Charter Party, except if certification is required as a result of the cargo carried or ports visited under this Charter Party in which case all expenses in connection therewith shall be for the account of the Charterers.

(g) _Smuggling_ - Any fines, taxes or imposts levied in the event of smuggling by the Master, Officers and/or Crew. The Vessel shall be off-hire for any time lost as a result thereof. See also Clause 13(f).

12. Master

The Master shall be conversant with the English language and, although appointed by the Owners, shall at all times during the currency of this Charter Party be under the orders and directions of the Charterers as regards employment, agency or other arrangements. The Master shall prosecute all voyages with due dispatch and supervise loading and discharging operations to ensure that the seaworthiness of the Vessel is not affected.

The Charterers recognise the principles stated in IMO Resolution A.443 (XI) as regards maritime safety and protection of the marine environment and shall not prevent the Master from taking any decision in this respect which in his professional judgement is necessary.

13. Charterers' Obligations

The Charterers shall keep and care for the cargo at loading and discharging ports, be responsible for the stevedoring operations enumerated under sub-clause 13(d), arrange any transhipment and properly deliver the cargo at destination.

The Charterers shall furnish the Master with full and timely instructions and unless otherwise agreed, they shall provide and pay for the costs of the following throughout the currency of this Charter Party:

(a) _Voyage Expenses_ - All port charges (including compulsory charges for shore watchmen and garbage removal), light and canal dues, pilotage, towage, consular charges, and all other charges and expenses relating to the cargo and/or to the Vessel as a result of her employment hereunder, other than charges or expenses provided for in Clause 11.

(b) _Bunker Fuel_ (See Clause 6). - All fuels except for quantities consumed while the Vessel is off-hire.

(c) _Agency Costs_ - All agency fees for normal ship's husbandry at all ports or places of call.

(d) _Stevedoring_ - All stevedoring operations during the currency of this Charter Party including receipt, loading, handling, stuffing containers, stowing, lashing, securing, unsecuring, unlashing, discharging, stripping containers, tallying and delivering of all cargo.

(e) _Advances to Master_ - Reasonable funds which, upon request by the Owners, are to be made available by Charterers' local agents to the Master for disbursements. The Charterers may deduct such advance funds from hire payments.

(f) _Contraband_ - Any fines, taxes or imposts levied in the event that contraband and/or unmanifested drugs and/or cargoes are found to have been shipped as part of the cargo and/or in containers on board. The Vessel shall remain on hire during any time lost as a result thereof. However, if it is established that the Master, Officers and/or Crew are involved in smuggling then any security required shall be provided by the Owners. See also Clause 11(g).

14. Owners' Requirements

(a) _Maintenance_ - Without prejudice to the provisions of Clause 9(a)(i), the Owners shall have the right to take the Vessel out of service at any time for emergency repairs, and by prior arrangement with the Charterers for routine maintenance, including drydocking.

(b) _General Average_ - General Average shall be adjusted, stated and settled at the place shown in Box 28 according to the York-Antwerp Rules 1994 or any subsequent modification thereto by an adjuster appointed by the Owners. Charter hire shall not contribute to General Average.

General Average shall be adjusted in any currency at the sole option of the Owners. Exchange into the currency of adjustment shall be calculated at the rate prevailing on the date of payment for disbursements and on the date of completion of discharge of the Vessel for allowances, contributory values etc.

The Charterers agree to co-operate with the Owners and their appointed adjuster by supplying manifest and other information and, where required, to endeavour to secure the assistance of the Charterers' local agents in the collection of security, at the Owners' expense.

(c) _Salvage_ - All salvage and assistance to other vessels shall be for the Owners' and the Charterers' equal benefit after deducting the Master's and Crew's proportion and all legal and other expenses including hire paid under the Charter Party for time lost in the salvage, damage to the Vessel and fuel consumed. The Charterers shall be bound by all measures taken by the Owners in order to secure payment of salvage and to settle its amount.

(d) _Lien_ - The Charterers warrant that they will not suffer, nor permit to be continued, any lien or encumbrance incurred by them or their agents, which might have priority over the title and interest of the Owners in the Vessel. In no event shall the Charterers procure, nor permit to be procured, for the Vessel, any supplies, necessaries or services without previously obtaining a statement signed by an authorised representative of the furnisher thereof, acknowledging that such supplies, necessaries or services are being furnished on the credit of the Charterers and not on the credit of the Vessel or of the Owners and that the furnisher claims no maritime lien on the Vessel therefor.

The Owners shall have a lien on all shipped cargo before or after discharge and on all sub-freights and/or sub-hire including deadfreight and demurrage, for any amount due under this Charter Party including but not limited to unpaid charter hire, unreimbursed Charterers' expenses initially paid by the Owners, and contributions in general average properly due.

The Charterers shall ensure that such lien is incorporated in all documents containing or evidencing Contracts of Carriage issued by them or on their behalf.

15. Charterers' Requirements

(a) _Plans_ - On concluding this Charter Party or as soon as practical thereafter the Owners shall provide the Charterers with copies of any operational plans or documents that the Charterers may reasonably request and which are necessary for the safe and efficient operation of the Vessel. All documents received by the Charterers shall be returned to the Owners on redelivery.

(b) _Flag and Funnel_ - If they so require, the Charterers shall, during the currency of this Charter Party, be allowed to fly their house flag and/or paint the funnel in the Charterers' colours. All alterations including re-instatement shall be effected in the Charterers' time and at their expense.

(c) _Communications Facilities_ - The Owners shall permit the Charterers' use of the Vessel's communication facilities at cost.

(d) _Logs_ - The Owners shall maintain full deck and engine room logs during the currency of this Charter Party and the Charterers shall have full access to all the Vessel's logs, rough and official, covering this period. The Owners undertake to produce all such documentation promptly upon written request of the Charterers and to allow them to make copies of relevant entries.

(e) _Replacement of Master and Officers_ - If the Charterers shall have reason to be dissatisfied with the conduct of the Master or Officers, the Owners shall, on receiving particulars of the complaint in writing, investigate same and, if necessary, replace the offending party or parties at their expense.

(f) *Supercargo* - The Owners shall provide and maintain a clean and adequate room for the Charterers' Supercargo if any, furnished to the same standard as officers' accommodation. The Supercargo shall be victualled with the Vessel's officers. The Charterers shall pay at the daily rate shown in Box 29 for his accommodation and victualling. The Supercargo shall be on board at the risk and expense of the Charterers and both Charterers and Supercargo shall sign the customary indemnity forms.

(g) *Victualling* - The Owners shall, when requested and authorised in writing by the Charterers or their agents, victual other officials and servants of the Charterers at the rate per person per meal shown in Box 30.

(h) *Representation* - Expenses for representation incurred by the Master for the Charterers' account and benefit shall be settled by the Charterers' payment of the amount stated in Box 31, per month or pro rata. The Charterers shall indemnify the Owners against all consequences and/or liabilities including customs fines which may result from such representation.

(i) *Sub-Letting* - The Charterers shall have the right to sub-let all or part of the Vessel whilst remaining responsible to the Owners for the performance of this Charter Party.

(j) *Inspections* - The Charterers shall, upon giving reasonable notice, have the right to a superficial inspection of the Vessel in their time and the Master shall within reason co-operate with the Charterers to facilitate their inspection of the Vessel. The Charterers shall pay for any and all expenses associated with such inspection and the Owners shall be entitled to receive a copy of the report.

(k) *Weather Routeing* - The Charterers may supply the Master with weather routeing information during the currency of this Charter Party. In this event the Master, though not obliged to follow routeing information, shall comply with the reporting procedure of the Charterers' weather routeing service.

(l) *Laying up* - At the written request of the Charterers, the Owners shall at any time provide an estimate of any economies which may be possible in the event of laying-up the Vessel. The Charterers shall then have the right to order the laying-up of the Vessel at any time and for any period of time at a safe berth or safe place in their option, and in the event of such laying-up the Owners shall promptly take reasonable steps to effect all the economies in operating costs. The laying-up port or place and laid-up arrangements shall be subject to approval by the Owners' insurers. Laying-up preparation and reactivation cost, and all expenses incurred shall be for the Charterers' account. The Charterers shall give sufficient notice of their intention in this respect to enable the Owners to make necessary arrangements for decommissioning and recommissioning. The Owners must give prompt credit to the Charterers for all economies achieved.

(m) *Cleaning* - The Charterers may request the Owners to direct the crew to sweep and/or wash and/or clean the holds between voyages and/or between cargoes against payment at the rate per hold stated in Box 32, provided the crew is able to undertake such work and is allowed to do so by local regulations. In connection with any such operation the Owners shall not be responsible if the Vessel's holds are not accepted or passed.
In lieu of cleaning the Charterers shall have the option to re-deliver the Vessel with unclean/unswept holds against the lump sum payment stated in Box 33 excluding the disposal of dunnage and/or waste, which shall be for Charterers' account.

16. Sundry Matters

(a) *Stowaways*

(i) The Charterers shall exercise due care and diligence in preventing stowaways from gaining access to the Vessel by means of secreting away in cargo or containers shipped by the Charterers.

(ii) If, despite the exercise of due care and diligence by the Charterers, stowaways have gained access to the Vessel by means of secreting away in the cargo and/or containers shipped by the Charterers, this shall amount to breach of charter for the consequences of which the Charterers shall be liable and shall hold the Owners harmless and shall keep them indemnified against all claims whatsoever which may arise and be made against them. Furthermore, all time lost and all expenses whatsoever and howsoever incurred, including fines, shall be for the Charterers' account and the Vessel shall remain on hire.

(iii) Should the Vessel be arrested as a result of the Charterers' breach of charter according to sub-clause (ii) above, the Charterers shall take all reasonable steps to secure that within a reasonable time, the Vessel is released and at their expense post bail or other security to obtain release of the Vessel.

(iv) If, despite the exercise of due care and diligence by the Owners, stowaways have gained access to the Vessel by means other than secreting away in the cargo and/or containers shipped by the Charterers, all time lost and all expenses whatsoever and howsoever incurred, including fines, shall be for the Owners' account.

(v) Should the Vessel be arrested as a result of stowaways having gained access to the Vessel by means other than secreting away in the cargo and/or containers shipped by the Charterers, the Owners shall take all reasonable steps to secure that within a reasonable time, the Vessel is released and at their expense post bail or other security to obtain release of the Vessel.

(b) *Stevedore Damage* - Notwithstanding anything contained herein to the contrary, the Charterers shall be liable for any and all damage to the Vessel caused by stevedores, provided the Master has notified the Charterers or their agents, in writing, within 24 hours of the occurrence or as soon as possible thereafter but latest when the damage could have been discovered by the exercise of due diligence.
The Master shall use his best efforts to obtain written acknowledgment by the party or parties causing damage unless the damage has been made good in the meantime.

(i) Stevedore damage affecting the Vessel's seaworthiness and/or the safety of the crew, proper working of the Vessel and/or her equipment, shall be repaired immediately by the Charterers and the Vessel is to remain on hire until such repairs are completed and, if required, passed by the Vessel's classification society.

(ii) Stevedore damage not affecting the Vessel's seaworthiness and/or the safety of the crew shall be repaired, at the Charterers' option, before or after redelivery concurrently with Owners' work. In the latter case no hire will be paid to the Owners except in so far as the time required for the repairs for which the Charterers are liable exceeds the time necessary to carry out the Owners' work.

(iii) The Owners shall have the option of requiring that stevedore damage affecting the trading capabilities of the Vessel is repaired before redelivery.

(c) *Fumigation* - Expenses in connection with fumigations and/or quarantine ordered because of cargo carried or ports visited while the Vessel is employed under this Charter Party shall be for the Charterers' account. Expenses in connection with all other fumigations and/or quarantine shall be for the Owners' account.

(d) *Anti-drug Clause* - The Charterers warrant to exercise the highest degree of care and diligence in preventing unmanifested narcotic drugs and/or any other illegal substances being loaded or concealed on board the Vessel.
Non-compliance with the provisions of this Clause shall amount to breach of warranty for the consequences of which the Charterers shall be liable and shall hold the Owners, the Master and the crew of the Vessel harmless and shall keep them indemnified against all claims whatsoever which may arise and be made against them individually or jointly. Furthermore, all time lost and all expenses incurred, including fines, as a result of the Charterers' breach of the provisions of this Clause shall be for the Charterers' account and the Vessel shall remain on hire.
Should the Vessel be arrested as a result of the Charterers' non-compliance with the provisions of this Clause, the Charterers shall at their expense take all reasonable steps to secure that within a reasonable time the Vessel is released and at their expense post bail to secure release of the Vessel.
The Owners shall remain responsible for all time lost and all expenses incurred, including fines, in the event that unmanifested narcotic drugs and other illegal substances are found in the possession or effects of the Vessel's personnel.

17. Bills of Lading, Waybills and Other Contracts of Carriage

(a) *Signing Contracts of Carriage*

(i) The Master shall sign bills of lading or waybills as presented in conformity with mate's receipts. If requested, the Owners may authorise the Charterers and/or their agents in writing to sign bills of lading, waybills, through bills of lading, or multimodal bills of lading (hereafter collectively referred to as Contracts of Carriage) on the Owners' and/or Master's behalf in conformity with mate's receipts without prejudice to the terms and conditions of the Charter Party.

(ii) In the event the Charterers and/or their agents, pursuant to the provisions of sub-clause 17(a)(i) above, sign Contracts of Carriage which extend the Owners' responsibility beyond the period during which the cargo is on board the Vessel the Charterers shall indemnify the Owners against any claims for loss, damage or expense which may result therefrom.

(iii) Neither the Charterers nor their agents shall permit the issue of any Contract of Carriage (whether or not signed on behalf of the Owners or on behalf of the Charterers or on behalf of any Sub-Charterers) incorporating, where not compulsorily applicable, the Hamburg Rules or any other legislation giving effect to the Hamburg Rules or any other legislation imposing liabilities in excess of Hague or Hague-Visby Rules.

(b) *Protective Clauses* - The Charterers warrant that Contracts of Carriage issued in respect of cargo under this Charter Party shall incorporate the clauses set out in Appendix A.

(c) *Deck Cargo* - Unless the cargo is stowed in fully closed containers, placed on board the Vessel in areas designed for the carriage of containers with class-approved container fittings, and secured to the Vessel by means of class-approved Vessel's lashing gear or material, Contracts of Carriage covering cargo carried on deck shall be claused: "Agreed to be shipped on deck at Charterers', Shippers' and Receivers' risk, and responsibility for loss, damage or expense howsoever caused".

(d) *Defence of Claims* - Should the Charterers issue or cause to be issued a Contract of Carriage in default of the provisions of this Clause 17, they shall be obliged upon written request by the Owners to take over, pay for the defence of and pay any liability established in respect of any claim brought against the Vessel and/or the Owners as a result of such default.

(e) *Payment and Indemnity* - The Charterers shall pay for, and/or indemnify the Owners against any loss, damage or expense which results from any breach of the provisions of this Clause 17.

18. Responsibilities

(a) *Cargo Claims*

(i) *Definition* - For the purpose of this Clause 18(a), Cargo Claim means a claim for loss, damage, shortage, (including slackage, ullage or pilferage), overcarriage of or delay to cargo including customs fines or fines in respect of such loss, damage, shortage, overcarriage or delay and includes:

(1) any legal costs or interest claimed by the original claimant making such a claim;

(2) all legal, Club correspondents' and experts' costs reasonably incurred in the defence of or in the settlement of the claim made by the original claimant, but shall not include any costs of whatsoever nature incurred in making a claim or in seeking an indemnity under this Charter Party.

(ii) *Claim Settlement* - It is a condition precedent to the right of recovery by either party under this Clause 18(a) that the party seeking indemnity shall have first properly settled or compromised and paid the claim.

(iii) *Owners' Liability* - The Owners shall be liable for any Cargo Claim arising or resulting from:

(1) failure of the Owners or their servants to exercise due diligence before or at the beginning of each voyage to make the Vessel seaworthy;

(2) failure of the Owners or their servants properly and carefully to carry, keep and care for the cargo while on board;

(3) unreasonable deviation from the voyage described in the Contract of Carriage unless such deviation is ordered or approved by the Charterers;

(4) errors in navigation or the management of the Vessel solely where the Contract of Carriage is subject to mandatory application of legislation giving effect to the Hamburg Rules.

(iv) *Charterers' Liability* - The Charterers shall be liable for any Cargo Claim arising or resulting from:

(1) the stevedoring operations enumerated under Clause 13(d) unless the Charterers prove that such Cargo Claim was caused by the unseaworthiness of the Vessel, in which case the Owners shall be liable;

(2) any transhipment in connection with through-transport or multimodal transport, save where the Charterers can prove that the circumstances giving rise to the Cargo Claim occurred after commencement of the loading of the cargo onto the Vessel and prior to its discharge;

(3) the carriage of cargo on deck unless such cargo is stowed in fully closed containers, placed on board the Vessel in areas designed for the carriage of containers with class-approved container fittings and secured to the Vessel by means of class-approved Vessel's lashing gear or material.

(v) *Shared Liability* - All Cargo Claims arising from other causes than those enumerated under sub-clauses (iii) and (iv), shall be shared equally between the Owners and the Charterers unless there is clear and irrefutable evidence that the claim arose out of pilferage or the act or neglect of one or the other party or their servants or sub-contractors, in which case that party shall bear the full claim.

(vi) *Charterers' Own Cargo* - If the cargo is the property of the Charterers, the Owners shall have the same responsibilities and benefits as they would have had under this Clause had the cargo been the property of a third party and carried under a Bill of Lading incorporating the Hague-Visby Rules.

(b) *Fines, etc.* - The Charterers shall also be liable to the Owners for any losses, damages, expenses, fines, penalties, or claims which the Owners may incur or suffer by reason of the cargo or the documentation relating thereto failing to comply with any relevant laws, regulations, directions or notices of port authorities or other authorities, or by reason of any infestation, contamination or condemnation of the cargo or of infestation, damage or contamination of the Vessel by the cargo.

(c) Deck cargo - The Charterers shall be liable to the Owners for any loss, damage, expense or delay to the Vessel howsoever caused and resulting from the carriage of cargo on deck save where the Charterers can prove that such loss, damage, expense or delay was the result of negligence on the part of the Owners and/or their servants.

(d) Death or Personal Injury - Claims for death or personal injury having a direct connection with the operation of the Vessel shall be borne by the Owners unless such claims are caused by defect of the cargo or by the act, neglect or default of the Charterers, their servants, agents or sub-contractors.

(e) Agency - The Owners authorise and empower the Charterers to act as the Owners' agents solely to ensure that, as against third parties, the Owners will have the benefit of any immunities, exemptions or liberties regarding the cargo or its carriage. Subject to the provisions of Clause 17 the Charterers shall have no authority to make any contracts imposing any obligations whatsoever upon the Owners in respect of the cargo or its carriage.

(f) Indemnity and Limitation - The Owners and the Charterers hereby agree to indemnify each other against all loss, damage or expenses arising or resulting from any obligation to pay claims, fines or penalties for which the other party is liable in accordance with this Charter Party. Both the Owners and the Charterers shall retain their right to limit their liability against the other party in respect of any claim brought by way of indemnity, notwithstanding that the other party has been denied the right to limit against any third party or has failed in whatever manner to exercise its rights of limitation.

(g) Time Bar - In respect of any Cargo Claims as between the Owners and the Charterers, brought under sub-clause 18(a), unless extensions of time have been sought or obtained from one party by the other or notice of arbitration has been given by either party, such claim(s) shall be deemed to be waived and absolutely time barred upon the expiry of two years reckoned from the date when the cargo was or should have been delivered. When the Hamburg Rules apply compulsorily the above time bar shall be extended to three years.

19. Exceptions

As between the Charterers and the Owners, responsibility for any loss, damage, delay or failure of performance under this Charter Party not dealt with in Clause 18(a), shall be subject to the following mutual exceptions:

Act of God, act of war, civil commotions, strikes, lockouts, restraint of princes and rulers, and quarantine restrictions.

In addition, any responsibility of the Owners not dealt with in Clause 18(a) shall be subject to the following exceptions:

Any act, neglect or default by the Master, pilots or other servants of the Owners in the navigation or management of the Vessel, fire or explosion not due to the personal fault of the Owners or their Manager, collision or stranding, unforeseeable breakdown of or any latent defect in the Vessel's hull, equipment or machinery.

The above provisions shall in no way affect the provisions as to off-hire in this Charter Party.

20. Insurances

(a) Hull and Machinery - The Owners warrant that the Vessel is insured for Hull, Machinery and basic War Risks purposes at the value stated in Box 34.

(b) Protection and Indemnity (P & I) - The Owners warrant that throughout the period of the Charter Party the Vessel will be fully covered for P&I risks, including through transport cover, with underwriters approved by the Charterers which approval shall not be unreasonably withheld.

The Charterers warrant that throughout the period of the Charter Party they will be covered for Charterers' liability risk by underwriters approved by the Owners which approval will not be unreasonably withheld.

21. War Risks ("Conwartime 1993")

(a) For the purpose of this Clause, the words:

(i) "Owners" shall include the shipowners, bareboat charterers, disponent owners, managers or other operators who are charged with the management of the Vessel, and the Master; and

(ii) "War Risks" shall include any war (whether actual or threatened), act of war, civil war, hostilities, revolution, rebellion, civil commotion, warlike operations, the laying of mines (whether actual or reported), acts of piracy, acts of terrorists, acts of hostility or malicious damage, blockades (whether imposed against all vessels or imposed selectively against vessels of certain flags or ownership, or against certain cargoes or crews or otherwise howsoever), by any person, body, terrorist or political group, or the Government of any state whatsoever, which, in the reasonable judgement of the Master and/or the Owners, may be dangerous or are likely to be or to become dangerous to the Vessel, her cargo, crew or other persons on board the Vessel.

(b) The Vessel, unless the written consent of the Owners be first obtained, shall not be ordered to or required to continue to or through, any port, place, area or zone (whether of land or sea), or any waterway or canal, where it appears that the Vessel, her cargo, crew or other persons on board the Vessel, in the reasonable judgement of the Master and/or the Owners, may be, or are likely to be, exposed to War Risks. Should the Vessel be within any such place as aforesaid, which only becomes dangerous, or is likely to be or to become dangerous, after her entry into it, she shall be at liberty to leave it.

(c) The Vessel shall not be required to load contraband cargo, or to pass through any blockade, whether such blockade be imposed on all vessels, or is imposed selectively in any way whatsoever against vessels of certain flags or ownership, or against certain cargoes or crews or otherwise howsoever, or to proceed to an area where she shall be subject, or is likely to be subject to a belligerent's right of search and/or confiscation.

(d) (i) The Owners may effect war risks insurance in respect of the Hull and Machinery of the Vessel and their other interests (including, but not limited to, loss of earnings and detention, the crew and their Protection and Indemnity Risks), and the premiums and/or calls therefor shall be for their account.

(ii) If the Underwriters of such insurance should require payment of premiums and/or calls because, pursuant to the Charterers' orders, the Vessel is within, or is due to enter and remain within, any area or areas which are specified by such Underwriters as being subject to additional premiums because of War Risks, then such premiums and/or calls shall be reimbursed by the Charterers to the Owners at the same time as the next payment of hire is due.

(e) If the Owners become liable under the terms of employment to pay to the crew any bonus or additional wages in respect of sailing into an area which is dangerous in the manner defined by the said terms, then such bonus or additional wages shall be reimbursed to the Owners by the Charterers at the same time as the next payment of hire is due.

(f) The Vessel shall have liberty:-

(i) to comply with all orders, directions, recommendations or advice as to departure, arrival, routes, sailing in convoy, ports of call, stoppages, destinations, discharge of cargo, delivery, or in any other way whatsoever, which are given by the Government of the Nation under whose flag the Vessel sails, or other Government to whose laws the Owners are subject, or any other Government, or any other body or group whatsoever acting with the power to compel compliance with their orders or directions;

(ii) to comply with the order, directions or recommendations of any war risks underwriters who have the authority to give the same under the terms of the war risks insurance;

(iii) to comply with the terms of any resolution of the Security Council of the United Nations, any directives of the European Community, the effective orders of any other Supranational body which has the right to issue and give the same, and with national laws aimed at enforcing the same to which the Owners are subject, and to obey the orders and directions of those who are charged with their enforcement;

(iv) to divert and discharge at any other port any cargo or part thereof which may render the Vessel liable to confiscation as a contraband carrier;

(v) to divert and call at any other port to change the crew or any part thereof or other persons on board the Vessel when there is reason to believe that they may be subject to internment, imprisonment or other sanctions.

(g) If in accordance with their rights under the foregoing provisions of this Clause, the Owners refuse to proceed to the loading or discharging ports, or any one or more of them, they shall immediately inform the Charterers. No cargo shall be discharged at any alternative port without first giving the Charterers notice of the Owners' intention to do so and requesting them to nominate a safe port for such discharge. Failing such nomination by the Charterers within 48 hours of the receipt of such notice and request, the Owners may discharge the cargo at any safe port of their own choice.

(h) If in compliance with any of the provisions of sub-clauses (b) to (g) of this Clause anything is done or not done, such shall not be deemed a deviation, but shall be considered as due fulfilment of this Charter Party.

22. Law and Arbitration

*) (a) This Charter Party shall be governed by and construed in accordance with English law and any dispute arising out of or in connection with this Charter Party shall be referred to arbitration in London in accordance with the Arbitration Act 1996 or any statutory modification or re-enactment thereof save to the extent necessary to give effect to the provisions of this Clause.

The arbitration shall be conducted in accordance with the London Maritime Arbitrators Association (LMAA) Terms current at the time when the arbitration proceedings are commenced.

The reference shall be to three arbitrators. A party wishing to refer a dispute to arbitration shall appoint its arbitrator and send notice of such appointment in writing to the other party requiring the other party to appoint its own arbitrator within 14 calendar days of that notice and stating that it will appoint its arbitrator as sole arbitrator unless the other party appoints its own arbitrator and gives notice that it has done so within the 14 days specified. If the other party does not appoint its own arbitrator and give notice that it has done so within the 14 days specified, the party referring a dispute to arbitration may, without the requirement of any further prior notice to the other party, appoint its arbitrator as sole arbitrator and shall advise the other party accordingly. The award of a sole arbitrator shall be binding on both parties as if he had been appointed by agreement.

Nothing herein shall prevent the parties agreeing in writing to vary these provisions to provide for the appointment of a sole arbitrator.

In cases where neither the claim nor any counterclaim exceeds the sum of USD 50,000 (or such other sum as the parties may agree) the arbitration shall be conducted in accordance with the LMAA Small Claims Procedure current at the time when the arbitration proceedings are commenced.

*) (b) This Charter Party shall be governed by and construed in accordance with Title 9 of the United States Code and the Maritime Law of the United States and any dispute arising out of or in connection with this Charter Party shall be referred to three persons at New York, one to be appointed by each of the parties hereto, and the third by the two so chosen; their decision or that of any two of them shall be final, and for the purposes of enforcing any award, judgement may be entered on an award by any court of competent jurisdiction. The proceedings shall be conducted in accordance with the rules of the Society of Maritime Arbitrators, Inc.

In cases where neither the claim nor any counterclaim exceeds the sum of USD 50,000 (or such other sum as the parties may agree) the arbitration shall be conducted in accordance with the Shortened Arbitration Procedure of the Society of Maritime Arbitrators, Inc. current at the time when the arbitration proceedings are commenced.

*) (c) This Charter Party shall be governed by and construed in accordance with the laws of the place mutually agreed by the parties and stated in Box 35 and any dispute arising out of or in connection with this Charter Party shall be referred to arbitration at the place stated in Box 35, subject to the procedures applicable there.

(d) If Box 35 in Part I is not appropriately filled in, sub-clause (a) of this Clause shall apply.

**) (a), (b) and (c) are alternatives; indicate alternative agreed in Box 35*

23. Commission

The Owners shall pay a commission at the rate stated in Box 36 to the Broker(s) stated in Box 36 on any hire paid under this Charter Party or any continuation or extension thereof. If the full hire is not paid owing to breach of Charter Party by either of the parties the party liable therefor shall indemnify the Brokers against their loss of commission.

Should the parties agree to cancel this Charter Party, the Owners shall indemnify the Brokers against any loss of commission but in such case the commission shall not exceed the brokerage on one year's hire.

In signing this Charter Party the Owners acknowledge their agreement with the brokers to pay the commissions described in this Clause.

24. Notices

Any notices as between the Owners and the Charterers shall be in writing and sent to the addresses stated in Boxes 2 and 3 as the case may be or to such other addresses as either party may designate to the other in writing.

"GENTIME" General Time Charter Party
Appendix A - Protective Clauses

A. WAR RISKS ("Voywar 1993")

(1) For the purpose of this Clause, the words:

(a) "Owners" shall include the shipowners, bareboat charterers, disponent owners, managers or other operators who are charged with the management of the Vessel, and the Master; and

(b) "War Risks" shall include any war (whether actual or threatened), act of war, civil war, hostilities, revolution, rebellion, civil commotion, warlike operations, the laying of mines (whether actual or reported), acts of piracy, acts of terrorists, acts of hostility or malicious damage, blockades (whether imposed against all vessels or imposed selectively against vessels of certain flags or ownership, or against certain cargoes or crews or otherwise howsoever), by any person, body, terrorist or political group, or the Government of any state whatsoever, which, in the reasonable judgement of the Master and/or the Owners, may be dangerous or are likely to be or to become dangerous to the Vessel, her cargo, crew or other persons on board the Vessel.

(2) If at any time before the Vessel commences loading, it appears that, in the reasonable judgement of the Master and/or the Owners, performance of the Contract of Carriage, or any part of it, may expose, or is likely to expose, the Vessel, her cargo, crew or other persons on board the Vessel to War Risks, the Owners may give notice to the Charterers cancelling this Contract of Carriage, or may refuse to perform such part of it as may expose, or may be likely to expose, the Vessel, her cargo, crew or other persons on board the Vessel to War Risks; provided always that if this Contract of Carriage provides that loading or discharging is to take place within a range of ports, and at the port or ports nominated by the Charterers the Vessel, her cargo, crew, or other persons on board the Vessel may be exposed, or may be likely to be exposed, to War Risks, the Owners shall first require the Charterers to nominate any other safe port which lies within the range for loading or discharging, and may only cancel this Contract of Carriage if the Charterers shall not have nominated such safe port or ports within 48 hours of receipt of notice of such requirement.

(3) The Owners shall not be required to continue to load cargo for any voyage, or to sign Bills of Lading for any port or place, or to proceed or continue on any voyage, or on any part thereof, or to proceed through any canal or waterway, or to proceed to or remain at any port or place whatsoever, where it appears, either after the loading of the cargo commences, or at any stage of the voyage thereafter before the discharge of the cargo is completed, that, in the reasonable judgement of the Master and/or the Owners, the Vessel, her cargo (or any part thereof), crew or other persons on board the Vessel (or any one or more of them) may be, or are likely to be, exposed to War Risks. If it should so appear, the Owners may by notice request the Charterers to nominate a safe port for the discharge of the cargo or any part thereof, and if within 48 hours of the receipt of such notice, the Charterers shall not have nominated such a port, the Owners may discharge the cargo at any safe port of their choice (including the port of loading) in complete fulfilment of the Contract of Carriage.
The Owners shall be entitled to recover from the Charterers the extra expenses of such discharge and, if the discharge takes place at any port other than the loading port, to receive the full freight as though the cargo had been carried to the discharging port and if the extra distance exceeds 100 miles, to additional freight which shall be the same percentage of the freight contracted for as the percentage which the extra distance represents to the distance of the normal and customary route, the Owners having a lien on the cargo for such expenses and freight.

(4) If at any stage of the voyage after the loading of the cargo commences, it appears that, in the reasonable judgement of the Master and/or the Owners, the Vessel, her cargo, crew or other persons on board the Vessel may be, or are likely to be, exposed to War Risks on any part of the route (including any canal or waterway) which is normally and customarily used in a voyage of the nature contracted for, and there is another longer route to the discharging port, the Owners shall give notice to the Charterers that this route will be taken. In this event the Owners shall be entitled, if the total extra distance exceeds 100 miles, to additional freight which shall be the same percentage of the freight contracted for as the percentage which the extra distance represents to the distance of the normal and customary route.

(5) The Vessel shall have liberty:-

(a) to comply with all orders, directions, recommendations or advice as to departure, arrival, routes, sailing in convoy, ports of call, stoppages, destinations, discharge of cargo, delivery or in any way whatsoever which are given by the Government of the Nation under whose flag the Vessel sails, or other Government to whose laws the Owners are subject, or any other Government which so requires, or any body or group acting with the power to compel compliance with their orders or directions;

(b) to comply with the orders, directions or recommendations of any war risks underwriters who have the authority to give the same under the terms of the war risks insurance;

(c) to comply with the terms of any resolution of the Security Council of the United Nations, any directives of the European Community, the effective orders of any other Supranational body which has the right to issue and give the same, and with national laws aimed at enforcing the same to which the Owners are subject, and to obey the orders and directions of those who are charged with their enforcement;

(d) to discharge at any other port any cargo or part thereof which may render the Vessel liable to confiscation as a contraband carrier;

(e) to call at any other port to change the crew or any part thereof or other persons on board the Vessel when there is reason to believe that they may be subject to internment, imprisonment or other sanctions;

(f) where cargo has not been loaded or has been discharged by the Owners under any provisions of this Clause, to load other cargo for the Owners' own benefit and carry it to any other port or ports whatsoever, whether backwards or forwards or in a contrary direction to the ordinary or customary route.

(6) If in compliance with any of the provisions of sub-clauses (2) to (5) of this Clause anything is done or not done, such shall not be deemed to be a deviation, but shall be considered as due fulfilment of the Contract of Carriage.

B. CLAUSE PARAMOUNT

The International Convention for the Unification of Certain Rules of Law relating to Bills of Lading signed at Brussels on 24 August 1924 ("the Hague Rules") as amended by the Protocol signed at Brussels on 23 February 1968 ("the Hague-Visby Rules") and as enacted in the country of shipment shall apply to this Contract. When the Hague-Visby Rules are not enacted in the country of shipment, the corresponding legislation in the country of destination shall apply, irrespective of whether such legislation may only regulate outbound shipments.

When there is no enactment of the Hague-Visby Rules in either the country of shipment or in the country of destination, the Hague-Visby Rules shall apply to this Contract, save where the Hague Rules as enacted in the country of shipment or if no such enactment is in place the Hague Rules as enacted in the country of destination apply compulsorily to this Contract.

The Protocol signed at Brussels on 21 December 1979 ("the SDR Protocol 1979") shall apply where the Hague-Visby Rules apply whether mandatorily or by this Contract.

The Carrier shall in no case be responsible for loss of or damage to cargo arising prior to loading, after discharging, or while the cargo is in the charge of another carrier, or with respect to deck cargo and live animals.

C. GENERAL AVERAGE

General Average shall be adjusted and settled at a port or place in the option of the Carrier according to the York-Antwerp Rules, 1994 or any subsequent amendment thereto.

D. HIMALAYA CLAUSE

It is hereby expressly agreed that no servant or agent of the Carrier (including every independent contractor from time to time employed by the Carrier) shall in any circumstances whatsoever be under any liability whatsoever to the Charterers, Shippers, Consignees, owner of the goods or to any holder of a Bill of Lading issued under this Charter Party, for any loss, damage or delay of whatsoever kind arising or resulting directly or indirectly from any act, neglect or default on his part while acting in the course of or in connection with his employment.

Without prejudice to the generality of the foregoing provisions in this clause, every exemption, limitation, condition and liberty herein contained and every right, exemption from liability, defence and immunity of whatsoever nature applicable to the Carrier or to which the Carrier is entitled hereunder, shall also be available and shall extend to protect every such servant or agent of the Carrier acting as aforesaid.

For the purpose of all the foregoing provisions of this clause the Carrier is or shall be deemed to be acting as agents or trustees on behalf of and for the benefit of all persons who might be his servants or agents from time to time (including independent contractors as aforesaid) and all such persons shall to this extent be or be deemed to be parties to this contract.

E. NEW JASON CLAUSE

In the event of accident, danger, damage or disaster before or after the commencement of the voyage resulting from any cause whatsoever, whether due to negligence or not, for which, or for the consequences of which, the Carrier is not responsible, by statute, contract, or otherwise, the goods, shippers, consignees, or owners of the goods shall contribute with the Carrier in general average to the payment of any sacrifices, losses, or expenses of a general average nature that may be made or incurred, and shall pay salvage and special charges incurred in respect of the goods.

If a salving vessel is owned or operated by the Carrier, salvage shall be paid for as fully as if salving vessel or vessels belonged to strangers. Such deposit as the Carrier or his agents may deem sufficient to cover the estimated contribution of the goods and any salvage and special charges thereon shall, if required, be made by the goods, shippers, consignees or owners of the goods to the Carrier before delivery.

F. BOTH-TO-BLAME COLLISION CLAUSE

If the Vessel comes into collision with another vessel as a result of the negligence of the other vessel and any act, neglect or default of the master, mariner, pilot or the servants of the Carrier in the navigation or in the management of the vessel, the owners of the goods carried hereunder will indemnify the Carrier against all loss or liability to the other or non-carrying vessel or her owners insofar as such loss or liability represents loss of, or damage to, or any claim whatsoever of the owners of said goods, paid or payable by the other or non-carrying vessel or her owners to the owners of said goods and set-off, recouped or recovered by the other or non-carrying vessel or her owners as part of their claim against the carrying Vessel or Carrier.

The foregoing provisions shall also apply where the owners, operators or those in charge of any vessels or objects other than, or in addition to, the colliding vessels or objects are at fault in respect to a collision or contact.

Index